Cause at Heart

Cause at Heart A Former Communist Remembers

Junius Irving Scales and
Richard Nickson

Foreword by
Telford Taylor

The University of Georgia Press
Athens and London

Designed by Kathi L. Dailey
Set in Mergenthaler Times Roman
with Helvetica display

The paper in this book meets the guidelines for
permanence and durability of the Committee on
Production Guidelines for Book Longevity of the
Council on Library Resources.

Printed in the United States of America

91 90 89 88 87   5 4 3 2 1

Library of Congress Cataloging in Publication Data

Scales, Junius Irving.
  Cause at heart.

  Includes index.
  1. Scales, Junius Irving. 2. Communists—
United States—Biography. 3. Communism—
United States—History—20th century. I. Nickson,
Richard, 1917– . II. Title.
HX84.S4A33 1987 335.43′092′4 [B] 86-7049
ISBN 0-8203-0890-0 (alk. paper)

British Library Cataloging in Publication Data
available.

Title-page illustrations are of the authors in 1947
and 1984. Both photographs by Lia Nickson.

Note

Several names have been changed in accord with the wishes of living persons; others have been changed or suppressed to avoid possible embarrassment or injury.

Certain words are employed in conformity with their use in a given period—notably the word *Negro,* in reference to a time when the word *black* was considered derogatory.

To the memory of Gladys

Contents

Foreword   by Telford Taylor

The trial, conviction, and imprisonment of Junius Scales was a major case testing American constitutional principles and values. These events triggered the writing of this book and comprise its concluding chapters. But the discerning reader will perceive that "crime and punishment" are the cap but not the core of the book. This is a story of growing up in the American South at a time of tension and transition, and might well have been entitled "The Education of Junius Scales."

I have read these early chapters with deep interest and, I hope, benefit. But my own background is so remote, geographically and otherwise, that I cannot comment meaningfully. I first met Junius Scales as a result of and in connection with his trial, and naturally I view those events through the eyes of a lawyer—his lawyer. Accordingly, I believe that I can best assist the reader to grasp the nationwide significance of the Scales trial by pointing out some features of the case and its aftermath with which the book does not deal.

Scales was indicted under the 1940 Smith Act, enacted by Congress over a presidential veto and supported by a coalition of legislators, some of whom were primarily concerned by Communist Party activities in the United States, and others by the presence of the Nazi German-American Bund in New York City. Neither of these organizations was mentioned in the Smith Act; its terms were general and made it a felony, punishable by imprisonment for ten years, to advocate, or to distribute literature advocating, overthrow of the United States government or any state government by force and violence; or to organize any society or group that advocates such violent overthrow, or be a

member or affiliate of any such society or group, with knowledge of its unlawful advocacy.

The Smith Act was not importantly used during or in the immediate aftermath of the Second World War. But the period of postwar optimism for an era
of good feeling between the Soviet and American governments was brief;
disagreements over the administration of occupied Germany, and Soviet domination and political oppression in Eastern Europe, provoked deep indignation
and fear among the American people. By 1948, both the Congress and the
executive branch had embarked on a far-flung program for the destruction of
the Communist Party and the suppression of communist influence in the
United States.

The Department of Justice was the principal executant of this program, and
the Smith Act its primary weapon. In July of 1948 most of the national leaders
of the Communist Party were indicted in New York City for conspiracy to
violate the "advocacy" and "organizing" clauses of the Smith Act. After a
tempestuous trial before Judge Harold Medina in the federal district court, all
were convicted, and most of them were sentenced to five-year prison terms.
On review of the case (known as the Dennis case) in the United States Supreme Court in 1951, challenges to the constitutionality of these provisions of
the Smith Act were rejected, and the convictions affirmed.

With the Smith Act thus constitutionally legitimatized, the Justice Department brought indictments against leading Communist Party officials in most
of the major cities, including Boston, Philadelphia, Pittsburgh, Baltimore,
Cleveland, Chicago, Denver, and Los Angeles. In all these cases the charges
were replicas of those in the Dennis case, conspiracy to violate the "advocacy" and "organizing" provisions of the Smith Act. Virtually all the defendants who were brought to trial were convicted.

While all this was going on, Scales was living the "underground" life
described in this book, until November 1954, when he was arrested and
brought to trial in his native Greensboro. His was the only Smith Act case
brought in a geographically southern city (I have used the qualifying adjective
because Greensboro is in important respects not a typically southern community). Furthermore, the charges against him were not those brought against the
defendants in the Dennis and other conspiracy cases. Scales was one of a
handful of Smith Act defendants who were not accused of conspiracy, and
whose indictments charged only an individual violation of the so-called
"membership clause"—the final clause, which punished being or becoming a
member or affiliate of a group with the knowledge that it advocated "overthrow or destruction of any government in the United States by force or
violence."

There followed Scales's first trial, his conviction and sentencing to a six-year prison term, and affirmance of his conviction by the federal Court of Appeals. The newspaper reports in New York were few and brief; I was vaguely aware of the case, but paid it no attention until near the end of 1955, when I received a telephone call from Francis Biddle in Washington. I had known Biddle slightly as solicitor general and attorney general, and became much better acquainted with him at the first Nuremberg war crimes trial, at which he was the principal American judge and I served as an associate prosecutor.

As recounted in the book, Scales had solicited Biddle's assistance in finding new counsel to seek review of his case in the United States Supreme Court. When Biddle telephoned, he inquired whether I would consider taking the case. He made no effort to persuade me, and I told him only that I was willing to see Scales and hear what he had to say. I did not ask Biddle why he had thought of me for the case; probably it was because I had recently and successfully represented Harry Bridges, president of the International Longshoremen's and Warehousemen's Union, by obtaining from the Supreme Court a reversal of his conviction for procuring naturalization by falsely denying membership in the Communist Party.

Given the public temper of the 1950s, I was well aware that many if not most lawyers would have declined to represent an acknowledged Communist Party official. But in my opinion the Smith Act in general and the membership clause in particular raised serious constitutional problems, and Scales, like any criminal defendant, deserved competent legal representation.

However, I had once before been approached by the Communist Party, to represent the "Hollywood Ten," artists and writers who had been convicted of contempt for refusing to answer questions about Communist affiliations put to them during a congressional committee investigation. After consideration, I had rejected the retainer when it became apparent that the Party insisted on a theory of defense with which I did not agree in principle, and which I thought the courts would surely reject, as indeed they did.

Accordingly, when Scales appeared at my office, accompanied by William Albertson and another senior official of the Communist Party (whose name I cannot recall), my primary concern was to discover any comparable obstacles to my taking Scales's case. I told my visitors that I would insist upon full control of the presentation of the case to the Supreme Court, and that I would not represent the Party, but Scales as an individual, to whom I would look for payment of my fees. These stipulations were readily agreed to, Scales appeared to me as a pleasant and sincere young man, and I took the case.

I knew from the outset that it would be a tough case to win. On the Supreme Court were six justices who had participated in the Dennis case, and of these four (Reed, Frankfurter, Burton, and Minton) had voted to uphold the convictions. The other two (Black and Douglas) had been the only dissenters, and I was fairly sure of their votes. The remaining three members were Chief Justice Warren, Justice Harlan, and Justice Clark, who had disqualified himself in the Dennis case because the indictments had been brought while he was attorney general, and who presumably would otherwise have joined the majority in the Dennis case.

Since it would have been foolhardy to ask the Court to overrule the Dennis decision, and since I needed five votes to win, it was apparent that in order to persuade the Court to declare the membership clause unconstitutional I would need to convince at least three justices (in addition to Black and Douglas) that the differences between the Dennis conspiracy indictments and Scales's membership clause indictment were so significant that the clause should be invalidated, even though the other provisions of the Smith Act remained in force.

I had some hope of persuading at least several of the justices to that effect. Overthrowing the government of the United States by force is no job for boys or lone revolutionaries. The majority justices in the Dennis case had relied heavily on the special danger of conspiratorial groups. But no such point could be applied against Scales, who was not charged with conspiracy. Furthermore, the defendants in the Dennis and similar cases were accused of conspiring to take *action* by advocating, and organizing groups to advocate, violent overthrow, and the Court had concluded that anyone who was proved to have so acted surely must have specifically intended to destroy the government. Scales, however, was charged with none of these things nor, indeed, with *any action at all*. The mere status of knowing membership in the type of organization denounced in the Smith Act comprised the entire offense. In the light of the First Amendment's protection of free speech and association, it appeared to me that the Court might have difficulty in sustaining a statute imposing heavy criminal penalties upon so tenuous a connection with unlawful activity.

When I examined the competent brief that Scales's previous counsel, David Rein of Washington, had submitted to the federal circuit court, I discovered additional promising grounds for attacking Scales's conviction. By far the most important of these arose out of the Internal Security Act, adopted by Congress in 1950, which embodied an anti-Communist legislative technique quite different from that of the Smith Act.

The Internal Security Act contained some criminal penalties, but relied primarily on exposure and quasi-outlawry of Communist Party members. The act established a "Subversive Activities Control Board" (SACB) to identify "Communist-Action" organizations such as the Communist Party itself. Once that was done, the organization, and all its members individually, were required to register publicly with the United States Attorney General. Thereafter, members of any organization required to register would be barred from employment by the United States government, by any labor union, or in any defense plant, and from holding a United States passport.

While the bill that became the Internal Security Act was pending in Congress, the legislators became aware that, since Communist Party members were liable to criminal prosecution under the membership clause of the Smith Act, compliance with a public registration requirement would be self-incriminating under the Smith Act. Since the Fifth Amendment to the Constitution provides that no person may be required to incriminate himself, Communist Party members would have a constitutional defense against enforcement of the registration provisions.

Deeming the registration requirements of great importance, the legislators amended the bill so as to provide that Communist membership "shall not constitute per se a violation" of either the Internal Security Act "or of any other criminal statute." This language, embodied in section 4(f) of the Internal Security Act, was avowedly adopted to immunize Communist Party members from prosecution under the Smith Act's membership clause, and thus to eliminate self-incrimination as a defense against required compliance with the Internal Security Act's registration requirements.

It appeared to me that section 4(f) gave Scales (and any other Communist indicted under only the membership clause) an explicit defense. But the federal circuit court, in an opinion by the eminent Judge John J. Parker (whom I had known and admired as the second American judge at Nuremberg), had rejected it when Rein invoked it on behalf of Scales. Judge Parker's reasons seemed to me flimsy, but I was well aware that anti-Communist feeling was running high, and that apparently unanswerable arguments might not carry the day.

Mr. Rein had made a number of other arguments, charging error in the trial court's evidentiary rulings and other mistakes in the conduct of the trial, which appeared to have substance. I adopted most of them, but decided not to present them as principal points. A Court decision that the membership clause was unconstitutional, or that the prosecution was barred by section 4(f) of the Internal Security Act, would result in dismissal of the indictment. Victory on the evidentiary or procedural points, on the other hand, would procure a reversal of the conviction but might leave it open to the prosecution to bring Scales to a second trial, at which the errors could be avoided.

The Supreme Court scheduled the Scales case to be argued in mid-October 1956, directly following the arguments in the Yates case—a Smith Act conspiracy case from Los Angeles that was to become the turning point in enforcement of the "advocacy" and "organizing" provisions of the Smith Act. In the Scales case, the government's argument was ably presented by my

Harvard Law School friend and classmate, John F. Davis. My own argument went, I thought, reasonably well, but despite extensive questioning from the bench I was unable to divine the trend of the Court as a whole. Obviously, however, the bench did not find either my case or the Yates case easy to decide, as nothing further was heard from the Court until June 3, 1957, when the Scales case was set for reargument the following October.

Two weeks later the Yates case was decided. Whereas in the Dennis case the Court had not passed on the sufficiency of the evidence against the defendants, in the Yates case the Court undertook that task, and the result was a fatal blow to the Justice Department's Smith Act campaign. The Court not only reversed all the convictions but also ruled that the prosecution lawyers had failed to prove that either the Communist Party as an entity, or the defendants individually, had sought to incite any persons to engage in or prepare for overthrowing the government by force or violence.

The Court's judgment ordered dismissal of the charges against five of the Yates defendants and remanded the case against the others to the trial court in Los Angeles, leaving the way open for a second trial. But there was no second trial; the prosecution was dropped, as it was eventually in all the pending Smith Act conspiracy-advocacy cases. The prosecution's evidence of Communist Party activities had been stereotyped, so the evidentiary deficiencies in the Los Angeles case, as found by the Supreme Court, were present in most if not all the others as well. The task of retrying all of them, under the standards of proof announced by the Court in the Yates case, must have appeared to the Department of Justice as too costly, time-consuming, and uncertain of outcome to warrant the effort. No more Smith Act conspiracy defendants went to prison, and no new such cases were brought, as the Justice Department shifted the focus of its attack against the Communist party to the Internal Security Act.

At first it appeared that the Yates decision was also good news for Scales and the few other membership clause defendants. Under that clause there could be no convictions without proof that the organization to which they belonged incited action directed toward violent overthrow of the government, and the Yates case had held that the proof against the Communist Party was insufficient. The prosecution itself had described the evidence in the Scales case about the Party as virtually the same as that in the Yates case. I could, therefore, look forward to the reargument of the Scales case with considerable optimism.

However, as a result of an unexpected prosecution move, the scheduled reargument never took place. During Scales's trial, Mr. Rein had asked the judge to order the prosecution to produce copies of reports made to the Federal Bureau of Investigation by two of the witnesses against Scales, in order to determine whether there were discrepancies between the reports and the witnesses' court testimony, which might discredit the witnesses' credibility. The judge denied the request, and this was one of the evidentiary rulings charged as error in Rein's brief in the circuit court and mine in the Supreme Court. On June 3, the same day that the Court ordered the Scales case reargued, it decided another case (the Jencks case, in which the defendant was accused of falsely denying membership in the Communist Party, in a report submitted to the National Labor Relations Board) that raised the same issue. The Court ruled that, in such circumstances, defendants are entitled by law to have the reports produced.

In light of the Jencks decision, it became plain that the Scales case was subject to reversal on the same ground. That, however, was the last thing I wanted. The Yates case had brightened the prospects of a reversal on constitutional grounds, which would have required a dismissal of Scales's indictment and, in all probability, ended his case. A reversal for failure to make available the witnesses' reports to the FBI, on the other hand, would lead only to a remand of the case to the district court, and the likelihood of a second trial.

But the Department of Justice, well aware of the danger that the Court would find Scales's conviction subject to the same infirmities as those in the Yates case, saw the Jencks case as an opportunity to avoid another stinging blow by getting the Scales case out of the Supreme Court and back to the district court in Greensboro. In September the solicitor general submitted to the Supreme Court a memorandum, admitting that the trial court had erred in refusing access to the FBI reports, and stating that the case "must be reversed for further proceedings in the light of the *Jencks* decision." Needless to say, I submitted a reply vigorously objecting to any such action, but on October 14, 1957, the Court announced that, in view of the solicitor general's "confession of error" in light of the Jencks case, the judgment of conviction was reversed. Thus no decision was rendered on the major issues in the Scales case, nor was there any barrier to a second trial.

While his Supreme Court case was in process, Scales, as recounted in his book, was passing through a painful crisis of mind and conscience. He had voiced to me his growing disenchantment with the Communist Party at the time of the Soviet invasion of Hungary. Early in 1957 he broke with the Party completely, and shortly after the Supreme Court reversed his conviction, his renunciation became publicly known.

This new circumstance naturally raised the question of whether the Justice Department would drop the case. Very likely that would have happened if Scales had gone before a congressional committee to confess the error of his ways and shown his contrition by giving full information about the Party, including the names of all those he knew to be, or to have been, members. But Scales had no such intentions. He still cherished the goals, such as unionization and racial equality, that had brought him into the Party and respected many of the individual Communists he had met during his Party career. Such an attitude foreclosed any expectation of official leniency.

But the Department of Justice had more general reasons for proceeding with the Scales case. No doubt there was a desire to confirm the constitutionality of the membership clause. Much more important, however, was the department's need to remove the threat that the *Yates* decision had raised to enforcement of the Internal Security Act.

Section 2 of that act declared that the "Communist movement in the United States is . . . seeking to advance a moment when . . . overthrow of the United States by force and violence may seem possible of achievement," and that the "Communist organization in the United States . . . present(s) a clear and present danger to the security of the United States." It was on the basis of such a description that the SACB was to declare the Communist Party to be a "Communist-action organization"—a declaration necessary in order to trigger the registration requirements and other penalties that would then be visited upon Party members. But this description hardly fit with Justice Harlan's opinion in the Yates case, describing the evidence that the Communist Party incited forcible action as "strikingly insufficient" because: "At best this voluminous record shows but a half dozen or so scattered incidents which, even under the loosest standards, could be deemed to show such advocacy. Most of these were not connected with any of the . . . [defendants], or occurred many years before the period covered by the indictment."

Thus it had become plain to the government that, if either the membership clause of the Smith Act, or the much more important Internal Security Act, was to be salvaged, the immediate necessity was to produce before the Supreme Court a case in which the evidence about the Communist Party would satisfy the Yates case standards and persuade the Supreme Court to find that the Party was an organization which incited the use of force and violence to overthrow the government. The Scales case was chosen as the vehicle for that purpose, and by the end of 1957 it was clear that the prosecution would be continued and that the trial would be held early in 1958.

These developments worked a basic change in my relations to Scales and his case. Win or lose, review of his first conviction in the Supreme Court had appeared as a one-shot undertaking. But the case had been neither won nor lost; it was back at square one. The next act of the drama would be the retrial in Greensboro, which to me was *terra incognita*. As a jury trial lawyer I was wholly inexperienced, and I had many commitments in the New York area. Furthermore, I was well aware that "foreign" lawyers rarely fare well before local juries, and I told Scales that I would take part in his trial only in collaboration with a southern lawyer, preferably one from Greensboro.

I drove to Greensboro with Scales as my passenger and had my first opportunity to cement our acquaintance, a process that confirmed my favorable appraisal of his personality and integrity. In Europe I was well traveled, but never before had I been south of Virginia, and I entered this (to me) strange new territory with some trepidation. The King Cotton Hotel (long since torn down) was certainly no Ritz. I knew no one in or near Greensboro, and I felt quite lonely as I prepared a motion to dismiss the indictment and had it typed by a public stenographer.

Meanwhile, Scales was pursuing his local contacts in search of a lawyer who might consider joining forces with me. What I would have done had he come back empty-handed I do not know, but for once fortune smiled on our enterprise.

That afternoon I found myself discussing the case with McNeill Smith, a senior partner in a leading Greensboro law firm. Despite a few awkward moments, caused by the use of words that did not mean in Greensboro what they meant in New York, we hit it off well, and eventually agreed to take the case together, on the basis that we would share the opening and closing statements to the jury, Smith would handle most of the witnesses from the Greensboro area whose testimony would concern Scales as an individual, and I would handle the imported government witnesses who would testify about the Communist Party, as well as the motions and other nonjury matters.

The successful outcome of my discussions with Smith was a great relief to me. In addition to Smith's counsel and collaboration, I had gained a base of operations—office space, telephone service, a law library—and the assistance of two able younger partners, Bynum Hunter and Richmond Bernhardt. Furthermore, southern hospitality put an end to loneliness; there were invitations to dinner, tennis to be played at the local club, and in those circles a far broader spectrum of social and political views than I had expected.

But if Greensboro was not Mobile, neither was it New York or Boston. Even in a northern city at that time, a jury acquittal of Scales would have been a long shot. In Greensboro, as I had expected, it appeared to be out of the question. The prosecutors were distant and obviously suspicious even of Smith; the clerks were civil but cool; the local press reporters and their editors were generally hostile; the jury was utterly "dead" in its reactions to our statements and witnesses. Judge Albert Bryan, a Virginian from Alexandria who was again assigned to try the case, was an experienced and technically competent jurist, but it was plain that he thought Scales guilty, and he gave us no breaks in his evidentiary rulings.

True to the government's major purpose, Scales's name was hardly mentioned during the first ten days of the trial, while the prosecution called a number of witnesses, who had not appeared in the first trial, to testify that the Communist Party leadership, at Party "schools" and other meetings, preached the doctrine that force and violence would be necessary in order to bring about overthrow of the capitalist government and the victory of socialism. It did not appear to me that the testimony was convincing or substantial, but there was no blinking the fact that the record on the Party was much fuller than that made at the first trial, and gave the government a basis, shaky though it might be, to argue that the Yates case standards had been met.

In putting in the defense case, we were seriously limited by our inability to call Scales himself to the witness box. No doubt he could have been a very effective witness in his own behalf, but had he testified, on cross-examination the prosecution lawyers would certainly have put questions the answers to which would necessarily have identified as Communists other members of the Party with whom Scales had worked, or about whom he had knowledge. If Scales had refused to answer, he would have lost credit with the jury and also been punished, presumably by incarceration, for contempt of the court. Answer such questions Scales would not, and under those circumstances there was no way to get the benefit of his testimony.

When the evidentiary proceedings were finished and both prosecution and defense had rested their cases, the hands of the Justice Department lawyers from Washington were again visible in the judge's charge to the jury. Obviously troubled that the language of the "membership clause" required nothing but membership in or affiliation with the Communist Party with knowledge of its unlawful purpose, the prosecution proposed to add other requirements. Thus, at the prosecution's request, the judge charged the jury that, in order to convict, they must find that Scales was not a "nominal" or "passive" but an "active" member of the Communist Party, and that in addition to his "knowledge" of the Party's aims, they must find that Scales had the "specific intent" to bring about violent overthrow of the government.

Superficially, it might appear that such contrived limitations would benefit Scales by requiring additional proof from the government. But everyone knew that these verbal alterations would not influence the jury one way or another, and probably would play no part in their deliberations. The prosecution had introduced these limitations, not out of any concern for the jury, but in an effort to bolster the content of the membership clause itself, against the time when the Supreme Court would again confront the question of its constitutionality.

To the anguish of the young lawyers from Smith's firm, who had preserved an optimism I could not share, the jury promptly found Scales guilty. Judge Bryan again sentenced him to imprisonment for six years. In June I went to

Asheville to argue the appeal in the Circuit Court of Appeals, and on October 6, 1958, that court affirmed Scales's conviction. A month later I submitted to the Supreme Court a petition for review of the case, and on December 15, 1958, just one year after Scales had publicly announced his separation from the Communist Party, the Supreme Court granted review, and the case was scheduled for argument in the spring of 1959.

Since my earlier presentation, the personnel of the Court had changed, I thought for the better. Three of the majority justices in the Dennis case (Reed, Burton, and Minton) had retired; the new justices were Brennan, Whittaker, and Stewart. None of them had as yet much of a track record, but at least they were not personally committed to the Dennis approach, and Brennan had already appeared to me as a great improvement on Minton. So far so good, but the other side of the coin was that the Yates decision had not been well received in congressional and other public circles, and I had an uncomfortable feeling that some of the justices might not be eager to render a judgment that would turn loose another Smith Act defendant.

When I argued the case in late April, my opponent was Solicitor General J. Lee Rankin. There was surprisingly little questioning from the bench, and I left the courtroom without a clue to the outcome.

Apparently the Court was as baffled as I was, for two months later an order was issued setting the case for reargument in November and specifying several questions to which "Counsel are requested to address themselves." These were whether the membership clause could "permissibly" be construed to include the requirements of "specific intent" and "active membership" (as the government was urging); whether the clause would be constitutionally valid if construed to exclude these requirements, or to include one or both of them; whether the doctrine of "clear and present danger" was applicable to the membership clause; and whether section 4(f) of the Internal Security Act barred Scales's prosecution.

But the case was not reargued in November, nor for almost a year thereafter. This time the postponement was due to the submission to the Court of the first major case arising under the Internal Security Act. The SACB had found that the Communist Party was a "Communist-action organization," and had ordered it to register with the attorney general, as required by the Act. The SACB's finding and order had been affirmed by the Court of Appeals for the District of Columbia. The Supreme Court granted review of the case and, recognizing that the issues in the Scales and SACB cases were related, scheduled both for argument at the opening of the next Court term in October of 1960.

These developments gave me no pleasure. The questions that the Court had listed for further consideration revealed that it was deeply divided, and that at least some of the justices were seriously considering the government's proposals for interpolations in the language of the membership clause and in section 4(f) of the Internal Security Act. The record concerning the Communist Party in the SACB case would be before the Court while considering the record in the Scales case.

Furthermore, in 1959 the Court decided another case, involving a Communist factor, in a way that boded Scales no good. Two years earlier the Court had set aside the contempt conviction of a witness, before the House Un-American Activities Committee, who refused to answer questions concerning the identity of certain former Communist Party members. But in June of 1959 the Court, by a five-to-four vote (the dissenters were Warren, Black, Douglas, and Brennan), had affirmed the contempt conviction of another witness before the Committee who had refused to answer questions about his own Communist connections. In his opinion for the majority, Justice Harlan had based the decision in large part "on the long and widely accepted view that the tenets of the Communist Party include the ultimate overthrow of the government by force and violence, a view which has been given final expression by Congress."

The reargument took place on October 10, 1960, exactly four years after my first appearance in the case. The following two days the Court heard argument in the SACB case, and in the only other "membership clause" case to reach the Supreme Court, in which the defendant was John Noto, an admitted Communist Party member from Buffalo. My impressions from these three days of arguments increased my anxieties about Scales's prospects. During my reargument both Justice Frankfurter (with whom I enjoyed an excellent personal relation) and Justice Harlan put questions or gave other indications which strongly suggested that they were receptive to the government's contentions. The very able lawyer representing the Communist Party, John J. Abt, also faced sharp questioning.

It was eight months later when the blow fell. On June 5, 1961, by a five-to-four vote, the Court affirmed Scales's conviction. The justices divided exactly as they had in the congressional investigation case decided two years earlier, and once again Justice Harlan wrote the opinion for the majority, which adopted all of the government's arguments, and in which Frankfurter, Clark, Whittaker, and Stewart concurred. Justices Black and Douglas would have held the membership clause invalid under the First Amendment, and they, together with Chief Justice Warren and Justice Brennan, thought that Scales's prosecution was barred by section 4(f) of the Internal Security Act.

On the same day and by the same division among the justices, the Court, in a very long opinion by Justice Frankfurter, declared constitutionally valid the SACB order requiring the Communist Party to register as a "Communist-action organization." Justice Black thought this requirement invalid under the

First Amendment, while the other three dissenters (Warren, Douglas, and Brennan) would have held it invalid under the Fifth Amendment's guaranty against forced self-incrimination.

My petition to the Court for reconsideration of their decision, as I expected, was denied, and Scales prepared to serve his sentence. Early in October he was taken to the Lewisburg penitentiary in Pennsylvania and started learning about the true inwardness of jails, as described in his book.

The distressingly anomalous nature of Scales's incarceration stimulated many prominent persons to urge commutation of his sentence. The numerous defendants in the Smith Act conspiracy cases that had been abandoned, most of whom had far outranked Scales, and many of whom were still active Party members, had escaped punishment. So had Noto, whose conviction under the membership clause was reversed by the Supreme Court; he had been tried prior to the Yates decision, and the evidence against the Communist Party in his case was comparable to that in the Yates record. Scales had been given a six-year sentence, while the topmost Communist leaders, convicted in the Dennis case, had benefited by the statutory maximum five-year penalty for conspiracy convictions.

Mac Smith did much more than I in Scales's behalf, by taking statements from the Greensboro jurors supporting his release, traveling to Lewisburg to take a statement from Scales himself, and lobbying the Justice Department. My only participation in the commutation campaign was to arrange a meeting with Deputy Attorney General Nicholas Katzenbach. He was cold, and very unresponsive to most of my arguments, but did agree that the length of Scales's sentence was unfair in comparison to that of the other Smith Act convicts. Meanwhile, a deluge of clemency recommendations was pouring in on the Washington authorities from James Wechsler, Jonathan Daniels, Archibald MacLeish, Eleanor Roosevelt, and many other notables. In December of 1962, after Scales had been fifteen months in prison, on the initiative of Attorney General Robert Kennedy, the sentence was commuted to time served, and Scales was home for Christmas.

Scales suffered an ordeal; I merely a disappointment. But it was a sharp one, the sharpest of my career at the bar. In part, of course, it was wounded ego. Scales was the only one of my some twenty-five clients who were criminal defendants that I failed to keep out of jail, and he was more deserving than all but a few of the others. I had an acute sense of failure, deepened by the fact that I had been armed with strong legal arguments in his behalf but had not succeeded in turning them to his advantage.

Once I had overcome the nervousness of my first few Supreme Court arguments, I greatly enjoyed them. But the aftermath has always been painful for me and, I suspect, for many others, as they reflect on their colloquies with the justices. Invariably I perceive brilliant *ripostes* that did not occur to me at the crucial moment. When one nevertheless wins the case, chagrin is, of course, soothed by the balm of victory. But I had lost, and to this day I fantasize, and suffer mental self-flagellation, over those lost dialectical opportunities of my Scales case arguments, particularly the third one.

In addition to my depression, I felt anger. As the four years that I was involved in the case passed, it increasingly appeared to me that Scales was being buffeted by events and circumstances that had nothing to do with him or the merits of his case. Why did the Supreme Court not decide the case, based as it was on a record and a judgment that squarely raised constitutional and statutory questions, when it first came up, instead of putting him through another trial and giving the prosecution another shot at the target? Why did brilliant and principled judges like Frankfurter and Harlan distort the language of the membership clause and section 4(f) by writing in new words and absurdly altering the original texts? Years earlier, in a case wherein comparable distortions were proposed to the Court at a time when William Howard Taft was chief justice, he had declined to construe the statute as if it had "a nose of wax." Why did Frankfurter and Harlan not heed that warning against judicial legislation? Such reflections reinforced my feeling that the political tensions of the time had generated forces that could not be overcome by briefs and arguments, however forceful.

In such a mood, it is hardly surprising that, during the next six years (1961–67), as cases involving the government's efforts to enforce the Internal Security Act came before the courts, I took malicious satisfaction in the defeats it sustained, as a direct result of the tactics it used in the Scales case. The Justice Department lawyers had badly overplayed their hand, and by 1967 the Internal Security Act was as dead as the Smith Act.

The procession of cases began when the government, relying on the Supreme Court's decision upholding the Internal Security Act's registration requirement, prosecuted the Communist Party for refusing to register, invoking the privilege against self-incrimination. In the federal district court, the Party was found guilty and fined $120,000. In February 1964 on appeal to the District of Columbia Court of Appeals, the conviction was reversed on the ground that the officers of the Communist Party had validly claimed the privilege, and that no other persons authorized to register the Party appeared to be available. The Supreme Court refused to review the case.

In reaching its decision, the court of appeals explicitly relied on the Communist Party officers' vulnerability to prosecution under the membership clause, as established in the Scales case, and on the insufficiency of section 4(f) of the Internal Security Act to protect the officers, as Justice Harlan had made clear in his opinion by alluding to Congress's failure "to protect the registration provisions of the Internal Security Act" by "wiping out the membership clause of the Smith Act, as applied to Communists."

In November of 1965 the Supreme Court unanimously dealt a further and final blow to the registration requirements as applied to individual party members. The SACB ordered William Albertson, and several other individuals whom the SACB had found to be Communist Party members, to register, and those so ordered brought suit to set aside the orders on the ground that their enforcement would violate the individuals' privilege against self-incrimination. The Supreme Court sustained this contention and set aside the orders, in an opinion by Justice Brennan. Once again, the insufficiency of section 4(f), as construed in the Scales case, was the determinative point.

Meanwhile, the personnel of the Court had changed. In 1962 Justice Whittaker resigned and was replaced by Byron White, and Justice Frankfurter, who suffered a stroke, was replaced by Arthur Goldberg. In 1965, when Goldberg left the bench to become ambassador to the United Nations, President Johnson appointed Abe Fortas. Especially on issues involving constitutional rights, Goldberg and Fortas generally joined the Warren-Black-Douglas-Brennan wing of the Court, thus significantly altering its ideological balance.

The advent of Justice Goldberg, in all likelihood, affected the division of the Court in June 1964, when it lopped off another branch of the Internal Security Act. Herbert Aptheker and Elizabeth Gurley Flynn, both well-known Communist Party officials, were holders of United States passports. In 1962 the State Department revoked their passports, pursuant to section 6 of the Internal Security Act, which made it unlawful for any member of a Communist organization to apply for or use a United States passport. The two individuals brought suit to enjoin the State Department's action. By a vote of six to three (Harlan, Clark, and White dissenting), the Supreme Court declared section 6 unconstitutional, on the ground that it abridged the right to travel, in violation of the Fifth Amendment's guaranty of liberty. In Justice Goldberg's opinion for the Court, he cited the Scales case, and pointed out that, unlike the membership clause as there construed, section 6 applied to all Communist Party members, including those who were not "active" and had no intention to overthrow the government by violence.

In December of 1967 section 5 of the Internal Security Act, making it unlawful for any members of a Communist-action organization "to engage in any employment in any defense facility," met a like fate. By a six-to-two vote, the Supreme Court held section 5 to be "an unconstitutional abridgment of the right of association protected by the First Amendment." Chief Justice Warren's opinion, like Justice Goldberg's in the passport case, relied on the fact that the statute in question, unlike the membership clause as interpreted in the

Scales case, punished Communist Party members even though they might be "passive or inactive" members having no unlawful aims.

Thus the Justice Department paid dearly for their victory in the Scales case. To fashion a basis upon which his conviction could be sustained, the department persuaded the Court to limit the scope of section 4(f) to a degree that proved fatal to the Internal Security Act's registration requirements, and to confine the membership clause to "active" Communists bent on violent revolution, criteria that the passport and defense employment prohibitions did not meet. The Internal Security Act joined the Smith Act as derelict legislation.

Of course, it would be a mistake to lay the demise of these laws exclusively on the Scales case. If the fears that generated the Smith, Internal Security, and Communist Control acts had remained at the level of intensity they reached in the 1950s and early 1960s, no doubt the government would have continued the legislative-judicial campaign, and in all probability could have made further headway. Even as things were, there is no doubt that the Smith Act cases drove thousands of members and sympathizers out of and away from the Party, and greatly diminished its importance. Its decline was expedited by what Scales saw as self-inflicted wounds, such as the invasion of Hungary.

No doubt, then, as public support diminished, the enforcement of these statutes would have dwindled and eventually ceased even if there had been no Scales case. But the decline was certainly accelerated by the Justice Department's exploding its own arsenal. In order to send to jail one man who had already left the Party, the government lawyers turned to legal devices that drew the teeth from the Internal Security Act, on which they had been relying to complete the destruction of the Communist Party.

In this book, Scales gives the reader his own appraisal of his years in the Party, on trial, and in prison. By a combination of fortitude, common sense, and a touch of luck he emerged in one piece and able to continue in the pursuit of happiness. Herein he gives us the fruits of experiences to which few others have been exposed, making no excuses for what he did with his life, and asking no sympathy.

Some may well feel that he deserves none. Others may find much to admire in his chosen course. The events that he describes took place long ago, and the young reader may find them hard to understand. Readers old enough to have lived through those years as adults are bound to have mixed reactions, and may find some of the author's attitudes offensive.

But I believe that the discerning reader will see that these failings, if such they be, are the product of a blunt sincerity. Scales truly had a "cause at heart," and because he found no "respectable" vehicle to advance it, he became a "rebel with a cause" by joining an avowedly revolutionary organization. His personal tragedy struck when he realized that the chosen vehicle was moving in directions which he found abhorrent, and he was left with opinions but no public cause.

Fortunately for him and his friends, he has been able to make the transition from public to private goals gracefully, thanks to his gallant late wife Gladys, and to music, for him as for me, *"du holde Kunst."*

June 1986

Introduction

This book opens with the arrest of Junius Irving Scales in 1954. Charged with violation of the membership clause of the 1940 Smith Act, the first federal peacetime sedition statute enacted in this country since 1798, he had his bond set at one hundred thousand dollars. His crime: belonging to the Communist Party, described in the government's charge as advocating the overthrow of the government by force and violence. Although his conviction in that test case was reversed by the Supreme Court on procedural grounds, the government brought him to trial all over again in 1958, one year after he had left the Party in disillusionment. Again he was sentenced to six years in prison, the heaviest penalty ever meted out under the Smith Act. He entered a maximum-security penitentiary soon after the conviction was upheld by a five-to-four decision of the Supreme Court and thus became the only American ever imprisoned for being a member of the Communist Party.

The Smith Act of 1940, officially the Alien Registration Act, made it unlawful for any person to be or become a member of or affiliate with any society, group, or assembly which teaches, advocates, or encourages the overthrow or destruction of any government in the United States by force and violence—an act that prohibits not conspiracy to overthrow the government but instead advocacy, organization of groups, and distribution of literature with the object of overthrowing the government. These statutes imported into our law the alien doctrine of guilt by association, a doctrine that had never been recognized by either the courts or the Department of Justice, a doctrine that had been regarded as abhorrent. A dozen years earlier—to little avail, as it would seem—Justice Louis Brandeis had warned, "The greatest dangers to

The authors Richard Nickson and Junius Scales, 1984 (Photo by Lia Nickson)

liberty lurk in insidious encroachments by men of zeal, well meaning but without understanding." Since that warning was given, a danger of equal magnitude has threatened our society: the acquiescence of the public in such encroachments—or, if not its acquiescence, its feeble show of remonstrance.

But so far in this dangerous century, Junius Scales, the man once imprisoned, has been relatively fortunate, as he would readily agree. He has not been incinerated by his fellows, or hanged or shot, or starved or frozen in a labor camp. All the same, this book explores his mounting misfortunes. Like ill-starred others, he has suffered some of the penalties inflicted on people who are motivated by beliefs that run counter to those of the majority. His memoir, with no programs or doctrines to advance, focuses on social and political matters, especially those of the South of the middle of this century, and offers the observations of a man who was deeply involved in issues that still remain pressing concerns.

Back in the 1950s, not long after Scales, in his mid-thirties, was arrested, the young Jimmy Porter of John Osborne's play *Look Back in Anger* sounded his complaint. "I suppose people of our generation aren't able to die for good causes any longer," said the angry Jimmy. "We had all that done for us, in the thirties and forties, when we were still kids. There aren't any good, brave causes left." For millions of young people, in this country alone, the search for such causes over the past four decades has been tagged by disillusionment, wracked by feelings of futility, and riddled with cynicism. This book depicts one man's selfless devotion to a cause—the cause of socialism, Communism; it depicts as well his bitter defeats and painful disillusionments.

Luckily for humanity, it always yields some few among its ranks, in every generation, who seek to reach beyond what others settle for or are constrained by. Among the transgressors who have been penalized and yet have survived there are those who, unbroken, seek to understand and report what happened. Readers are no doubt acquainted with reports of the kind that portray the author as wholly in the right. This would-be candid account of a victimization provides at least some contrast to the ardor of self-serving.

Self-interest being what it is—pervasive—there may be hordes among us of all ages unable to understand a commitment to a cause, whether secular or religious, that transcends personal ambition. To them, taking the world as one finds it is not only natural but comfortable, and ministering to one's own needs seems more than enough for a lifetime; to them, the few others for whom worldly ambition is negligible are enigmas usually labeled, and dismissed, as cranks. Still, a sneaking suspicion does lurk in the human conscience that "the world owes all its onward impulses to men ill at ease" (as Nathaniel Hawthorne once put it).

But being ill at ease in a world one never made by no means assures anyone of success in prompting onward impulses. Scales, like so many others, ultimately found the cause of Communism shackled and besmirched mainly because of the dogmatic insistence of his Party on presenting Soviet Russia as a model. He also bumped up against a hard fact of American life: our working class, unlike that of every other advanced capitalist country, has never produced a genuinely mass-based political party of its own. His memoir examines such salient obstacles as these to advancing the cause he embraced. It was not written, however, for the sake of blasting the ideas and ideals that propelled him.

Cynicism, following hot upon disillusionment, is all too easy to cultivate. Quick to join in jeering at all would-be world-betterers are some of those who have withdrawn from activist ranks because of the various injuries done them by those they had viewed as allies. Socialism and Communism have been dealt staggering blows by many of the leaders of parties and nations professing to govern in their name, so much so that for some these terms are getting to be linked with fascism. Thomas Mann, on the other hand, has argued, "Communism remains an idea—albeit a utopic one—with roots far longer than those of Marxism and Stalinism; its untarnished realization will never quite cease to present itself to humanity as a task and a demand. Fascism, however, is no idea at all; it is mere badness." Whether or not Communism can indeed be viewed as a utopian idea, clearly many besides Stalin and the Stalinoids have compounded corruption in the name of Communism. Even so, legions of the wise and eminent clung to their faith in Soviet Communism decade after decade, demonstrating that a secular creed can exert a spell every bit as mesmerizing as that of a religious one.

Judgments based on black-or-white evaluations bolster a variety of partisanship, even among the most humanistic. As Isaiah Berlin recently remarked about Albert Einstein, "His hatred of the cruelty and barbarity of reactionaries and fascists at times led him to believe that there were no enemies on the left—an illusion of many decent and generous people, some of whom have paid for it with their lives." Another sort of partisanship instilled in far more people the illusion that American Communists are all that the FBI and the House Un-American Activities Committee has branded them as being: sinister mercenaries bent on violence. An insider's account, such as this one, shows that small band of partisans to have been for the most part a far cry from the stereotypical "Commies" publicized by the McCarthyism and the mass media of yesterday and today. Zealots of freedom enmeshed in an ideology, they were so far from being exponents of "force and violence" that they once prompted Scott Fitzgerald to quip, "In order to bring on the revolution, it may be necessary to work inside the Communist Party."

And then the camaraderie, the being united in not only a cause but close friendships! "The real puzzle may be not that so many but that so few joined the Communist Party." So Murray Kempton, writing about balladeer Woody Guthrie, has observed, while explaining how "the Wobblies embodied the socialism of the boxcars and the hobo camps while the Communist Party represented the socialism of the hearth." The bugbears of yesterday certainly need not be viewed as seraphim today; the courageous merit of so many of them should nevertheless receive wider recognition—the more so when so many of the basic rights and humane values they fought for are being scorned and betrayed.

Scales, sorting out political foibles and errors—his own and those of some of his comrades—occasionally records effective and even successful activities. Since these took place where and when they did, they are the more remarkable. Though most of the relatively local causes were lost and their champions worsted, the outcries against injustices were heard and not forgotten, particularly such class injustices as the impoverishment of working people. The principle of militance in trade union activities in the South was staunchly advanced, chiefly by scouting racism and by linking blacks and whites in the organizing campaigns.

But the actions in the book are all remembered. They are the past: those days, those actions, swiftly receding from us. In his Nobel Lecture of 1980, Czeslaw Milosz declared, "Our planet that gets smaller every year is witnessing a process that escapes definition, characterized as a refusal to remember." It may be that by remembering and writing his remembrances Scales declares himself still an activist, even in effect practicing subversion: subverting the benumbing process deplored by Milosz. Still, the book was not written with the thought of attaining the lofty reaches of didacticism. Rather, the modest aim was to render as justly as possible that always unique account, one man's life as seen by himself.

So on the two of us worked together, with a shelf of books containing some bearing on the times and events that concerned us, as well as bulky courtroom transcripts and mounds of old newspapers and clippings of news stories and columns (mostly editorial) from a variety of journals. Besides these, there was quite a sampling of leaflets, programs, notices, and also, fortunately, an abundance of letters to and from Junius. Still another source of information for us, we surmised, might lie in that bulging repository of fact, fable, and malarkey bought and garnered over the years by the Federal Bureau of Investigation. After all, Junius had been spied on as relentlessly as had Martin Luther King, Jr. We thought it possible that the Scales file—legally available to us, for a price, by way of the Freedom of Information Act—just might prove helpful.

Upon learning, late in 1978, that the agency would allow over 5,000 pages concerning his case to be released and that their processing would cost $510, Junius requested a waiver or a reduction of the cost. Following the denial of

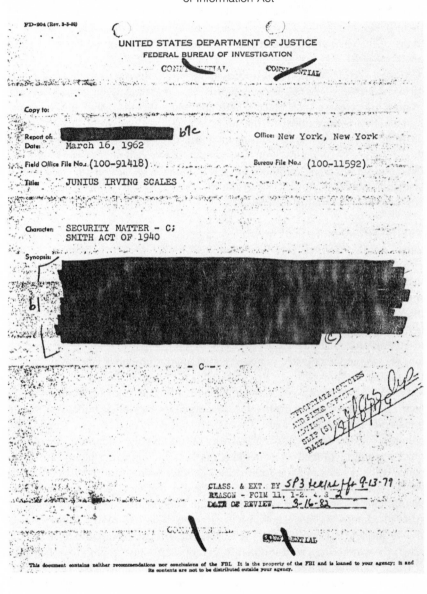

FD-204 (Rev. 3-3-59)

UNITED STATES DEPARTMENT OF JUSTICE
FEDERAL BUREAU OF INVESTIGATION
CONFIDENTIAL

Copy to:

Report of: Office: New York, New York
Date: March 16, 1962

Field Office File No.: (100-91418)   Bureau File No.: (100-11592)

Title: JUNIUS IRVING SCALES

Character: SECURITY MATTER - C;
             SMITH ACT OF 1940

Synopsis:

- C -

CLASS. & EXT. BY SP3
REASON - FCIM 11, 1-2.
DATE OF REVIEW   3-16-82

CONFIDENTIAL

This document contains neither recommendations nor conclusions of the FBI. It is the property of the FBI and is loaned to your agency; it and its contents are not to be distributed outside your agency.

that request, he received 341 pages of newspaper articles. Eight months later he requested further action and was informed, "You can expect to receive the first five volumes of material within the next several weeks." Four months later he complained that those five volumes had never reached him. When they did arrive, he asked for speedier processing of the remaining fifteen. But the processing required years, in the course of which twice as many pages were "reviewed" as were "released."

The money paid for those pages secured us precious little information. A preponderance of them yielded only the names of officiating FBI personnel together with this invariable description: "Confidential informant of known reliability." Each informant's name is routinely blacked out, and we cannot judge the reliability because all or most of each report is blacked out too. The information contained in the 5,000 blackened pages could readily be set down in 20 or fewer. In Part II of this book attention is called to the initial report of one of the informants, surprisingly released intact. Other than for that one dowdy item, we do not find ourselves indebted to the FBI for assistance in our work; we cannot honestly name the bureau as a collaborator.

One winter night late in the seventies, Junius, Gladys, my wife, Lia, and I found that our after-dinner conversation kept returning to a matter of some surprise to us: the fresh burst of interest in "the Scales case," with its bold, black headlines of yesteryear. Lewis Lipsitz, a professor at the University of North Carolina (Chapel Hill), had recently edited the transcript of Junius's second trial, and the Carolina Theatre Company was traveling about North Carolina performing the real-life dialogue to sizable audiences, twelve members of which were being asked at each performance to serve as jurors and render a verdict. Because of the publicity about those dramatic verdicts (so unlike the unanimous findings of the actual ones back in the 1950s), Junius was once more being interviewed by journalists—*young* journalists. Despite their sympathetic capabilities, the man being interviewed found it hard to bridge that wide gap of years, to explain what it was really like at the time.

Our conversation that night led to a sharp renewal of my wife's insistence that this valid interest in a significant piece of history should be supplied by the one person who knows it best. Surprisingly, Lia's proposal was not summarily dismissed, as it had been several times before. Junius was beginning to feel the worth of the argument, especially since it was further advanced by Gladys. He began to yield. At last he declared himself: "I'll write the book if Richard works with me on it."

So we set to work; and now after long years and lengthy interruptions the book is completed, and this is it.

R.N.

Part One

Every man who has a cause at heart is bound to act as if it depended on him alone, however well he may know his own unworthiness; and thus is action brought to birth from mere opinion.

William Morris, "Making the Best of It" (1881)

1

The Chase

My alarm wristwatch woke me before dawn. The gray light outlined a shabby, third-rate hotel room of a sort that had lately become familiar to me. I yawned and stretched on the lumpy mattress; bed and springs creaked and squeaked sympathetically.

It was November 18, 1954, and I was in Cincinnati. Cincinnati, Ohio, I thought sleepily. That meant I was registered as Oliver Ingram: first name beginning with the first letter of the state, last name beginning with the second and third letters of the city. That was a system I'd developed to avoid registering twice in the same hotel under different names and to ensure remembering my identity when in a strange place.

The air was chilling when I reluctantly abandoned the covers, slipped into shoes, and shuffled naked across the worn, stained carpet to close the window and turn on the radiator. Through the dirty panes I looked out on only a blank wall. Shuddering, I threw on my topcoat, which doubled as a bathrobe: I had to sleep bare because pajamas would have consumed too much packing space. After rounding up all my loose papers and literature from the rickety nightstand, I put them into a briefcase, double-locked it, and then hid it in the middle drawer of a small cigarette-burned chest. Taking all my keys and my soap and towel, I locked the room and hurried down the corridor to the shower.

When I returned, I shaved with a tiny electric razor and brushed my teeth with a compact folding toothbrush. My socks, underwear, and drip-dry white shirt, washed the night before, were hanging over the rust-stained basin. I put them on, got into my almost wrinkle-proof suit, and chose one of my two washable ties. The image reflected in the hazy mirror was, at least by intent, that of a struggling but respectable traveling salesman.

I reexamined a comprehensive interstate bus schedule and studied a street map of Cincinnati; having arrived the night before by bus and train from New York, I'd had little chance to grasp the layout of the city. Then, for compactness, I rearranged all the books, periodicals, and pamphlets in my expandable Swiss leather briefcase. With coaxing I even managed to fit the remaining clothes into their appointed places, rounding out fifteen pounds that appeared neither bulky nor conspicuous.

After checking the contents of my pockets and looking over the room to make sure I'd forgotten nothing, I put on my hat and topcoat, grabbed my briefcase, and rode the elevator down to the lobby. The key was dropped at the desk; the sleepy clerk looked to see that nothing was owing—"Come see us again, Mr. Ingram"—and I was out into the clammy cold of the street.

A restaurant around the corner (sighted the night before) proclaimed the best breakfast bargain in town. Concerned with keeping my expenses low, I decided to test that claim. Over greasy sunny-side-up eggs and bitter coffee I read with contemptuous satisfaction a story in the morning paper about Sen. Joseph McCarthy's pleading an injured elbow to try to delay or circumvent the Senate's impending censure hearings. Then, a block away, I caught a municipal bus to a highway intersection near the Ohio River, at the southern edge of the city, where a Greyhound bus was due to pass in fifteen minutes.

When it came, I paid for a one-way ticket to Memphis and occupied two seats more than halfway back. Taking out a scratchpad, I began noting the last three digits of the Ohio and Kentucky license plates in front of and behind me to see if I was being followed. After a half hour of intensive observation, I concluded that I was not. The driver had shown no interest in me, nor had the passengers. Reassured, I finished reading the newspaper and settled back with a book of poems, pausing only to study passengers as they got on.

And who was that spurious traveling salesman, living out of a briefcase under revolving aliases, continuously apprehensive of being observed?

He was a Man with a Mission. His immediate objective was to help save his country from the madness of McCarthyism; in the long run, he desired a socialist United States. To achieve his goals he had entered the labyrinth of Marxism-Leninism, accepted Stalin as his infallible leader, and learned to believe unbelievable things—lured and sustained by that will-o'-the-wisp, socialism. He was an organizer for the Communist Party of the USA, responsible for North Carolina, South Carolina, Virginia, Tennessee, and northern Mississippi. The Party had directed some three years earlier that because of government harassment and the "drift toward fascism" most of its native leaders were to become "unavailable" or "go underground," as the common expression went. And the blond, blue-eyed man in his middle thirties, bent intently over a book, was one of its chosen underground agents.

That man was me: Junius Irving Scales, from North Carolina, then happily married and the father of a baby girl. Looking back down the vista of years, I can now perhaps recapture something of the earlier days of my life, observing them with some indulgence, some pity, and certainly with some guilt and amazement—especially my encounter with a consuming ideology. This story I would like to tell with as much honesty as I—a not-disinterested recorder— am capable of.

I grew absorbed in the ecstasies and complexities of Gerard Manley Hopkins, the English poet-priest, whom I'd admired and puzzled over since my early college days. I sounded in my mind repeatedly: "I caught this morning morning's minion, king / dom of daylight's dauphin, dapple-dawn-drawn Falcon, in his riding / Of the rolling level underneath him steady air. . . ." I also relished the poet's tribute to Henry Purcell, and while the bus rolled through some heavily industrialized Kentucky landscape I sifted some comfort from the lyric reaction to man's fouling of nature in "God's Grandeur": "And for all this, nature is never spent; / There lives the dearest freshness deep down things. . . ."

That I should instead be doing political reading came as an uneasy thought, but one that I suppressed with a reassuring recollection of the pages of political material that I'd read the night before. When I'd begun traveling so far and wide by bus, the combination of exhaust fumes and motion had triggered acute nausea every time I'd tried to read. But I'd overcome the weakness with painful persistence, thereby gaining added hours of reading time, even time to convince myself that trying to understand a man like Hopkins provided a political challenge as well as an esthetic delight.

I turned to an early poem, "Heaven-Haven: A Nun Takes the Veil," written when the twenty-year-old poet was beginning to be attracted to the priesthood:

> I have desired to go
> > Where springs not fail,
> To fields where flies no sharp and sided hail
> > And a few lilies blow.
>
> > And I have asked to be
> > > Where no storms come,
> > Where the green swell is in the havens dumb,
> > > And out of the swing of the sea.

This justification, however exquisite, for pulling out of the world struck me as odd in one so seemingly compassionate and so obsessively Christian as

Hopkins. Such a withdrawing, a leaving of the world to shift for itself, without a qualm, ran counter to the parable of the good Samaritan. But perhaps, I thought, the idea of a "social conscience" would have seemed strange to Hopkins.

If I myself, I mused further, had chosen to pursue the life of a scholar, *I* might be where no storms could come. Even though I had no illusions about the contemporary academic world, knowing that it could be buffeted with "sharp and sided hail" and that no lilies blew there, I recognized that I was far better suited temperamentally to leading a scholarly, contemplative life than to rushing around trying to be a politician, a professional revolutionary.

Still, I told myself, the oppressive times I faced were not like those of Hopkins's England of 1864. And someone had to take on the practical task of reminding the people *now* of the need for the brotherhood of man—for socialism—no matter how poorly equipped he or she might be for the job. Moreover, so long as a handful of people stole the wealth of the world and left the working millions who created it in hungry want, while Negro Americans led lives blighted by bigotry, while organized slaughter was an accepted means of settling differences, while ignorant, small-souled politicians controlled the levers of power and bullied and coaxed the people into submission, no one with a conscience could unashamedly slip away from it all.

Thus I sought to reassure myself and to justify my bizarre manner of existence as the Greyhound continued to wind its way southward.

It was a long ride. By midafternoon the landscape had become gentler, flatter, and less autumnal. The road signs announced that Memphis was thirty-five miles away. The pad came out again, and the license plates, now mostly of Tennessee, were again checked. All seemed well.

A few miles before the city limits, confirming a Memphis street map, the overhead power lines for the municipal trolley began. I put on my hat and topcoat, fastened my briefcase, and waited. Soon the bus passed a trolley going in to Memphis. After a quarter of a mile I pulled the signal cord, left the bus, and boarded the trolley car.

I studied the traffic intently. As the surroundings grew more urban, the trees of Overton Park, a large area encircling the zoo, appeared. I left the trolley and walked rapidly along a path into the heavily wooded grounds. That section of the park was nearly deserted, and there was no way I could be followed by car.

Although the quiet peacefulness of the trees was inviting, I continued my quick pace, and when no one was in sight, I sprinted down the path to the south border of the park. When I reached the street, puffing, perspiring, and feeling my thirty-four years, I saw a bus just pulling up at a stop. I ran for it, caught it, and rode in to the familiar business district. I got off, entered a large store, and strode through it to the next block. There, at a cab stand, I took a taxi to a major intersection where several bus and trolley lines converged. Leaving the taxi, I took a bus in the direction from which I'd just come.

After about ten blocks I left the bus, trotted through an alley in the middle of the block, and came out on another street next to a movie theater, where I bought a ticket and hurried inside. I proceeded directly to the men's room, and with some urgency, since during my journey I'd not dared enter the bus stations.

For the next hour I sat in my cubicle sketching out a three- or four-day agenda of how I would spend my time in Memphis. I made notes on whom I'd like to see, in what order, and how I thought their work might fit into the overall local concentration on the textile and lumber industries. I wanted from each member a relaxed account of what was going on in his or her union, NAACP (National Association for the Advancement of Colored People) club, church, Democratic Party club, or campus. I was especially disturbed about the Smiths, the working-class couple I was to stay with. Why had they recently been dragging their feet so ineptly when they appeared to be respected and influential in a vital union local? I must figure out what was going on inside them. Maybe from my own factory experience I could give them some vision of what a factory could and should be like in a socialist America.

The Negro comrades seemed to be fine and solid, effective in both NAACP and their churches, but in their unions they tended to sound like Reds, clichés and all, whenever they spoke up. A get-together with them was always hazardous. They would have to be brought to the little house in a white working-class neighborhood under cover of darkness. Maybe somebody could borrow a car not known to the FBI to transport them in. I must check on that the first thing, and I must be sure to make my meeting with them worth the risk they were taking by entering a white neighborhood.

I asked myself what main point I should try to get across to everyone. I would argue that despite the toll of the Korean War and McCarthyism, it was still possible to wage an effective fight for political survival by functioning modestly in suitable organizations and by trying genuinely to strengthen them. They must all speak out bravely but in such a way as to carry people with them instead of scaring them away. I would try to keep that theme from being submerged by the dozens of organizational and personal problems that were certain to come up.

These had been scurrilous times, I brooded. Could the Party survive the attacks on it? Having part of the national leadership in jail and much of the remainder in hiding was producing havoc. The Party was losing touch with the people, and the hysterical phobia against Communists had become corrosive. Most of my mail in response to Party leaflets was either incredibly hostile (often threatening murder) or suspiciously friendly (FBI stoolies trying to make contact).

The Party had to survive, or what would happen to the country? Some of the best, most-talented people I knew were in the Party and would have the needed answers to the problems stumping the nation. Meantime, though Joe McCarthy himself was fading in importance, what about his ideological legacy—especially since the liberals seemed mostly too wishy-washy and too busy adding a "me too" to the anti-Communist chorus to fight for civil liberties? Chopped up and isolated as it was, the Party seemed indispensable, and I dared not despair.

I looked forward hopefully to seeing the Memphis comrades again after several months. Some of them had become especially dear to me: Fred, a resourceful New York Jewish intellectual with a love of music and a fine sense of humor, who headed the local organization; a cantankerous midwestern Irishman named Nick, the local organizational secretary, who had left college to try to aid the trade union movement; a Negro woman from northern Mississippi with a terse eloquence that would distinguish her in any company; and some young college students, whom I wished to get to know better during the visit. During my last stay Fred had taken me to a memorable recital by the mezzo-soprano Jennie Tourel, and there had also been some chances for socializing with the other comrades. But now Fred was under heavy FBI surveillance, had been fired from his job through FBI intervention, and might have to leave Memphis. During the present trip everything would be much different for me: I would have to remain holed up with the Smiths the entire time.

It was by then 6:15 and probably almost dark outside. I tucked away my notes and ascended the stairs to the back of the theater, where I first realized that I'd missed viewing an appalling soap opera. I remembered an inconspicuous diner around the corner and entered it, noting approvingly its dim lighting and few customers. In a booth at the rear I hungrily ate the ninety-five-cent blue-plate special.

The plan was for me to be picked up at 7:30 by the Smiths at the southwest corner of Jackson and McLean next to the McLean Baptist Church out near Memphis State. Although my maneuvers had shown that I was not being followed, I felt it would be a good idea to get near that corner a few minutes early just to observe it from a block or two away to see if all was clear. I quickly finished eating and left the diner.

The weather was mild, but heavy clouds were drifting low over the Mississippi, and it looked and felt like rain as I walked the two blocks to an intersection from which the trolley would take me right past my rendezvous.

The car was nearly empty, and I sat behind the driver where I could study the incoming passengers. Nothing unusual: only late workers and late shoppers hurrying home to dinner.

The business district slipped behind. and the trolley entered less-congested, mainly residential neighborhoods. Only three blocks before the church corner, a tall man wearing a brown suit and hat, with a puffy face, hanging lips, and quick eyes, stepped up into the car. As the man dropped his fare into the box, our eyes met.

A shock ran through me: I'd picked up a tail! Three suspicious-looking cars were following the trolley; one prowled ahead. The man in the brown suit got off in front of the church and spoke a word to the driver of one of the cars. He then climbed in the back seat, and the car continued to follow the trolley.

Only three persons besides me had known the appointed time and place: the Smiths and Nick, the organizational secretary, who had arranged matters with them. The meeting evidently had been betrayed, and an important and expensive trip had been wasted. Now, having found me, what would the FBI do? Innumerable times over the past three or four years they had harassed me, sometimes with the same sort of massive surveillance, sometimes with covert tailing. Always, as soon as the agents appeared, I'd experienced a nervous tingling in my spine and a shortness of breath born of fear and self-consciousness—reactions that I felt once more.

Eluding them in Memphis without a car was out of the question. The next move was theirs. Were they going to arrest me? I might as well find out.

I rode two blocks past the church and left the trolley. The clouds had thickened, a wind had sprung up, and rain was imminent. As I walked away from the trolley line down a quiet residential street, I could see the customary FBI surveillance pattern in operation: parked, darkened cars at intersections; cars cruising past and parking two blocks ahead; agents flopping down on car seats or floors as I walked by them. This time they were using unusually large forces—seven or eight cars.

I recognized that I must warn the local comrades that the FBI had known about the meeting place in advance so that they could decide whether someone had informed and, if so, who. To Nick I would have readily entrusted my life—I had indeed done so. The Smiths? Who could say what fear or pressure or greed might have done to them?

But that was not *my* concern at that juncture. It was 7:22. If the Smiths were on the level and were waiting for me, they could not fail to notice the swarm of FBI cars and would drive away. I decided to walk past the rendezvous precisely at 7:30. If the FBI planned to arrest me, it would arrest me, and the comrades would then know that the FBI had known beforehand about the meeting. If it didn't arrest me, I planned to cross the street, catch the trolley back downtown, take the train to New York, shake off my surveillance, notify the Memphis comrades what had happened, and arrange another meeting.

Meanwhile, determined to unload some things that might prove damaging to comrades and friends, I entered a street parallel to the avenue, walking back in the direction of the church. Midway in the block, equidistant from the nearest FBI cars, I rummaged through my shirt-pocket "front office" and pulled out a record of dues payments for Virginia, North and South Carolina, and Tennessee, some notes from a southern leadership meeting, and the notes I'd made that afternoon.

It began to rain. I took from my briefcase the plastic raincoat, the plastic cover for my hat, and a number of phony letterheads, business cards, and business letters of introduction that I carried to corroborate my various aliases. Then I put on the raincoat and plastic cover slowly, at the same time tearing the papers into tiny pieces. Rainwater was already rushing through the gutters. I dropped the torn bits over a storm sewer and saw them instantly disappear. With that accomplished, I strolled along at a leisurely pace as though enjoying the rain.

Suddenly I remembered a bright autumn morning fifteen years before, when I had been a Communist for only a few months. I had been going cheerfully to my job in the tax office in the county courthouse in my native Greensboro, North Carolina, when I looked up at barred windows on the top floor of the white stone building and stopped in my tracks. "My friends and I will go to jail someday," I had imagined in my idealistic innocence, "because our belief in the socialist world is something that these grim lawyers and smug pillars of society I work among will never tolerate; they will hunt us down and box us in, even though what we advocate they hear preached in church and even read about in the New Testament." I had felt a twinge of fear raise gooseflesh on my neck and scalp, even as I felt it then in Memphis, waiting that evening to take my lumps at last, like many another radical "do-gooder" and "bleeding heart." I had a fleeting moment of self-doubt during which I wondered how I could have allowed my adversaries to entangle something as beautiful as the advocacy of a better world in criminal proceedings; I myself must have botched the job somehow.

It was 7:28. As I walked past the apparently empty FBI car at the next intersection, I was overwhelmed with the helplessness of my situation. I was like an animal surrounded by hunters and with no bushes to hide in. Inside the peaceful lower-middle-class houses around me, people were finishing dinner, washing dishes, reading the paper, watching TV. Meanwhile, ahead of me, the gathering FBI cars were making their own traffic jam in the otherwise deserted, rainswept streets.

I had one block and one minute to go. "Oh, God!" I thought. "There are other papers and records I shouldn't be caught with." Could I still get rid of them? The bright lights of Jackson were already too close, and there was no storm sewer in the middle of the block. There was nothing I could do about anything.

As I reached the corner by the church and paused before crossing the street, car doors seemed to open everywhere, and a crowd of men with drawn revolvers converged on me. "We gotcha, Scales! Don't move! This is *it*! This is the end of the road!" My chest tightened, my heart froze.

Someone snatched my briefcase, and I was hustled into the back seat of a car with a man on each side of me. The man with the brown suit and the slack lips handcuffed me with my hands behind my back, so tightly that the cuffs bit into the flesh and cut off the circulation.

"You trying to cut my hands off?"

An uptight, Hollywood-style FBI man in the front seat, who seemed to be in charge, reached back and felt the cuffs. "For Crissakes, put 'em on in *front* and do it RIGHT! Stupid!"

Slack-lips fumbled for his handcuff key, but his hands trembled so violently that his rear-seat colleague, with a contemptuous sneer, removed and reapplied the cuffs.

Till then I'd been in a state of shock, but the discovery that my captors were nearly as nervous as I gave me confidence. In the grip of the confrontation that I'd anticipated and dreaded for years, I felt I must at least try to make my conduct worthy of my friends and my beliefs. Momentarily I thought of my wife's distress and how hard the future would be for her. Then I realized that despite the manacles I was in command of my faculties and should begin defending myself and what I stood for.

"Who are you guys anyway?"

"Who do you *think* we are?"

"You look like a bunch of gangsters to me."

Out came three FBI identity cards.

"In this light they could be coupons from a Quaker Oats box."

As the car sped along toward the business section, a flashlight remedied the deficiency.

"What am I charged with?"

"Smith Act. Membership clause. *You* know."

I knew all right: the Smith Act made it unlawful to conspire to teach and advocate the overthrow of the government by force and violence or to be a member of an organization that did. In contrast to most of the other Smith Act cases, in which the defendants were charged with *conspiracy to violate the*

Act—a charge which carried a maximum prison penalty of five years—I was to be charged with a direct violation of the Smith Act itself, which carried a maximum penalty of ten years in prison.

The boss picked up a radio telephone and announced pompously: "The operation is a success. Subject has been apprehended. Notify Director Hoover by radio immediately. We are bringing the prisoner in to headquarters."

They brought me in through the basement of the Sterick skyscraper, up the elevator to the eleventh floor, past a grim-looking scrubwoman in the corridor, to FBI headquarters. A big, glum color portrait of J. Edgar Hoover dominated the anteroom. There I was stripped to my underwear while several agents took my other clothes and belongings into another office. Two close-cropped, gray-suited agents began questioning me insistently.

"I'm not answering any questions. What kind of 'law enforcement' officers are you anyway? You don't identify yourselves, you don't tell me what I'm charged with, you don't tell me my constitutional rights, and you pick on each other. You ought to get yourselves organized. Now I'm not saying another word."

I listened in silence to the taunting, provocative questions, innuendoes, obscenities, while trying to assess the consequences of my arrest: the shock to my wife, my ailing mother, my three-year-old daughter, and my comrades, alongside the new crippling defense burden it would impose on the Party.

Eventually, I was told to put on my clothes for an 11:30 P.M. appearance before the U.S. commissioner. I asked to use the toilet. A young agent escorted me and stayed by my side as I stood, unsuccessful, at the urinal. "I know how it is," he said softly. "I can't pee either when someone's watching. I'll wait outside."

Another agent, as he put handcuffs on me before leaving the office, noticed my gnawed fingernails. "Occupational disease?" he asked. "Yes" was the reply.

By then, having observed the FBI from behind the scenes for more than three hours, I had formed some firm opinions about my captors. "These guys are nothing," I decided. "Inadequate lawyers afraid to practice law, pretending to be sleuths: drab, pliable, ambitious small-timers molded into humorless super-patriots; inefficient and incompetent in their seedy roles as political police; mainly helpless at investigative work; and chiefly dependent on informers. In general: petty, pretentious, half-educated, bigoted, fearful of authority, distrustful of one another, lacking in moral standards, largely dehumanized. What a crew!"

The fear of a few hours earlier had gone; familiarity had bred contempt; never again, I knew, would my heart skip a beat at *their* approach.

Reporters and photographers were waiting in the basement of the Sterick

Scales in custody. Memphis, November 18, 1954 (*Memphis Commercial Appeal*)

building, popping flashbulbs and shouting questions. They followed along to the federal building, where my appearance before the commissioner was brief. The North Carolina bench warrant for my arrest, dated that afternoon, was read aloud, and an extradition hearing was set.

The U.S. attorney asked that bail be set at one hundred thousand dollars because the defendant was "extremely dangerous" and "the internal security of the United States" required that sum. I asked softly: "May I point out that one hundred thousand dollars is such a fantastic and unreasonable figure that for one in my circumstances, it amounts to *denial* of bail and as such constitutes a violation of my constitutional rights?"

Mr. Commissioner, without any noticeable inner conflict, opted for internal security and set bail at a hundred thousand dollars.

Permission to make a telephone call was granted to me. Inside the office of U.S. Attorney Millsaps Fitzhugh I was seated at the great man's desk, facing a half-dozen FBI men at extension telephones. I wanted to reach someone in the Party's national leadership, most of whom were jailed or in hiding. Elizabeth Gurley Flynn, nearly seventy years old, was an experienced political prisoner and was then out of jail and active. Perhaps she or her sister Kathy would be home. I tried New York information and then made a collect call. No answer. I eventually reached George Blake Charney, the New York Party head, who had just been freed from his Smith Act term by the court of appeals because perjured testimony had been used against him.

"But I can't accept the call, operator. There must be some mistake. I don't *know* anyone in Tennessee," came a sleepy voice. It was 1:00 A.M. in New York.

"George, it's me—Junius Scales. I've been arrested on the membership clause."

Charney was concerned, reassuring, warm, and witty. The agents were incredulous at the joking and laughter. I carefully gave Charney the facts for a story in the *Daily Worker,* but he could not understand my insistence that the news story stipulate that I had been arrested at precisely 7:30 at the corner of Jackson and McLean. He agreed, however, and he assured me that my wife and daughter would be well taken care of.

Finally I asked, "George, have you any profound advice about what I should do?" A portentous pause. Then in an oracular tone: "In your place, I'd just sit tight!" Our dual explosions of laughter ended the conversation.

I left the federal building much relieved that Nick would learn when and where I had been captured and that my wife would not have to suffer alone. After some exchanges with reporters, I entered the FBI car in high spirits. Next stop was the Shelby County Jail, an old one.

Never having been in jail before, I was fearful of the unknown. The routine began: inventory of belongings, issuance of gray prison clothes (reeking of washing soda), signing of a receipt for the belongings. The FBI men left, and the two jailers began sharing the peculiar self-conscious chitchat of the breed, addressed to each other and designed to make the prisoner feel like an inanimate object. They interrupted their conversation from time to time to issue orders in gruff voices. Then away to a cellblock—fourteen separate locked cells opening into a "bullpen."

The whole area was lighted by two bare bulbs, which at least revealed that it was crowded. Two sleeping inmates were routed out and tripled-up on the floors of other cells. I was ordered alone into a five-by-eight-foot cage and told to stand back as, with a long preliminary rumble, the cell door thunderously shut.

It occurred to me that the animals in the Overton Park Zoo were housed better. But they weren't locked up because of their politics. I wondered how my fellow prisoners would react to a "dangerous" Red who threatened "the security of the United States." I decided I would worry about that when morning came.

The mattress on the floor smelled better than the one on the bunk, so I stretched out on it in my prison clothes, pulled a blanket over myself, and prepared for my first night barred off from my family and comrades. As I took off my glasses I looked into the shiny eye of an inquisitive little mouse that perched on the edge of my mattress and looked me over. Then to the accompaniment of snores and heavy breathing, I quickly fell asleep.

2

A Homecoming

The early light of dawn was just beginning to compete with the spooky light of the two bulbs when I awoke. I looked up at a row of high frosted-glass windows with vertical bars over them. Underneath, along the wall, was a walkway alongside the bars of the bullpen. Opening into the long bullpen were the barred fronts of fourteen cells.

It was still quiet, but from two cells down came a wheezy cough. Then up near the bullpen door a resounding fart drew a whispered protest: "Good God a'mighty! You ain't in here by yaself, ya know!" And quiet prevailed again until a distant door opened and closed. A muffled sound of voices accompanied by the jingling of many keys increased until two jailers came down the path outside the bullpen on soft-soled shoes and stopped opposite my cell. One held up a newspaper to the light and said softly, "Yeah, that's him. You know, this is the biggest thing to hit Memphis since Machine-Gun Kelly!"

"That's right," said his colleague. "And they had *him* in this *same* cell-block!"

Sensing that both history and the embodiment of the law looked down on me, I self-consciously put on my glasses. The first jailer moved on up to the end of the block, where he called into the first cell, "Hey, Craig, you an' Simmons an' Murphy come on out. I'm movin' you boys." The door-opening mechanism rumbled as the first door alone opened.

"Hey, Scales, you awake? We're movin' you to number one. Open ten, John." My cell door rolled open and I walked out. "All the way thisaway," the jailer called, moving up the walkway. I padded up to the first cell, where

16

the three dispossessed inmates stood, yawning and shivering. When the door to number one had clanged shut behind me, one of them asked the jailer, "Who's that guy?"

"He's a big Communist. I'll bring in the papers in a few minutes and you can see all about it. You all go on down to number ten now."

"*No-o* shit!" The prisoners tried to get a better look as they left for their new quarters.

I hurriedly washed up, thinking that I might soon be having a rough time. It had been a long while since I had been able to speak openly as a Communist, and all of a sudden I had no choice. Though feeling as tense as a piano string, I was resolved to look cool and calm.

An older jailer, addressed as "Chief," rattled a club across some of the bars and bellowed, "Everybody up!" He then pulled a lever and all the doors, save mine, roared open; about three dozen men, all white (Boss Crump ran a jim-crow town), drifted into the bullpen.

The word had spread, and everyone crowded up to see what a sure-enough Red looked like. Four or five copies of the *Memphis Commercial Appeal,* paid for the night before, arrived, and they all pressed close to see the front-page story and picture. "Hey, they got more stories and pictures in the second section," one reader called.

"Yeah. This is really gonna put the old town on the map!" a local booster responded.

One man handed me his paper. "Here, you can read mine. But save it for me." I thanked him warmly.

The *Commercial Appeal* was a paper remarkable for its good makeup, the large number of ads, the minimal amount of national and international news, and the provincialism and illiteracy of its local news and editorial matter. On this occasion its editors had gone all out with great gobs of photographs: Scales, three-quarter face; Scales, handcuffed, coming out of a door (with FBI agents); Scales, handcuffed, getting into a car (with FBI agents); where it happened, a big X on the sidewalk of the intersection where the arrest was made. The varied articles even included a "human-interest," "personal-observation" put-down by a heavy-handed staff writer. The perfervid ignorance of the stories, containing all the sober pomposity of the FBI, soon had me laughing and remembering a hilarious sketch by Mark Twain entitled "Journalism in Tennessee," which ridiculed the quality of the state's newspapers of some eighty-odd years earlier.

Breakfast, mainly oatmeal, arrived, and mine was pushed through a slot in my door. As I was washing down the last of it with what purported to be coffee, a rather simple-looking young man came up to my cage, squatted down, and seized the bars with both hands. He pressed his face up against them with an air of having waited quite long enough, and asked, "*Are* you a Communist?"

"Yes. Have been over fifteen years," I said cordially.

The young man was joined by four or five others who also squatted down. "Why?"

"Probably the same reason you're a Baptist or a Methodist; it's a matter of conscience."

"I'm a Baptist. Whaddaya mean 'conscience'?"

"Well, if something bad was going on that would hurt me and you and your family and neighbors, and you didn't do anything about it, it would be on your conscience, wouldn't it?"

"I spose."

"Well, it would be on mine too. But I'm *trying* to do something about war and poverty and unfairness, and I think the Communists are too. That's why I'm one of 'em."

"Hey, Scales, did you know Red Davis? Worked on the Inland Boatmen's Division of the National Maritime Union here on the River?" a tall, redheaded man in his thirties asked.

"Yes, I've met him."

"They say he was a Red. I worked with him, and he's a helluva good man."

"Well, we *couldn't* be as bad as the FBI and the boss men say we are."

For the next two hours the crowd grew and got steadily friendlier. Then I was taken out to a small office where I confronted a single FBI man, who was acting the role of Mr. Nice-Guy.

"We just want to clear up some odds and ends, Mr. Scales. If you could tell us—"

"I'm not going to tell you a damn thing. You tell *me* something. If I sign a waiver of extradition, do I forfeit any legal rights?"

"Well, I don't know what to advise you on that—"

"I didn't ask your advice; I asked you a question. You're a lawyer. You should know the answer."

"But I have no authority to discuss that subject."

"And I have no intention of discussing *your* subject. Let's just call it off." It was called off.

Later, four prisoners were brought in from the adjacent cellblock, which was even more crowded. As soon as the jailer had gone, one of the new arrivals edged over close to my cell. He was a tall fellow with a receding chin, a straight, no-lips mouth, and long, straight black hair starting in irregular, unkempt tufts just above his eyebrows. "Lemme at that Commie bastard!" he shouted suddenly. "I'll *kill* the nigger-lovin' sonofabitch!" He snaked his arm through the bars, grabbing at my throat. I leaned back out of reach while the man standing next to my assailant delivered him a karate chop across the bicep. The redhead snatched him back from the bars, and simultaneously a third man tripped him, decking him with a thud. A fourth man, a silent observer till then, stood over him and said, "I don't know what kinda crud *you* are, but anybody can see this man's a *gen'lman*. Now move away from here!"

When the jailer returned, the conversation had resumed around my cell, the Tuft-head was alone at the far end of the bullpen. By midafternoon the *Press-Scimitar* arrived with another big spread of stories. By suppertime I was sufficiently acquainted with a dozen or so of my visitors to know what they were in for. Redhead, for example, was charged with stealing a twenty-dollar roll of copper wire; the simple-looking kid was charged with stealing his sister-in-law's car ("I had permission," he said); the quiet guy was charged with vagrancy ("They couldn't think of nothing *else*"); and Tuft-head, I heard secondhand, was charged with holding up a filling station.

At eight-thirty everybody was locked back in cells; at nine the lights were put out; and quiet slowly prevailed. I welcomed a chance to think over my situation. I felt a dull, steady pain over the loss of my freedom, but there was nothing to be done about that for a while. I wondered if my wife, Gladys, was still working under an assumed name as a Macy's comparison shopper, as she had been since leaving North Carolina a few months before and moving into a Bronx apartment with her mother and three-year-old Barbara. In case she and the Party couldn't find a lawyer for me, I thought I had better prepare to handle my own extradition hearing, scheduled for Tuesday. I must decide whether to oppose extradition to North Carolina and what to do about my hundred-thousand-dollar bail, and I must demand a copy of the indictment. Feeling a reassuring security in my jailhouse community, I then drifted into a heavy sleep.

On Saturday morning the jail routine was comfortably familiar. While waiting for the guys to be let out for breakfast, I began jotting pencil notes on what I would argue on the bail issue. I thought I could make a strong case for reduction of bail. Even if I couldn't win it, I would at least embarrass my prosecutors while they were trying to tear the Constitution to shreds.

Though the papers carried more and more hostile nonsense about me, my new friends began visiting me more considerately, and I soon had a chance to talk with some of them alone. Before the morning was over I'd written two letters home for guys "shaky on spellin' " and another to a gouging lawyer who was trying to squeeze his client and take him for everything he owned.

In the early afternoon a telegram was delivered to me from Gladys: "DEAREST DARLING WE ARE DOING EVERYTHING POSSIBLE FOR YOU. EVERYONE HAS BEEN WONDERFUL. I LOVE YOU WITH ALL MY

HEART AND WILL ALWAYS BE AT YOUR SIDE. BARBARA IS FINE AND AN ANGEL. DONT WORRY ABOUT ANYTHING. LOVE FROM ALL. LETTER WILL FOLLOW." The fact that she had sent the telegram meant that she was no longer "under wraps," but I didn't know how to write to her. I assumed that she had got me a lawyer—the apparent meaning of "Don't worry about anything." But just in case good intentions didn't work out, I still prepared to handle matters for myself. Meantime, even that distant contact with Gladys, Barbara, and my friends had greatly warmed me.

As Sunday morning rolled around, I began to feel like a veteran jailbird. The routine was almost comfortable, and my new acquaintances seemed like old buddies. I now had a personal acquaintance with all my fellow prisoners except Tuft-head, who had been sulking and slinking around by himself. I was in the process of becoming some kind of oracle, and my advice was sought on all sorts of problems and for jailhouse-lawyering purposes. "He's a college man and he's been around besides," was the report.

Right after lunch, I received a letter from Fyke Farmer, a well-known Nashville lawyer who had achieved considerable fame by intervening in the Rosenberg case and winning a stay of execution. He said that Arnold Johnson (a prominent Party functionary) had called him Friday and that my wife had wanted him to come to Memphis for the Tuesday hearing. But he said that he felt the trip would be useless. He advised signing the removal order to North Carolina and recommended that all other questions be raised in the trial court in North Carolina. His advice seemed sensible to me, and I could see no reason not to handle the hearing myself.

On Monday morning, while lying awake, I began reflecting on the conditions in the jail. No doubt they were awful by comparison with almost any jail—especially the overcrowding, the poor food, and the wretched sanitation. During the day I spoke to a number of fellows about how hungry the papers seemed to be for any scrap of news about me or any word I might speak. Since reporters would be swarming over me, why not give them a list of gripes about the jail conditions? They were enthusiastic. One of them even figured out how to communicate with the men in the adjacent cellblock to get their gripes enumerated, complete with examples.

The morning mail brought a second telegram from Gladys saying that a North Carolina attorney whom I had retained two years earlier for such an eventuality would see me when I got to North Carolina. There was also a small envelope, addressed to me in block letters in green ink, which contained a leaflet signed by the Shelby County Communist Party protesting my arrest. Nick had come through, and the supportive message was welcome. The quick response of my Memphis friends was like a firm handshake right through the bars. To my delight, the next day's *Press-Scimitar* published a large photostat of the leaflet, giving it a circulation unprecedented for a Communist publication in the area.

An hour later an airmail, special delivery letter from Gladys arrived, full of reassuring family news. On the outside of the envelope was her name, in care of our assumed name, with our Bronx address. So I was no longer "down under" and had a name and an address again.

All afternoon and after supper, conferences were going on at cell number one as I prepared a classified list of grievances, richly illustrated from the personal experience of dozens of prisoners. Meantime, my suit and shirt had been given to me so that I could wash the shirt, because the jailer took to heart my telling him that the local press had been commenting rather gleefully on my soiled collar.

As soon as the guys had been locked in for the night, it was educate-the-rookie time. A naive young man named Charlie, a new arrival, was selected as the "student."

It happened that the sewer pipe for the toilets made a gradual descent from the first cell down through the fourteenth, and every flush from a higher cell roared through each lower cell at the toilet level. Occupying number fourteen was pretty much like camping by a millrace.

The young man, who had been locked in number twelve, was informed casually of a girlie magazine (nonexistent) with lurid pictures which nearly all the men claimed to have seen to their great satisfaction. When Number Twelve asked where it was, he was told, "Scales has it in number one, but maybe he'll send it down to you if he's finished with it."

"Hey, Scales," shouted the lad, "can I see your magazine?"

"Sure," I said. "Just stand at your john while I put it in the watertight can."

Several neighbors explained matter-of-factly that that was the way things were sent through the tube: the guy up above flushed once to clean the sewer; then at the sound of the second flush you poked your hand in the john and caught the can when it rushed down the pipe.

I flushed once. "OK, Charlie. All clear. Here it comes!" And I flushed again while thirty-six men all but gagged themselves and young Charlie gasped as a surge of water cascaded over his hand, out of his john, and onto his cell floor.

"Did you get it, Charlie?"

"No!" came the distressed reply, "but I'm wet plumb up to my shoulder!"

"You mean you lost our *girlie* mag?" came a chorus of outraged voices.

"Well, *hell*! I tried my *best*!" howled Charlie in anguish.

That was the end. Thirty-odd men roared, guffawed, snorted, and chuckled for the next five minutes. Even the sound of a legitimate flush could start off a chain of chortles.

The next morning I got into my street clothes and called on all to witness that my collar was shining white. Then I made two copies of my grievance list, one of which was smuggled to the neighboring cellblock by a member of a Negro clean-up crew that passed by (the only Negroes I had seen on the third floor, although there were many more Negroes than whites in the jail). One copy I left with Redhead, and the best one I put in my shirt pocket for the reporters.

About an hour after breakfast a jailer came for me, and I was given a big send-off with backslapping, handclasps, and a lot of "good lucks" and "give 'em hells." Out in the corridor I was handcuffed by two U.S. marshals to a prisoner from the neighboring block, a very disconsolate young man in his twenties, reputedly a bank robber.

We were driven to the federal building up on the riverfront. The car was parked some distance from the building, apparently to give TV, newsreel, and newspaper photographers plenty of time. As we approached the building, reporters closed in and brought us temporarily to a stop. I made a few remarks about the jail conditions and then handed a local reporter my list, saying, "Here. This is all documented and true. You can write a human-interest story after I've left."

Once inside, the bank robber and I were uncuffed and locked in a small room with barred windows. Then I was taken out and told that my lawyer wanted to see me. While I was surmising that the marshal had the wrong prisoner, a tall, pleasant, scholarly-looking man came forward, shook my hand, and introduced himself as Fyke Farmer.

I was puzzled, but Farmer explained that my wife seemed so concerned that he decided to come after all. I told him it was a real pleasure to have him and began to ply him with every legal question that had crossed my mind for the past four days. While we conversed intensely, a marshal came to say that I had a long-distance call from my wife in New York. Gladys sounded confident and delightful, and we talked affectionately for about three minutes. I thought of all the things I *must* say after we had hung up.

It was nearly 10:00 A.M. and time for the hearing to commence. Farmer and I went into the courtroom crowded with reporters and photographers. Farmer had advised keeping quiet, not fighting the bail issue or contesting the sufficiency of the indictment. I did as he said, and the hearing was soon over.

The incredible U.S. attorney, Millsaps Fitzhugh, once more mounted the battlements and rattled on about a hundred-thousand-dollar bond being necessary "in the interest of national security," and Mr. Commissioner solemnly intoned, "I feel it is proper in this case."

The indictment was read, but somehow no one had a copy for the defendant. A waiver of extradition, however, was offered to me, and on Farmer's

Hometown arrival, November 24, 1954
(*Greensboro Daily News*)

advice, I signed it. The commissioner asked me if I objected to photographers taking pictures. I did not. According to the United Press: "It was the signal for cameramen to take pictures while Scales sat calmly facing them. Scales smiled during the picture-taking when a photographer shouted, 'Give us a smile; look like you're happy!' "

By midafternoon, when I was returned to the jail, the *Press-Scimitar* had come out with a picture and a story about the hearing. The story stated, "Scales made a speech about the bad conditions in the Shelby County Jail and handed out a long list of grievances." Back in jail this was proof that I had been a good shop steward, that I had kept the faith. When I walked into the cellblock I was loudly cheered and then pounded on the back until I was dizzy. Between lock-in and lights-out, another "educational" session was held with another new arrival as the pupil. This time young Charlie enjoyed himself as much as the rest.

Before breakfast, the jailer handed me my street clothes again, and the word was that "Scales is goin' out this mawnin'." After finishing the meager oatmeal serving, I washed my nylon shirt, rolled it in my towel, and then waved it around to help it dry.

"That's right, Scales. You don't want that collar to get a bad press from the Carolina papers," Redhead said, grinning. Then the guys began gathering around my door as a sort of informal "testifying" meeting began, based, as one fellow put it, on "what to do about Scales's bum rap." The deliberations included "Play down that Communist issue, 'cause it'll hurt you with the public," "Just' take it easy an' be natural," "Jus' tell 'em the plain God's truth," and "Shee-yit! I don't think they got any goddam case a *tall!*"

The "meeting" was still going strong when the jailer came to get me. After shaking hands with nearly everyone and wishing them well, I said, "I sure wish you men were the jury; I'll never forget you!" I waved and was ushered out, wondering how I could have become so attached to a bunch of fellows I hadn't even known five days before.

A single marshal was waiting for me. I was handcuffed, a chain was wound around my middle, the continuing chain was looped around the handcuffs, and I was led on a leash to a car. Followed by a second marshal in another car, the marshal drove north out of the city, parallel to the river, to a military airport. There he drove up to a small quonset building surrounded by an assortment of military planes, and the follow-up marshal drove away. My driver had spoken very little during the ride, and I had been absorbed in my own thoughts.

I was escorted inside and handcuffed to a chair while the marshal talked to a tall, blond navy lieutenant wearing flying togs and a permanent beetling frown.

"That the Commie-bastard I'm sposed to carry?"

"Yeah. That's the prisoner," said the marshal.

"Oughta drop the sonvabitch in the river. Save the government money."

"How soon do we leave?" asked the marshal, slightly embarrassed.

"They're checkin' the plane now. Take you over the officers' mess for lunch. Shouldn' be long after that."

"I can't leave," said the marshal.

"Why not? He ain't going nowhere. Tries, I'll blow his goddam brains out."

"Regulations. I have to stay with him."

"Aw right. Have 'em send you a tray." He left and in about fifteen minutes an enlisted man wearing whites entered carrying a covered tray.

"What about him?" asked the enlisted man, nodding toward me. "Don't he get nothin'?"

"They'll have something for him at the other end," said the marshal vaguely, as he began stuffing his face.

Sometime before two o'clock the plane appeared to be ready. I was allowed to go to the toilet fully equipped with handcuffs and chains. Outside, by the plane, the pilot and the marshal strapped a parachute over my chains and then threw my topcoat loosely over everything.

"We hafta bail out, count five fast and pull the ripcord by your neck. Wait too long, you jerk ya goddam balls off."

I stared at the pilot in disgust. I couldn't *reach* the ripcord. I couldn't even blow my nose. The marshal helped me into the tiny cabin and methodically clapped a pair of leg-irons around my ankles, looped another chain several times around them, and connected both ends to my handcuffs and the chain around my waist. The marshal then climbed into the seat next to the pilot, who was checking his instruments.

"Oughta keelhaul him from a cable like a nigger. Oh! Shouldn'ta said that. You're a nigger-*lover*, ain't you?" The pilot glared at me balefully. I returned the look unfocusing, expressionless, and silent.

The props turned, the twin motors roared. The plane took off, circled half over the Mississippi, and headed east on the six-hundred-mile flight. As we climbed, it grew rapidly colder. The wind whistled around me as though I were out on the wing. Some ventilator had been left open by accident or design, while up in the snug cockpit two circulating heaters were blowing full blast.

After about four hundred miles we reached the Great Smokies, climbing still higher to clear the peaks. The snow was deep on the mountains below, and the temperature in the cabin must have been ten degrees or less. The wind had numbed my body. My hands had turned blue, and the manacles on my wrists and ankles burned like fire. My topcoat had slipped off my shoulders and down my back where I couldn't reach it. I was faint from hunger anyway, and I could feel my consciousness slowly melting away like an ice cube in the warm sun.

Somewhere, in a muddle, I could hear the pilot yakking over the radio with the Greensboro–High Point control tower. I forced my eyes open and looked foggily out the window. On the horizon was the Jefferson-Standard building, Greensboro's skyscaper. Below me, shining up like a mirror of my past life, was Lake Hamilton, and beside it the house where I had spent my childhood.

Part Two

Oh God help me now to cry out and
bear witness;
Help me to send forth a great cry at the
darkness;
Help me to waken my brother from his
dream of rage and fire;
Help me to cry out in defense of my
brother.
Hush; do not let a moment's delirium
Negate the decorum of a lifetime of
indifference.
If you should cry out there would be
nothing to say.
Hush; you would only waken the
others.

Thomas McGrath, from "The Restless Night"

3

Way Down Yonder

Watch out for him, Aunt Lou! It's muddy and slippery here," my mother called.

Aunt Lou held me tightly by the hand as we followed my mother from the car to witness the immense activity taking place at the edge of a newly made dirt road. Scores of Negro men in blue overalls and dozens of mules were excavating a huge basin, pulling drag pans full of dirt to one end, dumping it out, and circling back to where men with pickaxes, mattocks, and shovels were breaking new earth.

It was cold, and the smell of damp clay mixed with smoke from several bonfires, where roots, logs, branches, and debris blazed away. My mother, a beautiful woman in her early thirties, auburn-haired and smartly dressed, walked over to where the Negro foreman stood on a stump directing the mule traffic. "Howdy, Miz Scales," he said as he swept off his wide-brimmed hat.

"That's *Walter*!" I shouted as I pulled away from Aunt Lou and ran over to be picked up and hugged by the smiling, light-skinned man. Walter Holt, the foreman on most of my father's real estate development projects, lived in a big old house on a farm with a wife named Dosca and a little roly-poly boy named Alfred, who was about four or five.

"Now that part where they're pilin' up the dirt is gonna be the dam with a road on top of it; and over yonder is one of the feedin' streams and over thataway 'bout a quarter mile is the other one." While Walter took my mother to the white engineer, busy with his transit some distance away, Aunt Lou recaptured her charge and started back toward the car.

We made a strange sight. The old woman, small, black, wrinkled, her hair

Junius, 1924

Junius, 1928

nearly white, was clothed in a black dress down to her ankles, worn over numberless petticoats, and itself covered by a starched white apron tied in a big bow in the back. Around her shoulders was an old black cardigan sweater, and on her head was an immaculate white maid's cap. She'd been my nurse since the dawn of my memory. I, three or four years old, was wearing heavy knee-length socks, a navy blue double-breated overcoat with brass buttons, and a matching navy blue hat. My tight golden curls, carefully tended by Aunt Lou and much treasured by my mother, fell to my shoulders. My skin was unusually fair, and my eyelashes were exceptionally long. Admiring old ladies often told me, "My! you're pretty enough to be a girl!" to my great disgust. I had been born on March 26, 1920, to Alfred Moore Scales and his second wife, Mary Leigh Scales (née Pell).

As Aunt Lou led me along, trying to keep my shiny shoes away from muddy spots, her dim vision led us into the path of a mule team, and a young Negro driver swerved to miss us. "You better watch where you goin' wid dem mules, boy! This here Mist' *Scales's* chile. Mist' Scales, he own all dis lan' an' he buildin' all dese roads and things." She drew me to her protectively.

"Aw right, auntie, I jes' tryin to keep outa yo' way," the young man grinned.

Aunt Lou turned her attention to me. "Now, Uvvin, yo' daddy gettin' a big lake built here. Dere's gonna be water evvy *which*away, and den he gonna build anudder one 'bout a mile down de road."

But I was watching a six-mule team tugging on a chain around a large stump. The mules strained, the driver shouted, roots snapped, and the stump suddenly exploded from the ground, ripping up the earth all around it. Then I saw that the driver was Nereus Foster, a man in his mid-fifties with a shining, coal black face. He often came to garden at home in Irving Park, and I followed him around like a puppy under my nurse's watchful eye.

"Howdy, Aunt Lou. Howdy, Mist' Uvvin. How you all come on?"

"Oh, de Lawd's been good to me," Aunt Lou replied. "How's Miz Lula?" I had often visited "Miz Lula" at her home, where my mother took washing too fine to be entrusted to the laundry. She was as nice as her husband. At the last visit she had given me a biscuit with damson preserves and butter. And she boiled soap in a big black pot in her side yard.

Nereus would always allow that his "ole 'ooman" was fine except for her "rheumatiz," and today was no exception. "I bet you never rode a mule, did you, Mist' Uvvin?" I shook my head. Nereus unharnessed a mule, put a halter on it, and plumped me astride its bare back while Aunt Lou shouted, "Lawd-a-mussy! You hol' on tight, Uvvin!"

"He ain't gonna hurt hisself," Nereus said reassuringly. "He gotta learn to set a hawse like his daddy or his mama. You ain't skeered, is you, Mist' Uvvin?"

My mother, seeing her youngest on muleback, came running in alarm until she saw who was in charge and the ecstatic look on my face. When I'd ridden twice around in a circle, she announced that it was time to go home. She inquired of Nereus about Lula's health, got the usual "rheumatiz" information, expressed her sympathy, and led the way to the car. On the way home, she let me stand by her side on the front seat (held firmly from the back seat by Aunt Lou) so I could better see the new dirt roads and the beautiful forest which would soon become the town of Hamilton Lakes.

That was my earliest memory of Lake Hamilton. It became a lovely sixteen-acre lake several miles west of the then city limits of Greensboro. Before moving there my family had lived in a large brick house in Irving Park, in northern Greensboro. This was a residential area my father had developed many years earlier and named for his father, Colonel Junius Irving Scales (Confederate States of America), Presbyterian elder, lawyer, and North Carolina state senator. (Hamilton Lakes was named for Euphemia Hamilton Henderson Scales, the colonel's wife.)

Later, my father built a thirty-six-room Georgian mansion on Lake Hamilton, and we moved in early in 1927, when I was six years old. I grew up in that house and on a twelve-acre estate bordering the lake. I roamed the woods around it, swam in it, canoed on it, walked on its ice, explored its inlets and tributaries, saw thousands of days dawn over its waters and darken over the trees on its western banks, and watched the sun, the moon, and the stars undulate endlessly in its ripples; and I experienced many a poem and many a novel while stretched out in a burlap hammock in the forked branch of an ancient maple sixty feet above it.

Aunt Lou (Mrs. Louisa Trice) was senior among the servants. As my loving nurse, she referred to me as "her boy." She had been born in slavery in Greensboro in 1853, and she charmed me with stories of her childhood and youth—"de old-timey days." She told me once of seeing Joseph E. Johnston's Confederate army retreat through Greensboro in 1865: "The most horses an' wagons an' cannons an' guns you ever seed. They jes' kep' a-comin', and the mens looked plum whupped and wo' out. I was watchin' 'em most all day from in de yard cause I'se jes' twelve years ole and my muh wouldn' let me out." Such was her influence over me that I adopted her Negro dialect almost completely for a time. My mother, finding me one day seated primly in a chair in the kitchen, asked me why I was sitting in there. "I'se a-settin' heah 'cause Aint Lou sot me heah" was the reply.

Aggie or A.G. (Mrs. Agnes Craig), the tremendously accomplished up-

Colonel Junius Irving Scales, C.S.A.,
1832–1880 (Grandfather)

stairs maid, was proud of being part Indian. She was almost as concerned over the upbringing of the Scales children as she was over her own. She worked for my mother for more than thirty years.

Cooks and butlers changed from time to time, but the names Clyde, Elviro, Sara, and Martha always recalled for me much gentleness, insight, and patience. The two outdoor men I have mentioned, Walter Holt and Nereus Foster, taught me much about nature and gardening. Nereus, especially, with a beautiful ebony black face and graying hair, a noble preceptor and a tireless, sensitive teacher, won my deep affection and respect.

The Negro servants had a concept of how a young white boy should act, and they were kindly but firmly critical when I didn't live up to expectations. Once when Clyde, the butler, answered the front doorbell, I trotted up and became most inquisitive about the lady caller. A few hours later in my favorite haunts, the kitchen and the butler's pantry, I blushed and hung my head when I heard Clyde singing a little song, apparently to himself: "How long you gonna stay? Where you been? When you comin' again? What's your name and where you from?" But when he saw he'd got across his point about good manners, he stopped his work and gave me a "horsie-ride" on his shoulder.

My sister, Mary Leigh, and my brother, Archibald Henderson, five and three and a half years older than I, were close companions who studied together and played together, so that I saw surprisingly little of them in the large house. I actually spent more time with the grown-ups: my parents, my tutor, my Aunt Lucy, and my cousin Harry.

My mother's older sister, Aunt Lucy Pell, known to her niece and nephews affectionately as "Sis," worked tirelessly for the First Presbyterian Church. She never married. Incredibly selfless in her concern for others, this beloved member of the family came the closest of anyone I ever knew to putting Christianity into practice. Her entire life was given over to the needs of others. She began working for the church in the early twenties with the title of pastor's assistant. She acquired other titles, but in her forty years of devoted service she was the ever-bleeding heart, the full-time do-gooder, the living "soul" (and it needed one) of that huge church.

She had loved but once—and for her that meant always: my cousin Harry. They had intended to marry; but the financial reverses Harry suffered in the twenties, aggravated by the depression and his pride, put marriage out of his reach. She accepted that turn of events, brokenhearted, and almost no one knew her anguish.

Harry Cobb, nicknamed "Unk," was a sophisticated, very conservative Princeton graduate, a World War I veteran, and an unsuccessful lawyer who lived with my family most of the time for many years. Though he teased me, calling me "The Pest," he often talked to me as though I were a grown-up.

One of the traumas of my childhood was that, in the depths of the depression, my beloved Unk twice attempted suicide.

A newcomer to the family circle at the time of the move to Hamilton Lakes was our tutor, Miss Louie J. Williams, a retired schoolteacher from eastern North Carolina. Because of her last name, Harry nicknamed her "Bill," and thus she was addressed by her pupils. I thought her rigid: having learned to read at four, I'd already read many children's books and newspapers and comic strips; yet I was relentlessly assigned to study a primer about an obnoxious "little red hen."

One visitor whose stay was always a thrilling event for me was my Aunt Katherine, my father's younger sister. She was a socialite who moved in the highest society and enjoyed the company of the rich, the powerful, and the socially prominent of the world. She swept through life with the grandeur of an empress.

Granddaddy (my maternal grandfather) was an even more regular visitor. Edward Leigh Pell, directly descended from Pocahontas and John Rolfe, had been born in Richmond, Virginia, in 1861. One of his two distinguished brothers was the president of Converse College in Spartanburg, South Carolina; the other was an editor, lawyer, judge, and for many years the powerful corporation commissioner of North Carolina. Granddaddy was a fragile, sensitive, controlled, yet essentially quite emotional man. He cared nothing for material things and was never well-to-do, having grown up and raised his family in an impoverished South. He became a Methodist minister early in life but, finding the denomination restrictive, gave up Methodism after becoming a doctor of divinity. While remaining an ordained minister of the Methodist church, he refused pastorates and became an interdenominationalist, at home in most Protestant churches, who made his living by writing and lecturing on religious subjects.

About 1928 Aunt Lucy and my mother were stunned (and even somewhat scandalized) when their father announced that he had remarried—a music student, Florence West of London, Ontario, thirty-five years his junior. Granddaddy tactfully arranged for Florence to visit her relatives in Canada while he visited his daughters in Hamilton Lakes. Because he continued the practice over the years, I didn't meet Florence till much later.

My half-brothers and half-sisters were frequently home, and since other relatives often visited for weeks or months at a time, twelve at table was not an unusual occurrence. The dining room, large with a high ceiling and two French windows, boasted a resplendent crystal chandelier over its table. At lunch individual doilies were used along with the second silver service and simpler plates. But at dinner, when there was company, the table glowed—especially while Elviro was the butler. Elviro was a Filipino who had served in the U.S.

Navy and been impressed with the glitter of the captain's table on board ship. He loved the fine china and crystal and the sparkling best silver and would set a truly elegant table. His wife, Sara, the cook, would match the visual delight of Elviro's table with the quality of her traditional southern cooking. Sweet-potato pudding covered with marshmallows, scalloped oysters, fried chicken, hot cakes, lemon meringue pie, soft rolls, biscuits, corn bread, popovers—these were the merest beginnings of her culinary marvels. But my father believed that no matter how delicious the food, conversation was the most important thing at table, and under his inspiration the dining room rang with laughter, grew tense with the advocacy of opposing political and philosophical views, and relaxed with the exchange of amusing anecdotes.

Alfred Moore Scales was an imposing man, over six feet tall, ruddy in complexion, and handsome. His manner was gracious and warm. He was intelligent, well read, quick-witted, and often eloquent—the dominant spirit of any gathering.

His ancestry was distinguished. The first colonial forebear of his name, Hardwin Scales, had arrived in Jamestown, Virginia, in 1623. Youngest son of a Hertfordshire family, lacking an inheritance, he had decided to seek his fortune in the New World. The family had been in partial eclipse since the Wars of the Roses, at which time the head of Lord Scales, a notable but defeated general, had been displayed on London Bridge atop a pike. Lord Scales (immortalized in part three of Shakespeare's *Henry VI*) was of Norman descent, his ancestor d'Escaler having founded the family fortunes by fighting with William the Conqueror and receiving handsome rewards for his efforts. Lord Scales's sister was married to Edward IV and mothered the little princes murdered in the Tower of London.

In America, Hardwin Scales's progeny migrated to North Carolina and became well-to-do. There seemed to be a remarkable attraction between Scales men and Henderson women, for Alfred's father and uncle married Henderson sisters. Among his Henderson ancestors, his great-great-great-grandfather, Richard Henderson, had been a royal judge in North Carolina before the Revolution, formed the Transylvania Company (which owned Kentucky and part of Tennessee), and employed Daniel Boone to explore the territory; Leonard Henderson, son of Richard, was the first chief justice of the North Carolina Supreme Court.

Alfred's father had named him after his own elder brother, Alfred Moore Scales, congressman before and after the Civil War, Confederate general, and later, governor of North Carolina. The first Junius Irving Scales, Alfred's father, had emigrated in 1858 from North Carolina by wagon train, accompanied by numerous slaves, to Mississippi's Yazoo River valley, where he had acquired much land. When Mississippi seceded from the Union, he enlisted as a private and soon became colonel of the Thirtieth Mississippi Infantry Regiment. He fought at Chickamauga, apparently with reckless bravery (he was brevetted brigadier general), and was captured, spending the rest of the war in a prison camp on Johnson's Island in Lake Erie, near Sandusky, Ohio. If the camp was not quite an Andersonville, it nevertheless destroyed the young colonel's health. After the war, his fortune lost, he returned to North Carolina, first to farm and then to practice law with his brother and raise a large family. While he was a state senator, he dutifully managed his older brother's political campaigns. In 1880 he died at the age of forty-eight.

Alfred, then ten years old, grew up in Greensboro in genteel poverty. He attended the University of North Carolina at Chapel Hill, taught school, studied law, passed the bar, was elected a state senator at twenty-five, and became a successful lawyer with interests in life insurance and in real estate companies. By 1920 he had become several times a millionaire. His first wife died in 1912, and in 1914 he married Mary Leigh Pell of Richmond, Virginia, twenty-two years his junior. Since he was active in many areas, including politics, visitors were often prominent public figures. I once discomfited Wilson's secretary of the navy (later Roosevelt's ambassador to Mexico), Josephus Daniels, while sitting on his lap: after listening to him talk at close range with newly fitted dentures, I informed the famous editor, with the excitement of scientific discovery, that his teeth *clicked*!

There was much discussion of books in the family, and even Bill, after completing the "little red hen" torture, encouraged my reading. The library became my favorite room in the house. It contained more than three thousand books, which I catalogued completely in a ledger in a childish hand when I was ten. Long before that I'd read through thirty volumes of Mark Twain; six or seven of Dumas *père*; novels like *Lorna Doone, The Swiss Family Robinson, Treasure Island*; several poetry anthologies; and much of an India-paper edition of Tennyson. Once I'd discovered books, even though the nearest companion my own age lived a half mile away, I was never lonely. Or at least, if I was, I never realized it.

Not long after moving to Hamilton Lakes my father had severe financial reverses, owing to the real estate crash which preceded the 1929 stock market disaster by some two years. At about the same time he had a nervous breakdown, followed by a heart attack which left him a near invalid and ended his active business and public life. The family's social life decreased noticeably, but as far as I could tell there was no change in the style of living until 1934, when I was fourteen.

I became my father's frequent companion and, when the invalid was able to take walks again, always accompanied him. I gardened with him, read to him, and sought his views on every conceivable subject. My mother, in addition to

Alfred Moore Scales, 1870–1940 (Father)

Mary Leigh Pell Scales, 1892–1960 (Mother)

being a tireless nurse and companion, became my father's amanuensis in innumerable business matters and maintained his law office for several years.

No one in the family played an instrument; there was no piano in the house; and the family's isolation made music lessons out of the question. But I was a passionate listener. I studied radio programs for music broadcasts and for many years rarely missed a New York Philharmonic or Metropolitan Opera broadcast. I read avidly about music and became a knowledgeable dilettante before I entered public school. I continued to read omnivorously. Following my father's interest in Civil War literature, I read nearly two hundred of his books on the subject. To my great self-satisfaction, while on a visit to the famous battlefield in 1932, I was able to "straighten out" my father concerning the relative positions of the brigades of Lane and Scales (my great-uncle) on the third day of the battle of Gettysburg.

Though I became an ardent Confederate, I began to alter my views when I was twelve, after reading Herndon's *Life of Lincoln*. It seemed a well-documented fact that Lincoln was gentle, kind, modest, intelligent, and eloquent—attributes I had supposed to be completely lacking in "Yankees."

At about the age of twelve I began to find that I didn't always agree with my father: Abraham Lincoln, tastes in poetry, and attitudes toward music were early points of difference. I was astonished at the things a man fifty years older than I did *not* know. So I began to develop my own views: a less-cozy but more-stimulating state of affairs.

My brother and sister had left Bill's tutelage and were driven to public high school every day, beginning with their sophomore year. I found their talk of their friends and activities so fascinating that I was pleased when it was decided, a year later, in the fall of 1932, to enter me at Greensboro Central Junior High School as a freshman.

Upon entering public school I'd decided to use my first name because no one seemed to be able to spell Irving correctly: it usually came out Irvin, Ervin, Irwin, Erving, or the like. There were problems with Junius, too, which often became either Julius or Junior. But despite these twists, I would become Junius.

I was an unusual student. Exceptionally well prepared in most subjects, I was wretched in math. Nor had dawdling over lessons and daydreaming prepared me for the competitive rush in the classroom and the need to take notes. What was really strange was that my social morality was compounded of elements such as the ideals of southern gentlemanhood epitomized by Robert E. Lee; ideals of chivalry exemplified by King Arthur and his knights (by way of Howard Pyle's books); "golden rule" Christian ethics, uncritically accepted (contradictions and all) from Bible stories; the Bible itself (which I had read in its entirety); discussions with my pious Aunt Lucy and my devout grandfather; and a trusting and enthusiastic belief that the world was very beautiful and that most of the people in it were too. Having had more contact with my parents than with my older siblings also tended to make my secondhand knowledge of the world singularly dated. My father's youthful experience of the 1880s was a poor preparation for the depression 1930s.

Generally I found the teaching uninspiring, but there was a memorable exception. An English teacher named Louise Smith was a warmhearted, enlightened free spirit who had a way of rewarding any scholarly initiative by making the student feel ten feet tall. She thought for herself; her opinions were her own; and nothing delighted her more than seeing some sign of this process in her students. She encouraged my poetry reading and deepened my understanding of what I'd already read. She was my first really stimulating teacher.

For the most part, I begrudged the time my homework took from my varied reading, which I considered my real education. Although my grades were rather good, I felt no urge whatever to compete for them with the other students. Whatever I'd learned was adequate compensation for my efforts. In any event, living five miles from the city tended to isolate me and exclude me from normal social activities outside school—an exclusion that continued even after I moved to senior high as a sophomore.

In October 1934, when I'd started my junior year in high school, my parents closed the house and rented an apartment in Fort Lauderdale, Florida, until the following June. My father's health had deteriorated further, and the doctor thought a warm climate would be helpful. And besides, as I found out later, the house had been mortgaged heavily and the maintenance of it had become a weighty financial burden. My brother and sister were away at college. Aunt Lucy moved in with friends in Greensboro. Cousin Harry had found a job in Ohio. Bill went to live with relatives. Aunt Lou moved in with her sister in Greensboro on a pension. Nereus and Walter (both over sixty-five) were able to find light work that was adequate for their needs. A.G. was working for friends of the family.

I went to Fort Lauderdale with few regrets, regarding my change of locale as a happy adventure. Accompanying me were my books on music, my opera librettos, and my wonderful ten-tube radio.

The new school was jolting: as a fourteen-year-old junior I found that I was slightly younger than the average freshman. On the positive side was the diversity of the transient students who came from every state east of the Rockies and were interesting and stimulating to me. However, the school, large and expanding when I arrived, had shrunk by more than two-thirds six months later with the departure of tourists.

I began to feel my oats intellectually, and in consequence more disagreement and friction developed with my father. My mother became a distressed peacemaker as her son and husband began to find it hard to agree even on what kind of day it was. At school I found no mental companionship whatever and began more and more to feel set apart and alone in my concern with literature, art, and music. The "get-ahead" obsession with success that motivated many of my classmates was revolting to me. I thought like an adult but felt like a raw adolescent socially: I saw the absurdities and vanities of the accepted forms of social intercourse adopted by my peers, but I wanted to belong. I deeply craved friends with values and interests like my own, and even more wanted a friend like that who was a girl whom I could love.

Sometime during the winter my mother went back to Greensboro and stored the furniture. The house no longer belonged to the family. It must have been a bitter blow to my parents, but I was not disturbed. I set no store on material things (except my books and my precious radio). And what interested me was the future. The plan was to move in the fall to Chapel Hill, where my sister and brother would both be students at the University of North Carolina.

My childhood thus ending, the timeless vistas of my early years, with all their heightened feelings, remained fast in my memory as I prepared for the challenge of a new life in a new hometown.

4

Youth Grown Old

Shades of the prison-house begin to close
Upon the growing Boy . . .

Wordsworth, "Intimations of Immortality"

C hapel Hill in 1935 was a town of about five thousand people, and its sole
reason for existence was to serve as the business and residential adjunct
of the University of North Carolina (UNC). The university and the town were
so wedded that they were often referred to interchangeably, and it was—and
is—as common to hear a student say "I go to Chapel Hill" as "I go to the
university." The relationship began in 1795 when the university first opened
its doors. The campus 140 years later was full of ancient trees and even older
buildings, with newer structures sprawled around in every direction.

The business section was largely confined to one block of East Franklin
Street and mostly on the north side at that. Between Berman's Department
Store at one end and Abernethy's Intimate Bookshop at the other were a grocery, a movie theater, a couple of drugstores, several cafés and cafeterias, the
post office, two banks, and some odds and ends of shops. Except in the very
center of town, the sidewalks were of beige-colored sand or fine gravel.

The residential areas were large, and in the affluent sections the houses
were well spaced. Trees were everywhere, bordering the walks and streets and
surrounding the houses. The townspeople were in tolerant familiarity with one
another and proud of such a character as eighty-year-old Marcus Cicero Ste-
phens Noble, a dean emeritus of the School of Education and president of the
Bank of Chapel Hill, who drove down Franklin Street at five miles an hour,
beeping his antique horn every few feet. When the old man came to an intersection he would stop, put on the emergency brake, stand up in his topless,
thirty-year-old two-seater, check for traffic to right and to left, and then, when

not a moving car was in sight, proceed, slowly building his speed up to five miles an hour. Pedestrians would chuckle while children romped alongside and dogs barked.

Chapel Hill was as proud of its distinguished faculty as of its "characters," and almost everyone from the grocery clerk to the postman felt free to greet the university's famous president, Frank Porter Graham, with a cordial "Howdy, Doctor Frank!" knowing the salutation would be returned with equal warmth, and with their first names included. There was also a generally tolerant sufferance of not-so-pleasant characters—for example, a dragon of a matron who was so energetic and zealous in the hounding of sin that she somehow cajoled and bullied the aldermen into passing a town ordinance preventing *infants* from wearing sunsuits where they could be seen publicly.

The Negroes, who worked mostly as domestic servants and janitors, were jammed into an area northwest of the town's center. Relations between whites and Negroes appeared to be marked by patriarchal benevolence of the former toward the latter. Nevertheless, within three or four years several near-lynchings occurred and a real riot erupted, casting considerable doubt on both the good intentions of the whites and the presumed passivity of the Negroes.

When a fire was reported to the volunteer fire department, code numbers were blasted from a foghorn so that the whole town could know where the fire was. Two blasts, a pause, and two more blasts, for example, meant twenty-two; a quick look at the phone book would show that twenty-two designated "E. Franklin, near Dr. MacNider's." Immediately fire buffs of all ages started for the scene, especially if it were nearby. A bright, relatively harmless fire (such as the burning of an abandoned barn on the edge of town) would bring about a social occasion where grown-ups met acquaintances they hadn't seen for months, and they would chat and gossip as they watched the blaze. Lovers necked, children cavorted and got in the way of the firemen, and a pleasant entertainment was enjoyed by all.

All in all, Chapel Hill was a lovely place to live in, and there my family rented a huge house nearly a mile east of the business district. The walk into town was a delight: almost continuous shade in hot weather, the sight and sound of birds everywhere, and cordiality from everyone encountered (even the terrible dragon matron). In spring and summer the air was delicious with the fragrance of flowers and blooming trees. The heavy, seminal scent of mimosas penetrated everywhere. I was pleased with the new home and its spacious yard and garden, bordering on a vast woods known as Battle Park, and pleased, too, to have a large room of my own with a screened-in sleeping porch. Best of all, I acquired a record-playing attachment, which I channeled through my much-traveled radio, and some new records.

Being the new boy in school was by then no novelty. The high school had an easygoing atmosphere and by far the highest level of teaching I had encountered. Gradually fitting in with my cordial fellow students, I began to have normal social activities for the first time in my life.

The most interesting spot in town for me was Milton Abernethy's Intimate Bookshop. Ab, the proprietor, from Hickory, North Carolina, had long since become a legend, although he was only in his late twenties. He had been a radical antimilitarist at State College in Raleigh and had been expelled. He had made a trip to the Soviet Union which scandalized Chapel Hill. With his capable and energetic wife, Minna, he had issued in the early thirties a "little mag" of exceptional quality, *Contempo,* which had published Bernard Shaw, T. S. Eliot, Ezra Pound, William Faulkner, North Carolina's own Paul Green, and a host of other imposing writers.

The store was a dilapidated frame building on East Franklin Street between a vacant lot and the First Presbyterian Church. The stock of books was immense and incredibly varied. If one found an interesting book by a contemporary writer, it might very well have the author's autograph in it. When I mentioned this discovery with amazement, Abernethy promptly offered to have the volume of Milton I was then buying inscribed by its author. Ab's unpredictable, even erratic, manner contributed to the wary fascination with which he was generally regarded.

The treasure-house of books was a magnet for a number of the university's better professors and students. Two or three intense discussions would likely be going on at one time in different parts of the store. Distinguished writers would drop in on their way through the state, and I met there (within two or three years) figures as disparate as Allen Tate, Norman Thomas, Paul Green, Muriel Rukeyser, Clifford Odets, Ralph Bates, and W. H. Auden.

A high school companion, Bobby, like me found the bookstore irresistible; we spent much time there after school and on Saturdays. Imperceptibly, and completely without formalities, we became employees and rang up sales, ordered books, kept financial tallies, swept floors, got the mail, and generally took charge when Ab and Minna were not around. Most of all, we read. I had a platform fifteen feet above the floor, well hidden by piles of textbooks, where I often curled up and read for hours at a time.

At the back of the store was a print shop with the huge (abandoned) rotary press which had once printed *Contempo,* as well as a Linotype machine, several fonts of display hand type, and a letterpress. The proprietor was T. Olin Mathews, a printer, bachelor, bohemian, former socialist, and avid student of foreign languages. In exchange for some help with the letterpress, he taught me the rudiments of printing and always welcomed Bobby and me while regaling us with some choice, recently discovered item of esoteric and inconsequential information.

The bookstore, with its associations, was to be a major influence on me for years to come.

Meanwhile, my life grew less idyllic. The feeling of being apart from others had become aggravated. I'd stay aloof from everyone, including my family, buried in Tolstoy or Goethe or Balzac for days at a time. Then, with something close to desperation, I'd join my adolescent school buddies and we'd drive recklessly around town, taking along any girls foolish enough to go with us. Petting was self-conscious and tentative, much inhibited by neo-Victorian standards of social behavior.

Sexual frustration became more and more distressing. Nor was it helped by an overt homosexual advance made to me by a college instructor in his twenties. I was shocked and repelled by it, but most of all I was crushed by the realization of betrayal: I had thought the man's interest in me stemmed from a feeling of friendship and sympathetic intellectual and cultural interests. The very crassness of his approach during a hike in the woods showed that I had been gullible indeed and that my "friend" was merely interested in adding to his collection of teenage boys. My hurt was further complicated by the feeling that I had been "square" and gauche in running all the way home after having been propositioned.

The Sir Galahad who had entered public school at the age of twelve was to lose many more of his cherished illusions by the time he was fifteen. In any event, as exhortations or precepts, they were all probably a good deal more redolent of Victorian times than of the twentieth century.

When I was about twelve, Aunt Lucy gave me a handsome leather-bound Bible with my name printed on it in gold. I reread the New Testament and was deeply moved by the Gospels. I began to consider myself a Christian.

I assumed at first that the First Presbyterian Church of Greensboro, where my paternal grandfather had been an elder and where my father was the senior elder, was wholly dedicated to carrying out the principles which had so touched my heart. But the pastor, a close personal friend of my father and the family, was a frequent visitor, and I had "big ears." The talk that I heard, alongside my own observations, led me to several conclusions: the inner-church politicking, factional struggles, and backbiting would not have pleased Jesus; the money changers were firmly in control of the temple, and Jesus himself would not have received a cordial welcome to the church if he were a poorly dressed carpenter without social connections; the behavior of many of the elders, deacons, and sometimes the pastor himself could not by any stretching of credibility be described as "Christian"; Aunt Lucy, with her unstinting concern for the indigent, the infirm, and the wretched, had to struggle inside the organization to defend her activities—activities that furnished the church with a much better reputation than it deserved.

My father's reluctance to discuss the church with me and my mother's gentle ironies about the "Christian" behavior of some of the church leaders further cooled my ardor. My experiences in Sunday school ranged from a fairly interesting discussion of Saturday's football games to a perfunctory, embarrassed exhortation from the teacher to believe in Christ and "observe His Ten Commandments"—and then I stopped attending. I concluded that my grandfather, whom I loved and respected, was trying to save with his writing and lecturing a hopelessly foundering ship.

My own beliefs had evolved toward a private sort of Christian mysticism, precious but ephemeral, which might be tarnished if discussed or brought into the open. The supernatural and the mystical aspects gradually faded away, but the feeling for Christ the man remained. I thought that Christ's goodness and gentleness and most of his principles, even if unattainable in practice, should be the model for my own behavior and for the conduct of the society I lived in, even if we all fell greatly short.

But my distrust of self-proclaimed "Christians" and Christian churches had culminated in anticlericalism.

In my first public school year in Greensboro, I had looked around the room at my classmates, for whom I had such affection and admiration, and thought: When people like buoyant Bob King, glorious Eloise Hendrix, witty Billy Stern, charming Patsy Jones, brilliant Stafford Webb, warmhearted Bobby Moffett, thoughtful Mary Baker, and responsible Bernard Foster grow up, how can the world *not* be a fresh and wonderful place? With so much talent, sincerity, generosity, and idealism, how could they not sweep away the narrow-mindedness, the bigotry, the snobbery, and the greed which had trapped their parents' generation?

In Chapel Hill, as I observed my contemporaries in their homes, I began to discover, reluctantly, that quite often they did not even measure up to their parents. In school, for example, l saw the competitive struggle for high grades bring out the most shameless truckling to authority, bootlicking of teachers, and predatory putting-down of fellow students. At private social affairs I noticed the general exclusion of the poor and "the kids from Carrboro" (a little mill town adjoining Chapel Hill on the west), the existence of snobbish cliques within cliques within cliques, and the cultivation of remarkably refined techniques for hurting one another.

The idea that my generation was better gradually fell into ruins.

I had two painful experiences with bigotry.

At age five, reacting to some tutelage from an older boy in Irving Park, I shouted at Aunt Lou in a fit of petulance when she tried to brush my curls, "Take your old black, nigger hand off of me!" She looked as pained as if I had struck her over the head. Seeing this and sensing that I'd reopened unspeakable wounds, I burst into helpless, uncontrollable tears of shame and remorse. I was at last soothed by being hugged to the bosom of the old ex-slave, who petted me tenderly and said over and over as she rocked me, "Dat's *all* right; dat's *all* right!"

Soon after I entered public school at the age of twelve a kindly teacher spoke to me privately and asked how I was getting adjusted. "Fine," I replied. She said that I seemed to be popular with the other kids. Then she said that she had noticed that I seemed to be with Billy quite often. "I think you should spend less time with him," she said. "I don't think your parents would be too pleased if they knew you spent so much time with a little Jew. He's not your type." I felt bewildered that a decent, considerate teacher could see my charming, delightful, mischievous friend only as something called a Jew. I blushed, hung my head, and answered nothing. But I saw Billy more than ever and appreciated him even more because others picked on him. I also discovered with satisfaction that another boy I liked, Robert B., was also Jewish.

These two experiences jolted me anew when I first heard Beethoven's Ninth Symphony, with Schiller's grand words, "Alle Menschen werden Brüder" ("All mankind shall be brothers"); and I felt that it must be so—out of love, reason, and sheer necessity. But in Chapel Hill, one of the most enlightened communities in the South, I found bigotry against Negroes all-pervasive. They were not even a concern, except as a reservoir whence came domestic servants. By established custom, 20 percent of the population was consigned to poverty, indignity, and isolation because of skin color.

About the time of my high school graduation, I was part of a gang of girls and boys returning to Chapel Hill, jammed into a Model A Ford, from an afternoon of frolicking and swimming in Sparrow's Pool in Carrboro. As we crossed the railroad tracks in the middle of Carrboro we suddenly saw a large crowd of Negroes on one side of the highway and a crowd of whites on the other. I'd heard a vague report of the arrest, the previous night, of a Negro on an unspecified charge because he had been "uppity." Resentment in the Negro community apparently had boiled over—an almost unprecedented thing. The boy driving the Model A was so startled by the sight that he let the overloaded jalopy stall on the road directly in between the two groups, and it would not start again. The Negroes were silent, grim, defiant; the whites were raging, screaming, threatening. We were frightened. The other boys and I jumped out and pushed furiously until the motor sputtered and caught up. Then we rattled back to the snug security of Chapel Hill with much excited laughter and exclamations about "all those mean-looking jigaboos, and us stuck right in the middle!" One boy, full of bravado, said, "We oughta go back and throw some firecrackers in the middle of those Nigras; *then* they'd run!"

Later the police and the red-necks came down heavily on the Negroes, and sheer terror reigned in the Negro community for three days. My family was without a cook and a maid for that period because the two women didn't dare leave their homes. When I heard from them the stories of the violence and threats, I could only think guiltily of the words of Thomas Jefferson on the same subject a century and a quarter earlier: "I tremble when I remember there is a just God!"

The Jewish community in Chapel Hill was relatively small compared with that in Greensboro, but prejudice was apparent in the way most Jewish kids were ignored socially and in the ingrown way local Jews clung together for support and social life. I then had no close local ties with Jews, but I thought it shameful that at a time when the people of Moses, Jesus, Spinoza, Heine, Mendelssohn, Freud, and Einstein were undergoing unbelievable torment in Germany, a widespread, largely unspoken disparagement aggravated the customary indignities suffered by the Jews in Chapel Hill.

Brotherhood was not flourishing.

I valued music, literature, art, ideas, and (with some reservations) girls above everything. Because of my enthusiasm, I had a belief (unsupported by empirical evidence) that things of beauty, upon close acquaintance, would win the admiration and respect of almost anyone. Instead, I found that an aggressive philistinism was the norm among my contemporaries; that even some of my favorite companions only tolerated my "culture vulture" ways; that *culture* was an inflammatory word; and that its known devotees were suspected of effeminacy or, at best, snobbery.

Since I wanted to be liked and since I found so many things likable about my companions, I became something of an "underground longhair" and kept quiet about my interests. Moreover, I gradually adopted masks or false fronts to hide my intelligence, for I'd discovered that nothing was so likely to arouse animosity as identifiable intelligence. So I appeared to be "a good fellow," to have "a great sense of humor," to be "a lot of fun"; and all the while my intelligence was sitting to one side, sizing me up, criticizing, calling me an ass.

For the sake of being comfortable with amiable fools, philistines, and even some yahoos, with whom I was scarcely acquainted and whose views and attitudes I held in contempt, I kept silent while cherished values were scorned. Mockery of music, art, and poetry was commonplace. So were expressions of white chauvinism and anti-Semitism. Often my sexually frustrated companions would speak in the foulest terms of the character and person of some girl I adored (at a distance).

Chivalry died painfully, and Sir Galahad's banner trailed sadly in the mud.

Sixteen years old and at the end of my high school career, I still had no fixed objective, no ambitious goal. I would go on to college because I knew of nothing else to do. I believed I had no special talents. Music had passed me by because I had discovered it too late to pursue it seriously, or so I told myself. For writing I had evinced no particular bent, an opinion nourished by laziness and fear of failure. I decided that I was noncreative, merely an appreciative sponge, a dilettante. With such awareness of my inadequacies, I felt that my disillusionment and my self-loathing were complete.

Nevertheless, life went on, and graduation neared with all its high expectations. The usual preamble, the senior-class play, outfitted me with a leading role in a bloody murder mystery in which nearly the whole cast was done in. Afterward a few of my fellow graduates decided to celebrate with an all-night party complete with a bottle or two of champagne. Shortly before dawn, we walked in couples under bright stars to Gimghoul Castle, a local landmark on a promontory commanding an unparalleled view to the east. As we necked and talked enthusiastically of our futures, the night faded away and a glorious sunrise began. When the first rays came over the distant horizon, the boys (certainly I) suffered a first postgraduate disillusionment: the girls' faces, which had been so lovely and radiant the night before in the lamplight and beneath the stars, had turned a greenish gray under the merciless light of the early sun. It seemed to me that their youthful loveliness had departed, that their pretty faces had been replaced by haggard, makeup-smeared masks which proclaimed, with cruel mockery, previously unnoticed weaknesses of character. I was overwhelmed with a searing sense of the fragility, the transience, of human beauty, and for the first time I "saw the skull beneath the skin." Whatever the others may have felt, a depression drearily seized the group, and the boys soon escorted the girls home in near silence.

As the time for enrollment in the university approached, my morale declined steadily.

Then, just before the fall term began in September, I received an invitation from the university to attend, along with about two hundred others, a special "freshman retreat," which was supposed to be a valuable introduction to the "college experience." I accepted, at my parents' urging, and found myself borne on a heaving tide of fellow North Carolinians, all apparently from prominent families.

They represented the elite which had led the state for generations. Most came from families long noted for prominence in the Confederate army, politics, the ministries of Protestant churches, manufacturing, banking, lawyering, and the educational system. Such families had the inside track to preferred positions in the circles of power; their scions, if they performed satisfactorily, could expect to have entree into those circles and to achieve prominence in their chosen fields, and ultimately to have a hand in operating the levers of power in the state. Attendance at and graduation from the university was an important rung up the ladder of success, since connections could be made there which would provide "pull" in future undertakings, whether politics, business or the professions. All of those chosen ones knew what was at stake, having had it impressed upon them from childhood by their families. They were on their mettle.

Most of them seemed eager to "get off on the right foot," "make college count toward future success," and "carry on the great traditions of the university and the Old North State." Most of them seemed to vibrate at every sick platitude thrown at them by members of the administration and faculty; a great many of them appeared, to my embittered eye, to be smug, snobbish boors, determined to remember everyone else's name so that they could make "lots of college friendships which would be of enormous advantage in later life." They could scarcely wait for the term to commence so they could start "getting ahead."

The administrators and teachers who dispensed the drivel were well known to me: I'd been a guest in most of their homes without ever suspecting that they were capable of expressing themselves with such locker-room vulgarity or of pandering to such crass notions of what constituted success. Every speaker seemed to feel duty-bound to make some coy reference to the football team to show that he was a "regular guy." Near the end of the three days of speechifying, smokers, receptions, tours, how-to-get-ahead indoctrination, plugs for fraternities, urgings to "back up the team," and the like, a dean reminisced about his Chapel Hill student days and mentioned the "good old classics," Plato, Virgil, and Shakespeare, and how he had formed a lifelong habit of rereading them. This was the first and only mention of college study as a means of enlightenment or esthetic pleasure. The rest was all flimflam, the bridling of ignorant youth and whipping them on in a race for corrupt trophies. I felt trapped in an alien institution. I felt revulsion. I felt that there was nowhere to turn, no place to go.

I walked home from the campus grimly. No one was home. I went to my room and played my recording of Wagner's *Siegfried Idyll*. After its soaring serenity I listened with the utmost intensity to the "Liebestod" and its celebration of a passion I had never known. But I could know the ultimate peace which the music seemed to promise at the close.

I went to my parents' bathroom and studied the medicine chest. There were sleeping pills, some strychnine, and numerous narcotic prescriptions for my father's various heart ailments. I poured several dozen of the pills into my hand, popped them into my mouth, and washed them down with a glass of water. With some bitterness and much self-pity, I decided to write no note—no one understood me anyway.

I walked through the large garden to the edge of the woods, chose a grassy spot, lay down, and waited to see what death would be like. I was a little frightened by my action, but knowing it was irreversible, I was determined to drink in the beauty of the woods in my last minutes.

Oddly, nothing seemed to happen. I was not even drowsy, and yet I knew I had taken several times a lethal dose of strychnine alone, not to mention all the codeine and sleeping pills. Still, I must have goofed somehow. There was nothing for it but to go back to the medicine chest for more. As I got to my feet I was seized by violent nausea and vomited copiously. With my head spinning crazily, I staggered back into the house, climbed the stairs, and fell on my bed, losing consciousness as I touched it.

My mother's gentle, anxious voice roused me at ten o'clock to tell me that the cook had saved my food for me, and that since I had seemed so tired, she had let me sleep through dinner. "Thanks, Mom. I'm not hungry. Just tired." I turned over and slept for ten hours more.

The next morning I was sick with contrition at my heartlessness in not considering the distress I would have caused my family, and I was ashamed at having let sniveling self-pity overwhelm me. I resolved that no matter how ugly or unbearable life might seem or might become in the future, I would never again accept suicide as an alternative.

I buried my shame inside and kept my secret for many years. But underneath the shame, once the deed was all behind me, there lingered a sneaking, unconfessed grain of pride that I had had the guts to do it.

5

The Campus

We try to reap who do not sow:
We learn and learn and never know.

Student refrain

U nder heavy parental pressure I pledged to join my brother's fraternity. I soon found that my "brothers" liked neither my interest in music and literature nor my associates. One solicitous "brother" told me that when I wasn't "hanging around that goddam music building playing longhair records with a bunch of queers, I was in Abernethy's bookstore with a pack of radicals"; only the night before he'd seen me "drinking beer in Harry's with some awful-looking kikes from New York or New Jersey."

Breaking away, with my brother's approval, from the fraternity—and all that it stood for in the campus realm of things—was but one of a series of painful experiences during my freshman year. Lightened by one or two instructors only, that year passed in a haze of agitation and confusion. Ab's bookstore remained an oasis for me, one that also provided my closest ties with the rest of the world. There I read avant-garde books and listened to discussions on subjects I had never before dreamed of. I became acquainted with graduate students and junior faculty whose backgrounds, experiences, and outlooks were for me completely and exhilaratingly exotic.

At the same time I kept open the door to the cozy world of the university establishment. I socialized occasionally with my high school friends, because virtually all the women students at the university were juniors, seniors, or graduate students who were considerably older than I. Still virginal and miserably frustrated, I was able to make a pretense of greater suavity with girls my own age.

Nevertheless, the gap continued to widen between me and traditional southern values. I was distressed that so many southern students were oblivious of or indifferent to the cultural and intellectual currents of the day. Even though President Frank P. Graham's liberal administration had made UNC the "Athens of the South," and though the regionalist school of sociology, led by Howard Odum, was based in Chapel Hill, and though playwright Paul Green was in residence, much of the intellectual yeast at the university, at least for the undergraduates, was provided by outsiders from the North and West.

One Friday in early September as I was walking along the sidewalk of East Franklin Street toward Ab's bookstore, the youthful Presbyterian minister stopped me and said that he and his wife were having some young people in for tea at the manse the next afternoon. Would I be so kind as to bring Bobby and a couple of other local lads? He had a new tenant, a student, who had arrived a couple of weeks before the fall term had begun and who knew no one. Caught before I could think of an excuse, I agreed.

Bobby and I, showing up on schedule, encountered a room full of familiar local acquaintances, male and female, from high school and the university. The new tenant was introduced, a student transferring in his junior year, as an English major, from the University of New Mexico. His name was Richard Nickson, and he was from Roswell, New Mexico, where his father was a well-to-do hotel owner. By the time the party broke up, I, who had talked with no one else, was delighted with my new friend and assumed that he was as iconoclastic as I considered myself to be. I had not, however, reckoned with Richard's fiendish sense of humor (of which I have been the butt for most of my life). As we parted, Richard said in a pious tone, "I suppose I'll see you in church tomorrow?" Since I had only been inside the church twice since coming to Chapel Hill, I blushed and gagged, and my face fell noticeably as I stammered some excuse or other.

Having had some exposure to left-wing political thought, Richard succeeded in disabusing me of such notions as "Franco must be all right because he's leading the *rebels.*" I was still strikingly ignorant of world affairs since World War I, even though I enthusiastically agreed with my father's support of the New Deal at home and generally shared his loathing of the Fascists and Nazis and his dislike of the gray, repressive drabness of the Soviet Union.

Richard and I found another friend in Harold, from my hometown, who was an accomplished (though erratic) pianist and a graduate student in music. The three of us spent much time together, and Harold provided us with many new musical insights. Harold, a few years older than Richard, very wealthy, and a bit neurotic, was quite set in his ways. Intensely dedicated to mastering the piano, he spent many hours daily at his Steinway grand, setting himself a Spartan, somewhat mirthless regimen.

We heard much music together. Among the notable experiences was a recital by Roland Hayes (segregated, of course, in the auditorium of the North

Carolina College for Negroes in Durham), in which the great tenor sang Beethoven's "Adelaïde" with such exquisite art that I was moved to tears. Later in the same concert, two spirituals, "Were You There?" and "Little Boy, How Old Are You?" moved me again to tears, this time mingled with rage that Negroes had to hear this glorious music created by their ancestors and consummately performed by a great Negro artist, one of their own, while barred from the best seats in the house.

A performance in Greensboro of Mozart's *Così fan tutte,* creditably done by a traveling European company, was unforgettable for us. But almost as memorable as the music were two incidents associated with that event. Richard and I were invited to dine before the performance and to spend the night at Harold's luxurious home. I drove the forty-eight miles with Harold, while Richard, who had a late class, was to drive over later in the afternoon. While riding along, I told Harold of a marvelous book I had bought from Ab that morning: "He wanted three dollars for it, but I jewed him down to two!" Harold, who was Jewish, smiled sweetly and said in a gentle tone, "Don't you think you could find a *better* word to express bargaining?" I, who had never imagined that there was any relationship between *jew* (which I had thought a perfectly serviceable verb) and *Jew* (the noun), was mortified and shocked at that confrontation with my insensitivity.

That night at dinner I remarked, quite innocently, to Harold's father (a major textile tycoon) that I thought the current organizing drive of the CIO (Congress of Industrial Organizations) would have a salutary effect on the state. Harold choked with amusement behind his napkin, Richard gleefully kicked me in the shins, and the host graciously refrained from breaking the wine decanter over the head of his young guest.

In addition to these close friends, I had a wide acquaintanceship among the student body as a whole. Some, as I have indicated, were not interested in cultural or intellectual matters at all. These were just "nice fellows" I had got to know while participating in cross-country running, fencing, and intramural football and through chance encounters in classes. Many were pleasant and likable, although their college interests seemed to extend merely from football to basketball to dances.

Among the minority of undergraduates who actually read books, there were several noticeable trends.

There were numerous Thomas Wolfe idolators, somewhat given to sentimentality, Weltschmerz, and fine-sounding rhetoric. They were most often North Carolinians, since Wolfe grew up in Asheville, had attended the university, and generally typified their own somewhat vague and tepid revolt against the pettiness and restricted horizons of their hometowns. One of these devotees sat next to me in a course notable for the boredom which afflicted the teacher and the resultant dullness of the class sessions. One day for amusement, I, who had been reading one of Wolfe's books and was satiated with the florid, emotional style, scribbled a parody of one of its purpler passages. Then I rewrote it (making it, I thought, even more ironic and ridiculous) and passed it to this classmate. The young man read it several times, and to my embarrassment and dismay, mopped tears from his eyes, squeezed my shoulder appreciatively, and wrote in the margin, "Beautiful!"

There were a few purist esthetes who tended to withdraw into small groups to bewail or ridicule the vulgarity and philistinism of the student hordes. Homosexuals abounded among them. I knew and respected a slightly older student who had an ear for poetry, participated capably in a modern-dance group, acted occasionally with the Playmakers, and had a genuine love of music. He invited me to his rental on the outskirts of Chapel Hill one afternoon to hear his recording of Bach's *St. Matthew Passion,* a work unfamiliar to me. Arriving on my bicycle with the huge score (borrowed from the Music Library) tucked in my belt, I was ushered by my host into a darkened room. On one end of a large coffee table was a record player and the Bach recordings; in the middle was a massive candlestick supporting a huge multicolored candle (appropriate for a cathedral, and the sole source of light); at the other end was a white cloth on which was a plate of waferlike cookies and two small glasses of red wine, suggestive of a communion service. On the wall, revealed in the flickering light, was a reproduction of a suffering Christ by Rouault. As heart-rendingly moving as the music was, I was tormented by two requests I never dared make, lest I should fall among the philistines: "How about turning on the light so I can see the score?" and "Would you mind opening the window so I can breathe!"

Most exciting and exotic were the radical, Marxist-influenced, socially conscious fellows (mostly northern and Jewish), who had strongly held opinions on nearly everything and who were often disputatious and dogmatic. Some were self-involved caricatures of Odets's youthful revolutionaries, lacking in neither self-pity nor fatalism. Most of them loved to debate and discuss. Many, radiating intellectual curiosity, observed the southern scene with stimulating questions and criticism, as though they were Martians. A few were sensitive, thoughtful, serious students with passionate social consciences and appealing warmth. Many were thought to be Communists. Some were. Most were not.

There were mavericks who fitted into none of the groups, who were not doctrinaire, who seemed to suffer a great deal (unobtrusively), who were often immersed in some specialized discipline (especially music), and who had considerable depth and distinction of character.

Last among the literate students, and by far the largest category, were those benighted souls who led conventional lives, held conventional points of view and values, sponged up what was set before them in their course work, and maintained few or no interests other than their required subjects. Some quite bright ones, buried in specialized fields of study in which they attained considerable proficiency, expected to become professionals: doctors, lawyers, academics. Beyond these specialties, their intellectual and cultural torpor was astonishing; they rarely availed themselves even of the fairly meager cultural activities sponsored by the university. Others, equally bright, had been sent to college for a general education to acquire "polish" before they returned home to take over a family business, or to help them mature while they decided on a career. Their learning was more diffused. They passively absorbed what fell to their lot in liberal-arts electives, read what they were told, usually got high grades, and evinced little curiosity about the cultural and intellectual realms which lay beyond the textbook or the classroom. In fraternities they were considered brilliant students and were much in demand before exams and crucial tests. Though there were exceptions, I found such students uninteresting and indeed depressing, and I tended to avoid them, thereby further widening the gulf between my social peers and me.

Nevertheless, I did find attractive individuals in each group, though I did little during my sophomore year to advance my acquaintanceship with any of them because I was so taken up with Richard and, to a lesser extent, Harold. Besides, I was trying to make up for my ignorance of musical basics by singing in the Chapel Hill Choral Society and playing double bass in the University Symphony Orchestra.

"You see, Junius, these fellows could get expelled because they're nearly all northern and Jewish and radical. What we need on this letter is some good southern names from prominent families, like yours and mine—signatures for the sake of taking responsibility for the leaflets." The earnest young student then handed me the letter to read. A Voltairean defense of freedom of speech, it assumed responsibility for a leaflet distributed to the audience in Memorial Hall just before the speaker of the evening, George Derry, a professional anti-Communist, had appeared. I had read the notices in the *Daily Tar Heel* but had not been interested and had not attended.

"Well, what did this leaflet say that's got the Student Council so hot?" I asked.

"It just gave this guy's background from *Who's Who* and other respectable sources and said he was making a lot of money off of anti-Communism and had some disreputable associations, and that the audience should know it when it heard him. It didn't aim to stop him from speaking."

I looked over the names on the letter—all nice fellows I knew well from beer-and-bull sessions. It was Lee Manning Wiggins who had just handed me the letter in a corner of Ab's bookshop. Lee was a brilliant young fireball from Hartsville, South Carolina. His father was later to be undersecretary of the treasury and was a financier of great influence. Lee was a "mover and shaker"; he had a keen mind and wide-ranging intellectual interests, and he seemed afraid of nothing. I was quite fond of him and esteemed him as well. I signed.

The letter was published in the *Daily Tar Heel,* and a day or two later each signer received a stern summons to appear before the Student Council. We appeared. The council and its president were as hostile and angry as if Fort Sumter had been fired upon again. The charge was "behavior unbecoming a Carolina gentleman." The "defendants" stood firm: we had exercised our rights as citizens and students to expose little-known facts about a speaker; we had no more insulted him than if we had asked him embarrassing questions during the traditional question period. And what did the Student Council think it was, setting itself up to determine what behavior was becoming or unbecoming to a Carolina gentleman? Was that a *North* Carolina gentleman or a *South* Carolina gentleman? What if a Virginia or a New York gentleman were involved? Or what if a student didn't claim to be a gentleman at all? Was he bound by the offhand, unwritten dictate of the Student Council? What sort of ex post facto law was that?

The "defendants" enthusiastically reproved the council members and president for their censoriousness, their presumption, their lack of understanding of and concern for civil liberties, and their considerable deficiencies as logical thinkers. The "judges" complained defensively that it wasn't polite to distribute leaflets in that way, squirmed uncomfortably, realized they were licked, and concluded with a shamefaced "warning," openly laughed at by the recipients.

Having achieved a victory for free speech, we celebrated exuberantly in a nearby tavern. I was as exultant as the rest, except that I felt it was *not* good manners—or good politics—to distribute leaflets to an audience already assembled just before the speaker's appearance. They should have been handed out in the lobby or outside as the audience arrived or departed.

That had been my second foray into politics. The first, during my sophomore year, had been a vehement, and uncharacteristic, protest against a proposal for a compulsory Reserve Officers' Training Corps at the university.

Having heard from Richard that he would not return in 1938–39, I tried to fill the void left by his absence and scrutinized the campus scene more closely. Harold was back, but he had an assistantship in the Music Department that left him little free time. Even the Scales family had shrunk. Arch had graduated from law school, passed the bar, and left for a job in Washington, D.C. Although Mary Leigh was still living at home, a graduate student in dramatic art, the huge old house was far too large, so the family moved to a more comfortable, smaller one.

Meanwhile, the academic offerings for 1938–39 looked more interesting. I had completed the required general college courses and had decided to major in comparative literature. My department head and adviser was a cool, logical scholar and a superb teacher: Howard R. Huse, a distinguished authority on and translator of Dante.

My first course with him was the first half of a survey of French literature. The professor's insights into Villon, Ronsard, Montaigne, Pascal, La Fontaine, and Molière proved to be lifelong treasures, interspersed as they were with brilliant excursions into wide-ranging contemporary social criticism. He was a man of culture and refinement, a mature scholar with an inquiring mind and a gift for communicating his interests and inquiries to serious students. I decided to try to take one of his courses every quarter and enrolled in a course on Dante (in translation) which was so memorable that I later studied Italian under Huse in order to read *The Divine Comedy* in the original.

But very few courses were so stimulating as Huse's. After discussing the seeming provincialism and other deficiencies in cultural and intellectual affairs at Chapel Hill, Simons, a South Carolinian who wrote poetry, Irwin, a New Yorker who wrote stories, Lee Wiggins, who wrote poetry in addition to participating in every other imaginable activity, and I began planning a series of large seminars to which we would invite distinguished scholars and men of letters, both from the university and from nearby. The seminars, mostly open-ended, were launched with varying success, attended by as many as thirty students. A particularly remarkable one was conducted by the famous poet and critic Allen Tate, who then was teaching at the Women's College of the University of North Carolina in Greensboro. The series helped interested students get acquainted with many of the notable academic figures whose courses they would never take, and it lent some intellectual excitement to what was, for many, a dull grind.

My apparent interest in politics was responsible for an invitation to attend a student-labor conference in Durham sponsored by the state CIO and a number of liberal academic figures in both Negro and white colleges around the state. A ride was arranged for me in the car of Professor E. E. Ericson, an able English scholar and admired teacher who had been, a few years earlier, the center of a storm that rocked the university and the whole state.

Ericson had been invited to attend a dinner arranged by prominent Negro businessmen to honor James W. Ford, the Negro Communist candidate for the U.S. vice-presidency. He had attended—the only white person present. The fact became front-page news. He had broken bread not only with Negroes (horrible enough in itself), but with a *Red* Negro. The howls for his dismissal had grown ominously until Dr. Frank Graham silenced the uproar by saying, in effect, "If he goes, so do I!"

Riding in Ericson's car was something of an honor. Although I had sometimes spoken to him in the bookshop, this was my first chance to hear him talk politics. I found him well informed and provocative and was favorably impressed with him. The conference was also absorbing. Leo Huberman, a spellbinding left-wing economist, denounced segregation and pointed out its high cost to both labor and Negroes. A Negro college president and some CIO leaders also spoke, some of them emphasizing the importance of students in ending racial bigotry. I was startled and pleased to see a number of Negro students sitting in the audience, not jim crowed. I also noticed some white men and women mill workers listening attentively. My fellow students from Chapel Hill were nearly all northerners and were taking things in their stride; but for me, a new world seemed to be opening.

The conference recessed for dinner in the basement of the YWCA building. When I had been served, cafeteria style, I took my plate to a long table, occupied the first vacant chair—and discovered that I was seated next to a male Negro student from A & T College in Greensboro. We'd barely introduced ourselves when I was joined on my right by a breathtakingly beautiful Negro woman student from Bennett College in Greensboro (the daughter of its president). She was as charming and gracious as she looked, and I was soon at ease and conversing excitedly with my neighbors.

I had never known a Negro, except as a servant, and yet there I was in utter delight, defying all the taboos, customs, rules, and laws that kept the races apart, talking with complete naturalness as one student to another, as one young *person* to another! The remainder of the conference was a blur to me, and I didn't manage to meet any of the white workers (I had never known any of those, either). My companions must have noticed the impact of the meeting on me, because a day or two later I was asked by one of them to join the American Student Union.

The ASU had been formed earlier in the thirties by a merger of the Socialist-led Student League for Industrial Democracy and the Communist-led National Students League. I'd first heard of it when my high school in Chapel Hill had participated, somewhat perfunctorily, in the ASU's annual "peace strike." That annual rededication to peace every spring seemed to be almost its only local activity. I agreed to go to a meeting, and there I found twenty or twenty-five members in attendance, including several women. I liked the organization's literature and statement of purpose, the discussion, and the people. I joined.

There was concern among some segments of the faculty and student body over the Fascist gains in the Spanish civil war, and the ASU became the focal point of the anti-Fascist sentiment. Its membership grew rapidly through the winter and spring of 1939, during which time the writer Ralph Bates, returned from Loyalist Spain, spoke on the campus to great effect, aided by a powerful documentary film. Despite my hatred of militarism and my conviction that war was inimical to culture and everything human, I was ready, in view of the imminent victory of Fascism, to go to Spain to try to stop it there. To me, Fascism meant the dominance of the know-nothing, bigoted, hateful brutality that I knew locally; should it triumph on an international scale, it would make life intolerable. I was disappointed when I learned that the International Brigades were being disbanded and that volunteers were no longer wanted.

Embarrassed by my ignorance of world affairs, I began reading many books about politics, the most influential being Lewis Mumford's *Men Must Act,* Clifford Odets's plays, and *International Affairs* by R. Palme Dutt, a British Communist. I began to have a more favorable view of the Soviet Union because of its apparent support of Loyalist Spain. Richard, in his letters from New Mexico, seemed to share my views and concerns.

I continued to attend ASU meetings and soon began to realize that within that organization there was a sort of "wheel within a wheel." It seemed to me that if the big wheel (the ASU) ran by faith, the little wheel (the effective leadership) ran by the grace of the Communists. Hardly subtle in fighting for their positions, they had a propensity for presenting their arguments in the most doctrinaire and unappetizing forms. It seemed that they threw down a point of view with some hostility, expecting hostility in return, and resented any compromise or modification aimed at making their proposal more palatable to non-Communists—even if offered by someone who generally supported their position.

I soon figured out who the active Communists were, and I sought them out in ones and twos to see if I could get to the bottom of that much-denounced ideology and group. When I criticized their tactics or current politics, they talked freely enough, using many well-worn phrases, but when I inquired about their basic aspirations and beliefs, they were relatively tongue-tied and vague and seemed to be on shaky ground. One crony suggested, "You oughta talk to Sam. He's *good* on theory."

Sam was a midwesterner, stooped and frail of body with an unduly large head (covered by a mass of curly, untended hair), full lips, and a huge beak of a nose. "I look like an anti-Semitic caricature," he once told me despairingly. He had read widely and was often an astute critic. But he was full of self-pity, and his attempts at writing were drowned in sentimentality. There was an appealing gentleness, even tenderness, about him, and his goodwill and sincerity were evident. In fact, his heart was so much on his sleeve that he was frequently the butt of cruel remarks, even from his comrades.

I talked with Sam to little avail. He took Marx and Lenin on faith without having read much of either. Sam referred me to Al, who had read a bit more but had absorbed still less. Al was a New Englander with a severe physical handicap. He too was full of Weltschmerz and given to sentimentality in his writing, though his lifelong struggle with his ailment had given him considerable inner strength. His most appealing qualities were his unpretentious generosity and his sharp sense of humor, often directed at himself.

I had very nearly convinced Al of the philosophical unsoundness of Marxism as *he* had explained it when Al offered to lend me some books: *The Communist Manifesto* of Marx and Engels, *I Like America,* by Granville Hicks, and *The History of the Communist Party of the Soviet Union (Bolshevik).* The *Manifesto* aroused me, but it hardly seemed a guide to the world's problems eighty years later; Hicks's book was a likable, folksy accommodation of an intelligent man of letters to contemporary Communism; but the third work (the compendium of Stalinist ideology for a generation) was more repellent than attractive. I found the no-nonsense, no-words-wasted approach impressive, but the arrogance, the revealed-truth manner of giving out laws (which reminded me of the Book of Leviticus), and the cold, impersonal tone revolted me. I returned it mostly unread.

In the bookstore I met better-informed graduate students and junior faculty who were able to carry on relatively cogent discussions about Marxism. Several of the faculty wanted to recruit me to the Party; yet when Sam formally invited me to join early in March 1939, I was taken by surprise, thanked him, and said I would like to think it over for a while.

While I was making up my mind, I fell in with a bull session at a bistro with high-backed booths called the Tavern. A discussion raged over whether Communism was a morally adequate philosophy for a contemporary American. Many rounds of beer had been downed and many a fevered speech had been made when John, a long, lean, small-town North Carolinian (silent until then), said, "The thing I like about Communism is that it's like early Christianity before the Christians and the churches messed it up. If you want to fight for the poor and oppressed, and have peace on earth and goodwill toward your fellow man, it seems to me you have to be *some* kind of a Communist whether you join the Party or not."

I pondered for days what John had said. I agreed that the Communist movement seemed to come closest to my old dream of building the brotherhood of man, but I wondered whether it was necessary to join the Party to practice Christian/Communist principles. I hadn't noticed any exceptional degree of brotherhood among the student Communists, although they did show a certain camaraderie and a privileged sense of belonging which I found quite attractive. But on the other hand, if one really meant business, why not join the group that claimed to be the true practitioners of Communism? If they weren't what they claimed, one could always leave. The thought that my family would have a fit if they knew I was becoming a Red disturbed me. I decided that they need not know, and that I would give the Party a try.

I conveyed my decision to Sam and Al. Sam met me the next Sunday afternoon, and we walked a few blocks to a small apartment occupied by a young woman graduate student. Mary was a sturdy, freckled New Englander whose kind eyes twinkled with good humor. Ruth, the other young woman in the club (a term that had long before replaced *cell*), was from North Carolina. Small and frail, with a rather tough, cynical manner, she gave the impression that she had been knocked about a good bit. She was having a "heavy" affair with Woody, a blond New York Jewish lad who was two or three years her junior and also a member of the club. He was handsome, ingratiating, slick, and superficial. Roy, another Jewish New Yorker, was pimple-faced, unintellectual, talkative, funny, and deeply earnest about his Party commitment. John, from the Midwest, was handsome, intellectual, logical, unflappable, and reserved in manner; his adherence to the Party seemed based on his view that it represented the most rational approach to politics; his aloofness from others reflected his acute self-involvement. Danny, yet another New Yorker, tall and laconic, kept his thoughts so much to himself that his intelligence and sensitivity were not always apparent to the others. Max, a North Carolina Baptist, was rather stolid and slow, but he was unusually generous and sweet-natured and fiercely loyal to his comrades. Al and long, lean John were also present.

Ruth conducted the meeting, with the members in a semicircle, some on the floor. Some of the proposed agenda came from the "state leadership" by way of the "other club," which was composed of older people. This state leadership was mentioned in tones of awe and finality. It was explained to me that the student club was roughly a southern equivalent of the Young Communist League (YCL), which was, as its name suggests, the Communist youth organization. After a report on the world and national scene, drawn largely from the current *Communist,* the monthly organ of the Party, the members argued vehemently. I was impressed with the knowledge of politics—especially that of Sam and Midwest John. Then there was discussion of the club's work, focused mainly on the campus ASU club. There was much planning talk, but nothing got tied down organizationally, no responsibility was fixed, no clear plans were made. No one knew precisely what he or she was to do. I noted sourly (but silently) that with things left as they were, nothing would be done, the ASU would drift, and the previous discussion had been mere pretense.

Finally the last agenda item was reached: "Admission of new member." I filled out a brief application form and was told I would receive a Party card as soon as the DO (district organizer) signed it. I paid a few cents dues; Mary gave me a receipt; and I was *in*. It was explained that membership, in the South, was secret because of past and possibly future persecution of Communists. The fellows all shook hands and congratulated me, and the women each gave me a comradely hug and peck. Danny (who had a car) proposed that we all go out to celebrate in honor of the new recruit. But I had to decline. My mother, father, and sister expected me at home, where another kind of celebration awaited me: it was my nineteenth birthday.

A notable extracurricular event for me was a two-week visit to Chapel Hill by the playwright Clifford Odets. Odets, feeling stifled in New York, had come down for a rest. I met him in Ab's bookstore the day he arrived. He was anxious to meet some of the "socially conscious" students; could I arrange it? I could. I collected a political cross-section, from Lee, Simons, and Irwin on the right to Sam and Al on the left, to dine with the thirty-three-year-old celebrity. We jammed into a booth in the Tavern, had dinner, consumed cases of beer, and had much conversation that seemed profound at the time. The delightful evening sessions occurred almost nightly, with some personnel changes, while Odets's visit continued.

Odets was warm and appealing, unpretentious, and quite confiding. He told me that as soon as he had achieved some financial success, he hastened to buy the entire Everyman's Library and just savor having such marvelous books in his possession after a childhood and early youth nearly starved of books.

Sometimes his confidences could be almost embarrassing. One evening he excused himself temporarily from the beer session and asked me to accompany him to the telegraph office. As we walked, he spoke of the problems of his marriage to the film star Luise Rainer, and of how much he loved her. When we reached the telegraph office it had just closed, but the girl who ran it had attended high school with me and was kind enough to reopen for us. Odets composed, rather deliberately, a long, tender epistle to his wife, edited and corrected it, and then insisted that I read it and give my opinion—while the operator, who had a date, was gnawing her nails and looking daggers at me.

Odets seemed to need reassurance and approval of his conduct in the most intimate matters. He was also, at that time, most sensitive to criticism from the Communist left. Viewing the Communists as a sort of stern conscience, he was delighted when his work pleased them.

On the last night of his visit, a Saturday, a small group joined him, talking and drinking beer until the Tavern closed; then we adjourned to the University

Café next to the post office until about 2:00 A . M ., when the party broke up. Everyone was looped and beerily concerned over whether the others could get home unaided. Finally we reassured one another and straggled off, saying our farewells to Odets. I was the last to leave, and after a final handshake with a reeling Odets, bestrode my bicycle, rode down an embankment, crossed the wide street, rolled up another embankment, turned with a gallant wave and a "So long, Cliff!"—and ran squarely into a stone wall.

Another visitor was W. H. Auden, the British poet, who had been invited to speak at a Human Relations Institute and had been pitted against one Lawrence Dennis (who billed himself as "America's number one intellectual Fascist"). Auden made an ass of his opponent by a skillful combination of wit, reason, humanism, and a remarkably ingratiating way with the audience. His costume of shapeless tweed trousers and a baggy, unmatching tweed jacket looked as though it had been pilfered from a scarecrow after a season in sun and rain. Standing quite properly, he began his talk at a lectern before about twenty-five hundred people. As he warmed up, he hugged the top of the lectern with both arms and pushed his head forward, his unruly reddish thatch making him look like an aggressive rooster. Gradually he wound a leg around the middle of the lectern; then he uncoiled that one and tried the other. It was warm, so he unbuttoned his collar, slid his tie down, and removed his jacket. He abandoned the lectern altogether, advanced to a flight of stairs leading into the audience, and sat down on the top step. He concluded his remarks with his long legs crossed and drifting down one side of the stairs while he supported himself on his left arm, leaving his right hand free for an occasional gesture. He received probably the greatest ovation given at the three-day institute.

I had met him that morning at Ab's bookstore when, having arrived by bus, he'd dropped in to ask directions to Memorial Hall. Recognizing him from his picture, I'd greeted him in some awe: he was my favorite living poet after Eliot and the one closest to my own political outlook. I'd escorted him across campus to the hall, having left word for Lee and some of my other cronies to join me there.

After Auden's triumph, I introduced him to my friends and we all piled into Danny's car to give the poet a guided tour of Chapel Hill, sandwiching him between Danny and me in the front seat. Just as the tour ended and we parked in front of the bookshop, I felt a tremendous pinch on the behind which could only have come from Auden. After my first amazement, I suddenly realized that Auden was homosexual, and blushed fiery red. When he saw that I was embarrassed, he passed the whole thing off as if it had never happened, and we all went to lunch in a nearby café. There we spent the afternoon (with me discreetly seated on the opposite side of the table), listening to Auden's engaging talk about poets, poetry, and politics.

Although he had made no anti-Communist remarks in his speech, in private conversation he made no secret of his acute disillusionment with Communism, even though, he said, he still liked some Communists. That delighted Lee and Irwin and disappointed most of the rest. After seeing him off on the bus in the early evening, I regretted that I hadn't been able to get Auden to elaborate on the reasons for his disgust of Communism.

To my delight, Richard returned to Chapel Hill for the spring quarter. I eagerly filled him in on all my doings, political and otherwise, introduced him to my new cronies, and recruited him into the ASU. I would have asked him to join the Party, but I was having serious misgivings about it myself. I was fond of all the people in my club, with one exception, and got along well with them all. But I began to think that something must be wrong with an organization whose members professed such high ideals and accomplished so little in furthering them.

I began consciously comparing my comrades with the other students I knew, making use of Richard's reaction to them as an aid in maintaining my perspective. As to their individual talents, I thought them not remarkable. In intelligence and as students they were certainly above average. Their intellectual and cultural awareness was not exceptional, but there was little philistinism in any of them.

In their concern about matters of social justice, however, they were indeed exceptional. They would not tolerate white-chauvinist, anti-Semitic, or male-supremacist attitudes where they could do anything about them; they were passionate about the rights of working people; they hated the brutality of war and Fascism; and they believed that people, and the world, could be made better. Perhaps their staunch social conscience alone was reason to stick with them.

Still, it seemed to me that there were contradictory attitudes in the Party which tended to negate many good intentions. Within the ASU, for example, leading Party members, instead of trying to appeal to the less enlightened, to win them to a more advanced point of view, would wound or enrage someone in opposition by saying, "That's a reactionary position" or "You're talking like a Fascist!" That treatment of non-Communists arose sometimes from impatience or ignorance, sometimes from a need to support the stance that Communism had all the answers. But the failure to communicate and persuade made them turn in on themselves and talk jargon and clichés in comfort and without rebuke. Sam and Al, as examples, were sensible intellectuals, but the chief importance of membership in the Party for them seemed to be the high degree of acceptance and affection they found in the club as a sort of sheltered family and as a balm for their neuroses.

If the student club never managed to equal the sum of its parts, what of the rest of the Party? Nationally it had had great successes in organizing the unorganized and the unemployed into unions; it had formed the Abraham Lincoln Battalion to fight Franco; it had helped expose and oppose Fascism, Nazism, and white racism; it was forever prodding the New Deal to abet social welfare and social justice. These things were fine. But given the magnitude and the strength of the evils the Party opposed, how effective could it be in arousing the necessary millions to overcome them? It had garnered merely a hundred thousand votes for Earl Browder in the presidential election of 1936; yet everything good and progressive that it advocated still remained tied to support for the Soviet Union, in the manner of cheerleaders boosting a football team. Besides, I wasn't sure, from talking with persons who had been there, just how egalitarian the Soviet Union actually was.

Another thing which disturbed me was that I found it difficult and useless to talk with most of my acquaintances about my new Communist ideas. *Communism* was a dirty word in North Carolina, and few would even speak to a person thought to be a Communist. Many still supposed the Gastonia strike to have been a bloody Red insurrection. Their views on Negroes and labor unions were consistent with such attitudes. Usually they didn't know what I was talking about, and if they did, they were disturbed or even hostile. Yet I valued them and did not want to break with them; so I kept quiet about my views and, as a result, felt full of duplicity—almost as if I had a *Doppelgänger* like the protagonist in the Schubert-Heine song I loved. I was too unsure to declare myself openly a Communist, so why should I *be* a Communist till I was clearer in my views?

Finally, I was not reluctant to be in the right with a mere handful; I had reason enough to distrust the complacency and the tainted values of the majority. But before I committed myself fully to a movement which offered its adherents considerable opportunities for martyrdom, I wanted to be sure that I was in the right, that the rest of the handful had a truly humanist goal, and that they were genuinely devoted to that purpose. But from what I knew of it in June 1939, there was nothing purposeful about the Communist Party. I thought I would just quietly drop out in the fall.

6

Different
Drummers

Loyalty to petrified opinion never yet broke a chain or freed a human soul.

Mark Twain

O ne day early in July, while Ab and Minna were on vacation and Bobby and I were running the bookstore, Bobby kept the store while I went home to lunch. Upon my return he said, "Someone's been looking for you."

"Who?"

"Bart Logan. He came in right after you left." This man was something of a legend: he was district organizer of the Communist Party in North and South Carolina and had recently moved from Charlotte to Greensboro. Bobby had met him twice, but I had never even seen him. "He was looking around and asked if I knew whether any of his friends might be in town. I sort of casually mentioned a few names of people who are out of town. Then he asked if there were any students here that he might know—so I mentioned your name and said you'd be right back. Gosh, I didn't know *what* to say. *I'm* not supposed to know who's in and who isn't."

Then Bobby went to lunch. The heat was fierce and seemed to roll down from the high ceiling of the old frame building. Since there had been few customers all day, I propped the double front doors open, moved the phone where I could hear it, took a book, and sat in the shade on the square bench that boxed in an ancient tree in front of the shop.

Glancing up the street toward the post office, I saw a stranger approaching in the blazing sun—tall, thin, his shirt open at the collar, tie pulled down, cuffs turned up. He was about thirty-three, with dark hair, a high forehead, sensitive, expressive features, and extraordinarily piercing eyes. He had a careworn, even tragic, look about him that made me think of the Isaiah passage in Handel's *Messiah*: "a man of sorrows, and acquainted with grief."

"Are you Junius? I'm Bart." He held out a firm right hand.

"Glad to meet you at last," I said, shaking the hand.

Bart mopped the sweat off his face, and there was a pause as we tried to size each other up.

"I came over looking for help, but I can't find anybody. Would you care to give me a hand for two or three days?" I said I'd have to think up a good excuse to give my parents, who were alone at home since my sister had finished her graduate work and had taken a teaching job in eastern North Carolina. Bart was sure I could think up something. By the way, did I know how to run a mimeograph machine? No. Could I type? No, only hunt-and-peck. I was feeling worse than worthless.

"Well, we'll teach you," Bart said with a grin. "There's a textile strike in High Point where we have some people. 1 want to get out a leaflet in the Party's name, and we want to try to help the union with some of its problems. You can stay with my wife and me in Greensboro."

It sounded exciting. I "thought up something" and got my parents' approval, and Bobby was amenable to keeping shop alone. I took off for Greensboro with Bart, who was driving an old jalopy that he kept running by means of occasional doses of gasoline, a few kicks, a lot of oil, some swearing, and a great number of ingenious makeshift repairs. On the trip, which lasted about an hour and a half, I learned far more about Communism and the Communist Party than I had previously known.

I told Bart I'd been coming *un*recruited since joining in March, and explained why. "Can't much blame you for that," he said, pulling the corners of his mouth down while his eyes twinkled and smiled. "It's working people and Negroes that make the Party tick. They don't join it in a burst of idealism like a lot of students do. They join because they need it; because the Party teaches a person how to fight for his rights; it teaches him how to be a better person, and how to keep a rotten world from making him rotten too. And it even helps a guy to laugh a little. I'll show you some real Communists."

I pumped information from him on every subject I could remember that puzzled or bothered me. When Bart didn't know the answer, he said so and ventured an opinion or guess, clearly labeled as such. When he knew the answer, he spoke succinctly and colorfully, frequently using the Georgia country idiom which was native to him, for emphasis or illustration. He was a learned but modest man who scrupulously avoided highfalutin clichés. I was enraptured by his genuineness, his warmth, his humor, and his profound sincerity.

We drove to his home, a run-down little house on Prescott Street only yards from Green Hill Cemetery, where generations of my family were buried. Bart introduced his wife, Belle, a pretty woman of twenty-three with a sweet face

Bart Hunter Logan with his daughter, 1946

and dark blonde hair, the brand-new mother of a little girl named Elaine. At once I felt the warmest sympathy and affection for her, and within an hour I felt completely at ease with the family.

Belle had typed the stencil of a leaflet Bart had written, and Bart and I ran off five hundred copies. By late afternoon I considered that I was a master of mimeography. Belle served a dinner of boiled cabbage, white beans with fat-back, and corn pone. "My God!" Bart groaned. "I order caviar, oysters, rare prime ribs, and a bottle of Bordeaux, and *look* what my peasant woman gives me! Never marry a peasant, Junius, especially a *Georgia* peasant." Belle glowed lovingly back at him.

That night, when we had driven the seventeen miles to High Point, Bart parked in front of a business block on South Main Street and said, "Wait here, while I see if I can find Red."

Two minutes later he returned, accompanied by a lean, long-faced red-haired man, Kelly Y. ("Red") Hendrix. Red was a prominent leader of the Gastonia strike in 1929, was framed for the murder of Sheriff Aderholt, jumped bail, got to the Soviet Union and worked there for more than a year, returned to North Carolina, served four years in the state pen in Raleigh, and then went back to being a textile worker (when he could find a mill where he wasn't blacklisted). His face was deeply seamed with hard work (since child-hood), a great deal of suffering, and too much heavy drinking. At that time he was unemployed, although he had the title of chairman, Communist Party of the Carolinas. The strike at Highland Cotton Mill had attracted him like the old firehorse he was, and he had been in the thick of things—bucking up the spirits and militancy of the picket line, putting starch into the weak and waver-ing, eliciting flashes of humor from the dead-serious strike leaders.

Red was a personage to many of the workers, most of whom knew his history and respected him for it. Whether or not he was known to be a Com-munist, Red was admired as a charismatic leader with evidently vast strike experience. He and Bart got into the car to discuss the latest strike develop-ments and the Party leaflet.

Soon two strikers joined us in the car. Bill Gillen was tall, muscular, hand-some, with full lips and a mass of prematurely gray hair parted in the middle. Willie Held, who looked a little older, had wispy reddish blond hair, a florid complexion, a heavy lower jaw which gave him a slightly surly look, a chubby body, and shoulders that were beginning to stoop. Both men reflected the excitement, the anxieties, and the hopes of the strikers. Both were fathers; both their wives were strikers too. Victory and a union contract would let them all walk taller and upright, like human beings, and with a few cents more in their pockets. Defeat could mean firing, eviction from their homes in the company mill village, and worst of all, blacklisting in the industry in which they made their living. Even if they were not fired, they would have to eat crow, on the job and off, beyond human endurance; they could expect no mercy for their temerity.

The two strikers welcomed me cordially, and after I made a couple of useful suggestions, they sensed my commitment and emotion and made me feel like one of them. At the end of the discussion, Bill, who knew of the Scales family and its reputation for wealth and power, remarked to me that his father-in-law had worked for the past thirty-five years at Proximity Cotton Mill in Greensboro. "I know you know where that is," he added.

It then occurred to me that I'd lived the first six years of my life scarcely a mile from Proximity Mill, had heard its steam whistle several times a day, had lived eight more years only a few miles further away, and had never, to that day, even seen Proximity or the other enormous Cone mills. I was astounded to realize that immeasurable suffering, exploitation, and poverty had existed among thousands of people, right under my nose all my life, and I'd been totally unaware of it. Perhaps my class had even more to hide than I'd suspected, else why such fencing off, such barriers between the classes? How was it possible to grow up in the same geographical area and know so little of the lives of the working people—to meet the first workers I'd ever known when I was nineteen years old?

Bart and Red worked out with Bill and Willie numerous things they could do to help the strike. One was to set up an informal strike-welfare committee to help feed the strikers when their grocery money started to run out (such a need had apparently not been foreseen by the Textile Workers Union organizer). Another was to distribute the Party's leaflet pledging support of the strike in the mill village, where it would do the most good. Bill said he could get some kids—his daughters and some of their friends—to do the distribution house-to-house.

Finally Bart asked if they thought the union could use me at the union hall, in the office. I was a fair hunt-and-peck man on the typewriter and, Bart added with a smile, a semiprofessional on a mimeograph machine. Bill said that he'd introduce me as a friend of his family and that he thought they'd be "damn glad to have me."

Early next morning Bart dropped me off a couple of blocks from the union hall, and Bill met me and took me there. It was a huge loft with a large seating capacity and an office overlooking the street. There was a typewriter, a mimeograph machine, a table made with two sawhorses and a four-by-eight-foot sheet of plywood, a couple of crude benches, three chairs, and two desks, one of which had a CIO organizer seated at it.

A leaflet for the pickets to hand out was waiting to be mimeographed. I ran off a thousand copies and then stored the stencils, rolled lightly between newspaper, as Bart had taught me. All day workers came in and out until I thought I must have met half the work force at the mill. Until late afternoon I was swamped with work: typing, mimeographing, collating, tearing, folding, and cleaning the mimeograph machine. Then Willie stopped by and said to come with him, that he was going out to the mill to take his turn on the picket line, and that Bart and Red would be out there later to pick me up. The feeling on the picket line was good; there had been fewer scabs going into work than on the previous day and some anticipated violence against the pickets had not occurred. Management was talking with the negotiating committee, and things were looking hopeful. Willie introduced me to a number of his co-workers as "June Scales, a student from Chapel Hill" who had been helping out at the union hall all day. I was greeted warmly, and then my new acquaintances went with Willie to relieve others on the line.

Workers were standing around in groups across the street from the main mill gate, and listening carefully to their talk, I began to get the impression that not just a strike but something like a social revolution was taking place in that mill village. The workers were divided about two to one in favor of the CIO. Of those opposed to the union, about half were obligated to the company in one way or another: preferential jobs, better-than-average houses, big unpaid bills at the company store, hope of getting a son or daughter a job in the mill. Most of the rest either were aged or in poor health or were so crushed, so imbued with a cringing spirit, that they would oppose any move for self-betterment out of fear of the boss's retaliation.

One conversation that I overheard fascinated me. There was an interdenominational company church in the village with a minister paid by the company. The minister for a year past had been preaching fire-and-brimstone sermons proclaiming the CIO the antichrist. He split the congregation, and more than half quit the church. The company promptly fired the preacher, since he was not worth his pay as an anti-union propagandist with such a reduced audience.

After the union had come, most workers were not inclined to behave like frightened rabbits before the foremen. They were learning to stand up and speak for themselves, and they felt a new self-confidence. The women, especially, had been transformed, and their new militancy put additional backbone into the men. The union people had crossed the Rubicon; they had changed their lives and would never return to the old ways: the fear, the humiliation, the helplessness.

I felt as though I were getting a microcosmic preview of the kind of revolution I hoped to see and, I believed, the kind the Party was aiming at. Red aroused me from my reverie with a slap on the back and word that Bart was waiting for me around the corner in the car.

After another long day in the union office, working as before, typing press releases and mimeographing them, addressing envelopes and mailing them, lettering picket signs, meeting some state CIO brass, some Textile Workers Union brass, and lots more strikers, and receiving the thanks of the local president, I returned to Greensboro with Bart. After a much-needed night's rest, I took a bus for Chapel Hill the next morning.

The experience proved to be a milestone in my life. Having met Bart, Belle, Red, Willie, and Bill, having seen my first picket line, and having had a vision of the revolution to come, I had no further thought of dropping out of the Party. I had discovered the working class. Those were the people I wanted to stick with as long as I lived. As for the Highland Mill workers in particular, I liked and admired them enormously, and they seemed to accept me. I even felt reassured about the Soviet Union because of the account Red had given me of his sojourn there in the early thirties, at which time he'd seen a mixed picture but believed that most of the workers still had great hope for the future of the Revolution.

When I stepped off the bus, Chapel Hill seemed to have shrunk measurably in importance since my departure four days before. The places that seemed to matter the most were the factories around the state where working people in the union movement were fighting for their dignity and freedom. I could no longer look forward with any enthusiasm to the start of a new academic year in September. I still desired the life of a scholar-teacher, but that could wait. I wanted to plunge into Party and union activity and to join the working people and Negroes. But telling my parents, I feared, would disappoint them dreadfully.

A few days later, after dinner, my parents said they would like to speak with me. I joined them in the living room, and my father began by telling me that since Mary Leigh had left and there were only the three of us at home, they had considered taking a smaller house; we seemed to rattle around in twelve rooms. That was fine with me, I said.

But my father had not finished. "We have been thinking that since you are very young to be a rising senior, and you have been spending so much time on leftist causes, it might be a good thing for you to get out into the world a little and go to work for a year, and then finish your senior year." I couldn't have agreed more, and said so.

"Well, in that case, I think we'll accept Arch's offer and move back to Hamilton Lakes." Uncle Arch had written a day or two before to say that he intended to divide the rest of his days between his two daughters, who were both married to admirals and living on the West Coast, and to invite his brother to live in his house on Lake Hamilton indefinitely. The house, having been closed for nearly three years, would go to ruin unoccupied and would not likely be profitably salable for many years.

I was delighted. I could live in Hamilton Lakes, work in Greensboro, and see Bart and Belle all the time. And High Point was only a few miles away.

The family's move took place in August 1939. In anticipation of it my mother secured me a job through a family friend in the Guilford County Tax Department. I was to be a combination draftsman and checker of deed descriptions in a tax-revaluation project, and the pay was seventy-five dollars per month. Much of my working time was spent in the vault of the Register of Deeds checking property descriptions. The vault was also frequented by many of Greensboro's lawyers, especially those who were real estate wheeler-dealers. Since they were out of public view in the vault, they often operated at low levels of courtesy and civility. I formed a low opinion of many "pillars of society" thus observed at close range.

I tried to stay clear of the upper-class social circles I was familiar with in Greensboro. Two or three times a week, or oftener, I would buy something good to eat and go after work to visit Bart and Belle. Their financial straits were acute, forcing them on a bare subsistence diet. From the national office of the Party, Bart received a ten-dollar subsidy every week ("whether I need it or not," he said) with which he was, presumably, to feed himself, Belle, and little Elaine, pay the rent, and maintain a car.

One day when I showed up at their house, I found that Belle's young sister was visiting them. She was a country girl from north Georgia, about eighteen and altogether charming. I was much taken with her sweetness and naiveté and added yet another reason for visiting the Logan home.

The next time I dropped by I found Bart holding his ear against a feeble little radio to listen to a news broadcast. He said there had been some kind of report of a pact between Germany and the Soviet Union. "Fat chance!" I snorted. "That's about as likely as a snowstorm in hell." (Perhaps I was echoing the Party's leader, who only one month earlier had said, "There is as much chance of Russo-German agreement as of Earl Browder being elected president of the Chamber of Commerce.") Reassured at my own pronouncement, I turned my attention to Belle's sister, who looked uncommonly pretty. Thirty minutes later I was aroused from my calf-eyed enchantment by the announcement on the network news that Germany and the Soviet Union had indeed signed a nonaggression pact and that the Soviet radio was playing German songs and talking of the historic friendship between the two peoples.

We ate dinner in thoughtful silence. After a while, Bart said that the military situation must be dangerous in the extreme for the Soviet Union to eat crow like that. He felt that it must be a desperate bid for time in which to prepare to fight. He reasoned that whatever Stalin and the Soviet Party had done had been considered necessary for saving the Soviet Union. There was nothing for good Communists to do but take it on faith and wait for details and explanations.

I followed the events of the next week with horror: the Nazis' stepped-up bullying of the Poles, the desperate-sounding neutral appeals for peace, the invasion of Poland on September 1, the French and British declarations of war two days later. World War II had begun, and I felt hopeless at the coming bloodbath and prolonged season of beastliness that could only play havoc with humankind.

In a few days Bart embarked on a trip around the district to discuss the new political situation. By then it was becoming apparent that the Party membership nationally had accepted the drastic change of Soviet policy. Bart's itinerary would take him to Winston-Salem, Asheville, Charlotte, and various isolated points in the state and then to South Carolina. He asked me to be his emissary to the senior club in Chapel Hill (the students would not return till later in the month). I of course agreed and hitchhiked to Chapel Hill on a Friday after work.

I hunted up a couple of young instructors and asked them to get the club together for a discussion of the recent world events. On Sunday morning, when they met, I was taken aback by the adverse opinions about the Soviet Union expressed by many of the members. One of them felt that signing the pact had made world war a certainty. Others were dismayed by the sudden dissolution of the fight against Fascism. Was it to be left to Britain and France, cosigners of the Munich agreement only a year before? Another said the pact was certainly going to cost the club a number of recruits and that it would leave the Party alone and friendless.

I was a little annoyed that I had not considered any of those points. I promised myself to think carefully about them later. Meanwhile, since I was the focus of attention, I launched into a presentation of the point of view Bart had expressed on the evening we had heard the news. Apparently I was persuasive, because my position won the support of all but two, one of whom said he was going to consider withdrawing from the Party; the other said she wanted to "think *everything* over."

I felt important because I had won nearly all the club to my position in my first act of Party "leadership," and I was proud of myself—so proud that I never did get around to having a private think-session about those questions which had disturbed me.

When the academic year commenced at Chapel Hill, I hitchhiked over to see Richard and whatever student comrades had returned. In fact, almost every weekend found me back in Chapel Hill. The ASU was flourishing there, and I learned that there were several members at Women's College (WCUNC) in Greensboro. I lost no time in looking them up; they were very energetic and soon had an active chapter functioning once again at their school. There had been ASU clubs at two Greensboro Negro colleges: A & T (Agricultural and

Technical, which was just becoming co-ed) and Bennett (all women). I could not go to Bennett alone, of course, but I could and did go frequently, in the daytime, in the company of one or two young white women from WC. The president, Dr. David Jones, had given the organization his blessing (one of his daughters had been ASU southern vice-chairman), and in time there was a thriving chapter there. I visited the A & T campus mainly at night, with careful prearrangement, and was met in a car by Negro students. Any interracial activity observed by whites at that time would likely have been viewed with disbelief, the most profound animosity, or both.

In the three Greensboro chapters, student-welfare issues predominated, while in Chapter Hill, social and political matters held the students' attention. I thought it would be wonderful to have a huge interracial meeting in Greensboro of the membership of all four chapters to exchange views on their diverse interests and concerns; besides, I vividly remembered the effect on me of my first interracial meeting and hoped to make a similar experience available to my fellow ASU members. The first such meeting was held on a Sunday afternoon in a pleasant social hall at Bennett College. Chapel Hillians, armed with maps, drove over in several cars, heeding instructions from me: no carload without at least one woman. The WC women chartered a bus with a Negro driver. The A & T men just walked over.

Everyone was dressed in his or her Sunday best, but initially there was considerable social awkwardness. The Bennett women, hostesses in a totally new social situation, produced their best young-ladies'-finishing-school manner and somewhat overawed the others with their "correct" formality. There was also some prickliness among male students. Two white students returning to the gathering from the men's room approached a drinking fountain simultaneously with two Negro males. The whites stopped hesitantly, deferring to the Negroes. One of the latter, supposing the whites to be reluctant to drink from the fountain (it being unlawful to do so publicly anywhere in the state), commented sarcastically to his companion, "How *'bout* that? This *'colored'* drinking water don't taste like lemonade!" But after a half hour of conversation and much singing at the piano, things gradually loosened up, and then there were reports from each chapter on its activities. By the time the meeting had formally ended, refreshments had been served, and it was time to leave, the stiffness was gone; nearly all the students had made new friends and had new insight into their differently complexioned counterparts; and there was an atmosphere of unforgettable warmth.

A couple of months later a second, equally successful meeting was held at WC with the tacit approval of its dean. That time the A & T men chartered the bus and picked up the women from Bennett. A statewide ASU organization was set up, and I was elected its chairman.

Bart was pleased with my activity and told me affectionately that he had never expected half so much from "a dopey, scissor-bill intellectual who is still wet behind the ears." Belle observed with an amused but slightly quizzical look which said, "Why does Bart always talk so mean to good ole Junius?" Bart and Belle moved before Christmas to a larger but cheaper house on the south side of Greensboro. It was in bad shape: the roof leaked, the wind whistled through the cracks in the floor, and it was terribly hard to heat. Bart told me in advance not to plan anything for New Year's Eve, that there would be a surprise, and that I was expected for dinner. I showed up with a bottle of whiskey and a fancy dessert, hoping that the surprise was that Belle's sister had returned from Georgia. Instead, in Bart's armchair, I found a tall man with a shock of grayish blond hair, spectacles down on his nose, his long legs stretched out before him. That was Rob Hall, DO of the Alabama district, member of the national committee, and in charge of the Party in the whole South.

Rob had a rather terrifying, sardonic look about him until I noticed that when he pulled his mouth down disapprovingly, his eyes and the crow's-feet under them usually were smiling. Besides, his affection for Bart and Belle was so obvious that he won me over quickly. Listening to his Party gossip with Bart was fascinating: I heard talk of "Earl" (Browder) and "Roy" (Hudson), Browder's ubiquitous right-hand man; "Izzie" (Amter), straitlaced head of the New York Party; "Pop" (Mindel), the Party's foremost teacher; and many another Party great.

Rob was a big-time Communist. Well educated in the North, he was a native Alabaman and had spent most of his life in the South. He was an imposing-looking man, and his mental faculties were impressive too. He knew how to reduce complex questions to their fundamentals, and he could help people say what they intended without putting words into their mouths. His leadership was inspirational in the sense that after a long talk with him, despite his low-keyed manner, people had the feeling that they could do more, and better, than before. And usually they could. He felt obliged to know the individual Party members well, and he worked at it. Sensitive and kind, he never resorted to acting like a stuffed shirt.

His sense of humor was first-rate, and at dinner he had us all roaring at his drolleries. After dinner he questioned me closely about my background and what I was doing. He was en route to New York for discussions in the national office and said he would discuss student work with me on his return trip.

Though I was away from home a great deal, I relished the return to the scenes of my early life. Aunt Lucy moved back home and A.G. (Aggie) came to work for the family again; further, Mary Leigh and Archibald came home for the holidays, making it seem like a Christmas out of my childhood. The pleasantest thing about the move back, however, was that it was coincidental with a rapprochement between my father and me.

Since our move to Florida when I was fourteen, there had been friction between us. Mutual hardheadedness, disagreements over matters of taste, and, later on, political differences had kept us apart. Like many an adolescent, I couldn't forgive my father, fifty years my senior, for not having views contemporaneous with mine. Once when some dispute between us had gone on too long, my father had said, "You should respect your father." I had snapped back, "Respect can't be demanded; it has to be earned!" My father had been deeply offended, and I, though ashamed of myself, was too stubborn to say so.

My left-wing activity, largely concealed from my parents, gradually surfaced during the last months in Chapel Hill in connection with my ASU activity. Members were always dropping by to see me, and if it was all right with my mother, I sometimes invited them to lunch or dinner. Often my father found my ASU friends bright and stimulating; sometimes he was charmed with them. His special favorites were (unknown to him) Jewish, Communists, or both. But one fellow I invited to lunch mumbled inaudibly and hung his head; he was unkempt and dirty, pathetically shy, and simply hopeless conversationally. As might have been expected, everything went wrong.

Despite the fact that my father remained courteous and polite, I knew that he could scarcely wait for the young man's departure. Once he had gone, my father exploded, "I suppose *that's* a prime example of the kind of New York Jewish radical you run around with in your ASU!" When I replied that the lad was the barely liberal son of a Methodist minister from near Charlotte, my father laughed in spite of himself. That seemed to clear the air, and we began to discuss and argue about a variety of topics as we had not in years.

In Hamilton Lakes the discussions intensified and included Marxism and Communism, subjects in which my father was far more knowledgeable than I had supposed. To support my point of view, I would give him books of Marx, Engels, and Lenin. He would read them thoughtfully and then, upholding his Jeffersonian political faith, deliver a lively critique. Our debates were warm and friendly, and we teased each other without bitterness. I never said that I had joined the Party, and my father never asked, but probably he assumed that I had. He told me, "I haven't the slightest doubt of your moral character and I know your intentions are good, but *all* my experience tells me that you've chosen the wrong instrument to carry out your aims of human betterment." And he never let up on that admonition.

In attempting to assess my father objectively, I began to discover that he was a remarkable man. Born in the midst of Reconstruction of a distinguished but impoverished family, he had struggled for an education, had been admitted to the bar at the age of twenty-one, had been elected to the state senate at twenty-five, and had been reelected twice at wide intervals. He never lost an election and at one time or another could probably have been governor or U.S. senator; he declined an appointment as chief justice of the North Carolina Supreme Court, a position held by his great-grandfather. He was a liberal on the "race question," led (and lost) the fight for woman suffrage in North Carolina, and was probably the state's outstanding opponent of religious bigotry. He acquired great wealth without becoming a slave to it or making a vulgar display of it, and when he lost most of it he did not let the loss crush him. If, in his ten precarious years as a coronary invalid, a spectator of life, he occasionally felt some bitterness, it was not because his health, wealth, power, and influence had gone, but rather because of disillusionment with people he had mistakenly considered to be friends, and with institutions (including his church) which he believed had valued and honored him in the past largely for his money and power. Having himself a low opinion of material wealth, he seldom missed an opportunity to point out to his children the futility of its pursuit.

He did not allow bitterness to consume him or to poison his generous spirit. Perhaps the most striking things about his later years were his increased tolerance for opposing views; his restless intelligence, which forever explored new ideas and reevaluated accepted truths; the breadth of his cultural and intellectual interests; his exceptional personal charm in the face of continuous ill health; and his insight and warmth as a husband and father.

One Saturday afternoon in mid-January I was upstairs reading in my room. Rob Hall was to be at Bart's that night, and I was invited to dinner. A sweet young neighbor named Jean, a girl of thirteen (a favorite of the whole family from the age of two), had dropped in to visit my father and challenge him to a game of checkers. My mother had taken advantage of her presence to pay a brief, obligatory visit to an ailing neighbor.

Suddenly Jean called out in her high voice, "Irving, your father wants you to bring his heart medicine from the medicine chest right away!" I rushed to get it, dashed down the stairs, and found my father half reclining on a sofa holding his chest in pain. I administered the medicine according to instructions and then phoned the family doctor to come at once because my father was having a heart attack.

My mother returned, her face reflecting my father's pain when she saw him. The doctor arrived at a run. Jean, her face pale, left for home. After examining him for a few minutes the doctor agreed with the patient that he had had a close call. The patient needed to be in bed, so the doctor and I made a seat by grasping each other's wrists and carried him upstairs to his room. While we were getting him undressed he told me I was a good son, and while making a pleasantry to the doctor, he suddenly appeared to choke—and he was gone.

Waves of agony washed over me. My mother called softly to her husband. The doctor sobbed. After a while the doctor shook me out of my trance, saying: "You've got to take charge. There's a lot to do. Call Mary Leigh and Archibald, Miss Lucy, your father's sister, and the Admiral. I'll take care of everything else." I phoned Mary Leigh in eastern North Carolina and, when I heard the familiar voice, could only sob, "Daddy's *dead*!" For an hour I phoned and sent telegrams. Then I spoke to Belle and choked out my news. Aunt Lucy arrived trembling. Events seemed to take place with a nightmarish logic of their own.

Sometime the next day, before relatives began to arrive, my mother picked up my father's wallet and opened it tenderly to a little windowed compartment. There a tiny, yellowed newspaper clipping was neatly framed: "LOCAL YOUTH HONORED. Junius Irving Scales of Chapel Hill was recently elected vice president of the University's American Student Union organization."

After the funeral service, at the cemetery where my father was left with his ancestors, I saw faces in the crowd from out of my own past: Walter, Nereus, and a host of Negro ex-employees looking old and shriveled. Nereus came over to shake my hand and we embraced. I never saw him again; he died a few months later. As the family left the cemetery I saw a contingent of my WPA (Works Progress Administration) friends from my job, dressed in their Sunday clothes; they had taken off from work (being docked for the time, of course) to show their sympathy and friendship.

Back in Hamilton Lakes was a great throng of relatives and friends. My cousin Harry Cobb, looking relatively affluent but bloated and unhealthy, had somehow heard of my radicalism; he greeted my affection with cynicism and a harsh rebuff. In two years he would join his uncle in Green Hill Cemetery, and for many a year to come Aunt Lucy would keep his grave fresh with flowers. I saw my Uncle Arch for the last time, though he was to live another dozen years. Many relations and family friends were soon to die or drift permanently from my life.

My father had gone just when I loved and admired him most. I believed that he had understood what motivated me even though he had found Communism thoroughly repugnant. I was only beginning to realize the extent to which I relied on his standards and conduct as a guide to my own behavior. His death left me on my own. With my father had gone most of my ties to the past, leaving me determined to follow a new course which, in the face of a terrible, destructive war, offered the hope of a better world to come.

My Aunt Katherine stayed on for three weeks to look after my mother, whose own ailing heart was acting up and who was still numb with grief. Aunt Katherine put away her socialite affectations like so much costume jewelry and concentrated on being a loving friend to my mother, even preparing excellent meals on A.G.'s day off. At the end of her stay she insisted that my mother accompany her to Richmond for an extended visit at her home.

Since my mother needed to get away from Hamilton Lakes for a while, it was decided that I should rent a room in town until the spring term began in Chapel Hill and then quit my job and go back to college.

At the second ASU joint meeting (at WC), an intensive program of activity had been planned on behalf of self-help college students who were heavily dependent on the student job grants of the National Youth Administration (NYA). There was a move in Congress to eliminate the NYA jobs program, and the ASU decided to try to arouse the self-help students of the state in their own behalf. We worked up a list of nearly seventy schools and colleges and prepared a petition to congressmen and a covering letter explaining the situation and proposing a statewide conference. A mailing to the heads of student government at each college asked that replies be sent to an address in Chapel Hill. The startling number of replies, including hundreds of signed petitions, gave great impetus to the plans for a conference to be held in Chapel Hill.

Most of the excellent organizational work for the meeting was done by Steve, scion of a prominent southern Jewish family, and Monte from Massachusetts. Steve, whose curly black hair and heavy eyebrows accentuated his swarthy complexion, was a brilliant and charming intellectual, all of seventeen years old. Monte was a bright, longtime ASU activist. These two close friends argued themselves into becoming Marxists by way of an academic course in Hegel's philosophy which they both attended. It was therefore relatively easy for me to recruit Steve into the Party in the fall of 1939. Steve promptly went to work on his amiable buddy and recruited him.

The conference began at about 9:30 on a Sunday morning, in Garrard Hall, at the very hub of the campus, although at a time when the fewest students were stirring. More than eighteen colleges were represented, some by a single delegate, some by a whole group.

The number of Negro delegates far exceeded expectations. Most of them came obviously expecting to be jim crowed, but they had considered the cause worth the indignities. Instead, the host ASU members made a point of welcoming them with the most gracious social amenities. There were no "white" and "colored" signs over the toilets or drinking fountains (an unvarying southern fixture for public buildings in those days) because, of course, no one dreamed that Negroes would ever set foot in that building, aside from janitors. Groups of white students from Chapel Hill and WC mingled with Negro delegates as soon as they were registered and sat with them, thus assuring that there would be no jim-crow seating. Other ASU members, mostly women, attended to the numerous white delegates from more provincial schools, who might, it was feared, object to such unsegregated doings. They introduced them to other delegates, including Negroes, and studied their reactions for signs of hostility. Fortunately, the fears were groundless. Chairing the meeting, I opened with a businesslike presentation of the financial problem confronting several thousand North Carolina students who hoped to finish college. I outlined the need for a publicity and legislative campaign to petition congressmen, and I proposed that money be raised to pay the expenses of a student to lobby the North Carolina congressmen and to present the petitions.

Following the enthusiastic discussion, it was time for lunch. We had relied on timing, the element of surprise, and concealment to carry off the interracial character of the meeting, so it was essential that no Negroes leave the building. Accordingly, luncheon plans had been worked out carefully. The chair suggested that to conserve discussion time, sandwich orders be taken (a typed list was provided), the cost to be covered by the registration fee, and I announced that a huge pot of coffee with paper cups would shortly be available. Local ASU members took the orders and brought back the sandwiches in large cartons from the soda-and-sandwich counter of the YMCA next door. The purchase of the coffee and the loan of the coffeepot were arranged through a waitress there, a sometime date of one of the ASU fellows; she knew that a meeting was going on but hadn't the slightest idea that it was interracial—that was about as likely as seeing a battleship sail down the steps of the university library.

I became violently ill with food poisoning and was replaced in the chair by Monte. Steve was designated the lobbyist, and the delegates pledged themselves to raise money for expenses. The conference adjourned without incident, and the University of North Carolina campus had witnessed its first interracial student gathering. The expense money was raised, and Steve delivered five thousand signed petitions to North Carolina's congressmen. Meanwhile, local meetings of NYA-assisted students were held with wide support. The statewide campaign was so impressive that North Carolina's entire congressional delegation (in sharp contrast to those of other southern states) voted to restore the NYA budget cuts. With the NYA student program retained, thousands of students were able to complete their studies.

Shortly before leaving my job in the Tax Department, I had the first of what was to be more than a quarter century of encounters with the Federal Bureau of Investigation. Bart, of course, had often been harassed by the FBI. Two agents would sometimes sit in a car across the street from his house for two or three hours at a time; once, when I was present, they produced their credentials on his front porch and tried to interrogate him. The Logans' phone appeared to have been clumsily tapped, and their mail was frequently opened and crudely resealed.

One day in the corridor outside my second-floor office in the courthouse two men approached me. One introduced himself as "Morgan of the FBI," showed his identification, and introduced his colleague, Mr. So-and-so. After considerable beating about the bush, they said they were interested in purchasing a small piece of Land in Hamilton Lakes owned by my mother. Would I make them a drawing from a deed description which they had with them? I made the drawing; they left thanking me; and my mother never heard from them about the desired property. Their story was so implausible that Bart and I could only conclude that their objective was either to size me up or to intimidate me, or perhaps both. They certainly succeeded in jolting me.

I'd accompanied Bart to Party meetings in High Point a number of times and followed the concerns of those meetings closely. The textile workers had won a contract and Local 319 was flourishing, while Willie and Bill were engaged in union work almost around the clock. Red Hendrix had found work in a town nearby but spent most of his free time in High Point trying to make the Party club grow.

Meanwhile, Bart informed me that I had been co-opted onto the state committee of the Party and had been elected state treasurer. He turned over to me the Party's rather pathetic financial records, a supply of dues stamps, and some cryptic dues charts for the district, explaining with an evil chuckle, "Now Junius, in this job, you must understand, you're not only supposed to keep *track* of the Party funds, you're supposed to *provide* the Party funds."

As the beginning of the spring term of Chapel Hill approached, I began to dread the thought of being so far away from Bart and Belle. I would also miss the women at WC and my High Point comrades. There was still another wrench when I had to say goodbye to my friends at my job.

As a student in Chapel Hill once more, I needed a place to live. Since Richard was not pleased with his own quarters, we went out hunting for an apartment and found instead a minute, two-room cottage on North Street which was reasonable in rent and suitable for our needs.

My new girlfriend at that time was Liz, a tall, willowy North Carolina working-class woman, a few years older than I, who was working her way through college and who had joined the ASU because she believed in unions. During that term she and I spent much of our time together, and my courses, whatever they were, had only slight interest for me that spring.

But I did have time for politics, even campus politics. The university had an extreme degree of self-government and a corresponding amount of campus politicking. The campus was an excellent training ground for the state's future politicians. Every conceivable political dirty trick, deal, swindle, or frame-up in politics back home was, to some degree, duplicated in the university political apparatus. The amount of raw demagogy was appalling. Because I believed that Communists should be the most skillful politicians, I began to study closely the political games on campus.

The ASU, still the main focus of my attention, was becoming more and more divided along political lines. During the Christmas holidays Lee Wiggins had attended the national convention of the ASU, the only member from North Carolina to do so. Apparently he had been victimized there by both left and right factions. Joe Lash, leader of the anti-Communist forces, must have viewed the brilliant young southerner—somewhat naive, but articulate and strongly anti-Communist—as an ideal compromise candidate for the secondary post of national chairman. The pro-Communist forces looked him over and decided that he was relatively harmless and inexperienced, was lacking a strong base, and was therefore not unacceptable to them. In any case Lee, returning as national chairman with an inflated notion of his influence and attempting to throw his weight around rather imperiously, was overwhelmingly repudiated by the Chapel Hill chapter as well as by the state organization. That circumstance undoubtedly contributed to the factional bitterness.

The Soviet-German pact and the Soviet invasion of Finland, both defended by the Communists, exacerbated the differences between pro- and anti-Communists. Close friends drifted apart. Both sides needled their opponents hatefully. The ASU was sometimes a battleground, and some anti-Communists withdrew from it. As hostility grew, warmth and friendship gradually gave way to rigid, unreasoning partisanship, and both sides became blind to the fine, humane qualities they had formerly admired in one another.

Clifford Odets returned for a few days that spring. His newest play, *Night Music,* had just had an unsuccessful Broadway production, closing after only two weeks. Odets was upset and unhappy, saying that he simply *had* to get out of New York.

I had dinner with him and spent the rest of the evening talking with him alone over many a bottle of beer. Odets was miserable, he seemed even to have lost his old staying power with beer, for early in the evening he was literally crying into it. Although I respected his talent, admired him personally, and had a genuine affection for him, I would not, a twenty-year-old student, have presumed to claim him as a friend. But again Odets, to my acute embarrassment, discussed intimate matters without restraint, including his failing marital situation and his strained relations with some of his longtime co-workers in the theater.

I was surprised that Odets took in stride adverse criticism of *Night Music* by such renowned critics as Wolcott Gibbs, George Jean Nathan, Stark Young, and Joseph Wood Krutch, while a critical review by Alvah Bessie in *New Masses* (the cultural magazine controlled by the Party) reduced him to tears. I was again profoundly impressed by Odets's respect for the moral force of the Party, and felt once again reassured that I was on the right track.

Odets's response to the *New Masses* reproof was like that of a child reacting to an unjust punishment by an adored parent. Over and over he said that he had "explained to them at *New Masses* what I was trying to do, but they just couldn't seem to understand. I never claimed it was a *great* play," he sobbed beerily. "It's just a little diamond chip!"

A second visitor that spring who had a considerable influence on me was Anna Louise Strong, author of *I Change Worlds,* who, after living in the Soviet Union for many years, had become a recognized authority on it. Some nonleft organization had invited her to speak on the campus. She arrived, accompanied by her sister, and made it clear that she preferred to avoid the expense of a hotel and that she expected the local left to provide for her. Shortly after I heard of this situation, some consensus I never quite fathomed evicted Richard and me from our two-room cottage to make room for Anna Louise and her sister. They were two very large, ungainly women, who must have felt that the tiny rooms were closing in on them.

After her public speech, Anna Louise graciously consented to meet with a select group to answer questions about the Soviet Union. An incredible number of students jammed into the little cottage, where the speaker sat regally in the sole armchair. She had the aura of a prima donna and perhaps much of the imperiousness too. Her knowledge and experience were indeed vast, and she had a brusque but Olympian manner of replying to questions which had the effect of giving her answers a supreme authority.

I was especially struck by her clear indication that thirty-three years of socialism had begun to produce a new type of human being, Socialist Man; that a new attitude had developed toward money (vividly illustrated from her personal experience) as something to be spent, not hoarded; and that indeed a sort of unpretentious but genuine utopia was even then (in 1940) coming into being in the Soviet Union. Thus did she give yet another generation of wide-eyed radicals a chance to exclaim with Wordsworth:

Bliss was it in that dawn to be alive,
But to be young was very heaven!

At one point during the three days she remained, she gave a lively account of a meeting she had had with Stalin. To me she conveyed the impression that he was a giant among men, yet warm and human at the same time. Her firsthand testimony had all the more weight because she was an impressive woman with much of the rugged strength of her pioneer forebears, and perhaps something of their no-nonsense, I-can't-stand-a-fool attitude as well.

Bart had told me in confidence that if I were agreeable, he was considering sending me to a national Party training school. I said that of course I would like to go. He said that it was a once-in-a-lifetime opportunity, that he had gone to one, and that it had been an invaluable experience.

Not long afterward he announced that the school was definitely set and that I was to go. The district had a quota of three, and Bart had already picked Ron, a young union organizer and a southerner who would probably stay in the state. For the third choice, what did I think about Steve, Bart asked.

"He's wonderful!" I replied, but added that Steve had been in the Party only six or seven months and was only eighteen years old. I felt like a pompous ass when Bart reminded me that I had been in the Party but fourteen months and had just turned twenty. "What about Monte?" I asked, remembering that he had joined just after Steve.

"A great guy, but as New England as codfish," Bart said.

The unalterable date for showing up in New York for the school was the very date final exams were to begin in Chapel Hill. I had to invent an excuse to postpone my exams and take incompletes on all my courses. There was to be no correspondence with anyone for at least six weeks, and no one was to know the reason for my absence. I wrote my mother that I was going on a hitchhiking trip for a few weeks and left Richard to come up with additional excuses if she grew worried. Steve was busy making similar preparations.

Once the departure date arrived, Ron, Steve, and I found ourselves entrained, right on schedule, New York–bound, feeling honored and responsible. Each of us had memorized instructions from Bart for making a rendezvous with unknown comrades in New York. Youthful, clean-cut, and good-looking, we might have been taken for dedicated divinity students heading for a church retreat or idealistic Boy Scout counselors on their way to a summer camp.

7

The Party School

When I joined the Communist folk, I did what in
  me lay
To learn the grounds of their faith. I read day
  after day
Whatever books I could handle, and heard
  about and about
What talk was going amongst them; and I
  burned up doubt after doubt.

William Morris, *The Pilgrims of Hope* (1883)

The next morning, a bright day in May, we three were waiting impatiently in New York's Pennsylvania Station at a designated post near the information desk. A few minutes past the appointed hour a small man well into his fifties, with handsome features and a high forehead from which straight gray-white hair radiated, walked casually over to two young men standing at a post opposite us. He spoke to them briefly and they picked up their bags and waited. The man came over to us and spoke the phrase we had been told to expect, whereupon we replied with the agreed-on answer. "OK. Come with me," he said, with a trace of a foreign accent. He motioned to the other two men to follow. We walked silently down the long arcade to Seventh Avenue, into a small parking lot, and up to a large old sedan. The man opened the trunk and we put our bags in. He motioned us into the car, got into the driver's seat himself, and closed the door. "I'm Comrade George," he said. "And you are—?" He turned to Steve. "Comrade Steve." They shook hands. We all introduced ourselves by our first names.

We drove north out of the city for three or four hours. The conversation was desultory; Comrade George was concentrating on his driving and continually checked the rear-view mirror to see if we were being followed. When we were somewhere in western Massachusetts, he said, "I want you to close your eyes, please, comrades, until I tell you." We did and we then bounced on rough roads and turned considerably for ten or twelve minutes. The car stopped and the ignition was turned off. "OK," said George. Opening our eyes we saw a fair-sized, one-story frame farmhouse, a volleyball net in front of it, some meadowland, and forest all around.

Coming out to meet us was a tall stringbean of a man in his forties with a mournful face, sensitive features, and gentle, humorous eyes peering through horn-rimmed spectacles. "Hello, George. Hello; I'm Dave White." The latter greeting was graciously addressed to us newcomers. "You're the last to arrive and everyone is here, so let's go inside and get ourselves organized. You can take your bags into the room on your right."

We entered a large central room with wide windows on each side of the door and built-in sofas under each window. The room was dominated by a huge table with high-backed benches on each side and chairs at the ends. Wicker armchairs were scattered on both sides of the room, and a large book-case covered one wall, topped by an old phonograph.

We put our bags in two rooms packed with double-decked cots and returned to the living room, where we found George, Dave, seven young men, and a short, white-haired woman in her sixties. Dave invited us all to sit down at the table while he stood at one end. "I want to welcome you to this national training school of the Party," he said. "It is directed by the Party's national education commission and will be conducted by Comrade George Siskind and myself. I want you to meet Comrade Gordon, who has volunteered to cook for us. Comrade Gordon is a longtime revolutionary who was in the Party in Russia before most of us were born, and she took part in the Revolution of 1905." Comrade Gordon smiled proudly and nodded.

Then there followed an outline of the daily routine: up at 7:00; various chores, done in rotation; breakfast at 7:30; more chores and cleanup; group study at 8:15; at 9:15 a class; 10:15, fifteen minutes' recreation (volleyball); 10:30, group study; 11:30, class; 12:45, lunch; 2:00, study; 3:00, class; 4:00, recreation; 6:30, dinner; 7:30, reading and study or special program; 10:30, bed. No one was to leave the immediate area of the farmhouse except those assigned to the milk detail (white comrades only, to avoid attracting attention), who would walk to a farm nearby and pick up two and a half gallons of milk daily.

Each student was asked to tell a little about himself, covering his experience and class origins, and to pick the name he wanted to be known by. I said I was a student and that I had been a white-collar office worker; I supposed my class origins were big bourgeoisie and landed aristocracy. I was casting about for a first name when Ernie, the senior student, a twenty-nine-year-old Negro longshoreman, said, "He's white-headed. Call him 'Whitey.'" So I was known as Comrade Whitey.

The other students were from all over the South. Ray, a Negro of middle-class background, was twenty-four and the only married student; Bill, twenty-five, a union organizer from Ohio, had worked in the South for some years; Frank, twenty-three, was a student from a border state; Slim, twenty-seven, was a seaman and union leader; and so on. There were twelve students in all: eight white and four Negro.

We broke for dinner, and Slim and I volunteered to help Comrade Gordon. The dinner was delicious: creamy potato soup, followed by an excellent meat loaf with fresh vegetables from the garden just back of the house, and finally a triumphant peach cobbler. We students toasted Comrade Gordon with milk: she wasn't southern, but she was a helluva cook. She curtsied graciously.

After clearing the table and washing the dishes, we went to make our beds and organize our luggage. Several, exhausted from travel, fell into heavy sleep. Before the appointed bedtime, the lights were out and everyone was sleeping. The next morning George called us at seven. He was already fully dressed and went out for a walk in the lovely early morning air.

Everyone had nearly dressed when we noticed Steve still sleeping in his upper bunk. "Hey, Steve! Get your ass up or George is gonna serve it on the half shell!" I called into his ear. No response. He was shaken violently, but he still slept. Finally four of us pulled his mattress off the bed and bumped it down hard on the floor. Steve fought us away like a maddened bull, so we left him and went to breakfast.

"Where's Steve?" Dave asked.

"Still sleeping. Can't get him up."

The corners of George's mouth drew down as his eyebrows went up.

We were just clearing the breakfast things away when Steve walked in, all sheepish and apologetic. He ate alone while the cleanup continued. The class convened promptly at 8:15 while Steve was still choking down cold cereal.

George gave an outline of the school's curriculum and procedure. We would study the history of the Communist Party of the Soviet Union, using as a text the volume prepared by the Soviet Central Committee, along with other materials. We would also study the history of the Communist Party, USA; political economy, strategy and tactics; and, especially, the Negro question. There would be visitors who would serve as special lecturers; otherwise the teaching would be done by George and Dave. We would receive the *Daily Worker* and the *New York Times* every day (a day late). To facilitate study we would be divided into three groups of four each.

The assignments were made, and I was placed in a group with Ron and Frank; Steve was with Ernie and Slim. The groups were later named after Browder (the Party's general secretary), Foster (the national chairman), and Ruthenberg (a formerly Socialist founder of the Party).

The morning schedule was altered so that we could read the first chapter of the history of the CPSU, discuss it in the group, and then meet in the class. We all read about the conditions in czarist times, the antecedents of the Bolsheviks, Plekhanov, and Lenin's early writing and activities; then we discussed in the groups what we had read for its intrinsic interest and its relevance to the United States in 1940.

During the class George asked for a volunteer to summarize and comment on what he thought important in the chapter. Steve's hand was up instantly. Using carefully prepared notes, he gave a brilliant if slick lecture and wound up looking smug and proud of himself. George asked him if he had discussed all that with his group. No, he had not, was the reply.

"Comrades," George said, "This is not Communist behavior. Here we have a comrade who makes use of all of his student skills, learned in bourgeois educational institutions, not to enlighten and help his comrades, not to help *them* understand, but to make a speech in which *he* shines. He does this at the expense of both white and Negro comrades simply because he wants to look superior. He showed his willingness to exploit his comrades this morning when he chose to sleep late and indulge his petty-bourgeois individualism at our expense.

"But as to the assignment, comrades, Comrade Steve's behavior was *uncomradely* behavior. Comrades *share* their experience, their insight, their knowledge. They don't *hoard* it. This was self-indulgent; this was shoddy. Above all, it was shortsighted. In his group Comrade Steve deprived himself of the experience of the other comrades. Does he think he has nothing to learn from them? In comparison with the practical political experience, the trade union experience, of such comrades, he knows *nothing*!

"Comrades, if we are going to build a socialist world, we must first learn to behave like socialists to one another, to live as brothers, as comrades. The Party is a collective, a collective dedicated to organizing the working class and leading it to socialism—a *great* purpose. Inspired by our purpose, an individual member can transcend his own weaknesses. He can remake himself by living up to the demands of his goal and of the time he lives in.

"A Party school is a special collective designed to speed this process of development, to make great changes in specially selected cadres under controlled conditions, in a very short time. You have all been specially selected. You have all been sent here at great expense by your comrades. You are greatly valued by the Party. You must make this school count in our struggle, every moment of it. We have no *time* for petty-bourgeois vanity, for selfishness, for pettiness. Comrades, let us give to one another the *best* that we have to offer."

Steve's only immediate comment was a crushed "Wow!"

Everyday in the *Times* I read with growing distress about the collapse of France. It was excruciating to think of the land of Rabelais, Montaigne, Molière, Balzac, Berlioz, Cézanne, and the Communards lying prostrate, tortured and profaned by the antihuman Nazis.

One day at lunch I spoke about my distress, and I sensed that Dave had reacted to the news, to some degree, in the way I had. Dave was about to respond when George said, "Whitey, don't get carried away by romanticism. France is just another rotten imperialist nation with a vicious history in its colonies. The French have one of the most corrupt, degenerate, bourgeois-democratic governments in the world. They rejected collective security with the Soviet Union, they brought down disaster on themselves, and they don't deserve your sympathy." His face had turned hard and cruel, and no one answered him.

George Siskind was one of the Party's leading teachers. He probably would have been *the* leading teacher had it not been for "Pop" Mindel, whose sense of humor, insights, and greater urbanity made him far more popular with students and gave him the edge. The rumored rivalry was a sore subject with George.

Polish Jewish in origin, George had come to the United States in his youth, having had little formal education. He had read every word ever published of Marx, Engels, Lenin, and Stalin, and he was a walking concordance of their writings. Since its founding he had been involved in the inner workings of the Party in the United States. He was reputed to have spent years as a student in the Marx-Engels-Lenin Institute in Moscow and even to have worked briefly as an agent of the Communist International (Comintern). George did not say. He believed that no Party member should know more than was necessary about another, and his students did not need to know about his past. Whatever his history, he was a perfect English-speaking replica of an ideal Russian Bolshevik (Stalinist mold) of the thirties.

The same afternoon of George's diatribe on France, before dinner, Dave said to me alone, "I know how you feel about France, Whitey. What George says is true, but the French *are* a great people with a great culture, and I think they will eventually play a role in bringing down the Nazis." That sounded human, and it was the first anti-Nazi talk I had heard in the school. Somehow Dave and I drifted into a joyful discussion of Ronsard and tried to quote remembered lines to each other in less-than-perfect French.

David McKelvy White, whose father had been governor of Ohio in the thirties, had left the chair of poetry at Brooklyn College to haul a fifty-caliber machine gun on his frail back all over Spain as a member of the Abraham Lincoln Battalion of the International Brigades. Despite all the death and destruction he had witnessed, he had never hardened his heart. Determined as he was to become a steeled Bolshevik, he never found it necessary to be other than gentle, kind, and gracious.

The school's curriculum was intelligently organized to provide variety and frequent changes of focus. Dave gave three lectures on American history;

George lectured on the history of the Communist Party in the United States (largely on the basis of his personal participation and recollections). There was an extended project on the Negro question with lectures by Abner Berry and Ted Bassett, two prominent Negro Party leaders, and a weekend session on youth problems led by a young Negro leader, Henry Winston.

The heart of the instruction, however, was the study of the Soviet Communist Party, and the basic textbook was *The History of the Communist Party of the Soviet Union (Bolshevik),* prepared by a commission of the Soviet Party's Central Committee in the late thirties. The history, supervised and partially written by Stalin, was regarded by Communist parties everywhere as the supreme one-volume compendium of Marxist-Leninist theory. (Some years later, after Stalin's death, the book was said to contain many "errors" and was denounced and withdrawn by the Soviet Central Committee. At that time we knew nothing of the book's misrepresentation of events and individuals, nor were we aware that it was a gross falsification of fifty years of Russian history. And had we been told, no one would have believed it.)

The study of the *History* was supplemented by readings from the works of Lenin and Stalin and by lectures, usually delivered with great intensity by George. The students questioned and argued freely and became completely immersed in the ideological struggles of the Bolsheviks, which George attempted to make relevant to our own time and problems.

I still found the *History* a grim book, being as repelled by the terse, bloodless language as I had been when I tried to read it on my own. But as it got to be associated in my mind with the classroom discussions and the commentaries of George and Dave, it became for me the indispensable textbook of revolution. Day after day we pored over what we accepted as the true, detailed story of the Russian Communists guided by the genius of Lenin. As we saw the story evolve, Lenin acquired something very close to infallibility; later on, Stalin achieved only slightly less stature. What held us in awe was the picture presented to us of ceaseless struggle beginning in the 1890s: Lenin's fight for revolutionary and organizational principles, defeat in 1905, self-critical reevaluation, adversity, victory, new problems, traitors from within (Trotsky the arch-villain), their exposure and defeat by Stalin, and the building of socialism in one country. Emerging from this sweeping history was a picture of the Bolsheviks' selfless devotion to revolutionary duty, their clear-eyed, unsentimental humanism in fighting to destroy the inhuman exploitation of capitalism, and their ability to solve every problem and defeat every enemy.

We students felt that the Bolsheviks truly created and practiced "scientific" socialism. Knowing ourselves to be less than novices at building a new society, we felt we must learn from those real pros who had already built a heaven on earth. Consequently we regarded Soviet ideology as tested truth and believed that the Bolshevik experience offered guidance in every area of political work. In our naiveté we tended to make simple translations from the Russian experience to American problems, usually with ludicrous results—not unlike the leaflet issued by a Brooklyn Party club in the thirties which began, "Workers and peasants of Brownsville!"

As fascinating and impressive as the study of the Russian "success story" was for us all, George was never certain that he had impressed his charges sufficiently with the true position of the Soviet Union in the Communist world outlook. Forty years after the school, I found in my notes the following excerpt from one of his lectures, dealing with the dictatorship of the proletariat:

> The single country where the dictatorship of the proletariat has triumphed represents a wedge driven into world capitalism by the world proletariat. The USSR is the stronghold of the world proletariat; it cannot be looked on as merely a nation or a country; it is the most advanced position of the world proletariat in the struggle for a socialist world. When the Red Army marches, it is the international proletariat marching to extend its sphere of operations in the struggle against world imperialism. In the period of capitalist superiority in strength, the Party splits world imperialism by taking advantage of its inherent contradictions; it also builds up the strength of the USSR to provide the world working class with greater might. Stalin, the great genius of socialism, stands like a colossus of steel as the leader of the world proletariat.

The study of political economy was all too brief for me. Even so, I was satisfied that the machinery whereby the capitalists deprived the workers of the fruits of their labor had been substantially exposed. "Surplus value" became a fact of life to reckon with. In my political vocabulary, deviations of all sorts constituted a new bestiary, and I spoke familiarly of "right opportunism," "left sectarianism," and even more exotic varieties of devilment such as "khvostism" and "oblomovism." Dave's brief but searching exploration of dialectical materialism confirmed me in my philosophical materialism. I even resolved to have another go at Bishop Berkeley's *New Theory of Vision,* an essential exposition of philosophical idealism which had confounded me in my sophomore year at college.

To a man the students were stimulated and shaken by the school. The impact of what we learned academically was staggering, but the business of collective living was a revelation as well. Some of us parted reluctantly with the notion that gratification of our own desires was the paramount good and had difficulty in learning to respect the needs and desires of others. Nevertheless, we all became more altruistic and put aside much of the petty selfishness which had become a part of our lives.

In sum, if the party leadership wanted indoctrinated, devoted advocates who would put the "cause" above everything, they were beginning to get

their money's worth. We young scholars were all becoming hard-shelled ideologues, believing that our ideology incorporated all the wisdom and humanism of previous ages and convinced absolutely of the essential soundness of
Marxism-Leninism. We were becoming impervious to every opposing view.
Contrary ideas all seemed to have been drawn from poisoned wells: such stuff
was simply propaganda from the enemy class aimed at disrupting and confus-
ing the revolutionary working class.

Volleyball was the principal recreation of the school. As the days rolled by
and the intensity of the studies increased, the sport offered great relief from
pressures and tensions. But wily George used the game as a teaching aid.

One of the immutable facts of life at the school was that Ernie hogged the
ball and tried to make every shot himself. His "Ah got it!" was a warning
usually heeded by his teammates. Failure to let him have it could result in their
being knocked flat on the ground, because Ernie was big and powerful.
George was an exemplar of the collective approach; the ball should be passed
to the forecourt from the rear, *then* smacked over the net; the emphasis was on
retrieval, not smashes. George's strategy was so successful that the opposing
team, where Ernie was invariably the star, always lost. George claimed this
primacy as a victory of Socialist collectivism over bourgeois individualism.

Ernie became self-conscious about mauling and crippling his own teammates
and tried to make sure he had a great deal of space around him when he
bellowed his dread warning. One day after shouting an "Ah got it!" while
looking around, he waited too long and the ball hit him between the eyes with a
loud "splat," which was immediately followed by cheers from his teammates.

Near the end of the school, the intense, rigidly controlled atmosphere, the
constant pressure for self-criticism, the rigorous concentration on studies,
small irritations with one another, and sexual frustration all made themselves
felt on the volleyball court. There would be sarcastic comments on another's
inept play; balls would be slammed over the net with irresponsible violence;
taunts at the other team often got nasty. One day in the middle of a game,
when all these things were evident, George suddenly walked off the court.

Play stopped. "Aw George, come back!" "George, what'd we do?" came
the cries.

"I don't want to play with you until you learn to play like *comrades*! Now
let me see if you know how."

He stood on the sidelines until the irritation and ugliness were no longer in
evidence. Then he came back into the game without a word.

Comrade Gordon had her problems with a bunch of southerners whose eating tastes were largely unreconstructed and, in some cases, limited to what
would later be known as "soul food."

She was of Russian Jewish origin and was a superior mistress of the cuisine she had grown up with. Having survived her husband and children, she had volunteered to serve as cook for several Party schools. Her services were readily accepted by the education commission, not only because her immense culinary abilities were a significant morale factor, but also because her political acumen and trustworthiness were beyond question. She had taken much pleasure in the plaudits she had received in previous schools, and she expected to outdo herself for those "nice southern boy-es."

The first dinner had been a triumph, even if a trifle exotic. The first breakfast, cold cereal, fried eggs, bacon, soft rolls, and excellent coffee, was also well received, despite a unanimous feeling of deprivation at the absence of hominy grits. Dave guaranteed that grits would be provided, and Slim volunteered his assistance to Comrade Gordon in mastering the subleties involved in preparing that quintessential breakfast ingredient. Comrade Gordon accepted the offer, although she was puzzled at the insistence on a cereal which she had never even seen.

The disaster came at lunch: all four Negroes and half the white students left the main dish untouched: a superb Russian-style cabbage borscht with an exquisitely balanced sweet-and-sour flavor.

"Good God a'*mighty*! I don't mean no harm, Comrade Gordon, but that don't taste like no soup I *ever* ate!" Ernie grumbled in dismay.

Steve, Ron, and I (as well as Dave) had eaten our own and our unhappy neighbors' soup and had returned for thirds or fourths, but Comrade Gordon was incredulous and shocked at the majority attitude. "If dere not cabbage, dere not have *been* Russian Revolution! Ve vould have *starve* to death!" the old nineteen-fiver exclaimed indignantly.

Dave, speaking as one of the newly converted, said that everyone could profit from the expansion of his cultural horizons (including matters of cuisine) and that the school, like travel, offered a fine opportunity to explore an aspect of Russian and Jewish culture new to most of us. He suggested that those who had only tasted their soup should eat a whole bowlful before deciding what they thought of it.

The ploy worked. Even Ernie admitted that "once you get past the first spoonful, it's pretty damn good." Therefore, to a man, we responded with objectivity, and usually succumbed with enthusiasm, to cold beet borscht with sour cream, cold schav, cold fruit soup, cheese and meat blintzes, potato knishes, stuffed derma, gefilte fish with horseradish, spring salad (cottage cheese with scallions, radishes, and sour cream), and stuffed cabbage. As a matter of fact, by popular request the main dishes at the final commencement dinner were stuffed cabbage and a mountain of cheese blintzes (with sour cream).

Comrade Gordon also made progress. She pronounced hominy grits "de-leeshus," but a shocked Slim discovered that she ate it in a bowl and with *milk* and *sugar*! And Slim never did convince her of the merits of "red-eye" gravy.

She was a tough little woman. She was no traditional Jewish mama dedi-cated to stuffing and babying her "sons." She had long since eschewed senti-mentality, for she had seen much hardship, repression, and death, and she lived dignified and clear-eyed in the belief that individual survival and revolu-tionary success depended on self-sufficiency and ruthless honesty with com-rades. The Party had become her family, and her motherly feelings were ex-pressed in her intense and watchful concern over the "boy-es." That meant, primarily, seeing that they lived up to Party standards.

She always spoke frankly and to the point. "Vitey, if you don't know how vash dishes, zay zo. Don't chust slop dem around in vater. Here, I teach you." Or in reference to one of the day's class sessions, which she always attended when her work permitted, she said, "Vitey, I like ven you say, 'I don't know,' or ven you anzer vot you really know for true. But ven you try pretend, or talk baloney, you vaste everybody time."

Daily she studied our progress or lack of it and rejoiced or suffered accord-ingly. When she had one of us on KP, she frequently said what she thought would be helpful. For example, "Steevee, vy do you not try say theengs seemply, in few vorrds? You say *much* too many vorrds!"

Late in the school, when her cooking had conquered Ernie completely and he was gaining about four pounds a week, she noticed that he had popped the top button on his trousers. That night after bedtime she sent Dave in to fetch them, and the next morning Ernie found the button replaced. When he thanked her, she replied, "It vass a comradely obligation."

She loved poetry and music and would sometimes recite several lines in expressive Russian and say, "Dot's Pushkin" or "Dot's Nekrassov." I first heard bits of Tchaikovsky's *Eugene Onegin* while listening to her sing to her-self in the kitchen. I had never read Pushkin's poem from which the libretto was fashioned, so she told me the story and declaimed and sang much of Tatiana's letter scene from memory, having heard it in Moscow forty years before.

Cooking for fifteen would have been a tough job for a woman thirty years younger, but Comrade Gordon planned each day's meals like a military cam-paign; she had her work so incredibly well organized that she could conserve her strength, sit in on the discussion and lecture sessions, and still come up with creative ways of making each meal distinctive and memorable.

She considered herself a soldier of the Revolution and followed the Party's dictates without hesitation. Any questioning of Party attitudes, or those of its recognized leaders, was intolerable and was prima facie evidence in her eyes of disloyalty. Her own reminiscences about factional struggles in Russia before World War I and in the American Party in the twenties revealed a ferocity and hatred toward "deviationists" inconceivable in such a grandmotherly person. It gave me an uneasy feeling to think what might happen to me or any other Party member who might have an honest disagreement about Party policy. Would we have to face such hatred as this little old lady was capable of? And would Comrade George be any less relentless?

Dave had a complete recording of Marc Blitzstein's miniature opera *The Cradle Will Rock,* and played it through one evening on the old windup phonograph. Since the popular, catchy tunes and the politically sophisticated, tongue-in-cheek libretto made a great hit with the students, someone at every spare moment seemed to be playing one record or another from the album. George had listened to it unsmiling. Someone asked him if he didn't like it. "That kind of culture will *never* rock the cradle!" he snorted.

The lecturer-visitors were all well received: Henry Winston ("Winnie"), Ted Bassett, Harry Raymond (of the *Daily Worker*), Abner Berry, and finally our very own Rob Hall. Rob arrived toward the end of the school and got a private earful from George and Dave. At the dinner table that night he beamed with pleasure at all twelve of his charges and had something private and enthusiastic to say to each. The school had evidently gone well.

Shortly after Rob's departure, we were grouped by districts to prepare a plan of action to present to each district or state committee; then each one had to sweat over a "critical and self-critical evaluation" of the school and his participation in it. By that time even the poorest student could readily identify left and right deviations, distinguish a strategy from a tactic, explain the difference between value and price—but self-criticizing was tough, and the heavy introspection was fogging every brow.

Ron had for days been going around singing "Beautiful, beautiful brown eyes, I'll never love blue eyes again," with increasing mournfulness, and I suspected he was pining for his girlfriend. He showed his tension by drumming and rapping on the table or his notebook, and I showed mine by wanting to smack him for it. Besides, I had just about had it, as had everyone else. By way of relief, Ron began delivering a Ciceronian denunciation with me as the Catiline. The others listened with delight. Then, with inspired madness, Ron switched over to a sort of parody of an incitement to lynching. Negro and white responded with equal enthusiasm, and I finally had to run for it with the whole crew after me, whooping through the woods. Ernie circled around and ambushed me as Bill and Ray closed in from behind. Ron, the archfiend, was eloquently proposing innovative and creative tortures never before dreamed of, when suddenly there came a chilling cry: "Com*rades*!" It was George, white-faced and trembling with anger. "What is the meaning of this, comrades?"

"Well, George, we were just kidding around to get loosened up a little—" Slim began.

"Kidding about a lynch mob?" George thundered. For ten minutes we were chewed out, shamed, politically analyzed, and denounced. He nearly convinced us that we had betrayed the proletarian revolution, the working class, the Negro people, Comrade Browder, *and* Comrade Stalin. As we trooped back disconsolately to the house, Ron said in an awed voice, "My god! I guess we got a long way to go before we get to be Bolsheviks." And he spoke for the oppressed masses.

The next day, at our commencement exercises, everyone heartily concurred when Dave said, "A Party school constitutes an experience so trying that only prison and military combat are comparable."

At the commencement the three Carolinians were favorably evaluated. Dave's comment on Steve was: "There's nothing wrong with Steve except being eighteen and inexperienced; time will solve both problems."

The school and its six-week regimen had been unforgettable. The camaraderie and some of the funny incidents were delightful: Ray absentmindedly eating a spoonful of fresh horseradish; Steve, trying desperately to awaken himself on his second morning, putting his shirt on backward, and pulling his undershirt over the top of it; and ladies-man Slim solemnly criticizing the school on the final day for the failure to have women students, with such transparently ulterior motivation and such longing in his voice that even Comrade Gordon burst out laughing.

The school had given each of us an undreamed-of grasp of Marxist-Leninist theory, which I could no longer doubt was the *summum bonum*. It had convinced me that the Party *was* on the right track and that it *would* find an American road to socialism. I thought that with all I had learned I might have convinced even my father that I was on the right path, if only I could have talked with him then.

The school had swept me along, as it was meant to do, arousing in me a sort of exultation and decisively changing my plans for my future: henceforth the socialist revolution would be the determining force in my life.

I knew instinctively that there was a price to be paid. Organizing the working class would not be easy; it would take fanatical devotion and intense absorption. And there was no reason to believe that the ruling class would be gentle with me. Death, prison, torture, or combinations of the three were the historic lot of those who rebelled. I would take my chances. As with any dedicated fanatic, there would be a narrowing of focus, a delimiting of the horizon. I would be on a slim ration of music, literature, and art for a while to come. Perhaps I would even fall into parochial and sectarian ways of thinking, like Comrade Gordon, for example. I ventured to think that Comrade George, for all his knowledge and experience, sometimes lost his ability to assess the real world, as in his view of France or his reaction to the "lynch mob." If it could happen to George it could happen to me, certainly. But forewarned was forearmed.

Principally nagging at me were four thorny matters, although it would have been hard for me to put them in words then, and they did not dampen my singing spirits. They were, first, that I did not know what were the basic criticisms of the Party made by the Trotskyists, the social democrats, the socialists, and various liberals. Why didn't the school examine their attacks head on and refute them? That would have been creative and useful. Simply calling our opponents names was evasive of the real issues. The Party's ideology was impregnable; why wasn't it put to work on our critics? Secondly, our study of the trade union question revealed that unions were merely "schools for revolution" and that union objectives were "opportunist." I saw nothing opportunist about Local 319 in High Point; it was creating a social revolution right in the cotton mill village. Unions were having a revolutionary effect in the South wherever they were able to get a foothold. Were they useless if they were not under Communist leadership or failed to produce Communists? And what about the ASU, which had meant so much to me? Was it, as a "mass organization," only of consequence as a school for revolution, regardless of its good works and the social conscience it had developed in thousands of non-Communist members? Third, the Party was intolerant of dissent. I hoped I would never find myself in serious disagreement with the Party line, and I assured myself that in the long run, the essential humanism on which Communism rested would inevitably eliminate the Party's harshness toward those with differing opinions. Finally, there had been an air of indifference to wide-scale human suffering and death (as in the events in France). Cruelty seemed justifiable against great masses of people as long as they were identified as "counterrevolutionaries," "kulaks," "petty bourgeoisie," or the like. Could the basic Communist concern for people be distorted to accommodate to policy shifts? Once again I told myself that the fundamental altruism of Communism would necessarily correct and obliterate such contradictory attitudes and policies.

These were four seemingly tiny clouds on the horizon, and they wouldn't grow for many years—but they wouldn't go away either.

For me the school marked the beginning of a new life and the end of an old one. I was unalterably convinced that the Party held the key to the future: that it had the know-how to lead the way to a socialist America in the near future.

Quietly, without ceremony, and without mentioning it to anyone, I experienced an unparalleled thrill of dedication, as George had said, to a great purpose. I was going to become a professional revolutionary. So great was my exhilaration and so boundless was my youthful optimism that obstacles to my goal, such as my class background, my deficiencies as a practical politician, a public speaker, and a charismatic leader, and my temperamental deficiencies as an activist, all seemed trifles which I would readily surmount with the Party's aid.

I had taken sides! I had chosen to be with the wretched of the earth on their march to a better world. Behind me was the bog I had been sinking into at the university: the sweating away at university training for nothing in particular, for dubious rewards not worth the gaining. I was able to reject my own class and its worthless values. The loneliness that always besets the heretic and the outcast had no fears for me.

The forceful tide of my conviction was to sweep me on for more than sixteen years.

8

The Mill Village

America is . . . for the great mass of people—
the vast, surging, hopeful army of workers. . . .
The crowd of the grave working-men of our
world—they are the hope, the sole hope, the
sufficient hope of our democracy.

Walt Whitman

In an immense loft extending over several stores and businesses on South
Main Street in High Point, North Carolina, the regular Saturday night union
meeting of Local 319 of the Textile Workers Union of America (TWUA),
CIO, was in progress.

High Point was then a city of about thirty-five thousand, seventeen miles
southwest of Greensboro, the second city in Guilford County and a major
manufacturing center of textiles, hosiery, and furniture. The CIO had had a
strong impact on the area about a year and a half earlier when the workers of
Highland Cotton Mill organized, won union recognition, and transformed their
lives after a bitter and divisive strike. Highland was a cotton mill which bor-
dered on and dominated a large mill village. The rows of little frame houses, the
dirt paths, the unpaved streets, the trees, the general store, the barber shop, and
the interdenominational church were all company-owned and company-po-
liced. Over two thousand people lived there; approximately five hundred (at
least one from each household) worked in the mill and had twenty-five cents per
room deducted from their pay as house rent each week.

Unionization had brought about many changes in the village. For instance,
the large majority of the workers no longer lived in fear of the company's
power over them at work and at home, nor did they cringe at the constant
surveillance which persisted by means of a network of foremen, straw bosses,
and submissive informants. As noted earlier, most people had quit going to
church because the minister raved in the pulpit that the CIO was the antichrist,
come to lead the workers to perdition.

Among the pro-union workers the strike had released an avalanche of bitter resentment against their feudal-minded employer. They had won their strike with dogged courage and had achieved a new sense of their worth. They had discovered that they could think for themselves and speak for themselves. Encouraged by the union, many attended adult education classes offered by the WPA, studying such things as reading and writing, typing, bookkeeping, and American history. Many people found a new vitality and yearned for a life beyond the poverty and hardship which work in the cotton mill entailed.

During the strike, through the help they had received from other unionized workers, as well as from their own experience, the workers had a taste of what their unity could accomplish. But after a year or so, things had settled down to a continuous, tiresome struggle against a wily company to enforce the union contract. Most of the workers, one generation or less removed from the farm, retained much of the fierce individualism acquired in the lonely struggle to make a living from the soil. Because of this individualism, unity was difficult to maintain, and relations among the workers could become anarchic.

It was early November 1940, and several score workers sat in the well-lighted center of the hall on rickety folding chairs rented from a funeral parlor. They listened to a tense discussion of the company's obduracy in response to a grievance of the women in the spinning room, who were protesting an attempt to increase their already incredible workloads. Several spinners spoke eloquently, criticizing the chairman and other men on the grievance committee for a lack of backbone in handling their complaint. Some of the men were shocked at the temerity of these women, who, two years before, mostly submissive to their husbands and other men in positions of authority, would have been too unsure of themselves to say one word in public.

Virgie Lance, a small blond woman of about twenty-six, with blazing eyes and heavy eyebrows, spoke furiously and vividly about the attempt of time-study efficiency experts, carrying stopwatches, to intimidate and speed her up on the job. Virgie, because of her courage, magnetism, and passionate advocacy of unionism, was one of the true organizers of Local 319 and was the sole woman member of its executive committee. "Cowboy," her shy, supportive husband, observed her with amazed admiration, as if he had suddenly discovered himself married to Joan of Arc.

A striking woman, she would have been pretty, but as was the case with most women textile workers, a few years in the mill had put a mark on her. From standing long hours at spinning frames, her shoulders had begun to sag forward, her abdomen protruded, her complexion had become sallow, and already, as a defense against the flying lint which made one "spit cotton," she had adopted the practice of dipping snuff. The pinch of tobacco dust under the lower lip caused the saliva to flow freely, but it was as addictive as smoking, discolored the teeth, and gradually etched little brown lines around the mouth. Even dressed up and wearing makeup, Virgie looked nearly forty.

In the shadows were another two hundred people, some standing, some seated on benches. These were the families and friends of the union members: children, young people, and old folks. They were waiting for the meeting to adjourn so that the square dance, which always followed, could begin.

Old Shorty, the best caller anywhere around, stood near the stairs with the members of the string band, shifting his weight from one foot to the other. He had been a textile worker for nearly fifty years, starting when he was twelve, and had the stooped figure of a doffer of spinning frames. All week he worked at his killing job, inconspicuous and unnoticed, a pathetic-looking little old man. But on Saturday nights he put off his years, put on his neat, threadbare gray suit, walked a mile to the union hall from the village, and waited for the moment when he would get the microphone in his hand.

The public address system was at that moment being used by Buck Anderson, a tall, long-faced man, patient and solemn, who was the local's president. He had at last reached the final agenda item, "good and welfare," under which he had placed the report of the new organizing committee for the sake of winding up the meeting with a little "zing."

"Brothers and sisters, I'd like to say that you all know there's a lotta workin' people that don't know about the union and what-all it's done for us. So our new organizin' committee—Brother Held, Sister Yarboro, Brother Scales, and the rest—is tryin' to spread the union word so we can get some more of these plants, around High Point here, into the CIO and get more support for our own union. The committee's been workin' mighty hard lately, and I'm gonna ask Brother Held to report."

Willie Held, nervous at having to speak, made his way to the microphone, his full face even more florid than usual and the corners of his mouth pulled down. He announced that the committee had prepared a four-page mimeographed newspaper called *The Voice of 319,* written entirely by members of the local, who told in their own words what it was like, before and after the union came, at Highland Cotton Mill. "I believe you're gonna like it," he said, warming with enthusiasm. "I'm gonna ask Brother Scales here, who's the editor, to hand out a copy to everybody. I want you to read it yourselves and then give it to your kinfolks and friends who work in other mills. And we want anybody who would like to write for the paper to see somebody on the committee and write a piece for us. You don't have to write it yourself if you don't want to; Brother Scales can take down what you want to say and write it up for you. There'll be a stack of papers by the stairs so you can take as many as you want when you go. OK, June, you can pass 'em out. Thank you, Brother Anderson; that's the report."

While Brother Anderson praised the committee and the new paper, I handed out *The Voice of 319,* greeting the members by their first names. In less than four months I had come to love and respect those people, and I felt that I belonged among them. I had no doubt that they, the proletariat I had read so much about, would indeed, as I had been taught, rebuild the country and the world in a better mold. Meanwhile, most of the people had begun to accept me. It was generally known that I was a rich man's son, a Scales from Greensboro, and that I had gone to the university; many therefore viewed me with suspicion. What was *I* doing in a mill village? But my defenders pointed out that I put on no airs; had moved into the village with a respected family; had looked tirelessly for work (two days in a box factory, a week in a hosiery mill which promptly went out of business, at last steady work at nearby Hillcrest Mill); that I was friendly, polite, clean-living, and sober; that I worked hard for the union—and besides, dogs, children, teenage girls, and old people liked me. Two months earlier I had been voted full membership in Local 319, since there was no union at Hillcrest. Even though rumors persisted that I was tied up with the Communists—Red Hendrix and the like—no one could find anything sneaky or sinister about me, and I really *was* hell-bent for the union, so I couldn't be all bad, whatever I was up to.

I was greeted warmly by most and with cool politeness by a few. As I finished passing out the papers, the meeting was adjourned, folding chairs were stacked, benches were moved against the walls, and there was a buzz of excited talk as the band (two violins, two banjos, two guitars, and a bull fiddle) began tuning up on the platform. Old Shorty, his feet already tapping away despite himself while he relocated the PA amplifier, at last had the precious mike in his hand.

I sought out "my" family, the Gillens, and found them standing together on the edge of the dance area watching the preparations. Bill, a union stalwart since the strike, was standing beside his wife, Esther (née Parker), a pioneer union militant herself, perhaps a year younger. She had a handsome face and a sturdy build, looking far older than he as a result of working for fifteen years in the mills and bearing three daughters. Vera, the eldest, was a brunette beauty, apparently seventeen or eighteen; Carleen, eleven, was blonde and blue-eyed; eight-year-old Billie was a dark-eyed tomboy.

Excepting Bill, I had known them only since August. Bart Logan had driven me over to a Party meeting in High Point and had explained to the comrades that I wanted to become a textile worker and help the union movement. Bill had said that he could put me up overnight and that, while he would have to talk it over with his wife, he thought it would be all right if I stayed with them while looking for a job. Bill had taken me home and introduced me to the family. Esther liked me at once and said she'd be pleased to have me as a guest as long as I needed a place to stay. I was enchanted with them and accepted with enthusiasm, once they had agreed to let me pay five dollars a week, the prevailing rate in the village for a single man's room and board. When I had moved in, I had been received as a member of the family and treated with great kindness and affection. Even Scrappy, their little white mongrel, had wagged his approval.

The Gillens, like nearly everyone else at the dance, were shining clean, shampooed, free from lint, and dressed in their best clothes. Being clean and in clean clothes was no simple matter. There was reputedly only one bathtub in the village, in the head foreman's two-story house. And the laundry was done by hand during the week in big tin tubs with washboards, using water heated in pots, kettles, and buckets. Ironing was usually done with a flatiron also heated on the stove.

Bill and I had gone down to the company barber shop in the afternoon, where hundreds of other men had queued up throughout the day in their smelly workclothes, still with a week's accumulation of sweat, dirt, and lint. They each carried a brown grocery bag containing clean socks, shirt, underwear, and their Sunday-best suit. When our turn came, we each paid twenty-five cents and received a towel, a small bar of Lifebuoy soap, and the use of a shower stall and all the hot water we wanted. After Bill and I had showered and put on our clean clothes, we went home, where we had to wait on the front porch while the women bathed in the kitchen. There, as in kitchens all over the village, they heated water on top of the kerosene cooking stove and the little wood-and-coal laundry stove. The big corrugated tin washtub, placed in the middle of the floor and surrounded by newspapers to protect the linoleum, served as the bathtub. The youngest would bathe first, receiving successive dousings of warm water, then the next oldest, and so on.

The source of water was a single faucet three feet outside the kitchen door, which dripped into an ever-present mud puddle. When the bathing and shampooing were finished and the females were dressed and were attending to their hairdos, Esther would call, and Bill and I would come into the steaming kitchen, sweet-smelling with soap, and carry the tub of bathwater out to a ditch behind the privies, which stood in a row twenty feet behind each of the identical little houses.

After testing the PA system, Shorty gave the command: "Choose your partners for the first dance!" and waited patiently two or three minutes during which there was much rushing around, asking, refusing, and coy reluctance.

I hastened to ask beautiful Vera, who lately had been much in my thoughts, for the first dance; but she was in a perverse mood, and sensing that I was already attracted to her, decided to make me jealous. Casually declining my invitation, she accepted seconds later the offer of a young fellow who was startled, since she had previously treated him with nothing but contemptuous disdain. I was struggling with an acute attack of jealousy when little Billie announced that *she* was "gonna dance this one with old June." Esther promptly changed her mind for her and sent her off to dance in the corner with the under-ten small fry. I was nearly resigned to being a wallflower when I saw Carleen (or Corky, as the family called her) shyly trying to shrink behind a post. She smiled and blushed as I pulled her into the line on the dance floor.

Shorty chose an agile young matron to help him illustrate the pattern of the first dance. Although she towered over his five-foot frame, he was in complete charge, calling out his commands with perfect rhythm in a raspy, staccato singsong, executing difficult steps with consummate grace. His tiny feet fluttered and tapped as though they were entirely independent of the little hunched body, itself topped by a resolutely unsmiling face with contrasting eyes. The band struck up with the fiddles wailing nasally, tossing the tune to the twanging banjos and then taking it back again. The huge line began to move under Shorty's steady control.

As Carleen and I swung, hopped, shuffled, and sashayed through Shorty's intricate patterns, she said softly, "That Vera is so mean! She's just dancing with Linwood to get your goat. I think she's *awful*! Don't you feel bad, June." I was so touched by the insight and loyal concern of the little girl that as we circled each other, I gave her a hug and a peck on the nose, whereupon she blushed furiously and nearly lost her way in a complicated figure.

When Shorty had exhausted everyone, including himself, he brought the set to a resounding close, and everyone took a breather. As an interlude between square dances, the band offered something like a foxtrot, and a few tireless couples engaged in what was called "round" dancing. I joined a couple of my male Party comrades near a window, where we discussed union problems and talked about the possibility of running some labor candidates in the municipal elections, the chances of getting a Federal Housing Authority in High Point to build some low-cost housing, and whether we could organize some of the numerous small seamless-hosiery plants that always paid the lowest possible wages.

Life in the mill village was far from being a series of square dances. Five days a week I put on my denim jacket, stuck my sandwiches in the side pocket, said goodbye to Esther, walked through the village, open countryside, and woods a half mile to where the Hillcrest Throwing Company plant roared even more loudly than Highland Cotton Mill. Hillcrest was part of the enormous chain of Burlington Mills, its function being to process synthetic fibers, mainly rayon, converting them into finished yarn ready for weaving or knitting.

So vast was the Burlington Mills operation that the CIO and its Textile Workers Union had all but despaired of organizing it in the foreseeable future. Previously, I was told, when a Burlington plant *had* been organized, the company would close down the plant and transfer its functions one hundred or five hundred miles away, blacklisting the unionists for good measure. I therefore worked at Hillcrest to subsist while planning to direct my organizing efforts to cotton mills and seamless-hosiery plants where the CIO considered organization possible.

In 1940 the Burlington chain appeared to have developed to the highest degree the process of extracting the maximum amount of energy from each worker. The company's superintendents, supervisors, and even foremen had some training in textile chemistry and were encouraged to be dispassionate and statistically minded in the use they made of the hired hands. They were evaluated on their abilities as efficiency experts and were trained to be aloof from the workers. Occasionally they gave qualified praise for work well done (usually with comments about how it might have been done still better); their contemptuous condescension was reserved for the below-average or barely competent worker. Any hint of insubordination (they immediately smelled a potential union troublemaker) was dealt with by peremptory firing. If the shift foremen were regarded as heartless and inhuman by the workers, who knew them all too well, the belief was encouraged that the plant superintendents and other white-shirted, necktied divinities *were* human and might be appealed to for justice. Although there was no evidence to support that belief, beyond a few sympathetic words or a promise, when some problem was brought to their attention, to "look into it," there were many who were firmly convinced that the highest levels were on their side and who thought that there was a private understanding between themselves and a big boss.

Most of the workers were women under thirty (older women could rarely keep up the pace) who had had no previous industrial experience and often were fresh off the farms. They worked either as winders or as spinners.

Winders took a skein of continuous-filament rayon (hundreds of yards long), stretched it over a circular frame a foot or so in diameter, placed the frame in a rack above their heads where it could rotate, and passed the end of the filament through a guide and connected it to a bobbin that turned rapidly and wound the rayon evenly onto itself. Each winder carried a mechanical knotter, a complex device fitting into the hand which, when triggered, instantly tied a nearly invisible knot between the two ends of a filament, cutting off the leftover pieces at the same time. When a filament broke or a skein ran out, she had to use her knotter to get that bobbin filling again, and quickly, or her elaborately charted production would drop, as would her wages. In her pocket she carried a gauge to measure the fullness of the bobbin: if the bobbin got too full, the excess had to be rewound on another bobbin and she was penalized accordingly; if she removed the bobbin before it was sufficiently full, she would be suspected of cheating and would likely be fired if the infraction were repeated. The harvest of properly filled bobbins, placed on spindles in heavy, basketlike, metal trays, had to be removed frequently from her machine by "yarn boys" or "bobbin boys," as they were variously called; the trays were stacked on metal skids and then hauled by means of heavy hydraulic pull trucks to the spinning machines.

The spinners, also equipped with knotters and gauges, placed the bobbin of rayon filament on a sort of axle, guided the filament end through a series of guides and eyes, and connected it to a lighter-weight bobbin. A flyer, a wire device which whirled so fast it was invisible, put a twist of approximately thirty turns per inch in the filament, thereby strengthening it and transforming it into crepe yarn. The spinners did more knotting than the winders and had a desperate race to "keep the ends up" (i.e., to keep all the bobbins filling), since the filaments broke frequently. Skilled spinners were expected to operate two or three machine sides, depending on the type of work they were running. The bobbin men (no boy could stand such work) were required to keep a supply of the correct type of empty bobbins impaled on spiked boards at the bottoms of the machines; the spinners gradually replaced the empty bobbins with full ones of spun yarn.

For both winders and spinners, a shortage of filament or bobbins or an overaccumulation of finished work meant "ends down"—lost production— and hence lost incentive pay. Consequently, the women were often obliged to beg, wheedle, rage, or threaten the bobbin men, who got no incentive pay regardless of how much work they did. Some of the women even offered their bodies after hours in exchange for preferential treatment at their machines.

The yarn would not properly hold its twist unless it was baked in a steam chamber at a precise temperature for a period of time determined by the denier and other qualities of a particular lot of yarn. The steamer was an overheated, harassed worker who dashed about hauling skids at breakneck speeds with tons of yarn stacked on them, always looking at his watch or the big clock, trying to remember when he was due at which of the six steam chambers to remove a skid of yarn, and which load of unsteamed yarn he must steam next, and where. A clockwork-driven circular graph at each steam chamber told its history for twenty-four hours: how long and at what temperature each batch had been steamed and for how much time the chamber had been unused. The little circles of graph paper drove the steamer to exhaustion and mercilessly informed on him besides. Unused capacity was a major crime; "overcooking" a batch of yarn meant instant dismissal.

The male employees, other than bobbin men and the steamer, consisted of all the foremen, the warpers who prepared warps for weaving mills, a few machine fixers, and the packing and warehouse workers.

As I walked into the plant ten minutes before the four o'clock shift change, I recoiled at two things: the staggering noise, which made some lip reading and sign language a necessity, and the stifling heat with near-saturation-point humidity, considered ideal for the yarn. The physical shock of the noise was something one simply had to adjust to. The soggy heat would, in a half hour, have even the *seams* of my overalls soaked with perspiration; it could be coped with by taking half a dozen salt pills during the eight-hour shift, guzzling five Pepsi-Colas, and never passing by the water fountain without taking a substantial drink.

After strolling down the long aisle observing the winding machines, I started up the next aisle in the middle of the spinning frames, where I encountered my buddy and fellow bobbin man, Grover. Our practiced eyes told us that our dayside counterparts had given us a raw deal: the winding machines were loaded with trays of full bobbins, the bins were short of skeins, the spinners were running out of empty bobbins, and the boards at the bottoms of their machines were nearly all filled. It meant a tremendous surge of work for us at the start with no time to do the innumerable things which would have enabled us to organize and plan our work in advance, and to get the job "caught up" by seven-thirty, as was our custom.

Grover motioned me out of the plant onto the open ramp, to the warehouse where we could talk. His news was that our colleague, the steamer, had ruined three thousands dollars' worth of yarn by accidentally cooking it twice and had been fired at midnight the previous Friday. Grover knew about it because he had been waiting in his old Model A Ford to take his spinner girlfriend home and had heard the whole story from Ed, the ex-steamer.

Grover was twenty-three with a fifth-grade education; his current job was his first one off the farm. He had already been at Hillcrest three months when I had been hired, had generously shown me all he knew about the job, and had helped me out when my machines got swamped. Although Grover's muscles were rock-hard, he was not powerfully built; he tired easily and always seemed to be in poor health. His hair was sparse, his face angular and drawn, his teeth bad; he gave the impression of having looked old from infancy. He and I hit it off well and made our separate jobs a joint project, each constantly looking out for the other. We became so proficient at the backbreaking, high-pressure work that we systematically absented ourselves so that Jim, the shift foreman, would not think us too competent and find additional work for us.

We were popular with both winders and spinners because we always anticipated their needs and never caused them to have any costly "down time."

The shift-change siren wailed loudly (it was perhaps the only sound, short of a cannon shot, that could have been heard over the din of the machines), and the day workers streamed from the machines and up the aisles, screaming greetings and bits of gossip as they passed acquaintances on the night shift. The dayside bobbin men slunk guiltily past Grover and me with barely a greeting.

Faced with an appalling mess, we set out to overcome it. Grover got a long flatbed push truck; then the two of us began to fill the spiked boards with empty bobbins with such speed that our hands looked like mere blurs. When we had loaded a small mountain of the boards at one end of the truck, we started down the aisle between the two rows of spinning frames. I would grab a filled board of yarn from the bottom of a machine, replacing it with a board of empty bobbins on my next trip in. Grover was doing the same thing on the other side of the aisle.

When we were three-quarters finished with the spinning machines, I left the rest to Grover and dashed off to get a hydraulic truck and a skid so that I could unload the swamped winding machines and distribute the unspun filament to the spinning machines. This part of the job was a backbreaker because the filled trays from the winders weighed forty to fifty pounds, and as the four stacks on my skid grew, I had to reach them up as high as nine feet. Other fellows had ruptured themselves on those trays, but Grover had warned me of the danger on my first day and had shown me the proper lifting technique. When my skid was loaded, I went through the spinning machines again, putting the trays of filament bobbins on top of the machines and removing the empty ones; then I hauled the trays of empties over to the winding machines, where the winders were desperately in need of them to wind the skeins on. After an hour and a half of that rat race, Grover and I had only relieved the emergency; the basic work of our shift had barely started. We noticed Jim, our foreman, red-faced and sweating, trying to teach the steamer job to a hopelessly incompetent warehouseman, who seemed quite satisfied to let the foreman demonstrate how the job should be done while he remained a spectator. Grover laughed in my ear, "First time I seen *him* work since I been here. Serves him right for firing Ed."

I laughed and went off with a push truck to the spinning section, where Marie was running a side of short pieces—hundreds of nearly empty bobbins from the warps which were being rewound to prevent waste. Their running time was very short, and empty bobbins were accumulating by the hundreds. I took away the empties and distributed more pieces. Most spinners would have needed four hands and two knotters to keep even half the ends up on such material, but Marie was unperturbed. She was the pacesetter for the spinners, and the company reputedly paid her 20 percent additional, plus the regular incentives. She produced at least twice as much as any of her co-workers, making them all feel inadequate and clumsy. Although she was the foreman's pet, she had not one friend among the spinners, and Grover wouldn't even talk to her and avoided her whenever possible. Consequently, I usually took care of her six machine sides and, as I worked, would listen to her shouted condemnation of every other spinner. She was about twenty-seven, short, fat, with frizzy blond hair framing her frowning face and suspicious eyes. There was no lunch break at Hillcrest: the worker was expected to make his or her own lunch period by working extra hard and getting ahead of the work. Most workers, therefore, were content to gulp a sandwich in eight or ten minutes, but Marie would pull down a spring seat on the end of one of her machines, and eat two sandwiches and a piece of cake in exactly three minutes. No one could recall ever having seen her go to the ladies' room during a shift.

(A month later, just before Christmas, I noticed a more frightened look than usual in her eyes before the shift began, and she refused to talk even to me, the only person in the plant, aside from bosses, who would speak to her. Midway in the shift she sat down on the little spring seat, but instead of eating, she began screaming. The same high-pitched scream, repeated like a broken record, penetrated the plant until some of the women led her to the office. Later an ambulance took her away, and Hillcrest never saw her again. A neighbor reported that her husband had placed her in a state mental institution.)

Grover and I continued to work furiously to get caught up, without letting our haste show too much, because by then both of us were so adept at our jobs that it would have appeared deficient in style, and even undignified, to show signs of being harried or desperate. But on that occasion—the second time in a month—Grover began to get gray in the face and couldn't catch his breath, and there *was* a look of desperation on his face. I told him to go to the warehouse and rest while I redoubled my own efforts; Grover went reluctantly, but of necessity. By eight o'clock the job was caught up and I fetched Grover from the warehouse. Things were in good enough shape so that we could take a half hour off and go across the dirt road in front of the plant to the ramshackle "café," which sold pop, a few canned goods, and some packaged cake and sandwiches. There were tables and chairs, however, and Grover and I ate our lunches there nightly, spending a nickel apiece for a soda. On this night Grover couldn't eat his sandwiches; he was still short of breath and retained his ashen color. I compared our heartbeats and didn't like the choked, irregular one in my partner's chest. I made him promise to go to a doctor the next day and then found the address in the phone book of a well-regarded heart specialist. When we reentered the factory, the noise hit us like the shock-wave from an explosion.

Most of the winders and spinners were pleasant, and they welcomed us smilingly. Some were pretty and flirted charmingly, but Grover was not interested. About a month after I had started working at Hillcrest, a new spinner had appeared, just learning the job. Her name was Margaret; she was eighteen and very shy, lived on a farm about ten miles away, and had the face of a Raphael madonna, the body of a movie star, and the disposition of an angel. Grover's first sight of her, knotting up an end, with her bare arms upraised, standing gracefully on tiptoe, left him stunned by her beauty and resolutely in love with her. He proved so earnest and persistent that Margaret had soon gently rebuffed numerous other suitors in favor of him— "even if he is about as handsome as an old flop-eared hound dog," she said lovingly to me.

Before we had gone a quarter of the way through the spinning machines, Grover began running out of strength and panting heavily. I insisted that he go back to the warehouse and stay there till the shift ended. He refused. I pointed out that the foreman was too busy doing the steamer job to notice his absence. "I'm not gonna leave it all on you," Grover said doggedly. "You'd do it for me, wouldn't you?" I demanded. Before Grover could reply, I said, "Now *git* or I'll tell Margaret," giving him a friendly kick in the behind. Grover went. But I told Margaret anyway, since she knew something was wrong when Grover failed to show up at her machines.

(The next day she made Grover go to the recommended physician and accompanied him herself out of concern, and to lend him courage, since he had never in his life been in a doctor's office. The doctor told them that he had a serious heart condition which would be fatal unless he followed instructions, and said that he must quit his job at once and find a sedentary one. Shattered, clutching a sheaf of prescriptions, Grover first thought once he was alone with Margaret that he must break off their engagement: "I could drop dead tomorrow, and I ain't no more good for *nothin'*!" Gentle, retiring Margaret was not about to lose the man she loved on any such self-pitying pretext, and said so. If God took him, there was nothing she could do about it, she said, but nothing else was going to take him away from her. The following Saturday afternoon, Grover, in his old Model A, with Margaret and one of her sisters, picked me up at the Gillen home, and with festive gaiety we drove to a justice of the peace. Margaret's sister was the bridesmaid and I was the best man as the couple began their clouded future together.)

For the remainder of the shift, I worked like a powerful machine, with precision and no wasted motion. I was strong and self-confident, and as I worked, I felt elation. In my euphoria I realized that I was doing a superhuman job for my buddy. How glorious factory work would be, I thought, if you were working and creating for your buddies, male and female, and yourself. How marvelous if there were no cold-eyed sharks like Jim, or the dead-fish plant superintendent, or the self-important, visiting executives, personifying big corporations, who spoiled and took away all that you could achieve. That was what socialism was really all about! That was what the Communist Party was all about: work could be a joy, not a cruel necessity that sapped your strength, your time for living, your dignity and sense of worth. My heart sang within me as I dreamed that the future was going to *be* splendid and that the Party was going to lead the way as the Bolsheviks had in Russia.

I even mused rhapsodically that the kind of joy in work that I conceived of must actually have been enjoyed for two decades by my fellow workers in the Soviet Union.

I was still ecstatic when I noticed that it was almost a quarter to twelve. I rushed up to the warehouse, where I found Grover lying on a crate and brought him back, pale and a little trembly, but better. Jim walked through the machines with the third-shift foreman and came over to where Grover and I were standing, waiting for the siren. "You fellas did a fine job, especially considering what a mess the day side left you. I never saw the machines in better shape. Oh, by the way, Junius, tomorrow I want to teach you the steamer job."

The pressure of mill and political work during that half year left me small time for reflection and evaluation. Further, I was removed from my scattered friends of Chapel Hill days (Richard was on the other side of the continent, in California). Politics absorbed my attention and Bart's. Because of the raging war, our talks encompassed a good deal more than Party work in High Point. France was in the hands of the Nazis; Britain was being blitzed; the Soviet Union and Nazi Germany were in uneasy alliance; and the American Communist Party was vehemently opposing U.S. involvement in the "imperialist war." The little Party in North Carolina was trying to address itself to that stage of history.

Bart, in order to encourage one of his leading young cadres and to direct his thoughts into constructive paths, reminisced over my activities following the Party school the previous summer.

I had attended the Southern Summer School for Workers in Asheville, North Carolina, for three weeks. That school was a private institution (rather like the more famous Highlander Folk School in Tennessee), financed by both private funding and trade union support, which was designed to advance promising trade unionists from all over the South. I had found it invaluable in regaining some sense of reality after the Party school.

I had helped Bart with several issues of a mimeographed Party publication, issued about every six weeks in the name of the State Committee of the Communist Party of North Carolina. My contribution had been minor, serving as a sounding board, occasional copy editor, and mimeograph operator. Belle, who had become adept at stencil cutting, was by far the abler critic, always trying to keep the articles simple and down-to-earth.

I engaged in frequent polemics with the *High Point Enterprise* and other newspapers, attacking their warmongering editorial policies. Accepting the Party line without question, I felt apprehensive that the impending war would be horribly destructive of all things human and no more likely than World War I to make the world safe for democracy. But I was at a loss to suggest what might be done, short of war, to stop the forcible spread of Nazism. Instead of offering solutions, I usually lapsed into leftist rhetoric, coupled with an optimism I did not feel about "defeating the warmongers."

As state chairman of the League of Young Southerners (the youth division of the Southern Conference for Human Welfare), I had been instrumental in organizing, early in January, a peace meeting which involved a number of Local 319's leaders and activists. The meeting was held (not without some harassment by county authorities) on a Sunday afternoon in the main courtroom of the county building, and was addressed by my university friend Professor E. E. Ericson, who spoke in an effective populist style to more than two hundred people, denouncing the steps already taken toward a new war and questioning the motivations and objectives of those promoting it.

I had achieved some status in Local 319. I had been elected, along with Rob Parker, Willie Held, and a younger worker, to represent the local at a textile union–organizing conference in Atlanta. Willie and I both spoke out, one after the other, against the TWUA's president, Emil Rieve, who had maintained in his opening address that nothing could be done about the stretch-out (increase in the workload) until the greater part of the textile industry in the South had been organized. We pointed out that the stretch-out was the issue which most concerned the textile workers, organized or not. Organized mills like Highland, we said, were paying less for the amount of work done than they had before the CIO had organized them. The average wage at Highland was fourteen dollars per week, but the working pace had become so fierce that some workers could scarcely walk or talk at the end of a shift. Willie and I demanded an organizing drive directed at the mills near the established locals, using "Stop the stretch-out" and "Higher pay" as the main slogans. Willie said that President Rieve understood the problems of the mill owners better than those of the mill hands and that few, if any, of the top officers or organizers of the TWUA had ever worked in a mill or had any idea what the stretch-out was like. We added for good measure, dutifully (and disastrously) following the national Party line, that the TWUA should oppose involvement in the "imperialist war."

To our surprise, we received impassioned support on the stretch-out issue from delegates of locals in South Carolina and Alabama, and there was considerable excitement for a while. But Willie and I were attacked by such smooth labor bureaucrats as Rieve himself, George Baldanzi (the executive vice-president), William Pollock (the secretary-treasurer), and other staff members. Those old pros shifted the discussion to the "imperialist war" point and on that issue ultimately Red-baited the inexperienced rebels into isolation and silence. All the same, the rebels' standing was certainly not hurt in Local 319 when the delegates reported on what I referred to as the "un-organizing conference" at the next union meeting.

Looking back over those months, I saw a pitifully small achievement for one who wished to help lead a proletarian revolution; but Bart took a more positive view and praised my work, saying that one had to master walking before running.

Bart was concerned with my most important undertaking to date: the principal organizing role in a renewed effort to get local union workers into city and county politics. Willie and I, with some others (and with some covert guidance from Bart), had got the local's support for a campaign to elect two working people to the city council, one the secretary of the local, the other a furniture worker with a long pro-union history in his unorganized industry. With the primary election only a few days away, Bart was disturbed over the way things had been going. I myself felt that I had been outmaneuvered from the beginning by the local Democratic Party machine.

Shortly after the labor candidates filed in the Third and Fourth Wards, forcing a citywide primary, the board of elections ordered—with an absolute minimum of publicity—a new registration, thereby assuring that those who had voted in the previous election would be disfranchised unless they discovered that they must reregister. My plan to organize a campaign around the issue of worker representation in the city council was partly diverted into an effort to get people to reregister. The Democratic machine was so well entrenched that it had workers in even the Highland village beholden to it, and it used them to spread pessimism about the labor candidates' chances and to disrupt their activities. The candidates had not yet even printed campaign cards and were getting discouraged. There was every reason to believe that the campaign was not going well.

The Party nationally was attacking Roosevelt and the Democratic Party and was casting about for some way to stimulate the launching of a farmer-labor party in opposition. The national office therefore was encouraging the districts to support all manner of independent political movements and was awaiting

the High Point primary results with some interest. Bart said that he was beginning to agree with Willie's initial reaction that it had been a mistake to try to
organize a local labor party with only worker candidates, instead of trying to
enlist the participation of other sections of the population unhappy with machine rule.

Following this discussion, Bart made some practical suggestions, and I
went home determined to mount a fury of activity designed to assure at least a
respectable showing in the coming primary, even though Willie confided to
me that he didn't think the labor candidates would get a hundred votes. But
from then until the election Willie worked as though he himself were a candidate and expected to win. For two dollars we had two professional campaign
signs painted for the top of Willie's old car. Then we borrowed a portable
public address system with a turntable; chose a number of Woody Guthrie and
Pete Seeger records from my collection; and drove through working-class
neighborhoods urging people to register and vote while repeatedly stating the
location of the appropriate precinct and the hours for registration. We were
well received, and the records were immensely popular. The candidates became increasingly active, passing out newly printed cards at plant gates and in
front of grocery stores. The local having appropriated a small sum for radio
announcements, I also wrote and placed on the air brief spot ads which
aroused enthusiasm and comment, at least in the village.

Willie and I were more optimistic until we learned to our despair, on the
final day of registration, that scores of workers had attempted to register, only
to find precincts closed when they should have been open and election officials
unavailable. It appeared, in fact, that to be registered one needed to be personally acquainted with the registrar. Willie and I rounded up Buck Anderson,
president of the local; Virgie Lance, the vigorous and eloquent union leader
who was the only woman on its executive committee; Rob Parker, chairman
of the executive committee; and one of the candidates. They made angry
protests to the election board members, who replied smugly, without questioning the charges, that the matter would be corrected at once. That afternoon
a handful of people were registered—far too few, too late. Three days later,
when the primary was held, seven or eight car owners who had promised to
carry neighbors to the polls told me that 40 to 50 percent of those they took to
the polls were not properly registered and could not vote. Meanwhile, the
ward heelers hauled their privately registered, "dependable" voters to the
polls, being paid by the head for each one they delivered.

On the night of the election I took off from work, pleading sickness, and
dispatched a responsible crew of union people to each of the fifteen precincts
as certified watchers to keep the count honest. I went alone to the Fourth
Precinct in the county building, where I expected the worst results. But even I

was aghast when the precinct workers meticulously counted out seventy-one votes for the "regular" candidates and four for labor. When the poll watchers assembled in the village and added up their totals, the machine candidates had about 1,100 votes, the worker candidates, 150. The *High Point Enterprise,* which had consistently denied the existence of a machine, commented coyly that in view of the results, it was hard for Mr. Scales to maintain that a machine had defeated the labor candidates.

The national Party office was continually pushing Bart to "take appropriate action" on the numerous issues and campaigns to which it gave priority. The demands were frequently ludicrous, given the small Party membership and the limited possibilities for left-wing political activity in a conservative southern state with a small labor movement and no large cities. The pressure, however, could be intense, and the response was often a brave but much-inflated gesture. The formation meeting of the North Carolina Peace Committee as the state arm of the American Peace Mobilization, a Party-inspired and Party-controlled organization, was a case in point.

There was much playacting as close Party friends behaved like strangers to impress the "broad" non-Party people present, chiefly pacifists, church mavericks, and independent radicals, attracted there by a genuine concern for peace. I was elected chairman. I was already state chairman of the League of Young Southerners, the American Student Union, and the defunct Workers Alliance; Bart had wryly suggested that we form a State Chairmen's Association and elect me chairman of that as well. Nearly 50 percent of the other leading positions were filled by Party members; of the remainder, one was held by an extremely old man; another was held by a Negro minister whose ambivalent behavior aroused concern (much later he was discovered to have been an FBI informer). In addition to a general peace resolution, the meeting voted against the use of convoys to accompany lend-lease shipments to Britain and endorsed a congressional bill to repeal the poll tax. Because of good public relations work, there was a fair amount of newspaper publicity. Enough money was raised to mail American Peace Mobilization literature to a large list of North Carolinians—and that was about the extent of the organization's activities. The Party had appealed to itself, its friends, and stray individuals attracted by the specific issue, thereby producing another state peace committee for the national office's statistics. The charade was a good show and at least gave newer Party members a sense of influence and achievement. But to Professor Ericson, a friendly but astute critic, activity of this sort brought to mind a self-sucking cow.

In contrast to such dutiful self-agitation, the Party maintained an ongoing concern with the building of low-cost housing by the Federal Housing Authority (FHA). The original initiative had been taken by the Party, and for years it had remained a regular point on the agenda of the Party club's Sunday night meetings. Party members, avoiding leftist rhetoric, had convinced Local 319 and even the local trades council of the AFL of the project's desirability and lobbied for it constantly, always gaining new support, until at last the bureaucratic wheels moved and construction was set to begin. Local realtors who had opposed the FHA all along, fearing competition with their profitable slum housing and knowing that superior government buildings would force down slum rents, apparently got to the architects of the project and made certain that the new units would be substandard slums when completed. The plans called for every possible indignity to the tenants, including such items as coal bins in the living rooms.

A watchful comrade managed to get an advance look at the plans, and the Party was able to publicize this scandalous scheme in the local press. It then set up an ad hoc committee which petitioned the FHA to change the plans. A campaign for signatures on the petition proved an overwhelming success: more than eight thousand signatures were collected altogether, and the obnoxious plans were scrapped. Finally the project was built, setting greatly improved low-cost standards for High Point and providing scores of working-class families with the first decent homes they had ever known.

I changed roles often that spring. Within a week of the peace meeting, Bart sent me to Birmingham to a Party conference on youth work in the South. To get time off, I arranged a complicated swap with the day-shift and third-shift steamers and worked two straight days of double shifts—from 4:00 P.M. Wednesday to 8:00 A.M. Thursday and from 4:00 P.M. Thursday to 8:00 A.M. Friday. Bart met me Friday morning in front of Hillcrest and drove me, while I changed clothes in the back seat, to the railroad station, where I ran to catch the fast train to Birmingham. I was exhausted and had planned to sleep during the entire journey, but once aboard the train, I found myself sitting next to a pretty student I had known at Women's College in Greensboro. She was in a talkative mood, and I slept not a wink.

At the Birmingham station that afternoon I was met by Steve, who had become executive secretary of the League of Young Southerners and had been living in Alabama for several months. I had scarcely seen him since the Party school. He had worked in a cotton mill in Roanoke Rapids, North Carolina, for a few weeks, been fired for union activity, and been hired temporarily as a local business agent by the TWUA. Shortly afterward he had gone, with Party approval, to Alabama, where his task was to build a mostly white counterpart to the Marxist-oriented Southern Negro Youth Congress (SNYC). The SNYC, with a genuine mass base among Negro students and workers, had in its ranks some of the most dedicated and talented young Negroes in the South. It had been begun in Virginia in 1937 when five thousand Negro tobacco stemmers were organized and contracts were won for them in a number of plants. Subsequently it organized community drama and recreational groups throughout the Deep South and developed a brilliant and articulate group of leaders: Edward and Augusta Strong, James E. Jackson, Jr., Esther Cooper (later Jackson), Louis and Dorothy Burnham, Thelma Dale, and Raymond Tillman, to name only a few. They, in turn, nurtured a corps of proud, enlightened, capable young Negro militants whose influence would be felt for decades to come in the struggle for equal rights in the South.

Steve was exuberant about his job and his new friends. After giving me a quick tour of the central city, he drove me in a borrowed car to the home of some white friends, where I was to sleep during my stay. Later in the afternoon my host, Joseph Gelders, a Marxist intellectual of impressive aspect, escorted me on foot through a Negro section of the city en route to the business district. A comrade was to meet us there and take me to the Party conference. Gelders explained the extraordinary nature of "law" in Birmingham under Eugene ("Bull") Connor, the city police commissioner who was to become nationally infamous during the civil rights conflicts of the sixties. As we walked we saw in front of us an excited crowd of over three hundred Negroes milling about in front of a jim-crow movie theater. In the center of the crowd was a police patrol car. Gelders and I hurried up to it to find a young Negro man sprawled half into the back seat while a white policeman mercilessly pistol-whipped him. Gelders shouted, "What's going on here?" while I bellowed, "*Stop* it! You're killing him!" The startled officer interrupted the beating and, holding his bloody, unconscious victim by the collar, tried to justify his behavior to the two whites who sounded so authoritative.

Gelders, resembling a white-haired avenging angel, called to me, "Get witnesses. Names, addresses, phone numbers!" I stepped into the crowd and was mobbed by Negroes offering the desired information. Meanwhile a second patrol car containing two policemen pulled up across the street; it was followed by a third and a fourth. The first policeman, feeling braver, still with his pistol in his hand, dropped his prey and arrested Gelders for "failure to assist an officer" and yelled to his reinforcements to "get the other one!" The crowd surged angrily around the policeman holding Gelders while the other police tried to push their way to where I was standing with my pen and notebook writing down witnesses' names and addresses. The crowd immediately tightened up and became an impenetrable wall, and I was propelled like a leaf in a stream to the opposite edge of the throng, now swelled to at least five hundred.

People from the SNYC and the League of Young Southerners who had been circulating anti–poll tax petitions in the area arrived on the scene and hustled me and my fistful of addresses out of sight as the first patrol car roared off, siren howling, with Gelders handcuffed on the seat and the bleeding young Negro still unconscious on the floor. Steve arrived with a young civil liberties lawyer from Tennessee, Laurent Frantz, who coolly got the facts from me and hurried off to the police station. Steve took me a few blocks to a bare loft which served as the league office and began making phone calls to spread the news. In minutes young people, black and white, began swarming into the loft. Steve began composing a leaflet which was read and revised by others looking over his shoulder. Just before the stencil was cut someone came in with the identity of the victim and a statement from his family: the young man was an epileptic; he had had a violent seizure while watching a movie; the theater manager had panicked and called the police; the police had ministered to him after their fashion. Laurent Frantz called from the police station to say that Gelders was to be tried in a week; bail was set at three hundred dollars, and that sum had to be raised. The new information was quickly incorporated in the leaflet. Within two hours of the event the leaflet was being circulated in the Negro community, and Steve and I were attending the Party conference in a meeting room in a fraternal hall, rented for the occasion under a phony name.

Rob Hall, the southern Party director and Alabama district organizer, presided; Henry Winston, the Party's outstanding young Negro leader, represented the national office; and each district was represented by someone responsible for youth work as well as, in several cases, the district organizer. The leadership of the SNYC and other youth organizations was also represented. The meeting, a difficult and costly one to organize, was held under secretive conditions because of the ever-present fear of FBI or police surveillance.

Rob opened the proceedings with a minimum of formality, and I, having worked four shifts in two days and thus having gone nearly thirty hours without sleeping, and then having suffered the strains of the previous few hours, promptly fell asleep. The next thing I knew Steve was nudging me, and before I had quite regained consciousness Rob asked me to report on youth work in North Carolina. My mind went blank and I forgot everything I wanted to say, but Rob tactfully asked me how long (prior to the meeting, he emphasized) I had been without sleep. He then gently questioned me until I had said everything I had meant to say.

1 was much embarrassed by my clumsy account, especially when I had heard the fluent reports from Texas, Louisiana, Alabama, Virginia, and Florida. The Florida youth leader was exceptionally impressive, and his district organizer basked in reflected glory. Rob, however, seemed unimpressed by glibness and, after asking probing questions, soon determined that a youthful

revolution was not imminent in Florida. (Two months later that voluble youth leader absconded with a sizable portion of the Florida Party's treasury, took an attractive, redheaded young lady to Havana for a wild weekend, and was never seen again.)

The sessions continued through Saturday morning and afternoon and Sunday morning. The rest of the time I spent with Steve, Laurent, and Marge Gelders, my host's elder daughter. When that eventful weekend concluded I had gained two lifelong friends, who were married within a month. They and Steve put Henry Winston and me on the northbound train at 3:00 A.M., and I arrived back in High Point in plenty of time to get to work.

My shifts at Hillcrest were lonely without Grover, and the steamer job was a solitary struggle. Our two successors as bobbin men had soon become two and a half: one of the warehousemen had to help them for four hours every night. They worked at cross-purposes and earned the hatred of every winder and spinner. Every night, at the wail of the siren, I would meet Margaret and escort her to Grover's old jalopy, which she had learned to drive. On two nights each week Grover himself, off from his night watchman's job, would be waiting in the car for her, his face more sad and drawn, his strength failing.

There was one advantage to my brutal job as steamer: my shift foreman felt obligated, because of my hard work and efficiency, to let me swap shifts with the steamers on the other shifts. The other steamers usually had no objection; but if they did, I would pay them two dollars a shift—a small price, I thought, for a weekend extending from Friday morning to Monday afternoon.

Besides, nearly every weekend I was off to Chapel Hill; I had fallen in love with a young woman who lived there. She had graduated from Chapel Hill High School and was completing her freshman year at the university. She was eighteen, dark-haired, pretty, sweet, and gentle; she agreed with me politically; she was Jewish; she loved me as much as I loved her; and her name was Sylvia.

During our courtship I took Sylvia to visit Bart and Belle and to the union square dance, where she met my other friends. I was much taken by her family: her older sister, Anna, also a student at Chapel Hill, and her parents, who had had a tough time financially throughout their married life. Her father, a man of great vigor, was self-employed as a salesman of wholesale hosiery to merchants throughout the state and was subject to all the indignities reserved at that time for the non-rich Jew. The family was extraordinarily hospitable, and the daughters' friends were always welcome.

After a few weeks Sylvia and I decided to get married (to the temporary distress of her parents, who would have preferred a Jewish son-in-law). We set a wedding date in late June. Two days before the impending date I became so distraught at the immensity of the step I was taking that I lost track of time on my job and committed the unpardonable crime: I overcooked a whole skid of yarn. The superintendent himself summoned me, almost tearfully. The great man muttered about "inflexible rules" and having "to do things you don't like to" and then told me I was "fired—with regret." I was distressed and quickly told Bart of my disaster, feeling ashamed that I was not at least fired for union activity. Bart chuckled, saying that the job was enough to kill anyone and that he was going to propose that I quit anyway; he prescribed an immediate trip to Chapel Hill.

I hitchhiked the distance in record time and went to Sylvia's house, where she and a tense group of friends met me with the news that the Nazis had invaded the Soviet Union. We listened to the kitchen radio for hours till at last, to our relief, Churchill declared Britain's unequivocal support of the Soviet Union. Until then we had feared that the West would leave the Soviet Union to its fate. Any thought of peace vanished, and we all felt that the long-delayed confrontation with Fascism was at hand. (I was furious when I learned later that some student comrades had spent hours distributing peace literature on campus two days after the invasion had begun.)

On June 23 Sylvia and I, with Monte, Anna, and two young faculty friends, drove to South Carolina, where marriages could be performed without a waiting period. A justice of the peace conducted the ceremony, and that night I brought my bride back to her parents' house.

Bart phoned the next day and asked how I would like a sort of working honeymoon in New York. Since I had some savings, I said we would love it. Bart told me he would explain things when he picked us up in his jalopy that afternoon. He had been summoned to an urgent national Party conference to try to make some sense out of the confusion which had afflicted Party policy and activity for the past three days. We three arrived in New York following a fourteen-hour drive, and I, after checking into a cheap midtown hotel, called my former teacher, David McKelvy White, to tell him of my marriage. Dave insisted that we come at once to his Manhattan apartment so that he could meet the bride. After an hour's visit, Dave suddenly picked up a packed suitcase and walked out the door, calling over his shoulder, "This is your apartment as long as you're in town; there are the keys; the bed's made; the kitchen's stocked. Shut up and don't argue. I'll see you at the conference, Whitey." He closed the door and when we opened it, he had disappeared in the elevator.

The conference was presided over by Robert Minor, the acting general secretary while Browder was in prison for violation of a passport regulation. The new Party line was that the entire character of the war had changed, that with the entry of the Soviet Union it had become an anti-Fascist war, and that *everything* should be done to defeat Fascism. The Party's leaders were suffering a kind of psychological shock: for months the war had been denounced as imperialist; the most popular slogan had been "The Yanks are *not* coming!" Gil Green, the over-aged leader of the Young Communist League, shrewdly explored the need for readjustment, pointing out, in effect, that the Communists had become warmongers.

For me, meeting face to face with Party leaders who had been legendary was an exhilarating experience. William Z. Foster, Elizabeth Gurley Flynn, Jack Johnstone (all former trade union leaders), Jack Stachel, James W. Ford, John Gates, Gil Green, and Joseph Clark were among those who particularly impressed me. My old mentor George Siskind greeted me affectionately and sat with me; Henry Winston even took me to lunch in a Spanish restaurant. I felt that I was liked and respected by the leaders of my Party. After the conference my elation was increased when (on Rob Hall's initiative) my bride and I were invited to spend a week at Camp Unity (an upstate New York summer camp owned or controlled by the Party) as guests of the national office. At the end of a wonderful week, Sylvia and I bused back to High Point.

We found an apartment on Briggs Avenue, about a block from the main-line tracks of the Southern Railway and not far from Pickett Cotton Mill, where I got a job on the night shift, taking down yarn in the winding room. The work was hard, but compared with that at Hillcrest it seemed like a vacation.

The apartment, painted a dark, dirty yellow, was unfurnished except for a mattress given us by an acquaintance of mine at Hillcrest. The mattress looked fine, but the first night we used it, as soon as the light was out it came alive with bedbugs. The next morning Sylvia's parents arrived to see the new dwelling and helped me throw the mattress out the window. They generously bought us some basic furniture from the Salvation Army, and apple and orange crates did for the rest. The three small rooms included no bathroom; that was in the hall, shared with other tenants on the floor. Sylvia's resourcefulness and some paint on the walls and floor made the place livable.

I began concentrating my time and efforts on the area's seamless-hosiery workers. They would, I believed, respond favorably to a CIO organizing drive. Workers in the industry, mostly semiskilled, and wholly unorganized, usually received the bare minimum under the wages-and-hours law. Many of the plants were quite small, employing only fifteen or twenty workers. Capital costs being relatively low, small knitting mills sprang up and died with great frequency. Working conditions were usually bad; the employers' greed and fear of unionization caused them to force oppressive conditions on the workers, with whom it was difficult to discuss unionizing. They were afraid not only of losing their jobs but, even worse, of getting blacklisted in the industry, a circumstance which could keep them unemployed.

Through Willie, I had met several dedicated unionists who had known him for many years as a thoughtful radical, a realist, and a unionist of the highest integrity. They were boarders (most skilled of the hosiery trades), veterans in the industry, with a vast knowledge of the local mills, the bosses, the workers, and the stool pigeons and spies. They kept their eyes and ears open and were always searching for workers with guts, brains, and principles. When they had a good prospect, they would tell me all they knew about him or her and I would pay a visit, introduce myself, name an agreed-on mutual acquaintance, show my union card and my Local 319 credentials as a member of the organizing committee, and then discuss the union prospects in the worker's own plant. If the worker were a woman, Sylvia would often accompany me.

I was extremely cautious on my visits to new union prospects and on my keep-in-touch meetings with the old-timers. The FBI had repeatedly snooped around since I had been in High Point, and there was plenty of local employer-financed spy activity. I was careful to avoid exposing any of the workers and tried to disguise the fact that there was a potential organizing drive under way. There was an agreement with the old-timers that I would visit them once a month, going at night to their back doors, and that if anything urgent came up between visits I could be reached through Willie. In three months I had visited nearly a hundred "good prospects" and had the names of those extraordinary people on three-by-five index cards, with detailed information in my own homemade code. I stored my file index in a cardboard box, kept hidden up the chimney of our living room fireplace.

Meanwhile, Sylvia had become an industrial worker. She and Belle had both found jobs in a small factory sewing cloth work gloves. For the newlyweds, life was rapturous—full of love and purpose. We saw friends in the village, visited Bart and Belle, read, listened to music, worked, organized, went to square dances and union meetings, and were very happy—even though the imminence of war hung heavily over our lives.

I was fired from Pickett Cotton Mill for being a union member, just when I was beginning to feel at home and was learning to doff spinning frames. The action apparently resulted from a tip delivered by the bosses of the rival Highland Cotton Mill. I promptly got a job at a medium-sized seamless-hosiery mill on the other side of town, beginning as a lot boy (filling orders from retailers) and getting promoted to a shipping clerk. While at Thomas Hosiery Mill I intensified my organizing work and, since I had firsthand experience, increased my effectiveness. My hours at my new job (8:00 A.M. to 4:30 P.M.) enabled me to visit more often under cover of darkness.

My objective in organizing was to lay the basis of a campaign in the industry which I hoped would be undertaken by the American Federation of Hosiery Workers (AFHW), CIO. It was an old union with most of its membership made up of high-paid full-fashioned hosiery workers in the Northeast—wealthy labor-aristocrats compared with their impoverished southern cousins.

The AFHW had become interested in High Point chiefly because it had a local of full-fashioned workers there. I had bombarded the organizer who serviced that local, as well as the international office of the union, with reasons for conducting an organizing drive, pointing out repeatedly that there were eight thousand seamless-hosiery workers in the vicinity of High Point, that theirs was the lowest-paid industry with the most grievances, and that there had been frequent spontaneous attempts at organization—and one planned one—during the previous ten years.

My prodding apparently had some effect, because the AFHW sent down an experienced Pennsylvania organizer, a man in his late forties, to study the situation. He was an anti-Communist Socialist; when he called on me the night he arrived, he sat down on the sofa next to a copy of the *Daily Worker*. While Sylvia tried frantically to distract his attention, he picked it up and leafed through it. There was no need for any political pretense after that, and we avoided political discussions, tacitly agreeing not to agree.

Two or three nights a week I took him to visit some of my choice militants. At first he balked at my insistence that we park at least two blocks away from a worker's house and in some cases approach it up back alleys to the kitchen door. But when I told him of an organizer of those same workers who had been beaten nearly to death with apparent police collaboration only a few years earlier, when on our first visit he saw our host pull down the shades, turn off most of the lights, turn on the radio, and talk in whispers; and when two local goons followed his little coupe everywhere he went for two consecutive days—then the organizer raised no more objections about "conspiratorial behavior." In fact, he soon became expert at shaking a tail.

After four weeks of visiting and sizing up, we invited the organizer to Sunday dinner. In the midafternoon, over coffee, he said that he had visited a number of contacts given him by his international office and the area's TWUA organizer and had found a few "plain duds," many who were reliving past organizing attempts, and the remainder too scared to take any initiative. The only outstanding contacts were those I had taken him to. If his report favoring a massive organizing drive were to be accepted by his international leadership, and if he were to be placed in charge, would I be available to work full time on the organizing staff? I said I would, without reservation. The organizer asked Sylvia how she would feel about it, since she would be without a husband twelve to sixteen hours a day. She was stoically agreeable. Nothing was said about my being a Communist, so I assumed that the AFHW was willing to make use of me while I was indispensable and would dump me when I no longer was. This had happened often to Communists in CIO unions in the thirties, and it seemed to me a good exchange, if it meant organized hosiery workers in High Point.

As soon as the organizer had gone, Sylvia and I took a bus to Bart and Belle's house to tell our friends the glorious news. Returning home in the early evening, we had barely settled down when there came a knock at our door and Steve stood outside with Violet, his wife of three days. She was about eighteen, diminutive, with natural golden ringlets framing a lovely face. She and Steve rapidly recounted how they had met through the League of Young Southerners in Birmingham, had fallen in love at first sight, and had got married. Steve had quit his league job, and they were going to live in High Point, where Steve would get an industrial job. Meanwhile they needed a place to stay. Sylvia and I rigged them up a bed in our living room.

The next day Steve and Violet were off to see Bart and Belle and then to look for jobs. Sylvia and I went back to our workday routines. That night I visited and sent word to some of my best contacts, telling them of the probable organizing drive and asking them to start lining up the trustworthy men and women in their plants. Meanwhile, in my own plant, I began talking union to some carefully selected workers I had been observing for nearly three months. The response was positive.

The organizer returned in a couple of weeks and said that the drive was on, that he himself was in charge, and that a big send-off meeting was being planned the following month with all the AFHW international officers and hosiery worker delegates from Virginia and Tennessee; it was to take place in the TWUA union hall on a Sunday morning. I was busy for several days delivering the glad news to my hosiery friends around the city, and in my elation I spoke less guardedly in my own plant about the need for a union.

The great day came at last. At nine o'clock the international officers and the state director of the CIO arrived at the union hall. Already on hand were Local 319 president Buck Anderson, Rob Parker, and Willie, who had driven to the hall some of the union women volunteers who had agreed to prepare and serve lunch. Esther, Virgie, and several others were organizing the sandwich making, while covered hampers of fried chicken and huge containers of potato salad, prepared at home, waited promisingly for the lunch break. I was all over the place, full of exuberance: hugging the cooks, sampling the food, getting underfoot, and being thrown out of the improvised kitchen; then greeting the delegates, introducing people, meeting the officers. That was *my* day, the fruition of nearly six months of single-minded effort and the answer to a decade of lean hope for many hosiery workers.

Inspirational addresses were made to and applauded by a busload of organized hosiery workers from Virginia and another busload from eastern Tennessee. The local, unorganized workers did not dare attend, for they would have been spotted by the stool pigeons who sat in parked cars across the street from the union hall entrance, watching everyone who went in. The lunch break came and the cooks covered themselves with glory, while the rest of us stuffed ourselves.

After lunch the organizer got down to the details of the drive, introduced a staff of seven organizers from the North, and presented me as his second-in-command. The organizers would move to town in the following week, and the drive would officially commence in seven days. The meeting adjourned in the early afternoon so that the buses could get the workers back home in time to go to work on Monday morning. The hall rocked with enthusiasm, and I departed down the stairs in a glow of satisfaction a little after three o'clock. I was delighted to find Belle waiting for me in Bart's current jalopy with her sister Anne, Sylvia, and Violet. I told them the good news and, as we drove off, turned on the sputtery car radio to see if I could hear the remainder of the New York Philharmonic broadcast. Just as I tuned in the sound of my favorite orchestra, there was an interruption, and a CBS announcer said that the Japanese had bombed Pearl Harbor.

That night the organizer came by to say that he didn't know what would become of the drive, that it had been temporarily postponed, and that it looked hopeless to him. His president thought that rayon and other yarns would be "frozen" and placed at government disposal, a step that would cause widespread closing of hosiery mills until they could be placed on a war footing. He was greatly depressed. Finally he said, "I suppose you're glad you can have a crack at the Nazis now?"

"War's nothing to be glad about; it's just inevitable and I'd like to get it over with. We'll have to try to defend what's bad against what's worse," I replied gloomily. We shook hands, and he left. Later that night, Sylvia and I discussed with Bart whether I should enlist. Bart was sure that the hosiery drive was an early war casualty and that it would be a good thing if I volunteered. Sylvia objected to no avail.

At work the next day Pearl Harbor was the sole topic of conversation, and some of the younger fellows were already talking of going to Norfolk or Wilmington to look for high-paying jobs in the shipbuilding industry. On the lunch hour I crowded with the others around a tiny radio in the little one-horse café near the plant to hear President Roosevelt speak of the day "that will live in infamy" and announce that the country was at war. Not a word was spoken during the speech, and no one went back to work until it was over, even though the lunch hour had ended. Afterward we were a sober, silent lot of men and women, many of us with a grim sense of the ordeal the coming years of war would be bringing us.

At quitting time I went to the bus station in my work clothes, took a bus to Winston-Salem, and walked to the recruiting office upstairs in the post office.

The line moved rapidly. A sergeant took my name, address, and phone number and told me that I was accepted pending a physical examination and the filling out of forms, and that I was "furloughed" until 9:00 A.M., January 1, at which time I was to report for induction.

The next day I was back at work as usual. By Wednesday the government had indeed frozen all rayon, cotton, and other yarns. By Friday many hosiery mills were announcing their closing, and unemployed workers were heading to coastal cities looking for war work. Friday afternoon, just before quitting time, I was summoned to the office, and there a company official with pinkish, inflamed eyes and large hairy ears informed me, maliciously, that I was fired. (Perhaps I had talked unionism too widely and someone had informed, I thought.) "Why am I fired?" I demanded. I pointed out that I had been promoted and complimented on my work only the week before in front of a half dozen witnesses.

"I don't have to give you any reason!" said the pink-eyed one, "but just *maybe* you're in trouble with the government. That's all I'll say."

So it was the FBI that got me fired, I thought delightedly; no co-worker had ratted on me. I was so pleased that I laughed and said, "I'm not in trouble with the government. I *work* for the government. I joined the army on Monday."

The boss was nonplussed. "Well, in that case, I'll change this form to read, 'resigned to enlist in armed forces.' And I'd like to shake your hand, young man," he said, ablaze with patriotism as he stuck out a pudgy paw. I declined the handshake and said, "Give me my pay!"

My induction was too imminent for me to seek another job, so I decided to spend my remaining time in Hamilton Lakes with my mother. She had been a widow for almost two years, and I had been of precious little comfort to her during most of that time, making only hurried visits and upsetting her with my willful behavior and insistence on my independence. Though she had opposed my marriage, at Thanksgiving she had been polite to Sylvia and had begun to thaw out considerably by the time we left. So I hoped to leave for the army with relations improved all around.

It was a lovely visit. My mother, Archibald and his wife, Carolyn, Mary Leigh, Aunt Lucy, and A.G. were all very considerate of Sylvia. She won my mother over with her guileless charm and was herself caught up in the family's celebration of Christmas.

On the thirtieth we went to Chapel Hill to say goodbye to my in-laws and friends, and on New Year's Eve I was back in High Point saying my farewells to my hosiery contacts, my friends in the village, Willie and his family, and Bart and Belle. Long before daybreak on New Year's Day I breakfasted with

Steve and Violet and then went with sad-faced Sylvia to the bus station. As my bus headed for Winston-Salem, we waved to each other until we faded from view.

That day I passed my physical and was quartered in a local boarding house. The next day, January 2, 1942, I was taken by bus to Charlotte, where I was sworn in and became a private in the U.S. Army.

9

GI

Something still wrong in every system lurks,
Something imperfect haunts all human works.

Philip Freneau, "A Warning to America" (1792)

S oldiering began for me at Fort Jackson, South Carolina, with the customary snafu. For example, I was given the Army General Classification Test
while nearly delirious with fever from my smallpox vaccination and typhoid
shot; for several months I went from outfit to outfit classified as a medium-
grade moron. That was a fitting overture to the four-year saga of my thwarted
attempts to become an effective military anti-Nazi.

A troop train chugged me to Sheppard Field in Wichita Falls, Texas, where
I received intensive Air Corps basic training, the first of all too many basic
training courses. My one-month stay was made memorable by a one-hour visit
outside the field's gates with Richard Nickson, who had driven several hundred miles from New Mexico. Then one morning at 0300 hours, to the shrill-
ing of whistles, my fellow recruits and I were ordered out of the barracks, into
the glare of floodlights, to stand in formation while hundreds of names (mine
among them) were read out for shipment that day. A sleepy straggler, stumbling from a barracks halfway through the reading, was transfixed by a stare
from the first sergeant, who said over the public address system in a caressing
tone, "Soldier! You better give yo' heart an soul to Jesus, cause *ah'm* gonna
have yo' ass!"

Twenty-four hours later, as my troop train headed northeast through Tex-
arkana, the train wrecked: cars leaped the track, rails coiled and twisted as if
they were snakes, ties were tossed in the air like twigs, and glass shattered and
flew about the car, as did a few soldiers from upper berths. When the car came
to rest in total darkness, at a forty-five degree angle, a panicky silence ensued,
suddenly and comically broken by that most familiar of army announcements

Private Scales, 1942

to recruits, "All right, you guys, short-arm inspection! Skin it back and pull it forward!" An officer rushing through the train to inspect the damage found the car roaring with laughter and supposed his men to be hysterical from fright. The cause of the wreck was sabotage; I myself saw a log jammed into a half-open switch. We were told not to talk about it. In a few hours another train came and took us, roundabout, to Dow Field at Bangor, Maine, where the midafternoon temperature was ten below zero, and I still coughed up red Texas dust.

It soon became obvious that the FBI and/or army intelligence had caught up with me. On arrival I had been placed in a clerical job which called for a sergeant's rating and told I would get my stripes in a month. After a week, when I was already doing the job without supervision, I was summoned to the orderly room and informed by my commanding officer, a sinister first lieutenant, that I was removed from my job and assigned to the orderly room, with no specified duties. And the CO refused to say why I was removed.

For ten days, when I was not on KP, I was the Cinderella of the orderly room, shunned by the enlisted men and harassed by the CO. Then one afternoon a long, black, shiny, chauffeur-driven limousine, bearing a Maine license plate with the number 3, drew up outside. A footman opened the door and an impressive gentleman, impressively dressed, got out and walked into the orderly room. The CO, who had been watching openmouthed, jumped to his feet and all but groveled before the visitor. "I'm Arthur Hauck, president of the University of Maine. I want to see Private Junius Irving Scales. The general told me I would find him here."

"Why, y-y-yessir! He's right *here!*"

I came forward, introduced myself, and shook hands, ignoring the CO. The president suggested we talk in his car and led the way. He told me that he had just received a letter from two of his dearest friends (neighbors and friends of mine in Hamilton Lakes) saying that a young man they valued most highly was stationed in Bangor. Could I come to dinner the following day? I said I would be delighted. Hauck came back into the orderly room with me. "Lieutenant, I have invited Private Scales to dinner tomorrow. I shall send the car for him at 4:30. There *won't* be a problem, will there?"

"Why, *no* sir, none whatever!" the toady officer replied.

After that fairy-godmother visitation, I was given clerical duties and treated with common courtesy—and a certain amount of awe. Hauck turned out to be a delightful, unpretentious, and sophisticated man who quickly saw where my political sympathies lay. We had a pleasant and animated evening and I was invited back in ten days, when Hauck would be entertaining A. J. Muste, the well-known pacifist. Hauck chuckled in anticipation of the coming political conflict.

But I never made it. A heavy cold I had had since Texas had grown worse and I had gone on sick call. Slipped a couple of aspirins, I was promptly returned to duty, even though burning with fever. The next day, back on sick call, I was presumed to be malingering and was kept waiting for four hours. When my name was called at last, I got to my feet, fainted, vomited, and awoke in a hospital bed, diagnosed as having a "digestive disorder." I persuaded a nurse to send a collect telegram to my mother to say that I was hospitalized and could not call her that night as she had requested. An hour later my mother was on the phone asking the colonel in command of the hospital what was wrong with her son. The colonel, charmed by the gracious southern lady, said that he himself would go find out and call her back.

The colonel found an unconscious patient, with a fever of 106 degrees, expiring from untreated double pneumonia. Being a man of action, he not only administered an enormous dose of one of the newly discovered sulfa drugs, but sent MPs to the officers' club, to which my doctor (a first lieutenant) had hastened after admitting me. The doctor was brought, moderately looped and under arrest, to where the colonel was struggling to save his patient. He was given the choice of a court-martial or an immediate transfer with a letter of censure. The colonel said that his personal preference was for a firing squad. I remained unconscious for three days.

More than three weeks later, my buddy Walt (a veteran of Spain, who also was getting kicked around by army intelligence) quite literally put me on the train, because I was too weak to get aboard myself, and I went South to my mother's home to recuperate. Sylvia got two weeks off from her glove factory so she could stay with me. The days dropped away like falling petals as I slowly regained my strength. But drop they did, and I returned to Maine.

President Hauck entertained me for a splendid weekend in his Bar Harbor cottage, and I began, at last, to feel well again. Walt and I had a private celebration over the news that FDR had pardoned Earl Browder, general secretary of the Communist Party. Then in May, when spring had come, even to Maine, Walt and I were transferred without warning from the Air Corps to the Quartermaster Corps at Fort Ethan Allen near Burlington, Vermont.

The fort was a former cavalry post converted to field artillery; my outfit, quartered in an ancient brick barracks, was the basic service company or permanent party. When Walt and I arrived, a row of old tech sergeants and master sergeants, completing their required thirty years prior to retirement, sat on the long porch sunning themselves. Nearby was a street of brick noncommissioned officers' houses where they were quartered with their families. Across a parade ground was an even more impressive stretch of brick houses for officers. In that backwater the "old" army seemed to have survived the ravages of the new "citizen" army. The antiquated regular-army noncoms could scarcely tolerate the presence, as corporals and buck sergeants, of some physically unfit former National Guardsmen; the presence of draftees was an affliction to be borne, not discussed. The CO, a captain of German descent, had been newly transferred from the Field Artillery, under a bit of a cloud, for having carelessly blown up several of his men with a battery of howitzers.

A survey of newly arrived draftees suggested that some political expert in the New England area had chosen the outfit as a limbo for those soldiers suspected of disloyalty. The vast majority were German nationals drafted before Pearl Harbor; some were Wehrmacht veterans; some carried Nazi Party cards; some had acquired U.S. citizenship and were members of the German-American Bund; nearly all spoke of "President Rosenfeld" and were aggressively anti-Semitic. Also suspected of disloyalty and included in the mixture, with fine impartiality, were a rabbi from Bavaria, and Franz, the Jewish son of a cabinet minister of Prussia within the Weimar Republic. I was assigned to the post library, but I actually spent most of my time doing guard duty—about three times a week.

Sylvia, who had been lonely in High Point, decided to move to New York to be closer to me and to get a job in war industry. She was able to visit me in Burlington several times, and at Christmas, 1942, we were both guests in the home of my kindly old regular-army first sergeant. But nothing could obliterate our shared anguish during those months when the Nazis were having everything their own way. Would Moscow fall? How long could the Soviet Union take the full force of the Nazi assault? When would the United States really get into the war in the West?

Near desperation at times over my enforced inactivity, I had twice volunteered for immediate overseas duty. On the first occasion the request for volunteers was canceled; the second time, a handful who met the physical qualifications for the infantry were accepted—but the alphabetical list ended with someone named Russell. Most frustrating for me, while my friends and other soldiers were dying, was the fact that my war seemed to be primarily with army intelligence (G-2). Yet in other places Japanese-Americans, German refugees, and known Communists were allowed to function responsibly and were placed in combat outfits. There simply was no consistency in G-2 policy from one area to another.

Just after New Year's Day, 1943, G-2 struck again: Walt and I, along with six Nazis, were transferred to Camp Niantic, Connecticut, a small training camp for military police located on Long Island Sound, a few miles from New London. Also loaded with Nazi draftees, its sole merit for me was that it was close to Sylvia and New York. There, after a short MP stint, I was assigned to the dispensary as a medic.

The Medical Detachment, small and friendly, was hovered over by two amiable, aging doctors: a Jewish major and an Irish Catholic lieutenant colonel, both from Boston. The two were close friends and fond of the enlisted men placed under their benevolent protection—circumstances which gave rise to a most pleasant, familial atmosphere. I learned to be a "bedpan commando," to give immunization shots, to stitch wounds in emergencies, and to handle all the paperwork.

Almost every other weekend would find me in New York with Sylvia, who shared a large top-floor apartment on West Twenty-first Street with two other young married women. Their sole neighbors on the floor were Mary and Edwin Rolfe. Ed was a prominent left-wing poet, veteran of the Spanish civil war, and the author of an authoritative history of the Abraham Lincoln Battalion. Frail of health, stalwart of spirit, much beloved by his neighbors, he became a principal joy of the New York weekends. Mary, barely thirty, seemed almost a mother figure to me and to the young wives.

One day when things were quiet in the dispensary, the major and the lieutenant colonel called me into the office they shared and asked me, with fatherly concern, if there were anything I would care to tell them. They had gone to the camp commander to try to get sergeant's stripes for me and had been told, mysteriously, that I could not be promoted. Since I had agreed, in discussion with Bart before enlisting, that I would not reveal my Party membership, I told them only that I had been a Communist sympathizer and union organizer and that G-2 had hounded me for a year and a half. The two doctors, both rather conservative gentlemen, were indignant at G-2 and said that they were going to see what they could do about it through some of their high-ranking connections.

Walt and another friend, Elmer, had had similar experiences with proposed promotions, so the three of us got an audience with the camp commander, cited the treatment we had received in common, and told him that we were being discriminated against in violation of our constitutional and military rights, Elmer because he was a Communist, Walt because he had fought for the Loyalists in Spain, and I because I was a Communist sympathizer. The colonel heard us out and said that he would consult higher headquarters and see what he could do, but that it would probably take some time.

We anticipated few consequences from our protest. We expected the same harassment and discrimination to continue indefinitely. I had been accustomed to FBI prying since I was nineteen. Having my phone calls listened to and having my mail clumsily opened was bad enough in civilian life, but it was intolerable in the army. Mail was vital, and those faceless snoopers in G-2 delayed it for days. I had been told by a friend at Fort Ethan Allen that on an occasion when he had gone into the post intelligence office, the officer had

had my outgoing and incoming mail lying, opened and chronologically arranged, on opposite sides of his desk. Little tricks that Sylvia and I practiced from my Dow Field days on (such as drawing fine lines over the flap of an envelope after it was sealed) showed conclusively that each letter I mailed on the post, using the military franking privilege, had been opened before Sylvia received it. Her letters to me also were invariably opened before I saw them.

Being under observation, being stationed in isolated and inconsequential outposts with Nazis, being denied a chance at combat duty or responsible work elsewhere, being denied promotion—these were all onerous or even embittering conditions which called for vigorous protest. But neither most of my Communist friends nor I permitted such mistreatment to divert us from trying to do an exceptionally good job at whatever we were assigned. As Communists we had a primary commitment to the defeat of Fascism, and nothing was going to stop us from doing our solemn duty. Besides, we had an arrogant, elitist, and exaggerated notion of our superiority and were eager to show it off. Therefore we worked hard and creatively.

I pleased my elderly doctors by reorganizing the paperwork, the storage of supplies, the arrangement of the twenty-bed ward, and the officers' and enlisted men's work schedules for greater efficiency. Meanwhile, those kind old fellows had been busy in my behalf. Technically, I had been in the Quartermaster Corps on loan to the medics; at the end of May my officers triumphantly presented me with special orders transferring me to the Medical Detachment. They said they had been assured that I was no longer on the suspected list and they were going to get me promoted. Then early in June, to our surprise, Elmer, Walt, and I received orders transferring us out—Elmer and Walt to infantry outfits. I wrote to my mother from Mitchel Field on Long Island, "Here I am in the Air Force again after eighteen months, still a buck private—right back where I started from." I remained a week in a replacement center at Mitchel Field before being assigned to the Medical Detachment at a subpost of Mitchel Field, where there was a thirty-five-ward hospital.

Beginning as a morning-report clerk, I was promoted to corporal just before enlisted promotions were frozen in the First Air Force, and gradually over many months I became the de facto topkick of my outfit. My duties, in addition to the usual army administration for eight hundred men, included being personnel director for a huge hospital and demanded of me a sixteen-hour day and a six-day week. My objective was vastly improved morale and efficiency, and there seemed to be significant gains as the months passed.

I had heard much discussion of the new thinking that had been put forward in the Party by Earl Browder, and I was determined to try to get to the Party convention scheduled for May 1944. Taking a three-day pass, I went to New

Private Scales, 1943

York, hunted up Alice Burke, the Virginia Party leader, and with her assistance attended the sessions in uniform. I was much impressed by Browder, though I was a little put off by certain qualities which appeared to me as coldness and intellectual arrogance. Nonetheless, what Browder said made sense. Lessening the rigidity and discipline of the organization, rooting it in American political tradition and history, chopping away at its sectarian, doctrinaire fetishisms, dropping the Moscow-inspired nonsense about a Negro nation in the "black belt" and recognizing that the Negro people then wanted integration, deemphasizing the burden of esoteric Russian doctrine and history put upon the American Communist, stressing participation in American life and politics as they actually were, presenting the perspective of possible peaceful transition to socialism, projecting the possibility of a postwar world in which socialism and capitalism could coexist in peaceful competition—these were the main new directions indicated by Browder's report and summary remarks. In a matter of minutes the Party was dissolved and the Communist Political Association was created. Alice and other southern comrades disagreed with Browder's thinking and proposals, especially his estimate that segregation in the South would be eliminated with relative ease and his plan to transform the southern Party clubs into "people's educational institutes." I agreed with Alice about segregation but not about the Party clubs.

For days I pondered the meaning of the convention. Common sense told me that Browder was on the right track, that he had put the organization on a course which could ultimately make its program acceptable to a great portion of the population. Communists, in the future, could work more easily with liberals and others without so much hostility and such endless polemics.

At the same time, I felt a sense of loss at what I believed was the removal of professional revolutionaries, Bolshevik style, from the American Communist movement. The conception I had derived from the Party school of a selfless Party leader, totally immersed in the Party and dedicated to organizing an imminent revolution, had faded away like mist. The revolution, it seemed, was farther off—perhaps a lifetime or two away—and the practical work of bringing it about would be more prosaic than I had previously believed. Fanaticism in the cause of revolution would be out of place in the future; practical, patient mastery of the art of politics and tireless advocacy and explanation of the advantages of socialism would be needed. I was ready to tackle the new task I saw ahead: moving into the mainstream of American life. My army experience would be most helpful. Yet I knew I would miss the reverse side of political isolation and persecution: the feeling of being one of the elect, of self-denial in behalf of a great cause, of self-sacrifice for the good of mankind, the heady sense of being in the right with a mere handful of others. The problem, however, was how to be in the right with a great many others, and to me that was the goal to which Browder was pointing the way.

Before long, I made up my mind to return to college after the war, complete my senior year, go on to graduate school, get my Ph.D., and pursue an academic career as a teacher and scholar. I would try, in my chosen area of expertise, to become a true scholar and Marxist and to use what eminence I might achieve as a means of advancing the prestige and influence of the Communist movement.

The chief medical officer of the hospital, a colonel, had been very supportive of my innovations and, in an effort to reward me (since he could not promote me as an enlisted man), proudly told me he was sending me to Medical Administrative Officer Candidate School (OCS) with an eye to my return to Mitchel Field in three months as a second lieutenant. I had misgivings, and with good reason.

I excelled at the school in Camp Barkley, Texas: the second week I was platoon leader; the third week I was cadet company commander. At the end of that same week I was back at Mitchel Field. G-2 had revoked the orders that sent me to the school. In spite of indignant protests, organized by my mother, involving congressmen, senators, and many other prominent persons, the adjutant general simply declared that Corporal Scales was "not qualified," without specifying why. Finally the heat grew so intense that the army apparently made use of North Carolina's Sen. Robert R. Reynolds, chairman of the Senate Military Affairs Committee, to defuse the protest. The senator phoned my Uncle Arch (a retired admiral) and others and implied that there was more than met the eye in the incident, that there was a question of "Red leanings" on my part; he advised that the matter be dropped "in the interest of the war effort." Senator Reynolds, head of the crucial Senate committee for the conduct of the war, had been one of the country's foremost Nazi apologists almost to Pearl Harbor day.

Meanwhile, although Richard and Bart were still in the states, most of my other friends in service were overseas. Walt and Elmer were in Italy. Steve was in India. A childhood chum had started writing to me from North Africa. Monte was in France. Franz, my Ethan Allen buddy, had visited Sylvia and me in May 1944, the night before he was to be flown to England. For several months he had been getting intensive intelligence training, about which he could say nothing except that he had been called on the carpet for being a friend of mine and for having attended a "Communist meeting" with Sylvia and me. (The meeting had been a CIO victory rally in Central Park attended by more than a hundred thousand people and adressed by Philip Murray,

Sidney Hillman, David Dubinsky, and Paul Robeson.) During this visit Franz bubbled with excitement and high spirits. In late September I heard from a mutual friend that he had been parachuted behind enemy lines six days before D-day and had been killed.

One night while I was still in a depression over Franz's death and was sweating over selecting an overseas shipment of men from the Medical Detachment, it occurred to me that since the entire business was left to me (I even signed the orders for the CO, with his approval), I could put myself on an overseas shipment. A few days later there came an order for one 502 (chief administrative specialist), my military occupation specialty (MOS) for thirty months, to go to a Signal Corps detachment at Fort Hamilton in Brooklyn for overseas duty. I sent the request for special orders to base headquarters over my CO's signature, and the orders arrived routinely the following day, much to the consternation of the CO.

The Signal Corps outfit I was assigned to received a rush processing for immediate overseas shipment. The tension mounted as the detachment was marched to a railroad siding with heavy packs and our barracks bags. But while we were boarding the train there, an officer drove up in a staff car with special orders in triplicate. I had been transferred from the detachment back to Mitchel Field. As the train pulled away, I stood in my full field pack waving to my buddies, tears of fury running down my face.

(Months later I learned that my detachment had been moved into a North Sea port to take over its operation, but the army had failed to remove the Nazis first; my buddies were, every one, killed.)

My final stay in Mitchel Field was short. On a Friday orders arrived calling for twenty men to be sent to Army Air Force Overseas Replacement Depot (ORD) in Greensboro, North Carolina. Assuming that G-2 would soon be enjoying a weekend in the city, I picked myself and nineteen others. My stratagem proved successful, and on Sunday afternoon I had a pass from the ORD and was visiting my mother in Hamilton Lakes and phoning my wife, who had returned to Chapel Hill. I was part of a temporary replacement company of about two hundred, with nothing to do but sit around the barracks waiting for shipment to a port of embarkation. Having a painful right foot, I went on sick call to help pass the time. After being examined and X-rayed, I was told that I had four broken metatarsals (greenstick fractures) and was admitted to the hospital, where I remained for seven weeks. While I lay on my back, my group went overseas.

Once I was restored to duty, I was assigned to another group awaiting shipment. Again, as the group was boarding a train, I was taken off the shipment without explanation. I demanded to see the ORD adjutant and was given, by him, some doubletalk assurances that I would be sent overseas, that the problem was that no one wanted to take the responsibility. Two weeks later there was a repeat performance, except that I was removed from the shipment three hours before the group moved out and was left behind in an empty barracks.

I learned that there was an air inspector on the post who would listen to any grievance, had great remedial power, and could be seen without anyone's prior permission. I sought him out. He was an aging regular-army lieutenant colonel who listened impassively as I poured out my complaint. "So what do you want me to do?" he asked when I had finished.

"Send me overseas before the damn war is over!"

"Put your request in writing," said the air inspector, pushing a blank sheet of paper toward me.

I wrote: "I have been outrageously discriminated against by the army. I am a good soldier. I *demand* that I either be sent overseas immediately or given a court-martial."

I signed my rank, name, and serial number and pushed the paper to the officer, who read it and said, "You'll get action within three days." I saluted and left, wondering belatedly what kind of action he meant. Within forty-eight hours I was on a train bound for Camp Patrick Henry, the staging area for the port of Newport News, Virginia.

Soon I was crossing the Atlantic on the country's largest troopship, stashed well below the waterline, reading Rabelais and annoying my seasick neighbors with my chuckling. As we neared Gibraltar a series of alarms sounded, and the navy personnel announced the presence of enemy subs. Once at the "rock," alarms again sounded. Then that night, while many were wakeful with apprehension, an announcement came over the ship's public address system that President Roosevelt had died. I, like many another, forgot the alarms and wept late into the night.

All soldiers were allowed on deck as the ship entered Naples harbor, and we saw the city curving above the blue water, shining like gold in the late afternoon sun. For two weeks I was bivouacked at Caserta, twenty-odd miles to the north, where I observed one morning a lazy plane with swastikas on its wings flying over the camp area. "Just Jerry's observation milk run," was the unconcerned explanation. Before dawn on May 1, I was on a truck convoy over the Apennines, where every village we passed through was having a festive May Day celebration, led by the Communists and Socialists, in anticipation of victory. Just one week later V-E day was proclaimed: the war in Europe was over. "I don't know how they did it without us," another newly arrived GI remarked wryly.

My new outfit was Headquarters and Headquarters Squadron of Air Force General Depot No. 5, on the outskirts of Bari. There it began all over again. Soon after I was assigned as a clerk in the orderly room, my CO, a major and the intelligence officer for the whole area, called me into his office and, while leafing through a thick folder, advised me to limit my contacts with the local populace, especially political contacts. The CO next summoned to his office the first sergeant, who came out ten minutes later glaring at me as though I had leprosy. Fortunately, that topkick was shipped home after a month, and a friendly and inexperienced young staff sergeant was made first sergeant. Meanwhile, the outfit's personnel clerk was also sent home, and I assumed his duties, working half a day in the personnel section of depot headquarters and the rest of the time in the orderly room. I did the morning report (the first sergeant's prime responsibility), the payroll, and virtually all the personnel and orderly room work. The new topkick was a promoter who managed to have himself sent all over Italy on various larks which passed as "military business." When he was away, I had to stay near the orderly room during the day and therefore had to do my personnel work in the evenings.

Bari became, during the summer of 1945, a gathering point for the remnants of many Central European Jewish families, chiefly Viennese, who had somehow survived the concentration camps. I met two fellows, Ivo and Imre, each about twenty years old, who had been childhood friends in Vienna. Both had survived an Italian concentration camp; Ivo had remained imprisoned with his parents, while Imre had escaped and joined Tito's partisans, becoming a lieutenant. Imre had escaped across the Adriatic to Bari when the Communist partisans began shooting their non-Communist comrades.

The two lads and I became friends at once. Both were starry-eyed over the United States and aimed to emigrate there. (Later, sponsored by my mother, they became U.S. citizens.) I sought to destroy their illusions without success. They tried to destroy my illusions about Communism with equal unsuccess. (For example, while I could not doubt Imre's partisan story, I was sure it had been some local aberration that had undoubtedly been corrected later.)

"My friend Junius, the most *incredible* Communist you'll ever meet!" said Ivo as he introduced me to a group of young refugee friends who gathered on Saturday nights at Imre's lodgings, danced to a windup phonograph and a few records, drank wine or punch, and talked. The gathering consisted of three or four other young men and nine or ten young women, aged eighteen to twenty-two. Most of the young women had numbers tattooed on their wrists. They were survivors of Auschwitz by way of a German officers' brothel. Most were bright and sophisticated; several were pretty. They used little makeup, and all wore old British army uniforms with trousers. They also shared in common a sort of emotional vacuum, a profound cynicism, and varying degrees of paralyzed pessimism about the future. The young men were survivors of camps in Hungary and Rumania and seemed only slightly less scarred emotionally. I had an obligatory dance with each girl and then stood aside with Ivo, who was not much of a dancer either, and observed the group.

Nearly all had known each other in Vienna as children. Most were the sole living members of their families. Though barely adults, they had encountered more bitterness, horror, and suffering than their forebears could have had in ten generations. They had arrived alone and unwanted in a foreign country, surrounded by preoccupied people. They clung together because there were no other straws to cling to.

I was awed at the staggering odds which that battered handful, out of so many murdered millions, had surmounted to be there, in Imre's flat, dancing to Glenn Miller and Tommy Dorsey records. As they laughed and danced, they looked like any carefree, youthful group. But I had an oppressive feeling that I was watching a *danse macabre,* that the survivors had not quite survived, that death had permeated their being, and that the Nazis had essentially destroyed those haunted young relics of a dead past.

I tried to put aside my lugubrious feelings and began to discuss the future with the group. The single ray of hope any of them could see was to get to the United States and "start over," but even that ray was clouded by the years of red tape they anticipated before obtaining visas. As they attacked the pounds of cold cuts I had "liberated" from my mess hall, I asked them why they didn't go instead to one of the "New Democracies," Hungary, Poland, or Czechoslovakia, where the recently liberated people would be building a free and wonderful new life. I was dismayed at the unanimous expressions of revulsion from the young people who had just fled from firsthand experience with that "new life." "Only a cut above the Nazis—and it'll get worse," was the verdict. I noticed Imre and Ivo grinning "I-told-you-so" at me.

After thinking it over, I decided that their bourgeois backgrounds had blinded them to the glorious future of Eastern Europe.

Sometime in August 1945, the CO called me into his office to say that he had been watching me "like a hawk" and had informed the FBI that he considered me a "good American." He then asked if I would like to have a direct commission as a second lieutenant. I agreed, and the paperwork was filled out and approved; I appeared before a board of senior officers which gave its blessing and sent my papers to army headquarters in Naples for the approval of the commanding general. Fortunately for me, the news of the atomic bomb on Hiroshima caused the delay and then the cancellation of direct commissions.

As a consolation prize, I was made a sergeant and then, before I could get my stripes sewn on, a staff sergeant.

With V-J day, my desire to go home was overwhelming. Until then I was sustained by an enormous amount of work, regular attendance at the local opera, and the blessed companionship of Ivo and Imre. After V-J day, armed forces morale took a terrible nose dive: the war was over, there was no more fighting anywhere, and everyone wanted to go home. The army's gloomy forecast of a longtime shortage of troopships had all the GIs despairing. The venereal disease rate (always a good barometer for morale) rose 400 percent in a month; discipline, such as it was, went to pot.

Meanwhile, something bad had been going on back home with Earl Browder. *Stars and Stripes* had even carried a story that he was about to be ousted. A few clippings and oblique references in letters from Sylvia and her sister had left me more disturbed and confused than before. I would probably have to wait till I got home to find out what was going on; but I was profoundly concerned. Could this mean turning back the clock to the sectarian twenties and thirties and another crazy, hateful factional fight such as went on then? And what about the attempt really to involve the Party in American life and politics? Was that to fall by the wayside? What about Browder himself, that thoughtful man who had dispensed with so much doctrinal nonsense— was he to be scrapped? What a rotten break to be in Italy while everything appeared to be going to hell at home.

On a Friday I had been invited to Ivo's parents' apartment for dinner, so I went to the PX tent and persuaded the sergeant to sell me one of his rare cases (twenty-four cans) of good beer instead of the swill he usually sold. After filling my pockets with candy bars and cigarettes, I put my case of Pabst on my shoulder and headed for town.

Early for dinner at Ivo's, I sat on a bench on the Corso Cavour, a fancy avenue, to wait. There I head from the south a tremendous roar of shouting voices and rhythmic chanting. As it drew closer, I remembered that I had read in the local paper that the Communists were demonstrating, all over Italy, in support of the Constituent Assembly, then trying to write a constitution for the country. The parade must have been the Communist contingent from the industrial area south of Bari marching to meet the Communists from the slum area, Bari Vecchia (the only place in town where I could find the Communist paper *L'Unità*).

The Communists, numbering about three hundred, were marching nearly twenty-five abreast, the first two ranks ablaze with huge red flags. As they advanced through the fashionable quarter, they were being showered with insults, taunts, and threats: recently defanged Fascists fairly foamed at the mouth with frustrated hatred. The workingmen marched staunchly, grim and determined, dressed in their pitiful, threadbare best—to me a moving and heroic sight. Jeeps with U.S. and British MPs appeared a block above and a block below where I stood. Bits of garbage began to be added to the abuse poured on the marchers. I wondered if there were any way I could give them some show of support as a psychological boost. Looking into that sea of red flags, I saw a lone official Italian tricolor, and there flashed through my mind an army regulation which stated that it was proper to salute flags of friendly nations.

When the beleaguered workers drew near me, I stood on top of my beer case, drew myself to my most military bearing, and gave and held an exemplary military salute. Both marchers and spectators were electrified. The parade stopped and the Communists began shouting, "Viva il sargente americano! Viva l'armate americano!" ("Long live the American sergeant! Long live the American army!") I could see, out of the corner of my eye, the jeeploads of MPs taking note of me, so I snapped down my salute and raised my right hand in the clenched-fist Communist salute, while my comrades in the parade cheered. The leader struck up the revolutionary song of Italy, "Bandiera rossa," and they all joined in, their faces in smiles, their eyes sparkling. The two MP jeeps raced toward me and the parade leader motioned me through the ranks, between the red flags. Picking up my beer, I ran through the singing formation to the far side of the crowded Corso where the MPs could not reach me. When I got to the corner of Via Romita I turned, my case of Pabst still on my shoulder, joined loudly in the last line of the song, ("Evviva communismo e libertà!"), gave the clenched-fist salute once more, and in true Douglas Fairbanks style, dashed off down the narrow street as the workers, cheering, resumed their march, shouting defiantly, "Viva il costituente!" ("Long live the Constituent Assembly!")

I hustled down the deserted street, into a doorway and up three flights, arriving breathless at Ivo's flat. When I regaled the family and Imre with my adventure over dinner, Ivo entitled my story "Junius's International Incident."

I had the impression that the Italian people were as eager to have the British and Americans leave as those soldiers would have been delighted to go. The graffiti-laden walls of Italy, which had borne such slogans as "W Stalin" ("Long Live Stalin") at the time of European victory, and "M Tito" ("Death to Tito") during the long hassle over control of Trieste, had blossomed forth everywhere with "Fuori i stranieri!" ("Out with the foreigners!") Ironically, in view of the incitements and threats against the left made by both armies, only the Communists and Socialists still spoke of us as "armies of liberation." The welcome mat had been taken inside, and it was past time to leave.

On a blustery December day orders arrived transferring me to the Seventh Replacement Depot, the port of embarkation in Naples. I borrowed the jeep and driver of a friendly headquarters officer and rushed into Bari, where, luckily, I found Ivo and Imre. After a heavyhearted parting from those two remarkable friends, I packed my books and other belongings, said my farewells to my buddies in Headquarters Squadron, and that afternoon boarded a truck convoy which wound along the interminable, twisting road across the Apennines to Naples and the Seventh Repple Depple.

There I encountered an intolerable two-week delay during which the enlisted men, in a simmering rage, went around intentionally out of uniform and unshaved and firmly refused to salute officers, in protest against the snafu. At last, on Christmas Eve, I joined several thousand other angry, demoralized GIs boarding an aircraft carrier which had its hangar deck filled with five-deck canvas bunks.

The most noteworthy thing about the return voyage seemed so natural that it almost passed unnoticed: the ship was unsegregated. About 10 percent of the returning GIs were Negroes, and there was no noticeable racial friction whatever.

On January 2, 1946, we debarked at Newport News, where we were met by a band, congratulated by a general, and royally feasted. In a couple of days, I got on a train full of other North Carolina GIs, about a quarter of whom were Negroes, and we chugged along toward Fort Bragg at Fayetteville for final discharge procedures. As the train moved fitfully along before dawn, I could see, by the one functioning light bulb, sleeping Negroes and whites scattered about the coach haphazardly. The night before we had been laughing, telling stories, playing cards, and tensely discussing together our futures, each gripped by a mixture of fear and hopeful anticipation of the imminent return to civilian life. We had shared a profound and, for some, a terrible experience in a jim-crow army. It seemed only normal, with so much living and dying behind us, that we should meet at the end of it all, man to man, as equals.

Outside, the early light revealed the flat eastern Carolina landscape. At the first ray of the sun, the men began to wake up. Some shared cigarettes; others shared their recent dreams. The car soon buzzed with animated talk; we were back in home country. The train stopped briefly at a little village consisting of a dozen drab houses and a filling-station store. A white-haired man in overalls, denim jacket, and a railwayman's denim cap, carrying a lantern, got aboard and started through our car. He had a potbelly, a red neck, a red nose, and a surly look on his face. "G'mawnin' boys," he said as he lumbered along. There was a scattering of "Good mornings" in return. He stopped at the Negro staff sergeant seated on the aisle next to me and said loudly, "Boy! Git yo' feet outa my way!"

The sergeant's feet were not in his way; he was simply the highest-ranking Negro in the car, and furthermore he was sitting with a white man. The conversations ceased, and the railroad man walked on, muttering, "Some of you niggers tryin' to fuhgit yo' place. Won' take long to straighten *you* out." And he passed out of the car. There was an embarrassed silence. Then a Negro PFC, in a voice with the irony and weariness of centuries in it, said, "We's home again."

10

Gideon's Band Again

I wish to say . . . that you had better—all you people of the South—prepare yourselves for a settlement of this question. It must come up for settlement sooner than you are prepared for it, and the sooner you commence that preparation the better for you . . . this question is still to be settled—this Negro question, I mean. The end of that is not yet.

Captain John Brown at Harpers Ferry (1859)

I arrived in Chapel Hill late in the afternoon of January 8, 1946, wearing my army uniform, carrying two barracks bags, and displaying the "ruptured duck" honorable discharge button on my chest. I walked to my in-laws' house from the bus station and soon held in my arms my startled wife, who had thought I was still in Virginia. Thirty-six hours later I hitchhiked to Greensboro to convince my mother too that I was really intact and a civilian again. She was then almost fifty-four; her old heart condition had worsened, and she looked older.

When I returned to Chapel Hill I questioned Sylvia closely and read all the documents she had saved concerning Browder's removal from leadership in the summer of 1945. After I read Jacques Duclos's much-publicized article characterizing Browder's program as a "notorious revision of Marxism," my angry reaction was, "Even if he is the secretary of the French Party, what the hell does he know about us? And didn't he ever hear of *creative* Marxism?" I viewed with dismay the denunciations of Browder and his program by William Z. Foster, Eugene Dennis (the new general secretary), war hero Bob Thompson, and John Williamson. Most of those had been among Browder's principal lieutenants, so that it was all the more shocking to find such general condemnation, as though Browder had suddenly become a complete villain. Although the articles pretended to logical analysis, I sensed a scrambling for dissociation from Browder, and I guessed that there must have been an atmosphere in the national committee like that of a lynching bee.

Early one morning I hitched to New York, arriving at Anna and Monte's apartment near midnight. With Monte, who was studying at Columbia, I had my first reunion in more than three years. Since Monte too approved of Browder's imminent expulsion, I considered that my friend had been overseas too long. If only there were someone high in Party circles that I could talk with. Dave White, my friend and former teacher, would have been ideal; but Dave had died, apparently a suicide, about six months before, at the time of the hue and cry after Browder. I wondered how much Dave's despair over the ugly situation in the Party might have contributed to the tragedy.

I went to the Party's building near Union Square and into the Party book-store at 50 East Thirteenth Street, where I talked to Harry Lichtenstein, its manager. I had visited Harry all during the war, seeking the latest books and periodicals as well as news of what was going on in the Party. We had become friends. Kindly Harry, who only thirteen months before had been as ardent a Browderite as I, was then at a loss for words to describe the archfiend, and he insisted that I consult with John Gates. Without waiting for my assent, Harry led me through a dingy passage to the 35 East Twelfth Street entrance, intro-duced me to the Negro elevator operator, and told the latter that I was an old friend and comrade and that he should take me to the ninth floor and ask the receptionist to let me talk with Gates.

I entered the anteroom, familiar to me from before the war, and was soon buzzed through a locked door by the receptionist. I found my way to a small office occupied by the chairman of the Party's veterans' committee. Gates was a short, intense man with penetrating though humorous eyes and a no-non-sense manner. A hero of the civil war in Spain, he was newly discharged from a distinguished army career in World War II. I opened up with a cautious defense of Browder's broad, "popular-front" policies. For a good two hours Gates gave me practiced, forceful answers. He also observed with sym-pathetic candor that he himself had been enthusiastic about Browder's politi-cal line while in the service.

I made no such admission, for by then I was ashamed of it. The loyalty I had felt for Browder the man, and the enthusiasm I had had for his program, crumbled under Gates's pounding. As he explicated the matter, the Party's position was that regardless of his intentions Browder had taken the Party from the tried and tested path blazed by Lenin, Stalin, and the other Bolshe-viks. His was a line of class collaboration, of utopian and opportunist belief in the possibility of working with some elements of the capitalist class. Worst of all, he had dissolved the Leninist centralized structure of the Party and had left it little more than a debating society, incapable of moving with requisite disci-pline in crucial times. Powerless to refute Gates's arguments, I felt over-whelmed with a sense of guilt. Chief among my revolutionary sins I reckoned opportunism (I had let myself be seduced by a dream of not being at political odds with practically everyone in American life) and perhaps cowardice. After all, if the Party had to go entirely against the current, then I had run from a fight that had to be fought; I had even cheered while Browder dissolved the Bolshevik-style Party.

Somehow I managed to get out of the office, though not until Gates had made appointments for me with George Watt and Marvin Shachter for the next day. Then, sitting on a bench in Union Square, I tried to collect myself. I realized that I was so ashamed of my views of three hours before that I had not even told Gates that I had been at the convention that dissolved the Party. I could no longer trust myself politically; the Party *certainly* should not. My class background, my instincts, my intelligence—all had played me false. What did I, a product of the big bourgeoisie/landed aristocracy, a half-baked intellectual, know about politics? The Party was back to its old hard-nosed, against-the-stream stance, forecasting an economic crisis leading to a "revolutionary situation" in the near future. Every Communist should be at his post. Yet I felt no enthusiasm and less capacity for that commitment. I wondered if I even had the right to be in the Party after having been so wrong, so stupid, so corrupt.

As I held my head in my hands, slumped forward on a broken bench in the seedy park, I saw across the path a Bowery derelict sitting in the identical position, totally defeated. "Good God!" I thought, "I'm not that bad off!"

Still, what had happened to the political faith which had been the center of my existence for six and one-half years, which had given meaning and purpose to my life and had added moral fiber to my character? It had given me comrades and friends like Bart and Belle, Willie Held, Bill Gillen, Steve, Ron, Dave White, Ed Rolfe, some of my college chums, and many another. It had opened to me the world of the white working class and the Negro people, thereby enriching my life beyond description. It had placed me in a forward-looking elite of fine-grained, altruistic people, and perhaps above everything, it had given me access to the theory which would unlock the doors to a future of socialism, brotherhood, and peace.

How could I doubt the integrity of such a movement, even if individuals as fine as Browder went astray? Had not the Communists of the Soviet Union amazed the world and led their people to victory over Fascism? Were they not then helping to build a fresh new life for much of Central Europe? If anyone had offered me proof at that time that Stalin had caused the death of far more Communists than Hitler had; that in the "land of socialism" poets, artists, and intellectuals were murdered, browbeaten, and humiliated on a vast scale; that the presence of secret police was a terrible, ever-present fact of life in the whole Communist paradise—I would have laughed at such naiveté, such unquestioning vulnerability to capitalist propaganda.

Nothing had changed my blind faith. Though I had failed an important test, I still considered myself a conscientious, dedicated Communist. Of course I would stay in the Party and do my duty—but only what was asked of me, no more. I would not take a leading position again. I was sure that the Party's leaders knew infinitely more than I did. I would carry out Party policy, but thenceforth in political matters I would be a follower. I would pursue an academic career, as I had decided after the 1944 convention.

The next day I was back at the Party building. Previous visits had always been exciting for me, especially those to the ninth floor. That was where the entire national office of the Party was located, and "the Ninth Floor" was used as a synonym for the national leadership. That day, however, I wanted just to keep the appointments Gates had made for me and then clear out as quickly as possible. George Watt looked even younger than Gates. Thin, red-headed, sharp-featured, with a businesslike attitude, he too was a veteran of the Spanish civil war. After exchanging a few words with him, I could see that he, like Gates, was no commonplace Party bureaucrat but a quite remarkable man. Responsive as a tuning fork to other people, he had humorous crinkles at the corners of his eyes and a good honest laugh to go with them.

He treated his visitor as though I were a leading Party cadre. Not realizing that I was scarcely a week out of the army, Watt asked me about the Party in North and South Carolina—about the enormous new tobacco workers' union in the R. J. Reynolds plant in Winston-Salem and the National Maritime Union's progress in organizing the port of Charleston. Since I then knew much less about such matters than he did, he brought out some figures showing that at the last annual registration of membership, the Carolinas district had listed a startlingly low fifty-three members.

I was determined not to get involved in explaining why the figure was so low. Bart could account for it when he got out of the service. Meantime, it was Alice Burke's headache, for as the Virginia organizer, she was still the caretaker organizer in the Carolinas. Nevertheless, I knew what was wrong with the Party's figure. Alice had gone to reregister the membership only where there were functioning clubs, as in High Point, Chapel Hill, Asheville, and Winston-Salem. She could never have found a substantial part of the membership unless she had traveled two or three thousand miles seeking the isolated members scattered from the mountains to the sea, from the Virginia line to Georgia. Bart had ferreted many of them out in various imaginative ways: from watching letters to the editor in a score of newspapers, from following up on everyone who ever wrote to the *Daily Worker* or the *Worker* or who ordered books from International Publishers. Bart had all the comrades in the district alerted for anyone who challenged the status quo, and he would go to visit likely prospects himself, usually introducing himself as the Communist Party organizer. He encountered a lot of crackpots, some old-timers who were simply contentious for no particular reason, and some anticapitalist whites who were so obsessively racist that there was no common ground. But often he uncovered pure gold: old-time Debs Socialists or their descendants (Debs had had noteworthy, widely scattered support as early as the 1912 presidential election), a Negro railroad worker, a white sharecropper, a Negro farmer, an aged and distinguished poet and novelist, a small-town medical doctor, a Negro industrial worker, a retired editor and translator, and a score of others.

In 1939, 1940, and 1941 I had accompanied Bart on several meandering "circuit-riding" trips. We would drive for miles on a main road talking, and then Bart would fall silent and concentrate on landmarks like a bird dog sniffing out quail. He would make a turn and perhaps another two or three with increasing confidence until at last he would stop triumphantly in front of the house he had been looking for. On my first trip with him, our destination was the Rockingham County cabin of a white sharecropper named Roy. When Roy recognized Bart's jalopy, he, his wife, and all nine children ran in from the field where they were working and crowded around Bart, shaking his hand and hugging him. Bart knew each of the children by name and they all called him "Uncle Bart." The rest of the day was a holiday. The one-room cabin, made of logs chinked up with clay, had a partial loft, reached by a ladder, where the children slept. Everyone sat on benches at the table of rough boards over sawhorses while Roy and his wife and the older children questioned Bart about what was going on in the world and whether or not the Party thought there would be war in Europe. Bart answered in his low-keyed, laconic way and managed to keep the rapt attention of all but the youngest children. Roy insisted that we stay overnight because the next day was Sunday and there would be time to do more talking.

Roy had worked in the Loray Cotton Mills in Gastonia at the time of the 1929 strike. He had been a union man, had been blacklisted, and after the defeat of the strike had taken to sharecropping to keep from starving. He had worked with Red Hendrix and had respected him and the other Communists he had known; so that in 1938, when he saw something in a newspaper about Bart's being the Communist Party organizer and living in Greensboro, he hitched a ride to Greensboro and hunted Bart up at his house, fearing (with good reason) that using the mails would put the FBI on to him. Roy, highly respected by the other 'croppers in the area, had intentions of forming a sort of loose local union among them.

His children were tough and resourceful like pioneer children. Roy Junior, the eldest son, aged eighteen, was a little put off by my "city-slicker" clothes, but he nevertheless invited me to come along while he tried to get a rabbit for dinner. Roy Junior shot his rabbit and I broke down the reserve between us by taking his .22 and shooting two lined-up grains of corn off a fencepost at twenty-five feet without hitting the post.

Dinner was fatback and beans (reinforced by one rabbit and one squirrel) and first-rate corn pone. Bart and I slept, as did the whole family, on the dirt floor on canvas bags stuffed with corn shucks. The next morning Roy, Bart, and I shaved with cold well water, and everyone breakfasted on cornmeal mush. While Roy and Roy Junior were out asking some of their trusted neighbors over to meet Bart, I noticed a long, narrow wooden box covered with tarpaper and locked with a padlock. I learned that it was the family library, consisting of volume one of Marx's *Capital,* several other Marxist works, a Soviet novel, *How the Steel Was Tempered,* a Bible, a one-volume Shakespeare, and Palgrave's *Golden Treasury.* The locked box was to hide from the landowner the fact that a 'cropper family read books; the tarpaper was to protect against roof leaks.

When the neighbors assembled, Bart spoke naturally and without pretense of the advantages of sticking together, of what might be accomplished, and of the dangers involved. He won their complete trust, and after they had discussed problems and planned their first steps, one of the neighbors went out to his ancient flivver and took a quart of bootleg corn whiskey from under the seat. The men passed the mason jar around and around until it was empty.

Bart kept in touch with more than two dozen Party members (that I knew of) who belonged to no Party club but were influential and like yeast in their communities. The Negro farmer, for instance (who had once had Bart preach in his church), had organized some of his friends into what they called the "Community Party"—concerned with making their community better. That group was probably more effective than most Communist Party clubs; it had transformed the church to which they all belonged into a militant Negro defense organization as well as an exceptionally enlightened social service group, making use of many cooperative devices.

Whenever Bart visited those individual comrades (about two or three times a year), he was welcomed like spring after a hard winter. He would bring with him a tailor-made bundle of literature (including back issues of the *Worker*), because if they received the *Worker* or any other Communist publication by mail, they would automatically become suspect with the FBI. Of course, Bart's concern made the district look bad in the innumerable circulation drives aimed at increasing subscriptions to the *Worker.*

But how could I possibly explain all that to Watt, a sophisticated New York Communist who thought in terms of "sections" comprising many Party clubs. Bart would straighten things out when he got back, which should be soon. He had written to me in Italy saying that he liked Colorado so much that he and

Belle might just stay there—but he was probably joking. I took notes dutifully, saying that I would relay the various organizational matters either to Bart or to Alice, whomever I saw first.

Watt then introduced me to Marvin Schachter, who was in charge of the Party's youth work. He was about my age, a very well organized veteran, bubbling with statistics and enthusiasm over the prospects for Party work on the campuses. He wanted a full description of the situation at the University of North Carolina. When I told him I knew nothing about it, he promptly gave me a description and an estimate of the campus organizations which later proved to be remarkably accurate. He read the student newspaper, the *Daily Tar Heel,* thoroughly every day. His optimism was infectious, and I again made notes to pass on to someone responsible. A few days later I bused back to Chapel Hill.

The campus was transformed from its quiet, prewar days, when it had only twenty-five hundred to three thousand students, to a bustling place dotted with temporary frame army structures to make room for swollen departments and a student body of eight thousand. The nature of the student body had changed: veterans studying under the GI Bill dominated the campus and set the tone in classes and elsewhere. Fraternity supremacy had a temporary setback, for the veterans were mostly serious students in their mid-to-late twenties eager to get on with their interrupted or delayed careers. A large, low-rent "Victory Village" had been constructed of converted army barracks for the married vets, an area soon noisy with newly arrived infants.

The town of Chapel Hill had grown slightly and seemed much busier. The hub of it for me was still the Intimate Bookshop run by my friends Ab and Minna Abernethy. Ab was just out of the army, which had rewarded him for his past maverick radicalism by years of latrine duty in Texas. Minna had run the store so ably in his absence that customers frequently could *find* the book they were seeking instead of stumbling across it by chance like buried treasure.

Accompanying Sylvia to a meeting of the student chapter of the Southern Conference for Human Welfare (SCHW), I was amazed to find over eighty students present. The SCHW, formed in 1938, was an offspring of the New Deal, representing an alliance of liberals, radical populists, radicals, and other enlightened southerners dedicated to bringing the South into the twentieth century by opposing racist laws, customs, and attitudes and by attacking the region's economic backwardness— "the nation's number one economic problem," as FDR had called it. Sylvia was active in the student chapter, which had attracted many liberals. At the meeting I met several prewar acquaintances and was introduced by Sylvia to many of her friends. It seemed to me, in the liberal postwar climate, that the Southern Conference was an organization of great promise.

Sylvia and I soon developed a wide social circle ranging politically from barely liberal to Communist. Our new friends visited us frequently and were hospitably received at the home of Sylvia's parents, who delighted in the company of bright young people. During the war the wholesale hosiery business had prospered abundantly, and after a lifetime of lean years her father became in his late forties a truly successful small businessman, able at last to indulge his generosity in material ways. He and his wife insisted that we live with them rent-free, and I was treated more like a son than a son-in-law.

The spring quarter at the university did not begin until mid-March, and so for two months I read insatiably. My academic mentor, Professor H. R. Huse, encouraged me to continue my undergraduate major in comparative literature with a view to getting a doctorate in that discipline, and I decided to take his advice.

While waiting to begin my academic routine, I received the stunning news that Bart Logan had left the Party and with Belle and little Elaine was settling in Denver. I could get no details or reasons. I thought that perhaps the Browder expulsion had repelled him; whatever the cause, I knew that it must have been deeply considered over a long period of time, because that was Bart's way. Certainly he had not left from a lack of courage or steadfastness; the man was a rock. He had spent nearly nine months lying in Bull Connor's Birmingham jail with leg and wrist irons festering into his flesh, a casualty of Connor's war on the Reds. Then there had been six years of terrible poverty as district organizer in the Carolinas, during which time he and his family were often cold and hungry. Yet he had kept his sense of humor, exercised a profound influence over the individual members in his district, and won their love and admiration.

I wrote to him and Belle asking what it was all about. Bart replied that his decision had been arrived at gradually and was irrevocable; he declined to state his reasons, since they would lead to controversy and he was determined to try to influence no one else to follow his example. He was convinced, however, that the decision was the right one for him.

I felt puzzled and hurt, despite the friendly tone of the letter, because Bart had always shared his thoughts with me in the past, and he and Belle had been an important part of my life. Nevertheless, though it was usually considered a betrayal of common principles for someone in a responsible post to leave the Party, I never heard a disparaging remark made about Bart by anyone.

I had joined a Party club in Chapel Hill after returning from New York. It was a friendly, close-knit group which met about every two or three weeks and included townspeople, faculty, and students. At a typical meeting, when reports and discussion and the rest of the agenda were out of the way, coffee and cake would be served and a pleasant social evening would follow. Alice Burke usually managed to drop in every three months or so from Richmond to pick up dues money, leave literature, and discuss what were currently the Party's most urgent tasks. A visit from a district organizer was always an event of consequence, one which gave the members a chance to get the thinking of the national leadership. In between such visits the *Daily Worker* and the *Worker* were the lifeline for keeping up with the Party attitude on everything from world events to cultural affairs. In the latter area *New Masses* (later *Masses and Mainstream,* a monthly) was more specialized. *Political Affairs* (formerly *The Communist*), the Party's official journal, was the authoritative publication on theoretical and political matters.

In early spring I received a letter from Alice coolly summoning me to a district convention of the Party in Winston-Salem. Using the mails to call a district convention before the war would have been unthinkable, and I supposed that the power of the new tobacco workers' union, largely organized by the Party, had given Alice a feeling of security. But I disapproved of the procedure. In Bart's day, because of FBI surveillance, conventions and district committee meetings were held in unlikely locations—almost anywhere except in trees—and with careful word-of-mouth preparations. One comrade would be told to meet another at a certain time and place; a third comrade would meet them; and still a fourth would lead them all to the meeting place. The security of Party members in the South had always been precarious and needed to be protected, since exposure would likely lead to loss of jobs or harassment by Klan-type groups or local police. Whatever slight acceptance the Party had achieved because of the Soviet war role and its own dedication to the war effort, that acceptance was superficial and already eroding with the deterioration of American-Soviet relations and the Party's return to a hard line.

As a member of the prewar district committee, I was to attend the convention, and I was to have the club elect two additional delegates as well. It selected a housewife and a young student. Early on the following Sunday morning we three drove to Winston-Salem, where the convention assembled at nine o'clock in a Negro fraternal hall. There I met many old friends: Willie Held from High Point and others from Asheville, Durham, Charlotte, Greensboro, and South Carolina. But many of the faces were new. They belonged chiefly to members and union organizers of the new tobacco local in Winston-Salem and to a number of organizers from other CIO unions (especially of furniture, fur and leather, and maritime workers), then increasingly active in the district. A number of the organizers were not southerners, judging by their accents; and I found myself noting their missionary attitudes and wondering cynically how long they would be around. The Negro tobacco workers, especially three or four women, were impressively articulate and radiated a self-confidence and magnetism which had already made them effective leaders of their huge union, just as most of them had previously been in their churches.

Among the delegates from Winston-Salem was "Preacher," a white North Carolinian who had been friendly with me before the war. He had been attending a Protestant divinity school studying to become a minister when he became disillusioned, left school, and subsequently joined the Party. He had engaged Bart in endless philosophical discussions which Bart found tiresome and unproductive because Preacher expressed himself with difficulty and was about as active as a three-toed sloth. Nonetheless, he was not stupid, and his friendliness compensated for his otherworldliness. Preacher had served a brief time in the army during the war and then had drifted about until encouraged to take part in some of the preliminary organizing work among the Reynolds tobacco workers. During the war he had married a handsome Jewish woman named Betty, who had grown up in Party and Young Communist League circles in New York and exuded dedication to the Party, along with a pervasive bitterness about nearly everything else. I had first met her at the convention in 1944, to which she had been a delegate. There was usually a storm cloud on her face, and lightning lurked in her eye, ready to strike the unwary offender against the purity of the Party line or doctrine. She sifted the simplest utterances, especially those of Party leaders, for "incorrect" formulations, and depending on the circumstances, she would either reprove the malefactor on the spot or store up her indictment for a future confrontation; at the very least, she would enlighten Preacher when they were alone about the bad tendencies of so-and-so. Preacher's latent fundamentalist inclinations found happy grazing in the pastures of Marxism-Leninism, and he looked on his wife as a source of revelation about the comrades he had previously accepted so amiably and unsuspiciously. Betty had brought Sin into his Garden of Eden.

Chatting with them before the meeting began, I had my formulations corrected several times by Betty, who told me smilingly, in a sort of summation, "With your background, you have to watch out for bourgeois thinking, especially when you're in a student environment." A few minutes later, while I was talking with Willie, Alice Burke called me aside and suggested that I avoid Betty and Preacher, as they had become real troublemakers and were suspected of *factionalism,* a serious and very generalized Party sin. Alice added that they were considered hostile to the leadership and that an effort was being made to isolate them. That was a sour note to me. Not liking to be told with whom I should associate, I took a seat next to Preacher.

The convention was called to order and began with a report by Alice which covered the postwar situation in the world, the country, and the South and contained numerous obligatory references to the evils of "Browderism" and the need to "eradicate it from the Party." During several hours of discussion, the comrades spoke on a great many matters, including trade union questions and Negro rights, usually concluding with a denunciation of Browder and Browderism coupled with a *mea culpa* and a promise to be on guard against such deviations in the future. I, among the last to speak, confined my remarks to the need for organization of veterans, especially Negro veterans, in order to take advantage of the increased social and political consciousness they had acquired. I said nothing at all about Browder.

Betty was the next speaker and discoursed brilliantly on a wide range of subjects, giving me the impression that she had been preparing her "spontaneous" remarks for weeks. She complimented me on my "thoughtful" remarks about veterans and regretted that I had not expressed myself about Browderism, since she was sure that it must be a severe problem with students and intellectuals at Chapel Hill. I realized that I had greatly underestimated her; I marveled at the subtle way she made herself the mouthpiece for the Party rank and file as against the Party leadership and union brass hats. She tarred them collectively and individually with Browderism, citing actions and words going back as much as two years. It was not a head-on attack, just sly and insinuating; she pretended that the references to the past were merely to illustrate how pervasive and pernicious Browder's influence had been. It was clear that she had won the admiration of most of those present and had left Alice and the top union organizers looking slightly ridiculous. She had really needled me too, and I felt sure she remembered my enthusiasm for Browder's dissolution of the Party in the South at the 1944 convention.

Alice certainly had not forgotten. At the end of the meeting she presented a slate of nominees for the district committee, accompanying each name with laudatory characterizations and comments. When she came to my name, she said only that I was a native of the state and that I had served on the district committee before the war. Since it was so grudgingly made, I briefly considered declining the nomination, but vanity won out. Election to the district committee was the highest recognition the convention could bestow, and I thought I deserved it. Besides, I would lose face with the Chapel Hill comrades if I were not on the leading committee. I said nothing and was duly elected, as were all on Alice's list.

Despite my disgruntlement, I looked around the room and exulted in the people I saw gathered there; from what I could see, they were indeed a selfless Gideon's band. I felt my old pride at being one of them, a renewed sense of being among the elect. If some among them were occasionally hard to take, there was ample precedent. Jesus' apostles, after all, were full of human weaknesses which they transcended for the good of their cause. My differences with Alice aside, she was, on balance, a kind, courageous person and leader, and even so conniving and abrasive a comrade as Betty could probably be an asset to the movement. Things seemed to have advanced greatly since before the war: the Party had a major trade union base in tobacco and a number of new smaller ones; the tobacco union provided a real bridge to the Negro people never dreamed of before; and already, impressive Negro leadership was coming to the fore. The district had lost its organizer and the Party structure was in disarray, but the convention had petitioned the national committee to assign a new organizer soon.

I found my return to academic work disappointing. I had forgotten, after six years, how much of the promising material listed in the catalog of courses changed in the classroom to dull, unimaginative lecturing. For every H. R. Huse I encountered, there seemed to be ten routineers who treated their areas of expertise and their students with indifference, incompetence, or both. I found that getting reasonably good grades was no drain on my time; I was able to spend more of it on campus organizations.

The Southern Conference for Human Welfare chapter continued to grow, as did the American Veterans Committee (AVC) chapter which I had also joined. The AVC was one of two major campus organizations of veterans. The other, the United Veterans Associations, was the larger of the two and confined itself to issues such as the local administration of the GI Bill, veterans' housing on campus, and the like. The AVC, while also involved in bread-and-butter issues, was broader in its purview; its concerns ranged from the avoidance of World War III to combating racism. From the trade union movement I had acquired a mastery of Robert's *Rules of Order* and some skill in floor debate. Hence, despite my determination to stick to my studies and not be drawn into leading roles in any organizations, I soon found myself elected vice-chairman of the AVC. Moreover, once the Southern Conference for Human Welfare began setting up separate state committees throughout the South, I found myself on the board of the committee for North Carolina, partly because of my family name and partly because I had been the leader of its prewar youth division. That designation gave me a position of some weight in relation to the student chapter at Chapel Hill.

Meanwhile, the Chapel Hill Party had been growing by the week. New members, transferred in from other areas, sought me out. Many student veterans were seeking an organization which embodied their idealism, their impatience with the status quo, and their opposition to discrimination against Negroes and the drift toward cold war. The comrades and I spent days and nights recruiting such prospective Communists. Drawing on my experience with Bart, I believed that simply getting someone to join the Party amounted to little unless the follow-up included a huge educational effort, preferably on a one-to-one basis. Soon I was teaching several classes for new members, since my comrades considered me best qualified for this task.

As the Party grew, the single club had become four. Two clubs contained only students. Faculty, faculty wives, and white townspeople were in a third. Negro townspeople, newly recruited, were in a fourth club that was attended also by two or three students. The danger to Negro comrades in meeting with whites in a small town like Chapel Hill was extreme. Therefore contact was maintained principally by means of carefully planned social affairs to which Negroes were brought unobtrusively. For example, cars driven by whites would pick up Negro comrades at their homes and drive to the rear of the house of a white comrade in the absence of outside lights, and with shades drawn over all windows; then the Negroes would be taken in through the back door. Onerous as the procedure was, the very fact of social gatherings involving Negroes and whites in North Carolina in 1946 was richly rewarding to all and subversive in the extreme of the accepted southern way of life.

Partly because I was the only local member of the district committee, I was elected chairman of the Chapel Hill Party, a position I accepted reluctantly, stipulating that I would not continue in it after I became a graduate student in 1947. By the summer of 1946 my hands were full with Party affairs, the AVC, and the SCHW.

I would have liked to forget Browderism, but every Party resolution, directive, or article spoke of the need to root it out. Every weakness in Party work, collective or individual, was adroitly traced to that cardinal sin, and only six months after I had tried to defend Browder in the national office, I was denouncing Browderism as glibly as any Party bureaucrat, speaking dutifully of the fight against it when I attended district committee meetings. My depression had partially lifted, however, and my immersion in political and organizational matters was a pleasant alternative to the drudgery involved in the completion of my required undergraduate courses. It was satisfying to work in the AVC or the SCHW, where my work was respected even by my opponents, and it was also gratifying to work for the Party, where I was highly regarded by most of my comrades. My spirits were further raised by the return, after four years in the army, of Richard Nickson, to begin graduate work.

At that time I seldom tried to look far ahead politically. I was confident that the goal of socialism was worthy and that the Party leaders were ably plotting the course. Three principles guided me in day-to-day political activity: (1) the racist oppression of the Negro people must be eliminated; (2) the quality of life had to be improved, materially and spiritually, for everyone; and (3) the Soviet Union ("pioneer land of socialism," "home of the new socialist man," et cetera) and its leader Stalin could do no serious wrong.

During the summer the Party grew still more; two new student clubs were added, while the new members' classes increased. With so many clubs it was difficult to coordinate activities, so I attended a meeting of each club and asked that a member, usually the club leader, be designated to represent it on a city executive committee. The city exec met weekly, normally on Sunday or Monday before the clubs met, to work out common agenda items and to guarantee uniformity of policy on such matters as were pending in the AVC, the SCHW, or other campus organizations. Party members had previously crossed swords with each other in such organizations, but thereafter major questions were debated exhaustively in the Party clubs, and when a consensus was reached, each member was obligated to support the position agreed upon. The debates within the Party also gave me a chance to weed out some of the sectarian verbiage which showed itself and to point out how meaningless and repugnant Party jargon and clichés were to most people.

Shortly after the fall term began, Marvin Schachter paid me a visit and expressed pleasure and enthusiasm over the Party's student activity. There had been a number of new transfer members and an even larger number of recruits, the majority being southerners. Then at last a new district organizer had been assigned to the Carolinas; he was Sam Hall, a native Alabaman, a veteran, and a capable journalist with a natural populist flair. He showed up at my in-laws' house one night and introduced himself. He was in his late thirties, plump, alert, and amiable. I particularly liked his modesty and gentleness and his peculiarly southern brand of civility. The only thing I didn't like on that first visit was the news he relayed that Preacher and Betty were moving to Chapel Hill and that Preacher was going to enroll in the university. Betty having already given him a hard time, Sam could scarcely conceal his delight at getting them out of Winston-Salem, where, he said, they had everybody checking up on everyone else's "political purity."

In mid-September I received a letter from Esther Cooper, executive secretary of the Southern Negro Youth Congress (SNYC), inviting me to attend a large, three-day "youth legislature" in Columbia, South Carolina, and to give a fifteen-minute speech at one of the panel sessions. Aside from prominent southern Negro leaders, the participants were to include Adam Clayton Powell, Jr., a young progressive congressman from Harlem; W. E. B. Du Bois, at that time editor of the NAACP's *The Crisis;* and Paul Robeson, then at the peak of his fame and popularity. I had seen Robeson as Othello twice during the war and had heard him speak and sing. Of course I had to go. Sylvia couldn't leave her classes for so long, but I organized a carload of southern students representing the SCHW, including both men and women, Party and non-Party.

On a Thursday afternoon in October we set out, having arranged to cut Friday classes, and arrived in Columbia about 9:00 P.M. The first Negro man we saw on the street directed us to the Negro community and even told us where to register as soon as we mentioned that we were delegates to the youth meeting. Merely driving into the Negro community at night under the ever-watchful eyes of the police, white cab drivers, and the like made us all tense and silent. But so superb was the organization for the meeting that the community was a solid bastion of support, refuge, and welcome for the delegates. In the business and professional areas, at Allen University, in the working-class areas, the Negro people fairly buzzed with excitement. The white police force, though obviously hostile, remained discreetly aloof from the proceedings.

My group and I were entertained at the home of an official of Allen University with such social grace and affection that we felt as though we had entered a time machine and a future we had only dreamed of. I had been full of anxiety that some of the students might be insensitive to their Negro hosts. It was ticklish to be white, and southern at that, and to receive so much courtesy and kindness from a host and hostess who, in their lifetimes, had probably had few experiences with whites which were not in some way unpleasant, or worse. Yet that host and hostess were extending their hands without reservation or bitterness to whites. Those whites, knowing the unspeakable guilt of their kind toward Negroes over centuries, struggled to let their feelings be known without becoming effusive and therefore embarrassing to everyone. I soon saw that my own sentiments were shared to some degree by all the students, and my tensions relaxed in the sheer joy of communicating with Negroes as *people*.

The next day the meeting began with several panels. I made my speech at the education panel on the subject of ending segregation in white colleges—starting with the graduate schools—and was pleased with its reception. Party personalities, chiefly Negro, were prominent as panel speakers, including trade unionists, cultural figures, politicians, and others. In the main they made a great impression on the delegates, who were chiefly grass-roots Negro youth from all over the South (so numerous that the Party regulars present were lost among them).

The climax of the gathering came on Saturday night, when Paul Robeson was to speak and sing in the city auditorium. By that time the excitement and enthusiasm had built steadily. I was delighted to see the impact of the first day and a half on my fellow Chapel Hillians, who, overwhelmed with emotion and new impressions, were walking about with their eyes ablaze. As the audience filled every seat in the huge Township Auditorium, the program opened with a procession of the delegates and the audience standing and singing "The Star Spangled Banner." After an obligatory series of introductions and preliminaries, and speeches by Herbert Aptheker, a Communist historian specializing in Negro history, and Howard Fast, the popular novelist, the great man himself appeared.

A giant, he strode onto the crowded stage with a combination of dignity, grace, and responsive enthusiasm. By the time he reached the microphone he had established firm rapport with his audience, and when the gentle thunder of his greeting broke over us, it was as though each person there had been struck by the lightning of that smile, the grandeur of that presence. There were no formal phrases; he spoke straight to the hearts of all present. He spoke as one who knew the horror of living black in the white South; he spoke as a survivor to survivors. But he also spoke to those in the valley as one who, from the top of the mountain, could see far ahead, sharing his vision of struggle and future brotherhood, lending his courage, love, and strength to each one. The words flowed like a river, washing away from his listeners the pettiness and competitiveness of everyday life and bearing us along united in a transcendent determination to change life in the South, to take part in a new birth of freedom.

Then Robeson began to sing "No more auction block for me! No more, no more!" while in anguish and resolution a collective sob arose from the assemblage. For me and the four other white students, the incredible thing about this Negro meeting was the absence of racism among people who might justifiably have recoiled at the sight of a white skin. On the contrary, we were surrounded by friendship. Was there ever in the history of human oppression, I wondered, a people with such generosity of spirit, capable of such forgiveness for past crimes, so trusting that there were those with conscience and humanity among their oppressors?

> There is a balm in Gilead
> To make the wounded whole;
> There is a balm in Gilead
> To heal the sin-sick soul,

the glorious voice reassured.

I felt a crushing responsibility, personally, not to betray that trust, never to relax as long as there remained a legal vestige of racist oppression in the South, never to cease trying to change the hearts and minds of white people. Trust, I thought, was a fragile thing. How many times could a hand extended in friendship be ignored, rebuffed, wounded, before that trust became suspicion and, at last, bitterness and hatred? I felt fortunate to be young at the time when the Negroes had begun moving inexorably toward freedom while still offering me, a descendant of slave owners, a chance to participate.

> Git on board little chillun,
> Git on board little chillun,
> There's room for many a-more.

The Party had to rise to the challenge, seek out and arouse those white southerners with hearts and consciences, and bring them together with the ablest Negro leaders. Robeson was pronouncing the benediction with his version of a stark, sorrowful hymn:

> We are climbing Jacob's ladder,
> We are climbing Jacob's ladder,
> We are climbing Jacob's ladder,
> We're soldiers in this fight.

Then the audience rose to its feet as the organlike voice led them in a soaring rendition of James Weldon Johnson's Negro National Anthem:

> Lift every voice and sing
> Till earth and heaven ring.

There was nothing more to be said, and several thousand people filed out of the auditorium transfigured by a newfound pride in themselves as human beings.

As I, profoundly moved, inched out with the rest of the throng, a cooler, more detached part of me was trying to assess the meaning of that flash of lightning in Columbia. My Party training had taught me to think of the organizational follow-up to every inspirational occurrence. I knew that the other white students and I would go home with heightened consciousness of the Negro people's struggle. We would seek out and publicize the grossest examples of racial injustice and try to arouse a sense of outrage in our fellow whites; we would fight to break down segregation everywhere we could; we would set an example for other whites in our relations with Negroes.

But what about the nine hundred Negro delegates? What were those bright, radicalized young people going to do when *they* got back home to Negro ghettoes throughout the South? What handle could they grasp to take the next step for the liberation of their people? The meeting had shown that the Party, through the mainly Communist leadership of the SNYC, could organize and move the most militant and advanced young Negroes; it had shown that the SNYC could enlist the support of much of the Negro middle class, at least on special occasions; it had shown that inspirational leadership was plentiful—

but there was no answer to what could be done to move the quiescent, non-political, hardworking body of southern Negroes. Columbia was electrified on Saturday night, but on Monday morning a new work week would begin; the brilliant organizers of that great demonstration would have left town, and, once again, the indignity of being Negro in a brutally bigoted white city would be as it had been before. The delegates would return home with a glorious memory, while the fire kindled in them would gradually be snuffed in the monotony of day-to-day life—until the tactics were found to awaken the Negro masses.

While I was musing thus somberly and edging my way out of the main exit, Dorothy Burnham, one of the ablest of the SNYC leaders, crumpled into my hand a strip of yellow mimeographed paper which said, "The Southern Negro Youth Congress invites you to attend an informal reception in honor of Mr. Paul Robeson at the home of Dr. S. R. Higgins, Barhamville Road, immediately after this program." I clutched the paper as if it were gold, made my excuses to my fellow students, and caught a ride to the reception.

The impressive drawing room of the president of Allen University was already full of people, and I chatted with several I knew, including Herbert Aptheker, whose pioneering *American Negro Slave Revolts* had much impressed me. Hosea Hudson, a courageous Negro steel worker from Alabama, whom I had met before the war, greeted me and plied me with questions about the Negro workers in Winston-Salem. Louis Burnham, organizer of the SNYC, introduced me to Howard Fast, the left's most popular novelist, who had recently written *Freedom Road,* a novel about Reconstruction in South Carolina. With Fast was Leo Hurwitz (whom I knew by way of Ed and Mary Rolfe), a talented movie director who was interested in filming that novel with Robeson in the part of Gideon Jackson, the hero. A couple of other white intellectuals well known in Party circles were also present. While they were all talking, the outside door in the anteroom opened and the doorway was filled with Robeson's gigantic, glowing presence. A spontaneous gasp of admiration arose as everyone moved toward him.

Robeson was as genuine and magnetic socially as he had been on the stage. He managed to listen to every word spoken to him and to reply graciously. When I was introduced to him he made me feel like the guest of honor. The introductions were scarcely completed when two white Party intellectuals oozed up to him. "Oh Paul, you were simply *marvelous!*" gushed one. "You used *exactly* the right amount of feeling and emotion at *just* the right places," added the other. "Your timing was perfect, and you really got *to* them!" they concluded together. Shriveling with embarrassment, I saw Robeson recoil a bit as he replied coolly but politely, "Thank you. I'm glad you liked it."

I realized that I was in the presence of a man who suffered fools no more easily than many another, but who had such love for and confidence in his fellowman that he would not dispose of even the most intolerable ass with a sharp retort or a cutting put-down; he would suffer them with dignity and hope that whatever was good in them would win out, possibly aided by his example. He was, to borrow from his southern white detractors their ultimate encomium, "a fine, Christian gentleman."

When midnight was long past, when the host's punch had all been drunk and the reception was breaking up, I gathered up my courage as I helped Robeson on with his enormous overcoat and said softly, "Mr. Robeson, did you know that the largest Communist Party club in Winston-Salem is named the Paul Robeson Club?"

A smile broke over his face, glowing like sunrise, and the reverberant voice, suffused with surprise and pleasure, replied, "No, I did *not!* But I'm *mighty* proud to hear about it. *Thank* you!" And he crushed my hand in both of his.

At one of the panel sessions I had met a shy Negro furniture worker named George from Thomasville, North Carolina, a small town near High Point. The Thomasville Chair Company, where I had once been turned down for a job before the war, and where both wages and working conditions had long been intolerable, had been organized by the United Furniture Workers, CIO, and was currently being struck. George had been sent to the Columbia meeting to see what support he could raise for the destitute strikers. I was much moved by George's description of the people, Negro and white, men and women, walking the picket line around the enormous plant. George wanted me to make an appeal for funds at the final session. I felt that he would be far more eloquent than I could possibly be, but he said that he was having trouble with his false teeth, and that he froze up before big audiences; besides, he thought that a white southerner speaking before that gathering would make a big impression. I reluctantly agreed and cleared it with the SNYC leadership. When the chairman introduced me, I was almost paralyzed with stage fright, but I managed to get across what George had told me, adding that the Thomasville picket line was a symbol of the future and that such a struggle needed the support of every forward-looking southerner, Negro or white. I left the stage numbly, with applause washing over me while ushers collected several hundred dollars, much to George's delight. Before I could return to my seat, I was buttonholed by several reporters and was warmly congratulated by many delegates.

Late that afternoon I was given the most-prized honor I ever received: I was elected a vice-president of the SNYC by nearly nine hundred delegates—the first and only white officer in its history.

As the Chapel Hill delegation was saying its farewells to our host and hostess, we were at a loss for words until a young woman student hugged and kissed our hostess, saying, in her gentle southern accent, "I just can't tell you how much I love you and how grateful I am for getting to know you. I'll never forget you or this weekend." On the long drive back to Chapel Hill, when nearly everyone was dozing except the driver, the same young woman, sitting in the back seat next to me, whispered, her face aglow, that she wanted to join the Communist Party. To me, that seemed the reasonable thing for her to do.

11

Dust and Heat

Perhaps it is a universal truth that the loss of
liberty at home is to be charged to provisions
against danger, real or pretended, from
abroad.

James Madison (May 13, 1798)

Back in Chapel Hill the next day, I winced when I read newspaper accounts of "the scion of a prominent North Carolina family" making a plea for aid to striking furniture workers and subsequently being elected a leader of the Southern Negro Youth Congress, "a Negro organization." I felt as though my most private thoughts and emotions had been invaded by the publicity, and I blushed when student friends congratulated me. I had not yet learned to live with newspaper publicity and shrank every time I saw my name in print.

Shortly thereafter I found myself promoted to the executive committee of the Committee for North Carolina (CNC) of the Southern Conference for Human Welfare, probably because of my enthusiasm in campaigning for liberal candidates supported by the committee. The CNC had as its executive secretary Mary Price, a Greensboro native in her late thirties, who remembered me when I had been a small boy with golden ringlets and she had been a teenage girl, both of us attending the First Presbyterian Church. A capable and tireless organizer, she had activated some extraordinary people in support of the Southern Conference program, including Dr. Frank Graham, president of UNC and one of the founders of the Southern Conference, and Dr. Lee Sheppard of Raleigh, a Baptist minister who was chairman of the CNC. Other distinguished activists included a divinity professor at Duke University and several other prominent ministers, educators, lawyers, labor leaders, and even businessmen. The two outstanding Negro personalities on the CNC board were Dr. Charlotte Hawkins Brown and Dr. David D. Jones, both college presidents.

Dr. Brown was, and had been for decades, president of Palmer Memorial Institute at Sedalia, North Carolina, which had become a nationally famous Negro school under her leadership. She and Mary McLeod Bethune were the nation's outstanding Negro women educators. When I had first met her before the war, she had looked me over curiously in her grande dame fashion and had said with some emotion: "Young man, let me tell you a story. Many years ago when I was young and had just earned my Ph.D. in New England, I was offered the presidency at Sedalia. The board of trustees, which was all white, wanted to interview me and I came into the room somewhat ill at ease. They would have let me stand while they sat there, had not your father gotten me a chair and seated me. They spoke to me as though I were a cook and addressed me as 'Charlotte'—except for your father, who called me 'Doctor Brown,' then and for the rest of his life. He was the only member of that board I could speak to seriously about educational matters, or anything else for that matter. *You,* young man, have a lot to live up to." And she had taken my hand warmly. That incident endeared her to me, and my esteem for her grew over the years.

Dr. David Jones, then in his late fifties and president of Bennett College in Greensboro, also had some admiring recollections of my father. His two daughters had been stalwarts in the American Student Union at Bennett before the war, and his wife was a cultured and charming hostess; I had met the Negro composer and musicologist R. Nathaniel Dett in her drawing room. Dr. Jones was a passionate and articulate fighter for Negro rights, and both he and Dr. Brown, despite political and financial pressures from white boards of trustees, were staunch participants in the CNC's meetings and activities.

A proposal was made at one of the enlarged board meetings of the CNC that the committee support a bill either pending or to be introduced in the state legislature for the construction of a vast hospital in conjunction with the UNC Medical School. I inquired whether the proposed hospital was to be segregated, and if so, how many Negro patients would be accommodated and how many Negro doctors and nurses would be employed. As I made my inquiry I could see undisguised annoyance in the faces of several white liberals, who felt that I was being obstructionist and tiresome by raising the point.

President Graham himself answered me. The hospital was desperately needed by all the poor people of the state, and all would benefit from it. A certain percentage of beds would be reserved for Negro patients, but it would be segregated and there was no provision for Negro doctors or nurses on the staff. This was indeed shameful, but if a bill were to be introduced in the legislature calling for an unsegregated hospital it would surely be defeated and the proposed hospital would likely die aborning. But if the hospital were built it would be good for everyone, and the fight to desegregate it could begin.

Junius, chairing American Veterans Committee
meeting, Chapel Hill, 1947

That was a powerful argument, and I could see what I thought to be relieved, smug grins on the faces of those same liberals who obviously thought that Dr. Graham had extricated them from a sticky situation.

While I was trying to think of a response, Dr. Jones, who was sitting next to me, arose and walked tensely to the lectern. "I and my people would follow Dr. Graham to the ends of the earth," he said. "We respect and love him. But, my *God!*" His voice became an agonized roar and electrified his audience. "My GOD! How LONG must my people wait until the first faltering word is spoken by white men of goodwill saying that segregation is *criminal*—that it is *destroying* my people?" His impressive figure trembling with emotion, he appeared to want to say something else, but instead he returned to his seat amid a stunned silence and sat with his hand over his face.

As soon as I could suppress my own emotion, I broke the tension by improvising a substitute proposal: that the CNC endorse the construction of the hospital with the proviso that Negro doctors and nurses staff the Negro wards, since it was not only morally wrong to bar qualified Negro professionals from attending Negro patients but, in a tax-supported institution, probably unconstitutional as well. Further, because it was morally right, was necessary under the Constitution, and would entail a vast saving to the taxpayers of the state, wards and departments requiring special equipment and personnel—operating rooms, physiotherapy, X-ray, laboratories, postoperative care, cardiac care, and the like—should be unsegregated. That, I thought, while recognizing the prevailing political realities, would sharpen the issue, recommit the Southern Conference on moral grounds, and, by tying segregation to the high monetary cost it involved, embarrass some of the red-neck, know-nothing legislators who posed as guardians of the state treasury.

From that and many similar experiences, I found a gulf beginning to separate me from the majority of white liberals, who still clung to separate-but-equal delusions; were eager to avoid a confrontation on the "race issue"; shied away from a chance to fight segregation even on favorable ground; and were, all too often, ready to seek a "solution" by promising a future fight which usually did not take place. Those white liberals were mostly courageous, and they often took moral stances which expressed the true conscience of their time and place. What caused them to temporize and waver on issues involving Negro rights was the vested interest and the depth, scope, and sheer virulence of the bigotry they opposed. It was not easy to be called "nigger-lover" by one's neighbors, business associates, academic colleagues, fellow congregation members, or relatives. Nor was it easy to receive anonymous threats on one's life from some individual or group deeply convinced that liberals, highbrows, and radicals were betraying the common southern heritage, which was an inherent need and obligation to stick together with other whites to "hold down the nigger."

Nevertheless, in view of the infinitely greater sufferings, risks, and dangers endured by *every* Negro, I sought to be a gadfly to the liberals, even though fully aware of their difficulties. In that specific instance I was never sure in my heart which position was the better, but I was glad that I had responded to the emotion of my friend Dr. Jones. The haze of time has obscured the outcome of that afternoon's debate. Two things, however, are certain: Dr. Jones liked my proposal and the hospital was subsequently built—segregated.

I enjoyed my work in liberal organizations so much that I found the time I spent in Party organization oppressive. Like many unskilled leaders I tried to do everything myself: to attend every meeting of each club, to argue and explain every tactical matter. In my exhaustion I began to realize the self-defeating arrogance of my approach; I got an experienced northern woman student to be the city organizational secretary, relied much more on the club leaders, and began attending only one or two club meetings each week in addition to the city exec meetings. One of the rewards of my new procedure was that I saw an immediate flowering of potential leaders whose abilities I had underestimated.

My principal objective in the Party organization was to keep the students active in the campus organizations to which they belonged. There were few such problems with the Negro members or the white townspeople, but there were students who enjoyed the sympathetic warmth of Party society so much that they would have been glad to associate solely with other Communists. Such comrades found work in the Southern Conference, the AVC, or other groups "boring" and much preferred having endless bull sessions with comrades who were understanding and in complete agreement with them. I put a premium on "mass" work and frequently denounced what I called "purist theoreticians." I was fond of quoting Milton's *Areopagitica:* "I cannot praise a fugitive and cloistered virtue unexercised and unbreathed, that never sallies out and sees her adversary, but slinks out of the race, where that immortal garland is to be run for, not without dust and heat." I aimed at organizing a Gideon's band imbued with the desire and the ability to influence the broadest possible group of people.

The local Party's tactics in the mass organizations, such as the Southern Conference and the AVC, aimed to put forward as much of the Party's program as each organization's scope and its members' attitudes permitted. Implementing this goal involved working hard for the good of the organization, taking care not to push the members further than they were ready to go on any particular issue, eschewing petty squabbling over minor issues, and making creative proposals to further the organization's objectives.

That ideal of Party work was occasionally attained, but such achievements were partially undone by attitudes not easily controlled. Not surprisingly, because we were driven by a philosophy which claimed for itself the epitome of human wisdom and righteousness, Party members sometimes behaved condescendingly to our opposition and to the as-yet unconverted. Our conviction that we alone possessed the right line on every issue did not endear us even to those who were favorably inclined toward us. Arrogance rarely won true friends, and more often than not, a know-it-all attitude exacerbated differences with non-Party people. To overcome such disadvantages, I tried to train my forces to practice more suavity and tact. It occurred to me that I was actually teaching deception: how to hide our belief that, as Communists, we had all the answers and did not need to listen much to anyone else. That painful realization I tried to assuage by telling myself that Marxism-Leninism, used correctly, could indeed provide the right answers, but that good tactics required that we not boast about it and that we at least pretend to respect the opinions of others.

The Party forces were usually persuasive and successful on matters involving Negro rights, civil liberties, and economic matters, but less so in matters concerning peace and foreign policy. Truman had proclaimed his doctrine of Communist containment; later the Soviet Union had attacked the Marshall Plan, and the CPUSA had dutifully followed suit. Consequently, the campus Communists stood out in high relief in almost any debate involving U.S. foreign policy. The growing attacks on Communists in the labor movement and everywhere else made it increasingly difficult for us to avoid being isolated.

For example, the liberal national leadership of the AVC, in the spirit of Truman's loyalty oaths and the Taft-Hartley non-Communist affidavits, which anticipated the ambiance of McCarthyism, contrived and passed a resolution that invited an internal purge in the organization that would effectively bar Communists from membership. The leadership had been understandably annoyed by crude national Party tactics aimed at promoting a foreign policy based on peaceful coexistence with the Soviet Union and at forcing a more aggressive stand on Negro rights; it was therefore determined to "clean out the Communists." The resolution was to be submitted to each chapter for approval. In Chapel Hill, where the organization was more than 90 percent non-Communist, I led the opposition to the resolution, appealing for freedom of political belief and pointing out that the introduction of the resolution had brought a halt to most constructive work in chapters all over the country and had caused the membership to split and turn on itself.

The chairman had been absent for some weeks, so as vice-chairman I presided over the crucial meeting. I was scrupulously fair to my opponents, giving them the floor almost without limit. But because of my parliamentary experience I outmaneuvered them when they, sensing defeat, tried to delay the vote by parliamentary tricks. During the debate I would turn the chair over to the secretary, step down from the dais, and argue my points forcefully but in a gentlemanly manner, while my opponents grew loud, angry, and abusive. The vote was overwhelmingly against the resolution, even though there were only a handful of Communists present. Fearing that impatience among some of my less-experienced comrades might exacerbate the split in the AVC, I had asked several not to attend.

(A dozen years later, over a cup of coffee, the leading proponent of the resolution reminisced with me about how he and his allies had resorted to all sorts of skullduggery, including the preparation of a great number of false proxy votes and an attempt to falsify the tally of the vote—assuming from his perception of Communists that my supporters and I had attempted the same or similar deceptions. When I told him that I, like the majority, had behaved with complete honesty, he was genuinely surprised but saw nothing amiss in his own behavior. He felt that anything was justifiable so long as defeating the Communists was his objective. It never occurred to him that in his anti-Communist zeal he, like a great many of his countrymen, had fallen into the Communists' own specious reasoning: a worthy goal justifies any behavior.)

As I became better known on campus and identified by many as a Communist, Sylvia and I broadened our circle of acquaintances. Her parents' cozy little house, not far from the campus, became more and more a social center as I was sought out by many serious students, some of them intellectually curious about Marxism, some thinking that Communism might be the answer to the world's problems, some titillated by radical politics, and some finding my friends and me interesting or stimulating people. Every Friday night the Scaleses were at home and there was an open house; though alcohol was not served, tea, coffee, cookies, and conversation were always in plentiful supply. The conversation was often political but by no means exclusively so (though I usually found a political aspect of almost any topic), and the discussions were often very lively, sometimes continuing long into the night. There usually were far more non-Communists than Communists present—undergraduates, graduate students, and younger faculty, male and female. The social evenings helped to create a large circle of Party sympathizers, friends, and supporters in the community.

I enjoyed the Friday socializing greatly. The discussion and debate made me think more deeply about many questions, sharpened my wits, and made me more articulate. Besides, I enjoyed being the center of attention and the dominant presence in such lively groups. Best of all, the evenings were full of fun and friendliness.

Several of my student comrades, the ones who had "broken wings" of some sort, made great demands on my time. There was William, for example, a young veteran from a distinguished southern family who had suffered a mental crack-up in the Pacific just after the war ended. He was singularly vulnerable and unsure of himself, consulted me on every conceivable personal and political problem, and nearly succeeded in acquiring a free, if unskilled, psychiatrist.

There was also Harry, a veteran from eastern North Carolina, who had grown up knowing the ostracism of a six-family ghetto in a small town, collecting appalling emotional scars which were exacerbated by the anti-Semitism he encountered in his army career. He viewed the Party not only as the force for eliminating injustice in the glorious future, but as an instrument of vengeance for the cruel past and for punishment of the cruel present. Although often sweet-natured, he raged when he encountered opposition to Party positions anywhere, since he considered them to be self-evidently right; within the Party, when he perceived a "wrong" political view, he set out ruthlessly to crush the guilty one unless that one repented. Harry besieged me continually, not only with his personal problems, but with complaints and charges against his comrades, several of whom he wanted expelled from the Party.

Most comrades had never suffered comparable traumas, but they did bring problems of great variety to me. To some I was a father figure; to others I was a big brother, a stand-in psychiatrist, the pastor of the flock, a marriage counselor, a sympathetic shoulder to cry on; to many I was the experienced Party leader who had (or should have had) the answers to most problems. I tried to live up to some of the roles in which I was cast, trying at the same time to maintain the affectionate relationships I had with most of my comrades. Many of them felt close enough to me to discuss their sexual fears, difficulties, and inexperience, so much so that I wore out in a year's time my invaluable assistant, the expensive, hard-to-obtain sex manual *Ideal Marriage,* by Theodore H. Van de Velde.

The responsibilities of being the Party leader tended to separate me from those comrades I loved the most. There was never complete harmony within the Party. As in any large group there was always some friction, some smoldering resentment, some disguised hostility. As leader I could not let my personal feeling for certain comrades seem to imply political endorsement of them; I had to adopt a degree of aloofness toward everyone so that no one could doubt my political fairness and impartiality.

Betty and lazy, tongue-tied Preacher put my political impartiality to the test. They had left Winston-Salem angrier and feeling more sinned-against than ever. Sam Hall, his considerable patience stretched beyond endurance, had accused them of factional attempts to undermine the leadership in Winston-Salem, and he suspected them of worse. His charge was no doubt true. Betty (politically, Preacher was only a mute, inglorious clone) had purposefully cultivated dissatisfaction with both the Party and the union leadership, and when an occasion offered she would give eloquent voice to it with stinging criticism. There was always an element of truth in her denunciations, which was why they were effective. Her usual technique was to describe an ideal situation in the Party (with appropriate quotations from Lenin or Stalin), compare the then-existing situation scathingly with the ideal, ignore all the objective difficulties and limitations at hand, and put the blame squarely on the hardworking leadership—particularly Sam Hall.

In Chapel Hill Betty quickly adapted to the new environment and trained her guns on me. I had assigned Preacher and her to a sort of catchall club where I thought she might have less scope for her machinations. It contained a faculty wife, a prewar friend of mine, Harry, an out-of-state woman student, and a couple of relatively inactive graduate students. During the first meeting of this club that I attended after her arrival, she attacked me for a lack of collective leadership, dictatorial practices, and favoritism. No one was so contemptuous of "bourgeois democracy" as Betty, and her criticisms were profoundly cynical. But she was right. I *was* a sort of dictator and exercised profound authority over my Chapel Hill comrades. My prestige was great and some followed me blindly. Even though I was careful to have a vote in the city exec on most matters, there was no doubt that if I favored something and argued for it, I would have my way. If I proposed someone for a post, that person would be dutifully elected. If I wanted someone removed from a post, that person would be replaced.

Party leadership from top to bottom was a pyramid of dictatorships (known in Party jargon as "democratic centralism"), sometimes of a single person, sometimes of a coalition of two or three or more. Members did what they were told out of confidence and trust in their leaders and in turn felt free to make respectful suggestions and even criticisms of those leaders. In much the same relationship, I accepted Sam's leadership, knowing that he got his guidance from Nat Ross, the new southern director, who in turn got his guidance from the national committee, which was controlled by Foster and Dennis.

Because my lieutenants were largely inexperienced and new to the Party, I sometimes made decisions which bypassed them, and got their formal approval only after the fact. As to favoritism, it was true that I placed in leadership those most in agreement with me, especially those most effective with people outside the Party.

Her criticism was unanswerable, as Betty knew, and my reply was self-critical but lame. In consequence, I went to even greater lengths to see that decisions were made as collectively as possible. I also tried in personal discussion to see what really was gnawing at Betty, but she seemed to expect nothing less than unconditional surrender from me and became abusive and uncommunicative.

Sam placed me in an awkward position by instructing me to see that Betty held no responsible Party positions. Such an instruction, which assumed that I could "control" the membership (a common-enough practice in the Party), of course belied the pretense of inner-Party democracy. By carefully cultivating Harry and a few others, Betty got herself nominated for the city exec. Because of Sam's instruction, I could not take a chance that she might get elected. I was forced to tell the exec members that she was "considered untrustworthy" by higher authority—whereupon they maneuvered and pressured and made sure that she was defeated. I had not only, in an underhanded way, labeled her as suspect among a part of the membership, I had undermined open, frank discussion of the candidates and had made a mockery of the election of the leading committee.

I was caught between my Jeffersonian upbringing and my Party loyalty. I rationalized the situation by reassuring myself that the overall purpose justified a small departure from democratic (or decent) behavior, and that once there was an equitable and socialist United States and the preying capitalists had been defanged, there would be unprecedented democracy and an end to such intrigue and duplicity as I then found myself entangled in. As always, the glorious end justified the slimy means, and I had to squelch that persistent inner voice which suggested that perhaps the unsavory means was tainting the quality of the socialist goal.

Betty, shrewdly aware of my discomfiture over my unclean hands and of my reluctance to tangle with her, struck a martyr's pose and then boldly began to put forth her line that Foster and Dennis had slipped back into "Browder opportunism" and were not going seriously about the business of preparing for a socialist revolution. That was intolerable heresy and aroused me to combat. Pointing out the massive attack on the left in the trade unions and everywhere else, I asked scornfully where she saw a revolutionary situation developing in the United States in 1947. I suggested sarcastically that maybe she'd like to start giving the members close-order military drill so that they could all march on the state capitol building. She seized the bait and replied that military drill was a great deal more appropriate to the situation than my playing at politics and the other types of opportunism into which I was then leading the Party. After that exchange, she lost most of her support. But she still managed to cultivate conflict in the Party. In her own club she incited Harry to bring charges for expulsion against my prewar friend after he had sharply reproved Harry for his use of somber, turgid jargon and for his penchant for trying to expel other members. Nonsensical as the charges were, it was not easy to stop Harry once he found a mission. It took quite some doing to sidetrack the proceedings.

I had come to accept Betty as a sort of permanent cross to bear when Nat Ross, while on a visit to Chapel Hill with Sam, said that she and Preacher would have to be expelled. Expulsion had never occurred to me as a solution, especially since she had retreated somewhat and had quit trying to promote her "revolutionary" line, at least openly. It seemed too terrible and final, even though the two of them were scarcely on speaking terms with reality, were a little crazy, and could be intolerably nasty and vituperative. I had no doubt that they believed in socialism, and many of their past actions had indicated their devotion to the Party. Banishing them from that world of warmth, hope, and acceptance which had dominated their lives for years would be a cruel thing. Lenin, however, left no doubt: the Party must purge itself of unreliable or hostile elements, and they were both.

The expulsion process was strange and painful for all concerned. The state committee appointed a special trial committee in Chapel Hill. With Sam present as prosecutor, the trial began with written depositions from two or three Party leaders who had known Betty earlier and elsewhere. The depositions attempted, without any real evidence at all, to make a case that Betty had, along with other devilment, been informing to the FBI. Those charges fell, partly of their own weight and partly under Betty's impassioned defense. But ultimately the trial committee became unanimously convinced that her political line was from another world and that her attitude toward all Party leadership was destructive.

The trial sessions might have been created by the Dostoevski of *The Possessed*. To their judges the two defendants had gradually ceased being people and become symbols of evil. Witnesses, certain of their guilt, and using much hindsight, put sinister and sometimes grotesque interpretations on their most innocuous past actions and words. The defendants fought back gamely, often with reason and common sense on their side. I tried to preside over the sessions with informality and courtesy, but I developed a sickening feeling that I was presiding over a heresy trial—as indeed I was. The bitterness and venom generated at the trial were extraordinary. A prescient young woman student remarked innocently that if comrades could talk like that to each other, the future didn't look very hopeful for the brotherhood of man.

By the trial's end I had little resentment left for either Betty or Preacher. I had concluded that Preacher was a political simpleton, a sort of guileless fool, and that intriguing and plotting were as natural to Betty as to one of the Medici women. Before the final trial session Betty approached me without her usual animosity, saying that she could not live if she were expelled, that the Party was her whole life. There could be no doubt that her distress was genuine. But there was no way to turn back, and I hardened my heart. I tried to make peace with my conscience by reasoning that she was too embittered to be happy in the Party and that, in any event, the primary responsibility was on Sam and Nat—that the whole repugnant business was something to be endured for the good of the Party. The trial committee recommended expulsion, and the state committee formally expelled the two in August 1947.

Betty and Preacher moved away and later issued two atrociously written documents. The first, of twenty-odd pages, attacked the Party and rehashed their expulsion; the second, issued late in 1948, dealt with general political matters. The interesting thing about the second document was that its authors had been able to figure out, after having been out of the Party only a year, and having had to do their own thinking, that there was something profoundly phony in Stalin's denunciation of Tito and that the Soviet Union was behaving much like an imperialist power in Eastern Europe—deductions which were far beyond the capability of their erstwhile comrades.

Though I was still a "sheep" in matters of political strategy and policy, I did arrive at a few independent political observations and conclusions. After the Betty-Preacher trauma, I became convinced that the truly painful aspects of Party leadership were not the hatred, insults, and vituperation received from anti-Communists, but the disappointments in one's comrades, from whom so much was expected. Unkindness, pettiness, inhumane thinking, mean-spirited social attitudes, weathervane changes in political positions—those were the things, coming from one's beloved, idealistic, fellow humanists, that could break a Communist leader's heart.

As I grew politically wiser (or perhaps more jaded) in a few respects, I became more distrustful of political clichés or truisms which translated into sectarian political behavior. For instance, I rejected the widespread attitudes toward religion then prevalent in the Party, which ranged from the contemptuous to the militantly atheistic. I argued that the Negro churches had often been the backbone of resistance to oppression, that innumerable, unsung Negro ministers were discreet and eloquent tribunes of their people, and that many Negro Communists were religious. It was pointed out by a militantly antiracist southern white minister that eleven o'clock Sunday morning was the South's most segregated hour. I maintained that, even so, in the white churches it was still the best hour in the week for most of the congregation, perhaps the one time in the week when there was some consideration (however hypo-critical) of ethical questions; the time when a much-violated code of Christian ethics was dragged out of the mothballs and held out for emulation (to how-ever slight effect); and a time when one was exposed (however obliquely) to some ramification of the exhortation "Thou shalt love they neighbor as thy-self." I believed that in the South, on balance, white organized religion tilted slightly to the side of the angels. In any event, there was nothing to be gained by alienating a great many good people with pointless attacks on religion.

Though a philosophical materialist myself, within the Party I never dis-paraged religious beliefs because I had observed that even in some sophisti-cated students there often lurked considerable areas of religious feeling largely unsuspected by themselves. To overzealous "God-haters" I suggested that such excessive antireligious emotion might indicate an unresolved internal religious conflict, and I would assure them that no one would respect his or her Party loyalty the less because of the presence or absence of religious belief. On a practical level, I counseled tactful consideration.

It was a pleasure for me to put aside the pressures of student affairs and graduate studies, get out of Chapel Hill, and immerse myself in working-class concerns. Sometimes I would go with Sam Hall to Winston-Salem, where I would soon find myself awash in the complex problems of a giant left-led union local, predominantly Negro, fighting for its life against a company of enormous power that controlled the city and was doing everything it could to Red-bait and race-bait the union out of existence. The overwhelming prob-lems facing that heroic band of workers and organizers found me out of my political depth, but I welcomed the chance to try to help; and besides, no one else appeared to have all the answers either. I always returned to Chapel Hill with a feeling of refreshment and renewal after meeting with the tobacco workers' remarkable leaders.

I believed passionately that the fight to organize and maintain trade unions was near the heart of what the movement for socialism was all about, and I was forever trying to bring the working-class struggle closer to the student Communists. During the summer of 1947 I arranged to have a whole truck-load of students attend a union rally in Winston-Salem in the course of a thirty-nine-day strike against R. J. Reynolds Tobacco Company. At the rally, Paul Robeson sang to more than twelve thousand people jammed in and around a school yard in a Negro community. Again I was able to observe and feel the astounding human pride which that amazing artist could arouse in his listeners. As Robeson held the incredibly low final note of "Water Boy" like a pedal point on a great organ, a Negro worker next to me stood openmouthed and unbreathing until the sound died away; then he slapped his knee in ecstasy, shouting out, "Gah-ahd DAMN!" while tears coursed down his face. The students returned to Chapel Hill awed and exalted.

On other occasions I accompanied Sam to cities where there were organized shops in which the Party had forces and influence: furniture, leather, and textile. Sometimes I would go alone to High Point to see Esther, Willie, and other old friends. When I had first returned to the mill village after the war, the place had been unrecognizable. The union was still strong, real wages had increased dramatically, and the workers had climbed out of the poverty they had known before the war. Esther and most of the other workers had bought their houses from the company and were rebuilding and refurnishing them as fast as postwar consumer goods became available. Once the workers became homeowners, their individuality began to show in their houses, and the village lost the look of regimented uniformity it had once had.

Visiting the village filled me with nostalgia; I recalled my life there: its dedication and simplicity, the love, friendship, and joy I had known. Life had seemed cleaner, more honest, the future more secure. And even with all the poverty and the backbreaking factory work, I had been more at peace with myself.

By the middle of 1947 it was becoming increasingly difficult to be an American Communist. In the spring of 1946 I had listened with dismay to Churchill's Fulton, Missouri, speech as marking the end of the great alliance that had defeated Fascism and as sounding the prelude to the cold war. I had heard it on the very radio in my in-laws' kitchen on which I had listened to Churchill proclaim Britain's support of the Soviet Union at the beginning of the Nazi invasion in 1941. In 1947 the Truman Doctrine began the policy of "containment" of Communism. The Party's response was, of course, to put the blame for the cold war entirely on the Truman administration and to defend without exception Stalin's every aggressive or acquisitive act. Accordingly, anti-Communist feeling was on the rise and showed itself in innumerable ways. For example, my mail was frequently opened and clumsily resealed; the large weekly bundle of the *Worker* I received was invariably torn open and retied with string; neighbors reported being questioned about Sylvia and me by the FBI. In the press, editorial denunciations of Communism and Communists became more frequent and more intemperate.

Henry Wallace, the former vice-president and Truman's secretary of commerce, was widely revered by liberals. He opposed the cold war and advocated peaceful coexistence with the Soviet Union. When he resigned from the cabinet in protest against Truman's foreign policy, the Southern Conference for Human Welfare sponsored a speaking tour of the South for him. Although most Democrats then in office avoided him, most liberal Democrats were anxious to show their support. Dr. Frank Graham, as president of the university, wanted to honor Wallace as he passed through Chapel Hill en route to a major address in Raleigh. To avoid the attacks from conservative politicians around the state which would have occurred if the university had officially welcomed Wallace, Graham called me to his office and asked me to have the student chapter of the Southern Conference sponsor a reception for Wallace which he would attend, unofficially, as an old friend. He left all of the arrangements to me, saying, "He is a dear friend. I know I can count on you."

I supervised the arrangements, and the reception came off so much to the satisfaction of Graham that he invited me to drive with him and Wallace to Raleigh, where they were to have dinner at Josephus Daniels's home. For forty-five minutes I had the pleasure of their company while they reminisced about mutual friends and discussed the current pressures on liberals—the gracious Dr. Frank occasionally drawing me into the conversation.

That night, in the civic auditorium where Wallace addressed an unsegregated audience of over three thousand (picketed by organized racists), I was invited to sit on the stage next to Josephus Daniels, then eighty-five, who reminded me of some comments I had made at the age of four about his false teeth. Seated nearby was a lovely North Carolinian, the movie star Ava Gardner, who was visiting her sister in Smithfield. She was even more beautiful close-up than on the screen, and I was so entranced that I had to read the papers the next morning to find out exactly what it was that Henry Wallace had said.

A delegation of some thirty strikers from the Reynolds Tobacco (Camel Cigarette) union in Winston-Salem, wishing to present their case to Wallace, were waiting backstage after his address ended to meet him. I told Ava Gardner they were there and asked if she would like to meet them. "I'd *love* to!" she said. I took her backstage and introduced her to each striker by name. She had a firm handshake and some words of encouragement for each one, and after meeting them all and being much impressed by their purposeful dignity, she delighted them while standing in their midst by asking, "Does anyone have a cigarette? *Anything* but a Camel will do."

Meanwhile, Wallace was still swamped with well-wishers on the stage, and some university students were waiting in the auditorium to give me a ride back to Chapel Hill with them. A lovely, nubile young woman mounted the stage to look for me. As she stood on tiptoe trying to see where I might be, old Josephus Daniels tottered over to her and pinched her firmly on the behind.

That same young woman, Mary-Louise ("Lia") Huse, daughter of my favorite professor, became Richard's bride in August, and to the scandal of the academic community and the Episcopal rector, I, whose reputation had grown steadily redder, was the best man. At the wedding reception I was in fancy dress and feeling conspicuous and thoroughly useless when Phillips Russell, the university's professor of journalism and my friend for years, shouted across the crowded drawing room, "Hello Junius, you old Bolshevik! You don't *look* like a Bolshevik!"

Richard had acquired a master's degree as well as a bride and left Chapel Hill, creating a large hole in my life.

I had by then completed my undergraduate work and had received my B.A. degree in comparative literature. I had begun my graduate work without a pause, having decided on history as my discipline. I thought I could make myself more useful politically by deepening my understanding of American history of the last century and, more particularly, of southern history since the Civil War. Graduate work was proving far more demanding than my academic work up until then, and I had been under great pressure for time because of my growing Party and other political commitments.

Late in the summer I was shocked to hear on the radio that I had been named before the House Un-American Activities Committee as the leader of the Communists in Chapel Hill. Local 22 of the Food and Tobacco Workers Union in Winston-Salem had won its strike; and the company had apparently found the time opportune to have Ann Mathews, an informer, a minor member of the union staff, and a Party member, "tell all" before the committee. The main purpose of her testimony was to air her claim that Local 22 was dominated by the Communist Party; the information about me had probably been thrown in as an extra. When questioned by reporters, I refused to confirm or deny her statement, saying that in the pervasive political climate it was becoming an honor to be called a Communist and that it put me in good company. The incident blew over quickly as far as I was concerned. It seemed to have no appreciable effect on me in Chapel Hill, although it greatly disturbed my mother.

The cold war atmosphere was rising inexorably, and the hysteria against domestic Communists kept pace with it. I began to think that it might, in a very small way, help to stem that tide locally if I, a respectable married veteran, a member of a well-known family, and a generally reputable person, came forward as a "Communist sympathizer" to defend Communism and to speak my beliefs more frankly. I discussed the matter with Sylvia, who didn't care for the idea, considering it much like putting one's hand into a buzz saw. She also reminded me of my resolution to stay out of Party leadership and stick to my studies, to which my reply was that the Party was in an unparalleled crisis that could not have been foreseen.

Before I could discuss my idea with Nat and Sam, they exhorted me on

The authors. Best man Scales and bridegroom
Nickson, 1947 (Photo by Lia Nickson)

behalf of the national office to speak out openly as the head of the Communist Party in Chapel Hill. Despite my serious misgivings about my abilities as an official public spokesman, my great regrets at what I thought might be the end of my academic career, and the frenzied objections of my mother and the vigorous ones of my wife and others, I decided to take the dread step. I would then be able to speak without the feeling of duplicity I'd felt when I concealed my affiliation. I would also be able to draw fire away from my comrades, debate my opponents openly, and perhaps humanize the image of a Communist. After all, if the national leadership of the Party, as well as Nat and Sam, felt that I should become an open Communist, there was little else to discuss. The Party came first.

Before I made any plans, I attended an enlarged board meeting of the Committee for North Carolina. Certain that my public announcement of my Communist Party membership would cause the CNC some embarrassment because of my prominence in it, I hoped to lessen the harm by giving the organization a chance to decide what to do in advance of my action; especially, as a courtesy, I wanted to tell my colleagues of my intent rather than have them learn of it when it became news.

Before the meeting I drew aside Mary Price, the executive secretary, told her of my plans, and asked for a point of personal privilege near the end of the agenda. Though considerably shocked, she approved of my plans for telling the membership and asked if I intended to resign from the executive committee. I replied that I did not, at least not until it had been discussed and I saw that that was the desire of the meeting. The Southern Conference had had occasional Communist members in prominent local positions since its inception; indeed, the Party had played some minor role in its creation. There had been at that time tacit agreement that in the South, where reaction was so powerfully entrenched, there was no justification for barring any individual or group opposing reaction and supporting the Southern Conference program. Moreover, I did not want to resign precipitately, thereby implying that a Communist had no right to a position he had earned.

I expected considerable hostility, especially from the representatives of the Textile Workers Union of America, CIO, my old union in High Point, whose social-democratic leadership had been flirting with the CNC while making its full participation conditional, more or less, on the barring of Communists. When my point on the agenda was reached, I said that I viewed the intensifying cold war and the resulting attacks on American Communists with alarm, as symptomatic of a dangerously repressive political climate; that I had been a Communist for many years and saw in Communism the hope of a better future for everyone; that I was going to make my position public very soon, in the hope that I could, in a small way, answer some of the attacks on Communism;

and that, though I knew most of them disagreed with me, because of our long and friendly association I wanted them to hear about my plans from me rather than through the press or radio.

There was a stunned reaction. Then a woman TWUA representative who had known me most of my life denounced me bitterly and sarcastically. Non-Communists and even anti-Communists rose in my defense. The meeting ended in confusion and hostility, which later led to an open split, subsequent departures by many liberals, formation of an ADA (Americans for Democratic Action) organization largely concerned with attacking liberals less anti-Communist than its own members, and ultimately a narrowed SCHW which remained in the hands of the left wing and formed the framework for the Progressive Party in 1948.

For me the meeting led to some painful discoveries. The hatred and fear of Communism, even in so liberal an organization, was far greater than I'd imagined. Some who had liked and respected me as a "left-winger" hated me as a Communist. And I did not then understand why. I found that my candor caused more rage than reflection among my anti-Communist colleagues; they were unsure whether they were angrier at me for being a Communist or for telling them that I was one. Far from praising me for my present frankness, they condemned me for my past "deception"—for not having revealed my beliefs before.

In the general concern over the future of the organization there seemed to be a widespread wish among most foes and some friends that I would disintegrate, cease to be, cease to have been, even though I resigned from the executive committee. Thus I received a bitter foretaste of what would be the loneliness and isolation of a Communist leader during a prolonged period of anti-Communist hysteria alongside incredibly inept Communist tactics.

At the end of October 1947, a student committee prepared a Party leaflet concerning the inflationary prices of the time, titled "The Lowdown on High Prices," which was to have been issued under the name of the Student Section of the Communist Party of North Carolina. Sam's Party post office box in Winston-Salem was the return address.

I rarely took any part in the writing of Party leaflets or statements for which I was responsible. In part, I held back because I was gun-shy at putting any of my individuality into a Party document, having seen the printed utterances of numerous figures on the left dissected and used to illustrate their inmost hidden ideological sins. But mainly I felt inadequate at writing about Party policy. Then, and later, I was continually calling on those more gifted to help me formulate statements or write speeches.

On this occasion, however, I read the leaflet, approved it, and when the stencil was being cut, had the typist put at the bottom "Communist Party of Chapel Hill," and under it the inconspicuous lines, "Junius Scales, Chairman, P.O. Box 62, Chapel Hill, N.C." About a thousand leaflets were run off, and on the night of October 28 they were distributed in public places, on the campus, and through the mail.

The fateful step taken, I bade an unwitting farewell to my own and my family's privacy and peace of mind.

12

Debut and Debacle

n the spring of 1948, half a year later, I could look back with some detachment on what had at the time seemed a cataclysmic event. Reaction to the leaflet had been swift. Besieged for comment by the press, I issued a heartfelt statement with the following conclusion:

> I have had an opportunity of meeting many outstanding Communists, and I can say from long experience and close association that the Communists are the most human, the most principled, the most courageous, the most selfless people I have ever known.
>
> I am proud to be a member of a party which is democratic both in its own structure and in its outlook. As a southerner, I am especially glad to belong to the only organization which fights for the full and complete equality of the Negro people.
>
> Finally, I am glad that my party's patriotism expresses itself, not in hostility toward other countries, not in slavish veneration of the economic status quo, but in the practical struggle for the present needs and future welfare of the American people.

Most of the state press made much of the story, and a few papers printed the statement; some used banner headlines; all identified me as the son of a prominent Greensboro banker—one distinction my father had never had. The *Daily Tar Heel* was apparently thunderstruck at first; then it drizzled along fatuously day after day with columns, stories, and editorials seemingly designed to please the university's trustees and the ever-watchful state legislators. After five days a single issue of the student newspaper reported my attendance (top of the front page) at an International Relations Club meeting with a large audience "made tense by his presence," where I denounced the government's backing of Fascist regimes. The letter column contained a two-column "Open Reply to Scales," an enraged, all-too-prophetic threat to withdraw the Bill of Rights where Communists were concerned. Ironically, the lead editorial was a sympathetic if patronizing one on the death at sixty-nine of "Uncle George," a Negro janitor of thirty-five years' standing at the university, often exploited at pre-football-game pep rallies. Uncle George, though the editors were unaware of it, had long been an organizer and leader of a secret university janitors' union and a proud and active member of the Communist Party of Chapel Hill. On the same day the editorial was published, at a large funeral in a Negro church I led the gathering in the final prayer over the casket of my friend and comrade.

My new status as an admitted Communist appeared to have changed little in my relationship with those around me. I acted the same toward students, faculty, and townspeople, and their behavior, to my face, was much the same. My former high school acquaintances, except for one or two, still greeted me cordially and would stop on the street to chat (though they rarely talked politics); the window men in the post office, although they must have known that the FBI was opening my mail, addressed me by my first name as they had when I was a teenager; student acquaintances were generally cordial, although there was some recognition that I had become a celebrity; a few professors were cool or hostile, but others were friendlier than before. On balance, Chapel Hill took its first public Communist in its stride with little noticeable perturbation.

There were, however, some signs of a feeling of shock in the town, as though I had virtually declared war on my own community by revealing my Communist affiliation. The hostility I encountered ranged from intense ideological disagreement in some cases to ugly, simpleminded bigotry in a good many others. One day in the barbershop where I had had my hair cut over a period of a dozen years, a former high school chum who had ingeniously evaded the draft until the war was nearly over began loudly baiting me, questioning my loyalty to the United States because I thought so highly of the Soviet Union. All conversation ceased as the barbers and other customers listened, while I looked silently back at my denouncer; I could see my own barber in the double mirrors frantically signaling the fellow to be quiet. When my haircut was finished, I paid, tipped, and thanked my barber and then walked over to my antagonist and said softly, "My patriotism is as strong as yours, M——. And so is my war record." I left the silent shop, waited outside, confronted that ex-schoolmate, and received an apology from him. But although we shook hands, there was no sign of any reduction of his animosity.

Sylvia and I, sensing that pressures relating to my new status were begin-ning to weigh on her parents, decided to move from their house. Her father had bought two three-room mill houses adjacent to each other in Carrboro, about a mile farther west of the campus. He had them nicely spruced up, modernized, and painted, thereby acquiring his daughter and son-in-law as tenants for one of them; the house next door was rented to student friends of ours. With odds and ends of furniture, great ingenuity on Sylvia's part, and my large collection of books and records, we soon made the place look pleas-ant and hospitable.

My mother drove over to offer her assistance and her approval. She told me that my friends Ivo and Imre, still in Italy, had at last been cleared to come to the United States. But I had concluded from some cryptic correspondence from them to my mother that the police in Rome had been questioning them closely about their friendship with me. Therefore, when they did arrive in the United States, although my mother vouched for them and guaranteed their maintenance should they need it, I dared not communicate with them lest I be the cause of their deportation.

Life in graduate school went on much as before, with little antagonism from professors or students. Professor M. B. Garrett, who had known me for years and had once been my next-door neighbor, invited me into his office, where we talked for hours. The old man was concerned with my attitude toward "violent revolution"; I, who had never seriously conceived of such a thing happening in the United States, told him quite truthfully that I could see no advantage in achieving power by a coup d'etat, that power must have majority support behind it or become tyranny. The professor was pleased and suggested that I read several books, which he listed, on the Russian Revolu-tion; unfortunately, I never got around to doing so.

Another of my professors, R. D. W. Connor, who had been the first na-tional archivist, appointed by FDR, was also concerned about me and invited me into his office after a class session for a talk. Connor, then nearly seventy, had been a good friend of my father's and wanted to know what motivated the son of A. M. Scales to become a Communist. I told him that there were four main things: fear of war and Fascism; the plight of Negroes, especially in the South; the helpless, unorganized condition of most workers; and the belief that socialist redistribution of the wealth would be the basis of the brotherhood of man. These things were understandable, the professor thought, but how was my idea of justice to be attained? I repeated much of what I had told Professor Garrett, and Connor smiled. "I wish you would *write* your propa-ganda the way you talk to me instead of using that terrible jargon," he said. I assured him that I delegated the writing of Party material, but I could in no way explain why Party statements and leaflets, national or local, were so often strident, smug, and loaded with clichés. I then got Connor to talking about Roosevelt and listened delightedly to glowing reminiscences about him until we both realized that it had got dark outside and that we had talked away the afternoon.

In the Party there had been some changes. Sam Hall, returning to his native Alabama to lead the Party there, was replaced by a northerner, Eugene Morse, a tall, lean, handsome, thirty-eight-year-old veteran of the Abraham Lincoln Battalion in Spain and of the army in World War II. Long divorced, and most attractive to women, he never allowed his personal affairs to interfere with his responsibilities in the district, living a life almost monastic in its asceticism in between his occasional trips to New York. He was an experienced Party organizer and had also worked for a long time as a seaman and had been an activist in the National Maritime Union. Alongside the aura of inner strength that radiated from him, one of the notable things about Gene was that he experienced a genuine sense of discovery whenever he met a new comrade, as though he had found gold on his doorstep. He liked to sit and talk with him or her privately for three-quarters of an hour or so. Usually, after such a talk with Gene, comrades felt they had acquired a close, trustworthy friend who understood them and cared about them—and they were right. In only a few months he had gained the confidence of the membership and had helped many of his comrades perform beyond their usual capacities.

Gene and I became friends at once, and by the spring of 1948 had come to know each other so well that each knew what the other was thinking before he spoke his thoughts. Early in 1948 Gene proposed to the district committee that I be made district chairman of the Party, to be the number-two leader and the public spokesman. The district committee agreed, but I had serious misgivings and regaled Gene far into a night with a catalog of my inadequacies. "I know," was Gene's response. "We'll work on 'em."

The end of 1947 probably marked the peak of the Party's membership and influence in Chapel Hill and the Carolinas. In Eastern Europe the Soviet Union was tightening its control over the "New Democracies" and responding pugnaciously to the cold war moves of the West. In Western Europe the French and Italian Communist parties were leading big strike movements, and it seemed possible that one or the other might either take power or win a place in government. The American Party's leadership, perhaps feeling that great things were expected of Communist parties everywhere, decided to gamble on making a big advance by participating in the setting up of what they hoped would ultimately be a farmer-labor party built around the presidential candidacy of Henry Wallace.

The split Southern Conference for Human Welfare was being transformed, under the leadership of Clark Foreman, into the framework for the Wallace campaign in the South. The Party pushed for and achieved the dissolution of the Southern Negro Youth Congress in order to concentrate all its forces on the building of the Progressive Party—or the PP, as it was often called. In North Carolina a substantial petition campaign was necessary to get the PP on the ballot: ten thousand bona fide signatures. The Communist Party had the organized forces to achieve such a goal, and Gene Morse and I proceeded to make them available to the PP. In Chapel Hill the Southern Conference club, transforming itself into a Wallace-for-President club even before the founding convention of the PP in January, soon attracted strong support.

By January, Wallace's candidacy was taken quite seriously in North Carolina. The *Charlotte News,* for instance, ran a presidential popularity poll which showed, in that Republican area, Wallace and Eisenhower as the neck-and-neck popular favorites, far ahead of Truman and Dewey. From then on, however, Wallace's support declined, owing largely to popular identification of him with the Soviet Union and the Communists, racist attacks on him, organized disruption of his campaign, the strong traditional ties of voters to the two major parties, and the last-minute liberalization of the Truman administration.

I attended the PP founding convention as a private observer, partly to demonstrate that Communists were not barred and partly to see what kind of people would come. I spent much time with Esther Gillen, who, to my delight, had come from High Point. I was surprised to see so many new faces from every walk of life who had been moved to political activity by Henry Wallace's concern for peace, his New Deal aura, and his courage in demanding unsegregated audiences for his meetings in the South. It seemed to me that for the first time the Party was getting in touch with real grass-roots sections of the population in meaningful numbers. I dared to hope that the American Party was going to achieve the sort of "united front" that some of the European parties had secured in the thirties.

Scarcely a month later, however, the Communists in Czechoslovakia repudiated their united front with the forces represented by Benes and Masaryk and took power, isolating Benes and (as I was to learn many years later) probably murdering the more vigorous Masaryk. I, believing *Daily Worker* stories of treachery and intrigue, vigorously defended the Communist action in a campus debate. Having done my homework thoroughly, I sounded far more knowledgeable than my opponents, and of course I thought I was. But in June, when my particular hero, Tito, was expelled from the Cominform and denounced as the ultimate in evil, I had a few (unspoken) fears for some months that Stalin, all-knowing and peerless leader that he was, just might have stumbled somewhere.

As the summer approached, the optimism with which the Party members nationally had viewed the PP began to give way to some concern. There was no consequential farmer support in sight; the AFL unions and the right-led and center-led unions in the CIO clearly were not going to back Wallace. In the left-led CIO unions, there were bitter struggles between the Party leadership and Communist union leaders, the latter growing fearful that support for Wallace would antagonize their memberships and further isolate them within the CIO. Most adopted an it's-up-to-the-membership stance; the tobacco workers and furniture workers were among a handful of unions which endorsed Wallace. Among the Negro people there was great appreciation of Wallace's advanced position on Negro rights, but no clear indication that the Negro *vote* would go to Wallace.

Despite such warning signs, the Party began pouring its people into the PP to provide the forces to do the legwork of organizing the new party and, in North Carolina, of getting it on the ballot. Scores of Communist students devoted their summer to the exhausting work of canvassing industrial residential areas in teams, soliciting signatures on petitions. A great many non-Communist youths joined them, and dozens of PP volunteers from outside the state contributed their services. As the summer advanced, the young people rapidly developed campaigning technique and worked tirelessly and effectively.

I had a distressing sense of being outside the great activity, in which even Sylvia could participate freely, while I, as the public Party figure, was forced to remain on the sidelines. I watched the work with a critical eye and urged my comrades to list likely prospects they encountered for involvement in future projects.

Another of my activities that spring and summer was recording a number of radio speeches which I would then have played on leading stations from one end of the state to the other. The costs were modest and the response considerable, so Gene considered the money well invested. Gene was a particularly good money raiser (which I was not) and had built up a special fund, contributed by relatively comfortable Party members and some well-to-do sympathizers, to enable the Party to speak in its own name.

One of my obligations was to appear almost weekly, on or off campus, to address groups or to participate in debates or panel discussions. I was particularly in demand with church groups, appearing before the Baptist Young People's Union (BYPU) three or four times in one academic year. I challenged the BYPU members to outdo the Communist Party in working for the brotherhood of man, saying that if they did, I would leave the Party and join up with them. Although I was not a good speaker, being much too tense and self-conscious in prepared speeches, the give-and-take of discussion or question periods relaxed me and improved my effectiveness.

I was preoccupied with preparations for the district Party convention, which was to be attended by John Gates, editor of the *Daily Worker* and the *Worker* and a member of the Party's national committee. One day, while discussing places in which to hold the convention, Gene told me that he had asked the national office to relieve him of his assignment in the district. I was crushed by his announcement. Gene explained that he had only agreed to the assignment in the first place as an interim measure; that he had already stayed longer than he intended because of the feeling he had for the people of the district; that he had just turned thirty-nine and needed some time out to assess himself and think about where he was going; and that he would always stay in close touch with me wherever he went. Gene said that Bernie Friedland, the man who would replace him, had lots of trade union experience, was Jewish (from the Williamsburg area of Brooklyn), and was a very good man.

My academic work, meanwhile, was in disarray. I had completed most of the courses necessary for my master's degree, except for two or three on which I had taken "incomplete" grades under the pressure of events. I had planned to turn in required papers to the professors concerned within the allotted year's time and to receive credit for the courses. But the year was about to run out on two courses, and I had no time to spend on completing them. I had also reached an impasse with the History Department on the subject for my thesis. I wanted to write about the 1912 Debs presidential campaign, including a study of the state's Socialist Party of the time. Feeling a keen interest in those I considered to be my political antecedents, I hoped to base my thesis partly on a series of tape- or wire-recorded interviews with a dozen or so surviving Socialists of that period. Several of them had extensive files of letters, literature, and clippings which they had offered to me, and I believed that I could bring the period and the Socialists to life. Some of my professors, apparently through fear of being accused of giving aid and comfort to Communism, rejected the topic as "controversial," without giving me any further reason or suggesting any alternative. One professor-friend told me that several of his colleagues thought that my topic would fill a void in North Carolina history and could be of unique value. He also said that the university's board of trustees was anxious to get me out of graduate school, that they had been sniffing around several times to check on my status, and that my own brother-in-law, a leading member of the board, had said on learning of my incompletes, "We won't need to force him out; those incompletes will turn to Fs after a year; and if he's too busy to finish them, he'll automatically flunk out and solve our problem."

I decided to bow to the futility of my situation and give up my academic career. Shortly afterward, Gene proposed to the district committee that I be put on the Party payroll, and I was hired at a salary of twenty dollars a week.

Party members had never been so eager or so active. Morale was high, for most of them felt they were playing a part in history, helping along the emergence of a new party that would ultimately unite the working people of the United States. A nominating convention of the PP in the spring and a tour by Paul Robeson in June had been inspiring events. But in the struggle to get signatures for the ballot petitions, the PP workers early encountered bitter redneck hostility on local levels, ranging from harassment by deputy sheriffs to tire slashings by young toughs. The harassment appeared to be systematic and coordinated, and the PP workers had little doubt that the Democratic Party machine, at one level or another, was directing it.

At the end of July the campaigners were shocked by screaming headlines announcing that Mary Price, the North Carolina PP chairman and candidate for governor, had been accused before a Senate committee of aiding a self-proclaimed Russian spy. Elizabeth Bentley, while she was destroying the career of William Remington, a young Commerce Department official, said that she had riffled through Walter Lippmann's personal files looking for documents to give the Russians, abetted by Mary Price, Lippmann's then secretary. Her testimony was interrupted by Senator Clyde Hoey (Democrat of North Carolina), who pointed out with considerable satisfaction that Mary Price headed the Progressive Party in North Carolina. The accusation came to nothing, and later it occurred to many that had the charge been true, documents in Lippmann's office files would not likely have been of much interest to the Russians. But the espionage headlines had their effect, contributing to suspicion that the PP was under the control of the Communist Party.

That suspicion was only partially substantiated by fact. Although the Party had supplied most of the organized forces to launch the PP and get it on the ballot, Henry Wallace's dislike and distrust of Communists was always evidenced through his top aides. Party forces, therefore, had to walk a tightrope in order not to antagonize PP leaders devoted to Wallace or to alienate, through internal squabbling, the numerous new, independent people whose active participation the Communists wanted above everything else. While the Communists' organizational know-how and drive were useful and even necessary to the PP, and thus gave Party members considerable influence, they could have controlled the PP only at the cost of total isolation. They were far from having everything their own way—at least before election day.

It was probably because of events beyond its control that so much of the PP's early strength was undermined. For example, Wallace believed that the dominance of hard-line cold warriors in the U.S. government was the sole reason for the cold war and that a more farsighted and liberal administration could reach a quick accord with the Soviet Union. But the events in Eastern Europe in 1948 suggested that the cold war, no matter who had the initial responsibility, was being exacerbated by both sides and that Wallace's diagnosis was not valid. Truman's belated liberal posture toward labor and Negroes, especially his desegregation of the armed forces, and his gestures toward easing the cold war proved effective and lured away many Progressive votes. All in all, there was an increasing sense in the PP as the summer wore on that its base of support was slowly shrinking. Then the Department of Justice, probably to answer the Republican charge of being "soft on Communism," indicted the twelve top Party leaders under the Smith Act, accusing them of "conspiring to teach and advocate the violent overthrow" of the government.

I was meantime preparing for the Party convention. Keeping the number of delegates quite small (a mere twenty) to avoid an unwieldy gathering, I fixed on our house as the meeting place, largely because I thought the FBI would consider it the least likely spot. John Gates, representing the national committee, and Bernie, the district organizer-to-be, arrived from New York. On the big day everything went smoothly except for the general consternation caused by a student delegate who advocated preparations for leading the workers to "armed struggle"—a position much like that of Preacher and Betty a year before. The delegates and Gates were amazed and incensed by such craziness; the student was later expelled from the Party on my initiative.

Toward the close of the convention, Gene announced his departure (to the great distress and even the tears of those who had not already known it) and received some moving, spontaneous tributes from the delegates; John Gates thanked him, on behalf of the national committee, for his service in the Carolinas and then introduced Bernie, recommending him as the national committee's proposal for district organizer. Bernie, quite tense, spoke briefly but made a most favorable impression. Then the convention elected a new district committee, approved Bernie as district organizer, renamed me as district chairman, thanked the national committee for sending down Comrade Gates, and adjourned.

Gene was able to visit Carrboro again a few days later to say goodbye to Sylvia and me, and then he headed straight for New York. Three days later I received a telegram from the Party's general secretary: "GENE MORSE DIED TODAY. SPECIAL DELIVERY LETTER FOLLOWS—EUGENE DENNIS." Bernie, arriving with his wife, Bea, at almost the same time as the telegram, found me distraught and inconsolable. Dennis's letter arrived the next morning. Gene had gone to the national office, spent a day or so there, and said he was worn out and would like to go to Camp Unity in upstate New York for a few days. He was told to stay as long as he liked as the Party's guest. He arrived there in the afternoon, very overheated, and decided to go for a swim before checking in. He dived in the water and didn't come up; when a life-guard pulled him out a minute later, there was no heartbeat.

An hour behind the letter a second telegram said, "COME TO GENE'S FUNERAL DAY AFTER TOMORROW AT NATIONAL OFFICE EXPENSE— GENE DENNIS."

Henry Wallace was just then beginning a campaign tour through the South starting in Norfolk, Virginia. After stops in Richmond and Suffolk, he would proceed to Durham for a meeting that night in the local armory. The tour was conspicuously flouting segregation laws and customs, and I'd been warned that trouble was being planned. I felt that I must be present. That, I thought, would be Bernie's and Bea's introduction to the Southland. As Sylvia and I walked with them to the armory, we passed an alley in which a large black Lincoln sedan was parked; from it some well-dressed men were handing out money and placards to a group of twenty or so youths. The placards, on long sticks, bore such slogans as "Send Wallace Back to Russia," "Wallace—The Hitler of Today," and "We Don't Have Race Problems Here."

When we reached the armory, a crowd of fifteen hundred or so, approximately half Negro and half white, had already assembled; they were singing and in high spirits, and the seating was totally unsegregated. Those same young toughs, with their signs, burst in screaming and shouting. A melee ensued and the youths were ejected, considerably the worse for their invasion. Minutes later a side door suddenly crashed open, dramatically revealing a National Guard sergeant with a drawn .45, followed closely by several policemen and Henry Wallace. There was a tremendous, emotional ovation, and finally Wallace began to speak. In a few minutes the toughs, augmented by other local riffraff, pushed their way into the rear of the building, shouting, "Communist! Communist!" At the same time they set off several firecrackers in rapid succession, so that people up front thought they were shooting. After scoring several near misses with eggs thrown at the candidate, they once again were ejected, and Wallace was able to finish his speech. That same corps of twenty paid disrupters followed Wallace throughout the state for the remainder of his tour; PP workers grew to know them so well that they had a nickname for each one.

Sylvia, Bea, Bernie, and I had to catch a train in Raleigh to get to Gene's funeral, so we left as soon as the meeting was over—and we were fortunate. Many who were slow to leave had to fight for their lives against the hoodlum corps, white cab drivers, and assorted street characters who struck at them with clubs, stones, and knives, while the Durham police looked on impassively. Several from the audience had to be repaired extensively in local hospitals.

In New York the next day I went to the national office. There, on the ninth floor, exhausted, dejected, and miserable looking, I was met by Eugene Dennis. He put his arm around my shoulders, patted my arm sympathetically, tried to speak, choked out, "I'm glad you could come!" and retreated to his office wiping his eyes.

The next morning the funeral was held in a large memorial chapel in midtown Manhattan. Gene had no family—he had been raised by Catholics in a foster home—so the Party itself took charge of the farewell to one who was truly its devoted son and who, in his short life, had reflected much credit on it and had done many a good work in its name. For forty minutes before the ceremony an honor guard of four at the coffin was changed every two minutes. It consisted of veterans of World War II and the Abraham Lincoln Battalion; members of the national committee, including John Gates, Henry Winston, and Gene Dennis, and many other Party celebrities. The service consisted of tributes from four friends: Carl Vedro and Charles Loman, Brooklyn Party leaders; Blackie Myers, a former National Maritime Union leader; and me. In the rear of the hall, sobbing brokenhearted and alone, sat an extraordinarily beautiful woman in her mid-twenties, wearing an exquisitely tailored black dress and a heavy veil. She was well known to me; I had spent two evenings with her and Gene on my last trip to New York. Besides being beautiful, she was intelligent, socially conscious, and prominent in the *Social Register;* Gene had loved her to distraction, but thinking he could never bridge the differences in background, life-style, or values, he had almost despaired of marrying her.

Forty miles out on Long Island, in a cemetery where space seemed to be measured in centimeters, fifty people, including the woman in black, a friend of Gene's since childhood named Jerry, and me, watched the coffin lowered into the ground near a high hedge alive with small birds. At least one of those mourners would remember that grave and the vibrant radiance of the one who filled it as long as he lived.

In the remaining two months before election day, the PP campaigners in North Carolina labored ever harder, with a growing sense of frustration. Wallace's tour through the state was met everywhere with a combination of enthusiasm, fear, and violence. Some campaign stops took place under siege conditions, especially when the planners of violence had time for advance preparations. Eggs were thrown at Wallace; the same, or similar, tired placards were produced for newspaper photographers; campaign workers (including young specimens of "southern white womanhood") were attacked and threatened; their cars were vandalized; often the local newspaper accounts were grossly distorted.

After the tour was over, campaigners began encountering among liberal voters such attitudes as "Dewey's a sure disaster; Wallace is fine, but he ain't gonna make it; Truman ain't much, but you *can* live with him." As election day approached, many PP workers hoped blindly for a vote of 5 to 10 percent.

Bernie, settling in Chapel Hill with Bea, found himself in the midst of a complex weave of activity and problems. The Party's principal labor base, Local 22 in Winston-Salem, had no contract with Reynolds Tobacco; and the company had shrewdly cut the number of Negro workers to increase the proportion of whites; pressures (both segregationist and Red-baiting) on the white workers to withdraw from the union had so intensified as to make the local mostly Negro. There were severe problems in other left-led unions around the state, especially the locals of the Negro tobacco stemmers in eastern North and South Carolina. Bernie began an endless series of trips to Winston-Salem and elsewhere, usually taking me with him.

On election day Bernie assessed the prospects somberly, agreeing, "If the PP doesn't get 5 percent of the vote, we're in a bad way." Sylvia and I were invited to his house for dinner and to listen to election returns. When the radio reports by eleven o'clock showed a PP vote of about 1 percent nationally, and even less in North Carolina, Bernie, a near teetotaler, produced a bottle of scotch and said to me, who had scarcely tasted alcohol since the war, "I think we'd better have a drink."

13

Civil Rights and
Union Votes

The Progressive Party debacle left the Communist Party staggered and unable to make much sense of the election results or to provide answers to the question "Where do we go from here?" The Communists had hoped, in joining the PP movement, to help find a way out of isolation by establishing close working relations with the fresh, independent forces in the PP and winning their confidence. Ironically, after the election rout, the Party forces and the independent PP members were equally isolated; they found themselves politically, socially, and economically victimized in their communities, the whites widely considered to be "Commies," "nigger-lovers," or both; the Negroes judged to have strayed off the true path and to be unreliable guides. Many who had received their political baptism in the PP and had been enthusiastic a few months earlier lost interest in politics, or simply licked their wounds in seclusion. The Communists, familiar with defeat and accustomed to reacting to it in a disciplined way, tried not to show their demoralization.

But demoralization there was. In the absence of a penetrating analysis of the Party's policies, there was a turning inward in the Party, a seeking of the causes of defeat within one's comrades and oneself. I was a case in point. My first thought was whether, if I had been a more aggressive or inspirational leader, things might have gone better in the Carolinas. In the period following the election, I raked over all my deficiencies. In lonely isolation, I yet hoped, on the positive side, that I had begun to think in organizational terms about what was involved when a policy was adopted or a campaign undertaken—to consider and plan all the myriad things that must be done before anyone in the

Party did anything. That was a result of Gene's tutelage and Bernie's fresh example.

But in all the political and trade union problems I faced in the district I saw single trees, not the forest; elements of a problem, not the whole problem in its interrelations. I didn't think I was unintelligent, just not *political*. I knew I was expected to lead the Party in the district eventually, to be the district organizer, but I felt unworthy of the job. I was too unsure of my political stance; on many important matters my views would swing one way and another, depending on the point of view I had last encountered.

I had long considered that there was in the district a much abler, more talented potential DO than I, who had far more political experience and all the desirable qualities I lacked. That was my old friend Ron who had gone to the Party school with me. Ron, a southerner, was married, had children, and had been working effectively as a trade union organizer since the war. I thought the matter over and decided to visit him privately and tell him my thoughts. When I did, he adroitly changed the subject, and it was never mentioned between us again. Though I felt that he was not meeting his Party obligations, I realized that I was inextricably stuck with the job of Party leader-in-training and that I might as well make the best of it.

In the past I had sometimes felt that I was partly outside my job, that I was only partly engaged in the demands and challenges of my duties. I would go with Bernie to Winston-Salem, sit in long meetings with union comrades, listen to the complex problems, and think in distress, "My God, these questions are too important and too crucial to too many people. What the hell do *I* know about what Local 22 should do about its relations with the state CIO?" Then I would feel a sense of panic, lose the thread of the discussion, and come to with a jolt, hoping that Bernie knew what *he* was doing.

Fortunately, Bernie usually did know what he was doing and proved it again and again, brilliantly.

The problems Bernie grappled with in Winston-Salem derived from one of the outstanding organizing initiatives undertaken by Communist and left-wing forces in the CIO. Beginning in 1942, the CIO's catchall cannery and agricultural union, known as UCAPAWA (later Food, Tobacco, and Agricultural, or FTA), had sent organizers into Winston-Salem, then North Carolina's second-largest city, a real company town in which nearly everything was controlled by the R. J. Reynolds Tobacco Company and, to a far lesser degree, the Hanes knitting complex. Both corporations were notoriously anti-union.

The UCAPAWA organizers, along with local volunteers supplied by the Party, had tough sledding: meetings of fewer than ten workers were held secretly in workers' homes or in the basements of Negro churches; organizers were threatened and spied on; intimidation was so intense that pro-union workers would often be afraid to accept leaflets handed out at the plant gates by organizers they knew personally. At the end of the first year the union had only two hundred bona fide members out of more than ten thousand workers. Intimidation coupled with a newfangled paternalistic "stroking" of the workers made effective anti-union insurance for a while.

In mid-1943, however, the callous brutality of the company was dramatically displayed. A Negro worker became ill on the job and asked a company nurse to be sent home; she casually refused his request and told him to go back to work; a few minutes later he dropped dead. The news spread like a wind-blown forest fire. With the underground unionists taking the lead, the workers' fury was given direction; soon every plant where Negroes predominated was closed down, and before the day ended all plants were shut. Thousands of angry workers were in the streets and joined the union by the hundreds. By the end of 1943, despite every conceivable divisive racist tactic, Local 22 of UCAPAWA won a National Labor Relations Board (NLRB) election by a two-to-one majority, and after much stalling the company was forced to sign a contract with the union in the spring of 1944.

During the next four years the wages and the lives of Reynolds workers took a drastic turn for the better, the result of innumerable dogged struggles to enforce the negotiated contracts. Involved were several thousand Negro workers, a few score courageous white workers, and a superb elected stewards' council of about three hundred which led the struggles. By the end of 1946 the union had organized ten thousand to twelve thousand Negro workers in leaf houses (plants which did premanufacturing processing of tobacco) in the backward eastern "black-belt" areas of the state, in Charleston, South Carolina, and in Winston-Salem, right in Reynolds's own backyard. Through registration and voting campaigns, Local 22 began to play a role in politics: in 1946 it was instrumental in defeating a reactionary industrialist candidate for Congress; in 1947 Local 22 was responsible for electing a Negro minister to the Winston-Salem Board of Aldermen, the first Negro to serve in any such capacity in the South in the twentieth century.

The Reynolds strategy against Local 22 had been from the beginning to isolate Negro workers from white workers and to employ the standard divide-and-rule tactics of white supremacists. For example, in the 1947 strike, when one of the union's demands was to integrate Negro and white workers in all departments, leading officers of the company proclaimed, "This company is run by white southern gentlemen and we will close down before we will see nigger men working side-by-side with white women and drinking from the same fountain."

As cold war attitudes pervaded the domestic political atmosphere and as the Communist and leftist forces in the CIO became more and more isolated, the

Reynolds company added a second major weapon to its arsenal: Red-baiting. The Reynolds version of the situation in Winston-Salem seemed to be that black hordes were advancing on it in one direction while the Red Army was closing in from another. The two newspapers and the leading radio station, which regularly publicized the company viewpoint, were owned by a major stockholder and director of the company, Gordon Gray. His money reputedly bought him more than the usual baubles fancied by rich sons of rich fathers: he became secretary of the army and later, fortunately for a brief period, president of the University of North Carolina.

The Party was indeed involved in Local 22's affairs and had considerable control over its policies through the left-wing leadership of its parent union (FTA), through the Party membership of many of its most-respected leaders and members, and through the ability of the Party's district leadership to provide it with the sound and experienced trade union advice which had, in large measure, led to its existence and achievements. From the beginning the district had given its all for Local 22. It had, when necessary, fought the FTA leadership to secure the advancement to leadership of some of the most talented local Negro leaders, especially Negro women (including Moranda Smith, who became the FTA regional director). The Party, because it generally opposed the easy opportunism of organizing Negro workers while white workers were largely unorganized, owing to political, economic, and racial pressures applied by the company and the community, had insisted that the organizers from outside concentrate their efforts on organizing white workers.

The district leadership was keenly aware of the significance of the state's largest union local, which was in many ways far ahead of its time: interracial itself and openly challenging segregation; militant, dynamic, and democratic in the shop; politically active in the communities; a constant threat, by example, to the lackadaisical bureaucrats who ran most of the CIO textile locals and the jim-crowed AFL tobacco union in Durham, with their pathetically meager gains over the years. The existence of such a local and its vast leaf-house affiliates in a state which, less than two decades before, had crushed the white Gastonia textile strikers as though they had been invaders from a foreign shore was in itself a cause for wonderment. The Party's district committee included, increasingly, members of Local 22—Negro workers tested under fire, many of whom were able and charismatic mass leaders. The entire membership of the district shared a sense of pride—and amazement—at the continued existence of such a union, at the miracles of courage, hard work, ingenuity, and self-sacrifice that maintained it as a power on the workers' behalf for nearly a decade. During that time Local 22 stood up against bigotry, slander, greed, and brutality; and it faced insuperable wealth, force, propaganda, and a vast expertise in breaking, perverting, and bending the law. A later DO, viewing the aftermath of the one-sided struggle, commented, "It was like storming heaven itself."

The Party's sometime guidance of Local 22 was, however, inconsistent. From time to time grievous mistakes were made, often owing to the aberrations of national Party policy. The district Party leaders were, unwittingly, handcuffed by the policies of Stalin's Soviet Party, which cared nothing for the Communist parties of other countries except to the extent to which they could be immediately useful to the Soviet Union. The American Party (or at least its top leadership)—instead of devoting itself primarily to organizing the workers and Negroes and laying a basis for righting the wrongs suffered by them, instead of seeking allies and trying to unite the most aggrieved, most conscious, most concerned sections of the population into a movement for social and economic justice and peace, instead of fighting a principled fight to make the Bill of Rights a blazing reality—slavishly accepted the role assigned to it by Stalin and thereby narrowed and undercut every struggle in which it participated. It obtrusively glorified all things Soviet and equated the prospering (and expansion) of the Soviet Union with the advance of social revolution and the well-being of people everywhere; it accepted the dogma of Marxism-Leninism and shamelessly used it to justify any course of action whatever. "True" Marxism-Leninism was always what the Soviet Party, or the Soviet-controlled Comintern or Cominform, said it was.

The district leadership encountered conflicting attitudes from national Party leaders. Some hard-line sectarians, taking literally the orthodox Stalinist view that trade unions (along with their objectives) were intrinsically opportunist and reformist and useful principally as "schools for revolution," were rather cavalier about what happened to ten or twenty thousand organized workers. They were more concerned with carrying out a "correct, Marxist-Leninist revolutionary line" and "building the Party as the vanguard of the proletariat."

The thinking and priorities of such leaders inspired actions made to order for the union breakers, such as the Party's arranging to have Local 22 pass a resolution in support of striking workers in Italy. There were doubtless many strikes around the world which were deserving of support but which went unnoticed by Party brass in New York. The Italian strike, however, was Communist-led, and the resolution of support from thousands of southern Negroes was a fine example of "proletarian internationalism" that would surely make the American Party look good in *Pravda, Izvestia,* and *L'Unità.* The view was different in the *Winston-Salem Journal,* which publicized the resolution as further proof of Local 22's key position in the "international Communist conspiracy." The vagaries and shifting emphases of Marxist-Leninist theory even reinforced complacency in the Party when the company, attempting to isolate Local 22, began to drive wedges between the Negro middle class and the

Negro workers (after all, Communists were concerned with workers, not with the "unstable" middle class).

The district leadership had always insisted that the main responsibility of white organizers was to organize the white workers, since Local 22 would, in a sense, be only half a union so long as the company could keep a majority of the white workers out. Yet at least one prominent national figure in the Party argued that Negro workers "deserved primary attention" over "backward" whites. A corollary of his argument was that some white workers sympathetic to, or members of, the union were "white chauvinists" and not to be trusted, since the Party opposed all manifestations of racism. In the early days of the union it was often necessary for local Communists to explain to such people that because the entire fabric of white southern society was permeated with white-supremacist ideology, a white worker who was free of it would be rare indeed; that an approach so "pure" would only maintain the status quo; and that it was necessary to begin work where one was, not where one wished to be.

The situation Bernie found was dismal. The company, which had been busily mechanizing the all-Negro departments in order to reduce sharply the number of Negro workers, refused to bargain for a new contract upon the expiration of the one negotiated during the 1947 strike. The FTA was on the way to being expelled from the CIO along with other left-led unions. The AFL tobacco workers' union (TWIU) launched a campaign to organize Reynolds with a staff of more than twenty. It offered a union that would not "challenge southern traditions": one local for whites, one local for Negroes, and a third for Negro seasonal workers—"a real American union that could get along with the company."

At the same time the right and center forces in the CIO, eager to settle past grievances with the FTA and glad to demonstrate their anti-Communist zeal, sent a nondescript union, the United Transport Service Employees (UTSE, originally composed of redcaps), into the Winston-Salem scene like a vulture, to appeal to Negro workers on the basis of the CIO's reputation of concern for Negro rights (a reputation which, ironically, the CIO owed largely to the past efforts of such left-led unions as the FTA).

Bernie, after much discussion with worker Party members, outlined a strategy which was ultimately adopted by the local. Local 22 stood on its record of achievement; it reaffirmed its stand for one Negro-and-white local, for a union run democratically by its members—one which could stand up to the boss and neither run nor crawl when the company hollered, "Red!" Simultaneously, members of the local took to the streets with petition campaigns and demonstrations and won twelve hundred federal low-cost housing units and prevented the lifting of rent controls. "Trust the bridge that carried you over" was one of the Local 22 slogans.

A massive organizing free-for-all developed, with mass meetings, radio appeals, tons of leaflets, and countless house visits. When Local 22's mass meetings at plant gates proved immensely effective, the company prevailed on the board of aldermen to pass a "fire ordinance" which gave the police the power to break up any large meeting in order to keep the streets clear in case of a fire. Meanwhile, the AFL made considerable headway among the white workers, claiming five thousand signed cards. But if the AFL had really believed that it could "get along" with the Reynolds company, it had much to learn. In December 1949 the company gave hourly wage increases of five to twelve cents—the least to Negroes, the most to whites—demonstrating once again to the latter that they were the privileged favorites. As soon as that lesson had sunk in, the company fired eight or ten of the AFL's leading activists, and the AFL support dissipated rapidly.

The CIO union, which had been getting nowhere, was reinforced by the CIO's entire southern organizing staff under the direction of George Baldanzi, my old adversary in the textile union, who soon proved that he could not organize tobacco workers either. To exploit the Communist issue among Negro workers, the CIO prevailed on the distinguished Negro educator Dr. Mary McLeod Bethune, a strong anti-Communist, to endorse the UTSE and denounce Local 22. That ploy failed because of the indomitable Dr. Charlotte Hawkins Brown, the Negro educator who was even better known locally. Dr. Brown was no Communist sympathizer, but she had come to know many of Local 22's leaders in the Southern Conference for Human Welfare and had a deep admiration for them. A short time later she countered Dr. Bethune with a brilliant statement that ended with the local's admonition, "Trust the bridge that carried you over!"

Finally the NLRB election was held in March 1950, just two weeks after the FTA was formally expelled from the CIO. The results were

Local 22 (FTA)	3,323
AFL (TWIU)	1,514
CIO (UTSE)	541
No union	3,426

A runoff election was to be held between Local 22 and "no union" in two weeks. The company lost all restraint and used its power shamelessly. The local newspapers took on a hysterical tone. "Which do you want, Communism or Christianity?" one of them demanded. The company pressured the board of aldermen into adopting a resolution calling on the Reynolds workers to vote "no union." The mayor, in a barely disguised call for violence against the union, shouted over the local radio, "Let's drive Stalin's little songbirds from our doorsteps!" At the plants the company openly bullied and threatened pro-union workers. At the polls it had dozens of supervisors vote in violation of the NLRB rules. The runoff results were

Local 22	4,428
No union	4,381
Challenged	134

The challenges were nearly all made by the union against supervisory employees. Litigation over the challenged ballots lasted four months and featured a mountain of sworn affidavits by workers concerning the supervisory status of the challenged voters. The NLRB rejected every challenge without exception and in August 1950 announced a "no union" victory by sixty votes.

Though many a worker lost confidence in the probity of NLRB officials, there was no doubt that "Stalin's little songbirds" had suffered a severe defeat. But those who suffered most knew and cared next to nothing about Stalin or things Soviet. They were, however, profoundly knowledgeable about what it meant to work in helpless isolation in the plant of a company which was a law unto itself and valued a worker far less than a piece of machinery. For a few years they had known the material benefits, the self-confidence and fellowship, the freedom from fear, provided by the enlightened union of their own creation.

It is paradoxical that the organization of such a union was made possible by a political party whose ideal, the Soviet Union, had converted unions into managerial tools to facilitate the control and exploitation of workers. But at that time the extollers of Stalin were, perhaps willfully, ignorant of much else besides the truth about Soviet trade unions. Since that fateful election more than three decades have passed, and Winston-Salem is still a company town where "No smoking" signs are conspicuous by their scarcity. The nightmare of working in a giant open shop has become the common heritage of another generation of Reynolds workers, black and white. Many of those who fought for Local 22, now widely dispersed, and who have long since damned Stalin, his doctrine, and his Party, still think of that fight for unionization and dignity as one of the worthiest efforts of their lives. Many of them hope that good use will be made of their experience in years to come.

The inward-turning tendencies of the national Party leaders after the PP defeat were disastrous. Instead of evaluating the policies leading to the defeat, they sought its cause in the Party itself, in its composition (too many middle-class members, not enough Negroes, not enough industrial workers), and in its conduct (opportunism, ignorance of Marxist-Leninist theory, white chauvinism, insufficient discipline). In that time of increasing governmental and public repression, joined enthusiastically by large segments of the liberal community and the labor movement, the Party began its own hunt for heresy and unorthodoxy. The world Communist movement was still seething over the Yugoslav defiance of Stalin, and the problems of searching out the Titoist heresy filled Party literature at home and abroad. Thus, while congressional committees were making unemployed outcasts and pariahs of thousands of Communists and sympathizers, the Party was intimidating its members with its own brand of McCarthyism. Browderism was largely equated with Titoism, and the search for Browderites went on with renewed urgency.

By far the most significant of the inner-Party heresy hunts was the campaign against white chauvinism led by Pettis Perry, chairman of the Party's Negro Commission, between the end of 1949 and the middle of 1953. The Party had long held that Party membership for whites carried with it the obligation to rid oneself of all the traces of anti-Negro prejudice which were bound to persist where racism was both enshrined in the law and embedded in social custom. It was believed, with good reason, that without self-liberation from bigotry one could not be an effective fighter for socialism or successfully oppose segregation. The Party expected all members to eliminate from their minds and hearts such aberrations as white supremacy, anti-Semitism, male supremacy, and every other manifestation of racism or sexism. It took pride in its integrated character and its exemplary record of struggle for Negro rights.

Because the southern white Communist lived as part of a ruling white majority which was diseased with racism, and because he or she witnessed the humiliation and degradation of the Negro as a commonplace occurrence, the newly recruited white comrade, without much being said about it, would need to change many ingrained habits as a matter of simple decency. For example, he or she would pointedly pronounce the word *Nee-grow* as distinct from the very common *Nig-rah,* which was a grudging and offensive compromise between *nigger* and *Negro.* The white comrade would avoid using in the presence of Negroes such expressions as "Oh, boy!" or "Boy, did I have a good time!" since in the white-supremacist South a Negro man never advanced past "boy"-hood. *Negro* was carefully written with an initial capital because it was the usual practice of the southern press, into the late thirties, to dispense with the capital *N* as well as with *Mr., Mrs.,* or *Miss* where Negroes were concerned. That careful dissociation from the white majority by the southern white Communist in such particulars and, more important, in general attitude was so distinctive that an astute Communist-hunter (ranging from liberal to FBI agent) could often scent his prey by watching suspected whites for unusual politeness and sensitivity to Negroes.

Pettis Perry, a self-educated Negro worker, about sixty years old, was a pleasant, mild-mannered man, soft-spoken and likable. He began his campaign with an article in the monthly Party journal *Political Affairs,* which focused on white chauvinism within the Party. In a short time, at every level throughout the Party, zealous inquisitors began searching for evidences of white chauvinism in the white comrades. White comrades were quite often among the instigators. Perry himself traveled over the country demonstrating the evolving inquisitorial procedure: a priori any white member, and especially any white leader, was suspected (and probably guilty) of white chauvinism; Negro comrades were encouraged to describe the white-chauvinist words and deeds of white comrades; if a Negro comrade had observed none, it was implied that he or she was either weak or intimidated by the whites; if a white comrade resisted or denied charges, he or she was usually considered a "hard case" and mercilessly attacked and humiliated; a white comrade who soul-searched and self-criticized for real or imagined white chauvinism would be forgiven but remained on perpetual probation, at the mercy of any Negro or white comrade who might be nursing some resentment or frustration. The message seemed to be that with the proper technique and effort white chauvinism could always be "discovered."

In New York the leadership of an interracial youth club was severely disciplined because fried chicken and watermelon were served at a picnic—owing, it was argued, to patronizing, stereotyped thinking about the food preferences of Negroes. Use of such words as *blacklist* or *black sheep* was considered by zealots to be derogatory to Negroes. Although Perry's campaign certainly produced heightened sensitivity to white-chauvinist attitudes, in such a "lynch" atmosphere, it arose more from fear than from conscience, more from opportunism than from political responsibility or brotherly love. The campaign persisted with absurdity piled on craziness until few whites dared criticize Negro comrades for the grossest errors. Ultimately, irreparable damage was done to the trust and warmth which had previously existed between comrades.

Perry attended a district committee meeting in Winston-Salem after having spent a day or so talking to leading Negro comrades and trade unionists. Armed with the "evidence" he had gleaned, he plunged into an attack on the white leaders in the district, especially a white trade union organizer and Bernie. Occasionally one of his charges would hit near the mark; mostly they were monstrously wrong or mere nonsense. Months before, Bernie had tactfully pointed out to some leading Negro trade union comrades that to use the word *Jew* as a verb meaning to beat down a price, or as a noun meaning a crooked merchant, was a form of anti-Semitism; now his gentle words were chalked up as white chauvinism. Nearly all of Bernie's actions since he had been in the district were held up to sinister interpretation, until he began to wonder about his sanity and whether he was actually hearing what he heard.

I, inclined to believe the worst about myself anyway, was wounded and dismayed at the relatively minor accusations tossed my way. The maddening thing about Perry's charges was that there was always *some* element of truth in them which tended to disarm or paralyze anyone honestly trying to examine himself critically. I replied to the charges abjectly and in bewilderment. Bernie, instead of answering the absurdities, said that whatever his personal shortcomings, which he would be glad to discuss in the proper context, the political line and the work of the district were not, as implied, white chauvinist in content. Perry was somewhat set back by that reply and did not care to go into the work of the district. As a deviation detective he was not greatly interested in such problems as the survival of union locals or success in a score of political battles. He let matters rest for the time being, but he returned every few months and visited every large Party concentration in the district.

Bernie was so disturbed by this meeting that a short time later, in New York, he confronted Perry in the presence of two national leaders and again defended himself and the district so vigorously that Perry retreated. That was unusual for Perry, but he was only beginning his inquisition. Bernie's refusal to fall apart probably helped save the district from some of the future excesses of the white-chauvinism hunt; in other southern districts things were much worse.

Life in that troubled period was not easy for Sylvia. She suffered most of the difficulties and deprivations of my being a Party leader without any of the satisfactions. She had graduated from the university, and after the PP campaign, time hung heavily on her hands, especially as my duties kept me away from home more and more. The constraints of being married to a known Communist not only put her under pressure but tended to isolate her socially as well. Besides, she and I had never fully bridged the four-year gap in our marriage caused by my army service, and we had gradually, imperceptibly, drifted apart.

In the spring of 1949 she surprised me by announcing that she was leaving me, at least temporarily. She went to New York to live with her sister and brother-in-law and found a job. After two weeks of painful uncertainty I decided that I wanted a divorce. A divorce in New York at that time was a very expensive procedure and could be obtained only on grounds of adultery, which meant a sordid, rigged-evidence affair. The poor person's alternative was an annulment based in this case on the phony grounds that I had fraudulently promised her children, though never intending to have any. We proceeded with that cynical legal procedure, and the decree became final in December 1949.

I was much depressed at the dissolution of my marriage and certain that I would have to remain single for the rest of my life, since I could not imagine any woman willing to marry a man in my position, with such a grim-looking future. My plight was alleviated somewhat by the kindness of my former parents-in-law; Sylvia's father said to me, "No matter what you two damfools do, you're still going to be my son." And many comrades thoughtfully incorporated me into their social activities. Bea and Bernie fed me often and frequently suffered my morose company.

A by-product of my broken marriage was the acquisition of a remarkable roommate or, rather, housemate. Hans Freistadt was a young Austrian refugee who had become an American citizen after serving in the U.S. Army. He had attended the University of Chicago, where he achieved the distinction of being the only publicly known Communist on campus. His reputation preceded him when he transferred to UNC's Physics Department, on an Atomic Energy Commission (AEC) scholarship, as a candidate for a Ph.D. degree.

Hans was highly articulate, cool under fire, and (to his opponents) maddeningly rational and factual in debate. And debate he often did, speaking openly on campus as a Communist and taking my place on many occasions. I thought that he did a better job than I in many ways, and encouraged him. He received much attention from the press and from a few hostile student bigots who undoubtedly thought of him, as he said, as "that commie-Jew-bastard-furriner," an epithet that left him two nouns ahead of me. His innate decency and his intellect won him many admirers and defenders as well. Petty bureaucrats in the university sought to harass him, but they were limited because his academic work was exemplary.

In the spring of 1949 a U.S. senator (Hickenlooper, Republican of Iowa) discovered that Hans had an AEC scholarship to study theoretical physics and raised a vast alarm, like some latter-day Paul Revere. The Joint Atomic Energy Committee allowed Hans to appear before it; Hans distinguished himself by his logical testimony and gentlemanly demeanor; some of his congressional inquisitors distinguished themselves by their ignorance and boorishness and in one case by a sinister, though unsuccessful, attempt (of which Hans was unaware) to make him incriminate himself and set himself up for loss of citizenship and deportation. His AEC scholarship was shortly withdrawn and a teaching fellowship went unrenewed by the university. He completed his Ph.D. work with the aid of a private loan. Dr. Frank Graham had resigned as UNC president in March to accept an appointment to the U.S. Senate, so that the low-level bureaucrats were left without a restraining hand.

Because Hans was in a difficult financial situation, I invited him to move into my living room. He accepted and the two of us shared the three-room house in the utmost harmony, yet with considerable amusement at each other's eccentricities.

Hans remained for more than six months and proved to be a helpful companion. He found time to edit (and mostly write) a six-page periodical called the *Student Bulletin* which bore his name as editor on the masthead. With his personal stamp on every line, it was far superior in style and content to most of the leaflets appearing over my name, which were often poorly written and rather shrill. In his first issue he took up the cudgels for the admission of Harold Epps, a Negro, to the UNC Law School. With reasonableness and zeal he castigated acting university President Carmichael and Dean Brandis of the Law School for forcing the applicant into court instead of admitting him on the basis of his clear Fourteenth Amendment right. He dissected a racist editorial from the *Daily Tar Heel* opposing Epps's admission and pointed out irrefutably that it was a not-so-subtle call for violence by the Ku Klux Klan and its supporters. Another article ably summed up the issues in the Smith Act trial of the eleven Communist Party leaders, who had just been convicted, and managed to sound objective and not at all like the *Daily Worker*.

Before Hans received his Ph.D. in the spring of 1950, he was afflicted with some more national publicity. Some scientific work he had published had interested Einstein, who met with him briefly at Princeton. *Time* magazine had got hold of the story and made Hans sound like Einstein's heir-apparent. Hans laughed at the whole business and said that his work had no value for Einstein.

Despite his boyish looks (he was twenty-four years old), he got a job heading the Physics Department at the all-Negro Wilberforce University in Ohio. Fearing future recriminations, he informed the president of Wilberforce of his Communist affiliation and found the president willing to live with his politics to secure a man with such exceptional qualifications. But the Board of Bishops, responding to publicity initiated by a Durham newspaper, forced the president to rescind the appointment during the summer of 1950 while Hans was in Vienna visiting his father, a prominent Marxist intellectual whom he had not seen for many years. Ultimately, Hans took a teaching position at the Institute for Advanced Studies in Dublin and could only afford to return, late in 1951, to the country he had adopted in his youth with determination and dedication.

In January 1949 a UNC campus organization which customarily presented speakers of widely divergent viewpoints invited John Gates, one of the top Communist leaders and then on trial under the Smith Act, to speak on the campus. Gates accepted, but while he was flying to Chapel Hill, the university administration canceled the meeting (President Graham was reported to be out of town). At the appointed hour, Gates, Bernie, and I arrived at the darkened, locked Memorial Hall, where we encountered Hans and about a thousand students who had not yet heard of the cancellation. After a hurried consultation the diminutive Hans climbed on the pedestal of a pillar in front of the auditorium and in his penetrating voice announced that because the university administrators had so little regard for free speech, they had capitulated to outside political pressures and barred Gates from speaking on the campus; but there was no reason students could not walk two blocks to a public street and hear what the speaker had to say. The crowd, in a good-humored, frolicsome mood, roared approval.

As Gates, Bernie, Hans, and I led the way, the students whooping and cavorting around us, someone with humorous intent shouted, "Git a rope!" Hans and I knew our crowd and were unperturbed, but Bernie, feeling responsible for Gates and believing that he was going to see him lynched before his eyes, grabbed his arm protectively while his face turned ashen. Gates himself may have thought his last hour had come, for his lips were grimly compressed in a straight line as he looked directly in front of him. Finally we mounted a wide stone wall in front of a building on West Franklin Street where I had attended high school. I briefly introduced Gates, who began to speak with vocal cords which needed no amplifier. The only thing betraying his nervousness was that he began, "Here in the state of Georgia—" and the crowd roared with laughter. He went on to speak effectively, upholding American principles of justice, saying that a person was accountable for his acts, not his beliefs. As he spoke the crowd grew rapidly until there were about two thousand people, and local and state police had to reroute traffic. I noticed the arrival of some white cab drivers who had often been associated with goonery, and I warned Hans to keep a sharp lookout; we both pressed close to Gates.

A little man came up behind the wall, tugged at my pants cuff, and asked for a hand up. I pulled him up on the wall just behind Gates, whereupon he introduced himself as W. B. Debnam of "Debnam Views the News," a widely broadcast, ultra-right-wing radio news commentary sponsored, appropriately enough, by a fertilizer company. He wanted to arrange an interview with Gates after his speech; I said I would inquire. Meantime, Gates was saying that when someone was deprived of the right to speak, everyone was deprived of the right to listen, and he was glad that "here in the state of Georgia—" Again the crowd roared, and Gates, laughing himself, concluded his speech and, at my suggestion, began answering questions according to the university tradition.

I heard a thud and looked behind me, where I saw a cab driver of my acquaintance running away; on the ground, unconscious, lay Debnam, a water-soaked roll of toilet paper next to his head. Being sure that the missile was intended for Gates, I ended the question period quickly, told a policeman to take care of Debnam, and escorted Gates, surrounded by a cordon of well-disposed students, down the main business street of town.

Hundreds of people swarmed around us as we walked; and since local goons had already attempted violence on Gates, I was determined to get him out of the street. The Graham Memorial Building, where the *Daily Tar Heel* had its offices, was only a short distance away. As Gates was the editor of the *Daily Worker,* it seemed reasonable that he should pay a courtesy call on the *Daily Tar Heel* editor. The impromptu visit to the surprised student editor took place in the presence of some two hundred students while Bernie rushed to get his car and bring it close to one of the doors of the building; it was time for Gates to hurry to the airport in order to catch his plane.

That day, for Gates, had probably been a welcome respite from his seemingly endless trial. He could never explain why he had had such a fixation about the state of Georgia; perhaps it was a foreshadowing of the four years he would later spend in the Atlanta penitentiary.

We Communists spent much of our time trying to arouse the conscience of the community about court cases in which we believed that Negroes had been convicted despite inadequate evidence and because they were Negroes.

The Mississippi case of Willie McGee involved a Negro man convicted of raping a white woman who, according to the defense, had forced him to sleep with her for years and who charged him with rape when he attempted to break off the affair. For nearly five years the fight to save his life absorbed much of the energy and emotion of the Party members. (Jessica Mitford provides a vivid account of the struggle to save McGee in her book *A Fine Old Conflict.*) His execution in May 1951 caused us such anguish that it seemed almost as if a family member had been murdered. Afterward we read in our local papers and in national news magazines how the cynical Communists cared nothing for the man or his plight, or the plight of his people, but simply used him to stir up racial trouble and to advance the cause of international godless Communism.

Other cases among the many which deeply aroused southern Communists were those of Rosa Lee Ingram and the "Martinsville Seven," but in the Carolinas the civil rights case which brought the greatest sense of personal involvement was that of the two Daniels cousins.

Early in 1949 a white cab driver was found brutally murdered on a lonely road near Greenville, North Carolina. A woman's coat was spread on the ground near the cab, next to contraceptives, a woman's purse, and a glove.

Without investigating that evidence, the police descended on the Negro community. Two Negro boys, Bennie Daniels, sixteen, and his cousin Lloyd Ray Daniels, fifteen, were picked up because they had been seen with blood on their clothing. At the trial several witnesses testified that they had been bloodied in a fight; one of the witnesses was the man with whom they had fought. The evidence against them consisted of two long "confessions" filled with legalistic jargon and police gibberish, which they had never even read. One lad had never been to school a day in his life; the other had only reached the second grade.

Lloyd Ray described the signing of his confession. The officers, he said, told him that "if I wanted to see my mama again, I'd better own that Bennie and I did it. I had only three minutes. . . . I asked what they were going to do. They said, 'Kill you!' . . . I said, 'Yes.' " Bennie's story was similar: "The officers brought me a piece of paper with some printing on it. . . . They said, 'Nigger, if you don't write your name, we'll blow your damn' brains out.' So I wrote my name."

At the trial the woman's coat, glove, and purse were not introduced as evidence, although the motive for the killing was said to be robbery and the boys were said to have robbed the purse. No blood test was made of the bloodstains on the boys' clothing to determine their source, nor were any fingerprints introduced as evidence, even though the police had a fingerprint expert investigate the murder scene.

The local Party club called the little-publicized case to the leadership's attention after the cousins had been convicted and sentenced to die in the gas chamber. Because there was little time, the Party had to instigate the forming of an ad hoc Daniels Defense Committee to publicize the case and raise money for the appeal. Normally, efforts would have been made to involve the NAACP and to persuade it to take over the conduct of the case, but the NAACP leaders, generally staid and conservative, were wary of any case in which Reds were interested, whatever its merits. Worst of all, they could be maddeningly slow. Daniels Defense Committees sprang up around the state, generally where there were Communists to spark them.

Dozens of Communists were able to visit the cousins or their families and became profoundly involved personally in the case. The battle went on for many months and hope sprang eternal. The most infuriating and disheartening thing encountered was the indifference of so many "cultured," "educated" whites. The *Raleigh News and Observer,* for instance, printed a long "humorous" letter, elegantly written, in which the author compared killing the Daniels cousins to squashing frogs: it was a messy business; there was just no quiet or gentle way of doing it.

After a long legal struggle, despite nationwide protests, "due process" was exhausted and the cousins, grown to young manhood in prison, were executed.

The Party itself was under heavy attack on many fronts. The Smith Act trial of the Party's national board lasted nearly all of 1949 and almost turned the Party into a large defense committee. As soon as the national leaders were convicted, indictments were returned for the second-string leaders, to be followed at intervals by prosecutions of groups of regional leaders.

In the labor movement the left-led unions had mostly been forced out of the CIO by the end of 1949, and internecine warfare raged in many shops organized or led by the left, in a concerted right-center attempt to destroy the Party's power in the unions. In political arenas some liberals rivaled right-wing labor leaders in the fury of their attacks on Communists.

In Congress the Mundt-Nixon Bill, later adapted as the McCarran Act, was passed, and Truman's veto was overridden. Thus a "registration" procedure for leftists was set up, and the Washington scene was adorned with a Subversive Activities Control Board (SACB). The House Un-American Activities Committee and a similar Senate committee, operating with the procedural integrity of kangaroo courts, devastated the lives of hundreds of Communists, sympathizers, and liberals. The name and face of Senator McCarthy soon became well known in the land.

In North Carolina the state legislature was presented with the Shreve-Regan Bill, aimed at outlawing the Communist Party, which was so patently unconstitutional and so ineptly drawn that it embarrassed many anti-Communists and made it easy for me to deride it on the radio, in letters to newspapers, and in leaflets. Although it died neglected and despised, political observers, when it had been introduced, had given it a good chance to pass. At a subsequent session, another bill with the same objective, labeled the Anti-Klan Bill, eventually was passed.

At the beginning of the Korean War in 1950, all such attacks intensified. Harassment of left-wingers took place everywhere. Two Progressive Party members, graduates of different law schools, were not permitted to take the state bar examination because of their "leftist" views (one was cited specifically because he had referred to a Negro as "mister"). A young ex-student circulating the Stockholm Peace Petition (against the use of the atomic bomb) was arrested and charged with vagrancy, although he had over three hundred dollars in his pocket and was employed. At the university, Ph.D. candidates with Marxist views, particularly Jews, were advised to go elsewhere; if they refused, they encountered intolerable difficulties. Known PP activists lost their jobs at a great rate, in some cases as a result of FBI visits to their employers.

Subscribers to the *Worker* or *Daily Worker* usually received their paper with the wrapper ripped open. My mail was regularly delayed and had usually been opened. FBI agents made a practice of asking the neighbors of people they thought were Communists whether so-and-so acted suspiciously, entertained

Negroes, or slandered the government. For brief periods in 1950, I would find myself under the surveillance of six or eight FBI agents. On one such occasion I walked through the one-block business section of Chapel Hill tailed by three cars and two agents on foot; when my course took me across the campus, they abandoned their cars and stalked me on all sides, signaling each other as they hid behind trees and even a Confederate monument. Such fun-and-games at government expense were presumably intended to intimidate me; they could, however, be inconvenient, since it would be awkward to arrive at appointments leading a parade of FBI agents.

At the end of August 1949 I was exhausted and looked it, and was in need of a vacation—a fact called to my attention by comrades in Winston-Salem, Chapel Hill, and Durham. I was reluctant to take time off, and besides, I had scarcely any money and no idea where I might go. Bernie found a reason for me to go to New York on Party business, and once there, I discovered that he had arranged with the New York Party for me to go to Camp Unity (where I had spent my honeymoon eight years earlier) as its guest.

While still in the city I had a brief reunion with Richard and his wife, Lia, just returned from a year and a half in Europe. One night after dinner in the Village, where the Nicksons were staying, I fell into a protracted conversation with Richard, who was headed for Los Angeles and work on a Ph.D. at the University of Southern California. A score of years after that meeting, Lia remembers retiring late that night as we two friends continued our talk. She also remembers how, the next morning, her husband told her with troubled perplexity that I was altogether locked into my views and unwilling to entertain the advice that I return to graduate study in history.

Lia's recollection is right on target. And a day or two later, obsessively committed, I proceeded to Camp Unity. There, in the very first hour, I met a lovely young Jewish woman from Brooklyn (Flatbush). Gladys was twenty-five and, as a night student at Hunter College, was belatedly pursuing a B.A. degree while she worked by day to pay for her room, board, and tuition. I liked her at once and proceeded to monopolize her time. In a few days I more than liked her; I had fallen wholly in love with her. She was undaunted by the life I described to her and by the prospect that I might be in jail before long if the political situation continued to worsen. Before I returned home I had met her family: her mother (a widow), her brother, and her sister. Afterward, though my annulment would not be effective for three months, I began a serious courtship by mail, using complicated measures to prevent the FBI from reading our correspondence.

At Christmas, when I was legally single again, Gladys came down to see my family and friends and to be seen by them. Bea and Bernie had driven me to Raleigh to meet her train; and when I saw her diminutive, five-foot-two figure striding confidently down the platform, my heart pounded and I was sure *I* had chosen wisely—if only she could accept all that went with me. I still did not quite believe in the possibility of personal happiness for myself in a time so dismal.

We drove to Chapel Hill, where a great many student friends at a Christmas party were eagerly awaiting a look at my probable fiancée. She was a great success, for her good looks, her vivacious charm, and the impression of genuineness and strength of character she left with everyone. On Christmas Day in Hamilton Lakes she was similarly impressive to my family. For her part, much to my joy, she was pleased with the prospects; and in February 1950 she and I were married in New York in the municipal building, with Bea and Bernie as matron of honor and best man.

When we arrived at our Carrboro home late the next day, we were greeted by Hans, who was still packing his things, complying reluctantly with his notice of eviction from the living room—and perhaps hoping for a reprieve.

14

Rearguard Actions

For many Communists, the McCarthy years had a surreal, nightmarish quality. The entire Bill of Rights, and especially due process, seemed to us to be falling to pieces under the enthusiastic blows of cold warriors and Communist-hunters. With increasingly restricted association, we began to feel in our isolation that democracy was a lost cause and that we alone were fully awake to the danger, screaming our alarm soundlessly, while the great mass of Americans sleepwalked, scarcely caring, going about business as usual.

In the early fifties the Party was greatly concerned with civil liberties, often echoing Henry Wallace's dictum that either everyone has them or no one does. Previously the Party's civil liberties record had been spotty and self-serving, and the fact that it opposed free speech for Nazis, members of the Ku Klux Klan, and the like caused many to be skeptical. The Party had opposed the Smith Act when it had been passed in 1940, yet shortly afterward, during the war, when it was used against the hated Trotskyists, the Party had applauded the indictments. When the Party leadership was indicted in 1948, the Smith Act was denounced once more, as in 1940, as the essence of "thought control." When Japanese-Americans on the West Coast were rounded up and put into concentration camps "for the duration," there was little complaint from the Communists; perhaps the policy of "everything for victory" and similar procedures against national groups in the Soviet Union made for silence on the issue. In the fifties, when ominous preparations were being made to place Communists and left-wingers in concentration camps, many a warning was given to those who would listen. But because the Communists' hands were unclean, fewer and fewer would heed anything we might say—even when we were right.

The American Party, in concert with the Soviet Union and the large European Communist parties, was trying to launch a peace offensive to counter the intensified cold war policies of the U.S. government. But even when tied to opposing the use of the atomic bomb, that peace initiative was generally perceived by the American public as another move in support of Soviet foreign policy. Indeed, the Party's leadership elite so intended it, although many rank-and-file Communists were sincerely and primarily concerned with the horror of atomic war when they supported such activities as the Stockholm Peace Appeal, for which they gathered in North Carolina alone thousands of signatures.

The top Party leadership floundered in its efforts to maintain or regain the Party's fading influence, always giving top priority to keeping in perfect step with the Soviet Union's policies. It was easy to attribute the Party's reverses to the severity of the attacks made on it (the attackers ranging from the FBI to the ADA), the pervasive climate of cold war jingoism, the gradual fascistization of the country, and the enemies within (white chauvinists, deviationists, FBI spies); but it was much more difficult to get at the roots of the Party's isolation. For example, in 1951 William Z. Foster, the Party's chairman and most influential individual, believed that war between the United States and the Soviet Union was inevitable and that the American Party would be outlawed; many other leaders believed that a fascist America was likely. With such a bleak outlook prevailing, it is not surprising that little was done to help the Party mend its sectarian ways, end its isolation in the labor movement, or win new friends and influence. Instead, much of the time and thought of the national leaders was devoted to preparing an apparatus which would assure the continued functioning of the Party under the expected illegal conditions. Although it was not known to most Party members, large-scale preparations had been in progress since 1947.

Meanwhile, the deterioration of the Party continued nationally and throughout the South. In the Carolinas the membership had gradually declined. Local 22 was without NLRB certification, though it was still something of a force in the plants and the community. Its parent union, FTA, had merged with the Distributive Workers as a survival measure, and only a skeleton crew remained on the staff of Local 22; amid the general atmosphere of gloom and defeat the Winston-Salem Party had shrunk. The number of student members at Chapel Hill had considerably declined, owing to the departure of those who had completed their studies and the Party's inability to recruit a significant number of new students.

Bernie had been recalled from the Carolinas to serve as New York's state trade union director, an assignment of national importance; and he had been replaced by a younger but experienced New Yorker named Hank. The Party still had telling influence in some consequential trade unions: Local 10 (FTA) in the tobacco stemmeries of eastern North Carolina; a similar local in Charleston, South Carolina; sizable furniture locals in the Piedmont area of North Carolina; and assorted locals from the mountains to the coast (where a number of menhaden fishermen had been organized). There were fairly promising beginnings of Party-sponsored rank-and-file movements in AFL tobacco locals in Durham and in an important CIO textile local in the same city. In Chapel Hill off-campus activity was still flourishing in the Negro community, where some extremely able Negro and white Communists had managed to maintain an adult school which enjoyed broad community support. The school taught nearly anything its students requested—business skills (typing, bookkeeping), reading, writing, arithmetic, American history, Negro history, civics, painting, drawing—using mainly university undergraduate and graduate student volunteers as faculty. Although the Communists were the spark plugs, they were inconspicuous, managed to involve four or five non-Communists for every one of themselves, and secured the active support of several Negro ministers and their congregations. So great was the boost to community cohesion brought about by the school and its activities that it was an important factor in the election of a Negro to the town's governing body—after the Winston-Salem election, one of the first such events in the South. The Party in Durham had grown to more than twenty-five and seemed to be prospering. Scattered around North and South Carolina were geographically isolated individual Communists wielding considerable local influence, people with whom I kept in cautious contact, considering them treasurable Party forces.

The national leadership, anticipating the outlawing of the Party, had determined to retain an organization reduced to its hard core of trusted and tested members in addition to an underground leadership. The search for "weak links" and "rotten apples" inside the Party intensified. I myself, along with practically every leading cadre in the Party, was subjected to several security checks by the national review commission. They consisted mainly in the writing of autobiographies every year or so in response to questionnaires containing quite specific questions—even about one's sex life. An inscrutable Comrade Dora, sixtyish, of Russian background, with some earlier American trade union experience and some rumored past connections with the Communist International, was much in evidence as she compared earlier and later autobiographies for discrepancies. Party functionaries, considering themselves professional revolutionaries, submitted to such invasions of privacy without complaint, reasoning that since the Party had entrusted them with its leadership, they could trust the Party with the intimate facts of their lives for the sake of the Party's security.

At the next annual registration of the Party membership I was instructed to interview each member privately, asking a number of questions intended to be revealing of the overall character and personal history of the individual. Nothing was written down and the interviews remained with me, disclosed to no one, but the experience smacked more of the confessional than of politics and it was distasteful to both the interviewed and the interviewer. It was painful, for example, to have to ask my old buddy Willie if he had ever "engaged in extramarital sex," or to have to ask the same question of a young student wife or of a Negro woman fifteen years my senior. Most of the members were people I had known and loved for a long time, who trusted me and returned my affection. My occupying the role of inquisitor-confessor was distressing to me and injected a certain distance into some relationships. For my comrades this was not the Junius who rhapsodized imaginatively over what American socialism could be like, or who put routine Party tasks into a larger perspective; I seemed to be talking with an alien accent, and even if I gagged on it, I was doing it.

One question I had asked was, "Are you either homosexual or bisexual?" The number of affirmative replies was startling; they came from young and old, men and women, Negro and white, married and single, workers and students. Two prominent Negro unionists, two outstanding student leaders, and others exceptional in their ability and activity included themselves among the homosexuals. I had assumed, without giving it any serious thought, that several young men were homosexual, though it had never occurred to me that the Party had a "problem." But I had received an oral directive from the national office to drop all homosexuals from the Party, for the reason, ostensibly, that they were peculiarly vulnerable to blackmail by FBI or police and might easily be turned into informers.

I discussed the matter with Hank and we dragged our feet, nagged by the thought of disobeying a Party directive. While the percentage of the membership involved was fairly small, the quality of the individuals was generally exceptional. It was decided that I should explore the matter further. I visited a number of homosexual comrades, explained the Party's fears, and, to some, naively commended heterosexuality. Many felt guilty and out of step because of their sexual preferences; all were in torment because of the social pressures necessitating secrecy; all promised the utmost discretion, while some of the younger people declared their intention to attempt to "switch." My discussions convinced me of the complexity and diversity of the problem and of my own enormous ignorance of it. But I had learned enough to conclude that the

Party's position was wrong and superficial and, I thought, quite possibly a reflection of the bigoted thinking of some "security expert." What most impressed me was the homosexuals' willingness to reveal to the Party something so deeply hidden away. Such courage and such trust in the Party scarcely supported the theory of their vulnerability to blackmail. I felt that because homosexuals were a segment of the population subjected to prejudice and persecution, the Party should accept them freely (although encouraging them to become "straight" where it appeared emotionally feasible).

After much thought and discussion about the matter, Hank and I decided to make use of some advice I had once received from Henry Winston, the Party's national organization secretary. I had complained to him of the vast number of organizational directives I received from the national office which were mostly irrelevant to my district and which required time-costly responses. Winnie had said, "You have a wastebasket, don't you? Well, you've got to learn to use it more *creatively*." We decided to file the homosexuality directive, creatively, in that same trashcan.

I had become a happily married man, a fact which noticeably improved my morale. Within a few months Gladys and I had decided on parenthood despite the gathering storms that threatened us. She was working toward a B.A. degree in education, completing most of her work in about her eighth month of pregnancy. In the spring of 1951 she gave birth to Barbara Arline, who delighted and charmed us throughout her childhood. In all ways Gladys met ideally the standards expected of a Party functionary's wife: her husband's Party work came first, and she prepared and expected to shift for herself should it become necessary. That time was not far off.

The national leaders, guided by Foster, continued to prepare for the outlawing of the Party. To protect the organization's leadership, they devised three categories of cadres: (1) the "deep freeze," consisting of top leaders not yet arrested, people of great knowledge and experience—a sort of "brain trust"; (2) the "deep, deep freeze," trusted cadres removed from political activity, with changed identities and appearances, severed from all familiar haunts and associates (they were to be a source of leadership should other levels of leadership be discovered and arrested); and (3) the "operative but unavailable" leadership (known as "OBU" or simply as "the unavailables" or "the down-unders"), who traveled about a great deal, kept selective contact with trusted rank-and-file members and other unavailables, and maintained infrequent contact with some deep-freeze people. In practice, the unavailables provided the real leadership of the Party, in spite of frequent conflict with "legal" leaders and deep freeze pundits.

Hank and I at that time had only a vague idea of what the setup was to be.

Formerly the DO or the district secretariat (consisting of the DO, me, and one other) would meet periodically with the southern Party director to receive instructions and exchange views. Since the war, that director had been Nat Ross, a Columbia ex-graduate student who had gone to Bull Connor's Birmingham in the early thirties and had proved his courage and ability many times over in the company of such people as Rob Hall, Hosea Hudson, Bart Logan, and Sam Hall. Nat had succeeded to Rob Hall's post with high expectations: he knew and loved the South and was experienced in the ways of the Party. However, he was never given leeway to differentiate between national policy and its southern application or to make the needed case for "southern exceptionalism" with the mainly northern leadership. Beginning about the time of Pettis Perry's white-chauvinism witch-hunt, he began to be whipsawed between conflicting groups in the national leadership until he was rendered ineffectual. Unceremoniously removed as southern director and given a series of posts demeaning to one of his eminence in the Party, he received the assignments stoically and carried them out conscientiously and well, no matter how he may have suffered.

His successor as southern director was James E. Jackson, Jr., one of the founders and leaders of the Southern Negro Youth Congress in the thirties. From a well-to-do Negro family in Richmond, Virginia, he had recently received praise in some Party circles as a theoretician on the Negro question. Such praise had undoubtedly inflated his already considerable ego, and he had acquired a habit of striking an aloof, Byronic pose which, when accompanied by a heavy frown, was intended to indicate that he was engaged in deep thought. He was strong-willed and had decided to remake the Party in the South. When he first assumed his position, he was much given to issuing sweeping edicts which were not thought out and usually had to be reversed or extensively revised. To some it seemed as though he believed that commands to the membership could alter objective situations or restore the Party's lessened influence in the South.

His arrival at my Carrboro home in 1950, shortly after his appointment, was bizarre. His overactive imagination conjured up a major FBI plot in the middle of Chapel Hill because he misread some perfectly normal occurrences in and around a comrade's house. When he conspiratorially entered my house late at night, another comrade and I had to go retrieve his car, which he had abandoned in near panic. Not embarrassed for long by his misadventure, he soon adopted the air of a feudal lord sizing up a new fiefdom, and I had a premonition that the comfortable and sensible independence that the district had enjoyed under previous southern directors was nearing its end.

Soon a period of wide-ranging drop-everything-else-and-do-this directives began. The gatherings of southern district leaders had, under Nat, allowed each one some chance to speak his or her piece. Contrariwise, Jim would from time to time summon the various southern leaders to meetings which consisted largely of immense reports from him, with backup from his chief lieutenant, Ed Strong, his former colleague in the Southern Negro Youth Congress and an eloquent and inspirational speaker. Jim appeared to expect, and indeed received, much adulation from those assembled. Having presented his thinking on a number of subjects, he obviously expected the discussion to concern the application of his line, not doubts about it or proposals to modify it or add to it.

Observation of Hosea Hudson at those meetings proved distressing. Hosea was a near-legendary figure in the Party, and with reason. In the twenties and thirties, as a Negro steel worker, a Communist, and a union leader, he had performed prodigies of bravery, common sense, and devotion to principle in organizing Negro workers and in leading struggles for the rights of Negro workers and sharecroppers in Alabama. As was usual with Communist mass leaders, his faithful adherence to narrow, sectarian Party policies had cost him his base and gradually isolated him. Years later, he had made himself a self-appointed hatchet man for Nat, always coming down heavily on anyone opposing the line with national authority behind it and always receiving at least a large part of his income from the Party. After Nat's removal he never had a good word to say for him and often indulged in mean-spirited remarks at his expense. Such unworthy behavior was the ripe fruit of Hosea's observation of Party infighting over the years and his survival of it. Shrewdly, he saw a winner in Jim and managed never to be in opposition to him or Ed. Though Hosea stayed likable, capable of wise contributions to discussions, and, in his way, devoted to the Party, a couple of the leaders (including me) believed, perhaps uncharitably, that his prime motivations had become maintaining his status as a Party hero by recounting his exploits, remaining on the inside of Party activity out of vanity, and, at his advanced age, staying on the Party payroll.

I had a painful personal experience with Jim's leadership style in the summer of 1951. Jim met with me alone and informed me that I was to be, forthwith, in the deep, deep freeze leadership category; I was to go to Houston, Texas, without a word to anyone, severing all ties, and build myself a new life under a new identity. I was to avoid anything close to left-wing politics; I was to correspond with no friends or relatives; I would be contacted twice a year by a Party representative; my wife could join me in six months if all went well. I was to leave North Carolina within one week. No one was to know my destination, and l was to discuss nothing of what had been said with anyone (except a minimum of information to Gladys), not even with Hank, who would, he said, be told separately. I pointed out that I had all my roots in

North Carolina and had an unspoken commitment to my comrades to tough it out with them; that my mother was aging and in poor health and might well die of the shock if I were to disappear; that my daughter was not yet three months old; and that, in any case, such a step required careful thought and planning, not a week's notice.

Jim said that I was being asked to make sacrifices for the good of the Party and that my wife and daughter would be provided for. He made no mention of my mother. The Party, he added, did not make such a request lightly, and it did so because it was sure it could rely on me. Wishing to hear no further discussion, he repeated the instructions and departed.

In a state of shock, I communicated with Hank by an emergency phone code we had set up, and two hours later he met me in Chapel Hill. Abandoning the district's car, we walked through the university arboretum, popular with lovers because of its circuitous paths and dense foliage, while I violated Jim's instructions and told Hank the entire conversation excepting the destination. Hank, never having succumbed to Jim's charm, lost his usual poise, swore furiously, told me to hold tight and say nothing to Gladys, and flew to New York that afternoon. There he demanded a meeting with Henry Winston, due to surrender within twenty-four hours in federal court to begin serving his Smith Act sentence. He told Winnie the story and Winnie promptly countermanded Jim's order. Hank returned the next day, July 2, 1951, angry but triumphant.

While we were rejoicing over the good news for me, a report came over the radio that of the eleven top Communists supposed to surrender at the federal courthouse in Foley Square, four of them, Henry Winston, Gil Green, Bob Thompson, and Gus Hall, failed to appear and had forfeited bail. That was yet another signal to the Party membership that its leadership considered the situation so dismal that they were preparing for illegal conditions. A short time later Jim himself was indicted under the Smith Act, but he avoided arrest and disappeared.

Meanwhile, not everything in the Carolinas revolved around security planning and underground talk. One morning in the mid-summer of 1951 a comrade handed me a tiny clipping from an inner page of the *Greensboro Daily News* which told of a Negro man convicted in Yanceyville of rape without ever having touched the white woman who charged him. Yanceyville was a one-horse town, the county seat of Caswell, a poor farm county with a Deep South atmosphere. The last time Yanceyville had been much in the news was when four Negroes had been lynched on the courthouse lawn many years before.

I went to a pay phone and called my friend Louis Austin, the Negro editor of the *Carolina Times,* a colorful weekly newspaper for Negroes which was operated on a shoestring. Published in Durham, seat of one of the South's outstanding concentrations of Negro business, the paper was widely read by Negroes and had considerable influence. Austin, who had been a candidate for office on the Progressive Party ticket, had admired and defended Paul Robeson unstintingly over many years. He never lacked for courage, especially where civil rights were concerned.

I read the clipping to him and asked what he knew about it. "That's funny," he responded. "I just got a call about it a half-hour ago. Why don't you come over and let's talk?" I hitched over to Durham and was soon sitting in Austin's office. He said that a Negro tradesman in Yanceyville had called him that morning to ask him to publicize the case. Louis had wanted to go up and get the story but was tied down and couldn't. How would I like to go instead? "You just got yourself a reporter!" was the answer. I called a Negro student, one of my ablest Party lieutenants, and asked if he could borrow a car and a good camera and meet me in an hour. Being occupied with urgent matters, he could not. I then called Mace, a young white doctor of my acquaintance, and asked him the same question. He could and did.

As we drove northwest out of Durham, I briefed Mace about our mission and watched him beam with delight. In Yanceyville, he drove into an alley behind a run-down storefront and parked next to a black panel truck. Austin had called ahead to arrange things, and the Negro businessman was waiting for us. We transferred to the panel truck and Mace memorized detailed instructions on how to reach the tenant farm where Mack Ingram, the supposed rapist, lived. We drove a long way over bumpy roads, and then walked together to Ingram's little shack of a house. It was not long before Ingram, a dignified man, was convinced that his visitors were there to help him; and he and his wife, surrounded by most of their nine children, spoke freely. I noted down the facts while Mace prepared the camera.

Leaving Mace to his pictures, I drove the truck a short distance (the owner had thoughtfully obliterated his business name on the sides with black watercolor paint) and casually interviewed the "rape" victim, Willie Jean Boswell, and some of her family. I heard Ingram's story confirmed by his excitable and somewhat hysterical "victim," and Mace and I returned the truck to its owner and jubilantly headed back to Durham where Austin awaited us. I had already composed the story in my head while riding and scribbled it off longhand in Louis' office for Mace to type. Austin was so delighted that he literally "tore out the whole front page" and devoted page one entirely to my story and Mace's photographs.

I was concerned with how to give the case national publicity and how to get the NAACP to represent Ingram on appeal. Austin had a bright idea: he called the *New York Post* and asked to speak to Ted Poston, at that time the only

Negro reporter on that paper. "Ted, Louis Austin in Durham. I've got a great story for you. I'm going to put on the friend that got it for me (he's a white guy) and we're both agreed it's *your* story." I got on the phone, using the pseudonym which Louis had assigned me as a by-line, and dictated the entire story to Poston, who rewrote it more sensationally and got it prominently into the *Post*. Austin then took me to the little all-Negro print shop that printed his paper and introduced me to everyone by my pseudonym, whereupon I was the recipient of some heartwarming handshakes and backslaps.

Back at home in Carrboro that night, I wrote a press release (with timely propaganda clichés) which I sent to the state's main newspapers and wire services on Party stationery:

July 12, 1951

Chapel Hill, N.C.—Junius Scales, Chairman of the Carolinas District of the Communist Party, today issued the following statement:

Few events in recent decades have brought more shame on our state than the white-supremacist outrage perpetrated in recorder's court on June 18 in Yanceyville.

Mr. Mack Ingram, a 44-year-old Negro farmer and father of nine children was sentenced by Judge R. O. Vernon to two years on the roads on a charge of "attempted assault" on a white woman. The supposed "victim," 18-year-old Willie Jean Boswell, admitted on the witness stand that Ingram never spoke to her, never touched her, and never came closer to her than 75 feet. She said he "*looked*" at her.

The trial was held a few days after there had been considerable local talk of lynching Ingram. The court was conducted in an outrageous manner by a judge who never completed high school and a solicitor named Horton who sneeringly referred to Ingram as a "nigger" and a "damn' black grizzly." In that court a separate jim-crow Bible is used to swear in Negro witnesses.

Caswell County "justice" is primarily a white-supremacy instrument for beating down the Negro people of the community and keeping them struggling to make a living as sharecroppers and tenant farmers.

Encouraged by the national wave of reactionary attacks on the Communist leaders and other advocates of peace and equal rights for the Negro people, Caswell County's racist bigshots simply disregard both law and the Constitution. Such corrupt contempt for human rights and decency by the courts leaves no one secure under the law—Negro *or* white.

Every honest citizen should call on Governor Kerr Scott to fulfill his duty as chief magistrate and to conduct a thorough investigation and cleanup of the legal machinery in Caswell County.

Few papers made extensive use of that press release, but in a day or two, thanks to the *Post* story, the State Department in Washington was reportedly besieged from around the world for information about the "seventy-five-foot rape," and Yanceyville had become big news. One state paper ran a front-page story on the case, carried a second statement by me demanding that the governor investigate "the break down of law and order in Caswell County," and a statement from the state NAACP denouncing me and saying that it was going to represent Ingram on appeal, in part to prevent the Communists from making political capital from the case.

When I dropped in on Louis Austin a couple of days later with a collection of clippings and press releases to celebrate the turn of events with him, the editor jestingly offered to hire me as his first white reporter, "just to help break down the color line." Ultimately Mack Ingram's conviction was reversed by the state supreme court, and the NAACP justifiably boasted of its role in his vindication.

The FBI was devoting more and more of its time to the Party. One day in Durham, Hank and I found ourselves closely followed by two FBI cars. One car tailgated ours at a distance of eight to fifteen feet while the other would occasionally pull in front of us. The performance lasted about two hours and had no apparent motive other than intimidation. In Carrboro, FBI lookouts, as neighbors later admitted to Gladys, moved into nearby houses with a clear view of the Scales home; the cars of our visitors were often ostentatiously followed when they left.

The arrogance of the FBI agents was extraordinary. Once when my mother had driven over from Hamilton Lakes for a visit, they not only followed her but tailgated her car for forty-eight miles back to Greensboro. Nearby public pay phones were watched or tapped, so that making a phone call was a complicated undertaking. The unpredictable followings became an annoyance and sometimes prevented my attending meetings or keeping appointments.

Others besides the FBI were interested in me. One Sunday afternoon when Gladys was in Chapel Hill with Barbara, I saw through a window a long, low truck with seven or eight men in it driving at about four or five miles an hour around and around the small block on which our house was situated. Since two crosses had been burned in our yard in the past year, both times when I was at home and asleep, I deduced from a study through the window of the grim-faced, mean-eyed lot in the truck that it was bent on similar mischief. I noted that, uncharacteristically, the FBI was nowhere in evidence. Taking a double-barreled shotgun (lacking its firing pins) which had belonged to my father, some rags, a ramrod, an oil can, and a twelve-year-old box of shells, I casually went out and sat on the front steps of the porch. Paying no attention to the truck, which had slowed almost to a stop, I loaded the gun in leisurely fashion and pretended to sight it on a bush in the yard. Noticing a marked increase in the truck's speed, I field-stripped the gun and quickly oiled and cleaned it, never once even looking at the truck, which was then moving briskly. I advanced to the street while the house blocked their view of me and stared into their eyes as they approached and drew alongside me; then I pointedly pulled out my pen, wrote down their license number after they had passed, indifferently turned my back on them, and sauntered back to the house. That was their final circuit; they disappeared from view; I never saw them again.

In the fall of 1951 Carl, formerly Foster's secretary, who had also worked closely with Jim and Ed, informed me that I was to become "operational but unavailable," which would mean leaving home, moving about considerably, staying some of the time with sympathizers (Party and non-Party personal friends), and traveling cautiously between cities and towns. The worst of it was that it meant seeing Gladys and Barbara only about every month or six weeks, and then away from home at carefully chosen spots.

That time the instructions seemed reasonable under the conditions of such intensive FBI harassment. Gladys and I asked her mother, who was retired, to come live with us to help look after the baby. She readily gave up her Brooklyn apartment and seemed pleased that she was needed. And soon after her arrival, I said goodbye and commenced my life underground.

I first visited with a couple in Durham who had dropped out of the Party two years before but remained friends. I spent a week with them and kept all my appointments without once encountering the FBI. Those same friends then drove me to a highway outside Durham, and there I flagged a bus which took me to Asheville without my entering a bus station. On the outskirts of Asheville I left the bus and found a comrade at his place of work; he called a mutual friend who drove me (on the floor of his car) to a home where I was able to meet with clubs and individuals for a few days. I got out of town by flagging a bus on the highway to High Point. A comrade there drove me to Thomasville, where I spent three days. Then I was driven to Winston-Salem for a district committee meeting.

Hank was in the process of moving into the deep freeze category: he got a traveling sales job some distance away, a new identity, and tried to keep some track of things from a distance. But he met with me rarely and only with careful prearrangement. I became the DO, elected by the district committee. I felt a certain pride in my new position, but far more humility at the responsibility I owed to so many people so dear to me. There was also some fear at the realization that there was no Bart, nor Sam, nor Gene, nor Bernie, nor Hank to lean on. I had to stand on my own feet and rely on my own resources.

Fortunately there was Olive. She was a Negro woman a few years my senior who for years had been the strongest member of the district committee and then had served incomparably on the three-member secretariat. She had been the heart and soul of Local 22 (if such a statement could have been made about any one person), and she was much the same to the Party. No one in the district equaled her in her broad grasp of issues, her natural avoidance of narrow, sectarian language and attitudes; no one was so understanding of human foibles, inconsistencies, and weaknesses; no one had such undoubted personal integrity. She had been and would continue to be both my ablest critic and my strongest support.

(It is a troubling thing that at this writing, in 1986, so much about the life of this splendid woman must be suppressed lest her identity become known and she or her family and friends suffer possible retribution or unanticipated ugly consequences. The same thing is true of the people mentioned below and, indeed, of many of those noted throughout this book. The trepidation is principally that of the authors. Those who have themselves suffered through a period of profound repression can seldom afford to be carefree or unguarded about discussing their own or others' political pasts. The spirit of McCarthyism is far from dead; therefore one must still fear for those companion survivors of that period and be mindful of the fears that still haunt some of them, and such considerations delimit the candor of this attempt at personal history.)

Of my prewar comrades, few leaders remained in the district. Ron had moved to the West; Steve was currently out of the country; Willie had become less active. But fine postwar figures had grown into leadership. C.C., a capable trade unionist with an impressive education, was one of the strong white leaders. W.A., John, and Bill were white North Carolinians who had interrupted graduate studies to take on Party assignments. W.A., my ablest lieutenant, had entered the trade union movement at a crucial time and place. John, W.A.'s longtime buddy, had a remarkable talent for inspiring students. Possessed of a fine sense of organization and a witty and sociable disposition, he radiated charm and humor. After a Party meeting, if a piano was handy, he would lead his comrades by the hour in singing hymns remembered from his Baptist childhood; if I forgot the words to something esoteric like "There is a Fountain Filled with Blood," he would look up despairingly from the keyboard and say, "What else can you expect from a damn Presbyterian?" Bill was the dynamo of the Party's textile concentration; for all his modesty, he was a keen, relentless analyst.

Among Negro comrades, besides the splendid group from Local 22 and Pat, the student leader, there were two remarkable Georges, one a furniture worker and union leader and the other a railroad worker, both deservedly admired by their co-workers and beloved of their Party comrades. One of the Georges was so mild, shy, and sweet-natured that it was startling to hear him galvanize a union meeting with fiery oratory or to see him leading a picket line of Negro and white workers, his soft eyes glowing like coals while he shouted with the force and righteousness of a wrathful angel. Milt, a rank-and-file tobacco worker, had a whole family as principled and admirable as he himself. Mamie, an eastern North Carolina tobacco worker, over sixty, had character and ability enough to make her fit company for such as Sojourner Truth and Harriet Tubman.

Among other women, there were two Marys, Frances, Rebecca, Sylvia, Phyllis—students, housewives, workers—all people of unusual strength and goodness. The Party was also rich in older people of both sexes, many of whom were reservoirs of experience and common sense. While all had their share of human failings and weaknesses, there were dozens of truly remarkable people and even more who seemed less than remarkable only because they were in such extraordinary company.

Such was the band of the Party faithful who were the source of whatever strength and confidence I possessed as I assumed my harrowing job. Despite all the pressure and anguish of the times, all the half-baked ideological mishmash, and all the misplaced trust in a "workers' paradise" and a Party that could do no wrong, there was within that organization an immense amount of intelligence, social concern, and love. That love was not only for other Party members, but for their countrymen and all humanity. If many wondered why they were so cut off from others and so widely condemned by them, none could put it all together and figure out the reason. Thus they hopefully followed their blind DO as I followed *my* blind leaders—most of us bound for disastrous disillusionment.

15

Down and Under

The demands we place on members place them almost in the category of abnormal people, with no regard for health, family, or contact with the masses.

John Williamson, Member, National Secretariat, CPUSA

By 1952 FBI harassment was extended to some of the second-echelon leadership. It took some getting used to, both for the recipients and for members of their families. It was disconcerting to have two agents sitting in front of one's house for hours at a time and at night periodically shining lights into the yard. It was even more unnerving to be tailgated while driving.

Techniques gradually evolved which served as partial countermeasures. One night I was spotted by the FBI while riding with W.A. near the latter's home. I planned to attend a meeting there and then spend the night. With two cars in pursuit, W.A. speeded up suddenly, turning several corners on two wheels. Caught by surprise, the agents followed, two blocks behind, and rounded a corner to find W.A.'s car stopped by a heavily wooded lot and W.A. pulling the car door shut on the side where I had been sitting. As W.A. drove away, with me on the floor, he could see the agents charging into the thicket with flashlights shining. W.A. proceeded home, parked his car as usual in his driveway, noting another FBI car parked down the block. He entered his house, where the participants in the meeting had already gathered, turning off the porch light as he did so. A few minutes later, under cover of darkness, I quietly entered through the kitchen door and conducted the meeting as intended.

A couple of months later, expecting that I would be under surveillance when he met me in his car, W.A. performed a similar maneuver, stopping by a wooded area where another comrade was waiting in his car. The FBI arrived in time to see the doors of *both* cars closing as they moved off in different directions. Determined not to be fooled again, the agents divided their forces and pursued each car. A minute later I, standing in the woods, was picked up by a third comrade, who drove me to a meeting on the opposite side of town.

If I was alone and picked up a tail, I either pretended not to notice until I could get assistance from friends with cars or, if the agents were clumsy, I would try a ploy similar to one that once worked in Durham. I entered a large department store, got on an elevator as the doors were closing, removed a raincoat and hat I had been wearing, requested a shopping bag to put them in, purchased a cheap baseball cap, and walked unnoticed out of the store, right past one of the agents who had been following me.

Once I was subjected to "saturation" surveillance in a small town, Reidsville, about thirty miles north of Greensboro. I had gone there late in the afternoon to retain a sort of maverick-liberal-populist attorney whom I had known well for many years. I wanted to have him available should I (or any other Communist) be arrested on any charge. When I stepped off the bus I thought I recognized an FBI agent on the platform and walked purposefully down the street to see what would happen. Within fifteen minutes, by keeping track of the last three numbers (or letters) on license plates, I had ascertained that at least four cars were leapfrogging around me. Apparently the FBI had enlisted the aid of the local police force, for they joined in the game with two prowl cars. I had dinner in a restaurant, called my lawyer acquaintance, stated my business, and told him that I was accompanied by a procession of FBI and police cars. The attorney was clearly skeptical about my being tailed, ascribing my perceptions to political paranoia, but asked me to meet him at his office in a few minutes. He readily agreed to be retained and asked for $250, a painfully large sum, which I paid him.

The lawyer was astonished to see from his window a great congestion of cars, including the police cars, on the quiet little street in front of his office, and he was perhaps even more surprised when they all dispersed as I left the building. Since I had nearly a two-hour wait before the next bus going to Greensboro, I strolled up and down the town's main street in the company of my entourage, thinking that if they did plan to pick me up, it would be amusing to be arrested on Scales Street, named for my great-uncle.

Not having seen my mother for some time, I called her from a pay phone and asked if she could meet me at a highway intersection, which I identified cryptically so that no one else could have known where I meant. When I got off my bus, she was waiting for me and so was the FBI. The agents had evidently tapped my mother's phone and followed her there. They then trailed us back to Hamilton Lakes. I had a pleasant visit for two or three days with my mother and Aunt Lucy while two FBI cars camped out in the street on either side of the house. At regular fifteen-minute intervals the car on the left would give a soft "beep-beep" on the horn, whereupon the car on the right would drive off, circle Lake Hamilton for a mile or so, and take up the previous position of the other car. The car that had beeped would drive slowly past the house, at night always sweeping the yard with a powerful searchlight. After a while the beep-beeping began to keep my mother awake, and the outrageousness of it upset her so much that I felt compelled to leave. Taking my briefcase, I walked out the back door through some thick woods, across a cornfield, through some more woods, along a path leading into a dirt road, and thence to a paved road. There I caught a Greensboro trolley which took me through the city to the eastern outskirts, where I hitched a ride to Raleigh.

About a day later, when Aunt Lucy, who still worked as director of religious education at the First Presbyterian Church, was on her way home, her car was forced off the road by angry FBI agents, who flashed their identity cards in her face and demanded roughly that she tell them how I had left and where I had gone. The saintly woman truthfully answered that she did not know, since her sister had not told her. After spending the night in Raleigh with an old Socialist friend, I had called my mother from the lobby of the Sir Walter Hotel and told her that I was well and not to worry. I had assumed that the phone was still tapped, that the call would be intercepted, and that the FBI would then cease its around-the-clock performance in front of her home. Apparently all was as I had assumed, except that having learned that their quarry had eluded them the FBI agents vented their frustration on my Aunt Lucy.

After making my call, I rode a city bus to the edge of town just in time to catch a bus to Rocky Mount, where an all-Negro Party club was expecting me. At the bus station I took a manila envelope full of Party literature from my briefcase, locked the briefcase, and checked it in a coin booth, along with the jacket to my suit. I bought a cheap straw hat, rolled my sleeves halfway, put the envelope under my arm and a pencil behind my ear, and, with a clipboard in my hand, confidently entered the Negro community. It was a Friday afternoon, and I resembled the many white insurance salesmen and collectors making their weekly rounds. On going to the house of a comrade, I was assured sotto voce by his wife that everything was OK and that my people were waiting for me at a certain house. Leaving her a "receipt," I went to the designated house, was invited in "for a glass of lemonade," greeted and embraced my comrades, and spent the meeting discussing union, civil rights, and Party problems. The next day, in Wilson and Greenville, I repeated the performance with the Party clubs there, leaving the straw hat with the hostess comrade at the last meeting until my next visit.

I had increasing difficulty in setting up meetings with Gladys and our daughter, and sometimes my efforts ended in failure. It was necessary to get them "cleaned" of FBI agents before they could be taken to a rendezvous, and that involved at least two cars. Sometimes the rendezvous would be at a comrade's or friend's home, or sometimes I would arrange for a comrade to drop us off at a highway motel and come back for us two days later. That procedure, however, attracted attention, and the FBI caught on to it at least once.

The FBI gained an early informer in Ralph Long, a Durham native and former Chapel Hill student valued in the Party mainly because of his working-class background. He later had bouts of sheer terror lest he be exposed as a Communist, relaying his fears to his comrades when he was drunk, and even suggesting that maybe he should go to the FBI. Because of such incidents, his habitual drunkenness, and his extreme emotional instability, he was gently told in 1948 that he was being dropped from the Party pending his rehabilitation.

His debut as an informer came in 1952 when he testified against a former textile worker and president of the Maryland CIO at a Smith Act conspiracy trial in Baltimore. According to the defendant, Long made a "complete ass" of himself. Two months later he published a series of sensational articles in the *Durham Sun,* possibly in exchange for a job as a sportswriter for that paper. After that, he was of little use to the FBI or anyone else. He seemed to disintegrate. He lost his hard-won job and became a public nuisance, with dozens of convictions in Durham for public drunkenness, disorderly conduct, and assault and battery. In 1954, scarcely three weeks after his twenty-first conviction for drunkenness, he was taken from either the gutter or the jail to perform before a session of the House Un-American Activities Committee. There, having no fear of being cross-examined, he fingered and virtually destroyed the career of a former classmate at Chapel Hill who had befriended and aided him when he had aspired to be a playwright. His testimony was full of factual errors of such a nature (especially concerning the number of Party clubs and members in Chapel Hill) as to cast doubt on whether he had indeed told all to the FBI. Yet there was no trace of any moral restraint on him in the eagerness with which he named names or in his unctuous concern to speak the "patriotic" pieties the committee wanted to hear.

While I was "unavailable," I once met him face to face on a city bus in Durham. He was in an appalling condition, apparently drunk, with his eyes red, his face bloated, and his mouth drooling at the corners. He kept telling me with evangelical fervor that the FBI was "a tough bunch; they tortured me for days; they're gonna *getcha* and they'll grind you down; they'll *grind* you down!" I commented that they certainly hadn't left much of *him,* and got off at the next stop.

Ralph Clontz, a native of Charlotte and then a law student at Duke University, wrote to me in the summer of 1948, with FBI encouragement, to express his interest in the Communist Party. I routinely sent him a box of literature and invited him to visit me in Carrboro if he wished further information. He came in September and aroused in his host a vague feeling of irritation and unease. I handled him politely but cautiously and answered all his questions. He came again in December armed with questions and notes. When he asked early on about the Party's attitude toward force and violence and whether it would be necessary in order to take power, I was immediately suspicious and on guard: the Party's national leaders had been indicted only four or five months before on the charge of "conspiracy to teach and advocate the violent overthrow of the government." I carefully related to Clontz the position I had arrived at a year or two before and had since consistently taken, both publicly and privately: that without the support of the majority of the American people on the principal issues of the time, the Party could not hope to gain or retain power; that the ballot would probably be the major weapon in achieving power; that although the ruling class largely controlled the levers of power, especially communications and police, it was still possible to reach the masses of people through an educational process if a solid base were gained in the unions and other popular organizations; that the capitalist system might well paralyze itself with its built-in economic crises; that although Communists would try to defend themselves when and if physically attacked, there was no force greater than that of an idea whose time had come; and that, as Lenin had said, we were not "putschists" and had no thought of violence in a bid for power. I probably added, as I usually did, that if the Party after a generation or so under bourgeois democratic conditions and enjoying full legality could not convince the American people if the superiority of socialism, it would deservedly fade from the political scene.

Whether my position was "correct" in accordance with American Party theoreticians, I did not know. The question had rarely been raised prior to the Smith Act indictments, and the Party's position was fuzzy and ambiguous, allowing for a directly opposed interpretation, depending on one's choice and interpretation of Marxist classics. I had simply worked out my own position, beginning about the time of the expulsion of Preacher and Betty, and basing it on my understanding of Marxism-Leninism in the light of American history and traditions—and no Party leader ever told me I was wrong.

As I was to find out later, Clontz turned over to the FBI "notes" purporting to show that in the first half hour of my second meeting with him I had stated that the ballot was useless, that ideas could accomplish nothing, that the government had closed the Party off from converting the masses to Communism by any educational process, that force alone could bring the Communists to power. In other words, he attributed to me the very views for which I had helped expel members, including Preacher and Betty, from the Party.

Whether Clontz prepared such a report in the hope of gaining financial support from the FBI or whether, as an ambitious lawyer-to-be who understood the requirements for a Smith Act conviction, he wanted to show it the sort of made-to-order evidence he could provide, in the hope of becoming a right-wing hero and promoting his career, I never knew. Certainly no FBI agent with a brain could have believed that a Party leader would have made such statements to a total stranger, especially in the light of the Smith Act indictments.

Nevertheless, because of Hank's and my ambivalence, Clontz was a persistent and unwelcome presence for years. Bernie met him and immediately distrusted him. Every comrade who met him at public meetings described him in such terms as "repulsive" and "phony," saying that he went around with a notebook trying to get the name and address of anyone who would talk to him. One non-Party friend warned me that he had known Clontz when a child, that he recalled him as the bully of his block and a "foul ball." I still hoped that despite appearances the hostile-looking, slick-talking, vulgar fellow might just be on the level.

By 1950, having spent much time with him and believing him to be largely devoid of feeling, I was becoming convinced that he *was* an FBI informant. Hank, however, met with him several times and gave him some chores to do. Clontz performed his tasks efficiently and promptly, thereby bringing joy to Hank's heart. "I like his style of work," Hank said, still suffering from the rather leisurely approach to assignments of his Carolina comrades. Hank decided to retain Clontz, once he had passed the bar, as the Party's lawyer for minor legal matters. He intended thus to establish a lawyer-client relationship which would severely limit Clontz's effectiveness if he *were* an FBI agent, but if Hank ever formalized such a relationship, he neglected to record it in writing or in the presence of witnesses. Meanwhile, Hank thought Clontz might just as well be an at-large member of the Party, meeting solely with me or with him. I agreed, reasoning that it was better to take a chance with what the guy could do to us individually than to live with the thought of having possibly turned away an honest man.

Being thus confined to meetings with Hank and me, Clontz was making no headway in meeting new Party members. He did, however, compile copious data on conversations with me—data that proved, when he chose later to produce them, to be sometimes fairly accurate, sometimes warped and twisted beyond recognition, sometimes transformed into their opposite, sometimes gratuitously invented, and all seemingly tailor-made for possible use against me in court. Finally, at the end of 1950, he went to New York to spy on the Jefferson School, a Party-run institution which taught courses in Marxism-Leninism and related subjects. Sporadically contacting Hank or me until we went underground, he continued to pester Gladys with inquiries after 1951 until he made his debut as a professional witness in 1953.

The southern Party leadership, after Jim Jackson went into hiding, had some problems of continuity. Carl, who had visited the district several times after 1950 and had won the trust and respect of the comrades, served for a time as Jim's surrogate in the field. The leading body, the Southern Regional Committee (SRC), had been set up with Jim as titular head and Ed as second-in-command. It consisted, over several years, of Sam Hall, the Alabama DO; Hosea Hudson; Carl, who later had to be relieved because of his wife's illness; a young Negro known as Daddy-O, who was co-opted onto the committee late in its existence; and Frannie, a young former leader in Westchester County in New York, who acted as a courier and arranged organizational matters for the committee; and me. Other DOs were sometimes included in the meetings as the occasion demanded.

Alice Burke, late in her second decade as the Virginia DO, had finally left the South for personal reasons. Bob, her successor, a relatively inexperienced New Yorker, had a great many problems in Virginia with a badly bruised Party organization; I was sent to help out and ultimately to assume overall responsibility for the district, visiting the state regularly and frequently. Shortly after that addition to my duties, the Tennessee Party fell into disarray, its acting DO having left the state. I therefore became the DO of Tennessee too. Because Memphis was the real urban center for northern Mississippi, that area also was added to my travels and responsibilities.

My visits with Gladys and our daughter became steadily harder to arrange, and as the difficulties grew, so did the time between meetings.

The hue and cry after me was considerable, with editorialists and columnists gunning for my hide. The irrationality of some of the attacks was astounding. During the Korean War, for example, the *Raleigh News and Observer,* in an editorial by the liberal editor Jonathan Daniels (son of Josephus, and FDR's last press secretary), argued that the Party and I were trying to injure the university by using my Chapel Hill post office box (which I had maintained for years) as a return address for Party leaflets. Daniels evidently got his inspiration from a news story given a big play in his paper two days earlier, which began with an account of a protest to the same effect by some Rocky Mount alumni and ended with a snide account of an interview with Gladys, pointedly noting that she was from Brooklyn, New York (in those days a southern journalistic euphemism for saying that she was Jewish). I replied, in part: "By noting that such Communist Party leaflets bear a post office box address in Chapel Hill (one short mile from my residence) the editorial deduces a sinister plot to 'give the impression' that

Junius, Gladys, and Barbara, 1953

my 'propaganda comes from the University.' Through similar logic, if the box were in Raleigh, we might give some fuddled brain 'the impression' that our material comes from *The News and Observer* or perhaps the Governor's office."

My letter was published only because I delivered it in person to Daniels (whom I had never met) in his office and took him to task for his unfairness and faulty reasoning. He heard me out and then said that although our families had been friends for generations he had no use for me; he then expanded on his intense personal dislike of me. I threw my letter on the desk, saying that I hadn't come to exchange personal insults and that I expected he would publish it because, being his father's son, he probably possessed "*some* sort of conscience." It was published, but in a most grudging, demeaning way, next to a letter from the state's most vocal racist and reactionary, John Clark, and accompanied by a second editorial defending the first one and equating Clark and me as "extremists." Such was the stance of the state's most liberal newspaper in those troubled times.

An objective close to the hearts of Carolina Communists since the twenties had been the organization of the textile workers, the most important group of industrial workers in either state and probably the most ostracized, despised, overworked, and underpaid. When I had first joined the Party, I had heard at first hand from Red Hendrix the bloody story of how the Communist-led union was crushed at Gastonia in 1929. Gastonia represented the culmination of roughly seventeen years of sporadic efforts, chiefly by the AFL, to gain an organizational foothold among textile workers in the South. It also epitomized the evils present in the industry.

Child labor was customary and the captains of the textile industry were tireless and effective fighters against all legislation aimed at eliminating or regulating it. Red Hendrix had become a textile worker as a child; most of my older co-workers in High Point had also worked in mills since childhood. A fifty-five- or sixty-hour work week (and longer) was commonplace. In the twenties, when the industry was in the doldrums, the mill owners increased their earnings by instituting clumsy imitations of Ford assembly-line efficiency methods. Waste motions were eliminated and each worker was given more machines to tend. The workers called the new system "speed-up" and "stretch-out." Pay was incredibly low; the work was hard and injurious to the health. The policies of mill owners toward the workers ranged from patronizing, patriarchal sternness to a relationship suggestive of slave owner and slaves. Where the workers lived in company-owned mill villages the tyranny was most complete.

Comfortable middle- and upper-class people liked to believe that in such

huge dominions as the Cone Mills in Greensboro the workers were treated
with generosity and beneficence. But in 1930, inspired by a speech delivered
in Greensboro by William Green, president of the AFL, a number of workers
joined the United Textile Workers. The Cone management promptly discharged about forty union members, some of whom had worked at Cone for
thirty years, and evicted them and their families from their mill-village
homes. The *Raleigh News and Observer,* then edited by Josephus Daniels,
printed objective, detailed accounts. The company straightway fired and
evicted some thirty or forty subscribers of the *News and Observer.* Later, in
the depths of the depression, unorganized and desperate textile workers attempted a widespread textile strike by driving caravans of cars (known as
"flying columns") from mill to mill asking the workers to join them. I was
later told by some Cone workers how it felt to awake one morning to find that
their kindly employers had placed National Guard troops and machine guns all
over the roofs of the mills.

In 1937 the CIO formed a Textile Workers Organizing Committee (TWOC),
which in 1940 became the Textile Workers Union of America (TWUA), under
the control of social-democratic unionists (Sidney Hillman, Emil Rieve,
George Baldanzi). Those leaders, having encountered Communists in northern textile centers, may well have had reasons for hating and distrusting them;
and those encounters, alongside ideological opposition, no doubt accounted
for the union leaders' obsessive anti-Communism and their profound aversion
to the brand of militant, confrontation-style, participatory unionism often
found in Communist-led unions.

From personal experience with their brand of "cooperative" unionism, I
was convinced that they, and especially George Baldanzi, who was the most
active leader of the TWUA in the South during its first thirteen years of
failure, had little understanding of the true condition of the textile workers. He
seemed not to grasp the acute deprivation they suffered, or the stacked deck
they faced in the mills, or the difficulties confronting their unions in the communities, owing to the widespread absence of democratic rights for poor people in the South. The impetuous and seemingly rash militancy of the newly
organized workers frightened Baldanzi and his staff, and he was quick to
suspect Communist incitement behind every outburst of worker indignation.
In an area of sharp confrontation with an implacable enemy, and at a time of
acute suffering for the workers, there was little room for mediation. The situation was not unlike that in Kentucky in which Florence Reese, a miner's wife,
bluntly posed the alternatives:

> Down in Harlan County, there ain't no neutrals there;
> You'll either be a union man or a thug for J. H. Blair.
> Which side are you on? Which side are you on?

Yet Baldanzi was forever trying to reason with the textile giants, to persuade them to cooperate with the union for their "mutual benefit." Apparently he never learned that the big textile corporations look on even a docile union as a total nuisance and a dangerous enemy—a fact his present-day successors likewise seem slow to learn.

In the late forties the Communists were looking for a place to make a modest beginning at propagating an alternative brand of textile unionism. Local 319 in High Point, once considered a radical, militant local, had deteriorated seriously in strength and become relatively quiescent (the TWUA *was* proficient at putting out fires). The Cone Mills in Greensboro were unorganized, and there were insufficient Party forces nearby. Finally it was decided to concentrate on the Erwin Mills in Durham, part of a major firm which had been organized by the TWUA into a large local. A handful of students and ex-students devoted their available time to studying the company, the union, the union contract, and the textile industry. A few got jobs in the mill and lived nearby. Eventually they managed to get to know some of the most militant and respected union workers, who freely voiced their shop grievances and general dissatisfaction with the union. The Party began publishing under its own name in 1949 a mimeographed paper called the *Textile Workers' Voice,* which at first was rather general in its comments, betraying a lack of inside knowledge of what went on in the plants. Some Party people then began to reveal themselves as Communists to certain trusted workers; the workers in turn supplied them with much information and even wrote pieces for the paper or helped to distribute it. One old-timer, intimidated by past blacklisting, became an informer to play it safe, but nevertheless provided the Communists with valid information and may, on balance, have done us more good than harm.

The workers in the plant received the paper with enthusiasm because it regularly roasted the company, mercilessly exposing its crassness and greed with the utmost specificity, often in the actual language of a worker directly affected. Simultaneously it exposed the pusillanimous behavior of the union's top brass vis-à-vis the company. The paper promised to tell the truth about what was going on in the plants and it kept that promise; unfortunately, nearly every other issue would contain some item about the lot of workers in the Soviet Union or the Soviet role in maintaining world peace, items which were barefaced (though unintentional) lies.

Baldanzi, the company, and the local press frequently denounced the Communist paper; but each month it would make its appearance and be passed from hand to hand, posted in washrooms, left under windshield wipers, and placed on front porches. The vast majority of workers, with good reason, believed what it said—at least about matters in the shop and union. With the

Party's improved ties, the little paper's uncertain "you" in speaking to the workers became in time an authoritative "we" and concerned itself with everything from exposing the company's insidious incentive schemes and Rieve's or Baldanzi's collaborationist support of them to a vehement protest against filthy women's and men's rest rooms in the plants (complete with accurate and vivid details).

At the end of its first year the *Textile Workers' Voice* spelled out the kind of unionism the Party stood for in the textile industry:

UNIONS RUN BY THE WORKERS—and for the workers' benefit, not stooge outfits helping the company.

WAGE INCREASES—get part of the big profits the textile bosses are socking away, and help feed our families.

FIGHTING THE STRETCHOUT—do away with the whole rotten incentive system, standards, 4-weeks trial, and the rest of the sell-out. Get a union contract that isn't full of holes—one that will end time studies and speed-up.

UNITY OF WHITE AND NEGRO—in place of hatred and prejudice, cooperation and brotherhood. Only by working together can we all go forward to better days in the South.

Despite infiltration by company spies and FBI informants, the textile club and its paper continued year after year, gaining influence and, incidentally, providing me with the greatest pleasure and satisfaction I got from my Party work in that period.

I rode buses and trains so much that I became a master of the Trailways and Greyhound timetables and knew all the out-of-the-way railroad passenger services in four states. In my new territories, where I was less likely to be recognized, I often stayed at the tourist homes which lined the highways in the residential areas of most cities; cheaper than hotels, they were also not so easily watched by the FBI. On other occasions I was forced to use small, third-rate hotels. On long trips I would usually travel at night, sleeping on the bus or train because of the greater security, as well as the economy of saving the cost of a night's lodging. The growing pressures of the times dictated that I move more cautiously and take greater care to avoid the FBI.

Was I accomplishing anything by giving up my career, living wretchedly away from my family, existing like a fugitive? If I had doubts, they were of my adequacy for the job I had taken on. Though the Party was slowly disintegrating, and though its best policies were gaining at a glacial rate, I never really doubted that the Party was fundamentally right (as the Chinese had most recently seemed to confirm by their successful revolution) and that it carried the hope of a better future within its battered ranks. Creative Party members in my districts occasionally were able to stimulate a few people concerning such important issues as Negro rights, civil liberties, economic issues, and peace. Strangely, they were often comrades whom I considered to be deficient in Marxist-Leninist theory. Inspired by a discussion in a Party club, such a comrade would go to a union meeting, an NAACP gathering, or a church and speak from his or her heart about an issue which the Party had said was important. Shunning jargon and clichés and forgetting about "correct formulations," he or she would still win meaningful support. If I could suggest follow-up steps which would avoid leaving my comrades in an exposed position, could gain them wider support, and then could consolidate the step organizationally, I would feel that my efforts had been worthwhile.

If I myself got discouraged, there was always a new McCarthyite outrage or some racist horror to rouse me with indignation. If I began to feel cynical, there was always the unpretentious goodness and decency of many of my comrades to humble and shame me. Visits to the homes of comrades or sympathizers would bring simultaneously a poignant thrill of enjoyment at some commonplace ritual, such as reading a story to the children or putting them to bed.

Could the Party make measurable progress toward building a sane and altruistic society during my lifetime? I thought so. The Party's line was good. What could be morally wrong with demanding equal rights for Negroes, opposing McCarthyism, insisting that production be on a commonsense basis with a fair slice of the wealth for working people, advocating peace in the world? Those things, I believed, were what a majority wanted—or would want when they understood them. With proper educational and organizational work, why couldn't we Communists consolidate that popular program and achieve those goals? The "nigger-lover" charge against us (a plus among Negroes) was effective mainly in the South, and decreasingly so there; besides, it was a badge of honor. But the "Soviet agent" characterization was always effective, even when there was no anti-Communist war on. All the same, the Party at every opportunity continued to obtrude its admiration for the Soviet Union into every issue. Party policies were nearly always justified by quotations from Marx, Engels, Lenin, and Stalin and presented in language that sounded phony and dehumanized, like a bad translation from the Russian. There was a painful resemblance between Party literature and that of certain evangelical religious groups, with their revealed truth, fervid use of Bible passages, and reliance on doctrinal jargon. Was the Party becoming an ingrown sect rather than a political force? Could the pervasive Soviet-worship and the smell of rigid doctrine be what was turning people away?

I began to incline toward a head-in-the-sand attitude about the Soviet Union and discussed it as little as possible. "Don't worry about defending the Soviet Union. They've *built* socialism; they're doing fine. Let's concentrate on what we can do here," I would say, thinking that my comrades might alienate fewer people and expose themselves less if they soft-pedaled this side of their thinking.

Further, I had a feeling that all was not well with the Soviet Union. Certainly something was wrong in the protracted drive against Titoism, with its series of treason trials, and in the relations between the Soviet Union and the "New Democracies," as the Soviet-dominated Central European countries were still unsmilingly called in Communist circles. From discussions I had had with scientifically trained comrades and sympathizers, I was also disturbed at the official endorsement in the Soviet Union of the genetics theories of Trofim D. Lysenko and the ruthless attacks on Mendelian genetics and its defenders, as well as on virtually all schools of psychology except Pavlov's. Zhdanov's foray into the policing of music, art, and literature grew more disturbing with the passage of years, especially when I read some of the highly touted postwar Soviet novels available in English translation from importers. Those formula-ridden, Pollyannaish examples of "socialist realism" seemed a disastrous comedown from nineteenth-century Russian literature and the varied Soviet literature of the 1920s. As a result of my worries about the Soviet Union, I noticed that when I reported on the political situation to comrades, I spent less and less time on the international situation, usually mentioning the triumphs of the Chinese Party as a morale booster and quickly moving on to the situation at home.

When it came to my teaching of Marxist-Leninist theory, I still carried with me in my briefcase a selection of classics, but in planning study courses for clubs or individuals, I no longer picked a single classic as a fount of truth applicable to most current problems. I began by selecting the current problem and then cited those passages which I thought threw light on it. But the old books lacked their former magic. A Party isolated, reviled, and generally held in disrepute could not fall back on quotations from revolutionaries of other lands and other times. It needed to give forthright programs and answers to its fellow countrymen, programs and answers growing from its own experience, formulated in its own native language. Why couldn't our Party do that? Why couldn't *I*? Had we lost the ability to think for ourselves?

An event that dismayed American Communists everywhere was the execution of Ethel and Julius Rosenberg. While there was an unspoken guess that the Rosenbergs might have been Communists, few in the Party doubted their innocence of the charges. I had heard from mutual friends that the Rosenbergs

had belonged to the Young Communist League at one time, but I never entertained the thought that the Soviet Union would have endangered the Party by
trying to recruit any American Communist as a spy.

(Many years later, when I came to understand the exploitation of the Communist parties of other nations by the Soviet Party, I would join perhaps scores
of other former Communist leaders in sweating over the question "What
would I have done, back then, if the Soviet Union, the workers' socialist
vanguard, had asked *me* to spy for it?" Can I say with absolute certainty that I
would have said no? I hope and believe that I can.)

Communists participated belatedly but desperately in the fight to prevent
the Rosenbergs' execution. In the climactic days of June 1953, we watched in
disbelief as Eisenhower smugly denied clemency; as Attorney General
Brownell zealously combated every effort made for a stay or a full judicial
review; and as the majority of the Vinson Supreme Court disgraced itself by
removing the last barrier to execution. The day of the execution is burned into
the memory of multitudes, certainly of every Communist then alive. As with
Pearl Harbor day, there are few who cannot remember, more than a third of a
century later, where they were and what they were doing. I was in Roanoke,
Virginia, and heard the news from a portable radio on the hood of a car
surrounded by a hushed group. I spent that night walking the streets of
Roanoke and the floor of my hotel room.

A couple of days later I met with a comrade in eastern Tennessee, an ex-
miner, and heard with sympathy how he, in his rage and frustration that night,
had climbed to a mountaintop and set off charge after charge of dynamite until
long past midnight.

The Southern Regional Committee met and functioned on a regular and
carefully prepared basis. New York was the frequent site of its meetings because of the large Party forces there and the relative ease with which one could
shake an FBI tail in the subways or on the city streets. Usually, security
arrangements were smooth, efficient, and intelligent. The meetings themselves were less satisfactory. Jim, though a "fugitive from justice," still ruled
through his deputy, Ed, who met with him at intervals and, without ever
mentioning that he had seen him, relayed his thinking and instructions to the
SRC. Ed was a far more able organizer than his mentor and far pleasanter to
deal with. Although he sometimes adopted Jim's superior approach toward
comrades, I grew fond of him, admiring his keen mind and his articulate way
of presenting Jim's and his own thinking. Still, there was an ingrown, inward-
looking quality to the leadership which I had never encountered with any of
the Carolina DOs. There was a good deal of theory spinning, and a number of
the drives launched had overly ambitious goals, not based on the actual forces

available. And there were awkward clashes, with some of those present following what I considered to be an ignorant, leftist policy.

I, for example, along with others, had early been keen on having the southern Party members work in the NAACP to help build that organization and to help overcome its stodginess; I had helped implement the policy in the Carolinas. I had stressed that Party forces should not try to take over chapters or push them into untenable positions, but should participate in the organization wholeheartedly with the aim of building it up as the leading Negro-defense bulwark in the South. My approach met considerable opposition at first: the NAACP was a "middle-class outfit"; it should be transformed; it was anti-Communist and it Red-baited; the Party shouldn't tail behind a bourgeois organization. Then eventually my position was adopted and became gospel, without even a self-critical backward look.

The southern Party had precious little ability to execute any of the grandiose plans which Jim in his isolation might create for it. The Party in Alabama was threadbare. Florida was full of aged northern Jewish retirees scarcely suited for much activity. Georgia was paralyzed. Louisiana and Texas, with once-effective organizations, were only shadows of their former estate. The partial wrecking of the southern Party and the loss of most of its trade union base were reflected in its leading committee. Sam Hall, harassed and weary, was largely unable to maintain sufficient contact with his scattered members to come to grips with the fundamental problems of his district. Later he developed a malignant brain tumor, lingered for six months after surgery, and died under an assumed name in a New York hospital. Hosea Hudson had lost touch with activity in his old haunts and was becoming a monument, respected by all his comrades for his role in the thirties and early forties; he was prone to reiteration of the truths he had learned so painfully.

Jim and Ed were both generals without much of an army. Genuine mass leaders of Negro youth in the thirties, they had invested their talents and aspirations in the Party after the war and soon found themselves isolated and powerless outside it, and not very comfortable with the shrinking membership. Nevertheless, they bravely set themselves the task of rebuilding the Party in the South. If they set about their task with more passion than reason, it was perhaps because they, who had known the exaltation of giving inspirational leadership to hundreds of Negro youth, found themselves a few years later hunted and politically impotent, while their people seemed destined for more decades of the repression and degradation they had known for so long. And if both were given to authoritarian attitudes and practices and other forms of self-indulgence, those excesses seemed, under the circumstances, to be understandable and forgivable.

I, though relatively inexperienced and deficient in many ways as a leader, had been taught by my able predecessors as DO to look for political answers to problems and always to bring adopted programs down to local and individual cases. I was, consequently, skeptical about the success of campaigns to solve such organizational problems as reregistration of the membership by rhetoric or command. Furthermore, I was forever trying to discuss trade union problems at a time when most southern DOs had nearly forgotten their vanished influence in unions. Those differences in concerns and attitude gave me a slight feeling of disharmony with the rest of the committee, although I was then unable to pinpoint any basic differences with my comrades.

Since I was faced with a multitude of union problems in my four states, I urged for a year and a half a full discussion of trade union questions in the committee, but when the discussion finally came, I found that no one had any significant thoughts on the subject. I was forced to chart my own course, as I had been doing, drawing when possible on the vast experience of the Carolina district's own unionists. The discussion convinced me that most of the southern Party districts were in such disarray that they had virtually no approach to trade unions, even where Party members belonged to locals. Such evidence of loss of political perspective made me less respectful of my colleagues' superior experience.

Party leadership was inherently painful. For me the worst ordeal came when, as the Party's surrogate, I was forced to put pressure on a comrade to do something he or she was reluctant to agree to. Whether it involved disabusing someone of an "incorrect" political attitude, urging the contribution of more money to the Party's annual fund drive, or persuading someone to carry out a distasteful assignment, the confrontation nearly always hurt me worse than my comrade.

The most distressing such occasion took place early in 1954 and involved my old friend Willie in High Point. Ed had been appalled at the decline in Party registration figures for 1953. He made a speech to the SRC in which he said he could not tolerate such a loss of membership, that it could shortly amount to the liquidation of the Party, and that he would meet with each DO for an individual accounting for each member not reregistered. Though the decline in my districts had been quite small, when Ed heard that Willie had been in the Party since the mid-thirties, he demanded in his polished, clipped speech to know "precisely on what basis" I had allowed such a comrade to drop out. Ed pressed the attack in his best schoolmaster style: What had been Willie's reasons? Had l struggled with him? Ultimately I was pilloried for not having reregistered Willie; an implication of white chauvinism was thrown in, since Willie was a white textile worker, a category the Party was supposed to be concentrating on. Hosea, responsible for no district, threw in his two cents, emphasizing the white-chauvinist aspect and suggesting that I was too "soft."

A few days later, in High Point, Willie picked me up in his car in response to a telephone signal. He was cordial and asked what was up. I said I wanted him to reconsider his refusal to register. His face turned gloomy. He said he had been through all that before: his heart wasn't in the Party any more; he didn't think the leadership knew what it was doing; sending the leadership underground had been foolishness; the bail jumping of some of the leaders was wrong; the Party's attacks on the left-wing union leaders was crazy; the Party was going nowhere, a lost cause; and if he was needed for anything that made sense, I knew where he lived. Though I saw some truth in every point he made, I systematically wore him down, misusing argument, persuasion, references to his Party loyalty, his past courage, and even our friendship. Finally, without a word, Willie reached for his wallet and paid his dues for a year in advance, and while driving me where I wanted to go, he spoke only of family matters and mutual friends. When we had parted, I felt that I had bullied a friend and had betrayed our friendship—for nothing. The statistics showed one more member in the Party, but that was a lie. Willie had lost confidence in the movement and was truly lost to it. When next I reported to Ed and was complimented on reregistering Willie, I felt as though I had just received thirty pieces of silver.

Gladys's situation in Carrboro was becoming untenable. For a time she had worked in a furniture store in Durham while her mother took care of Barbara; but she was fired when Ralph Clontz, making his debut as an informer in a proceeding against the Jefferson School, stated that I had told him that Gladys would lead the Party if I should disappear. She secured another job as window trimmer in the Durham store of a nationwide clothing chain. The manager liked her work and refused to fire her when FBI agents urged that he do so. FBI pressure on the company's main store was likewise resisted. But she, Barbara, and her mother were totally isolated except for my former in-laws and two or three students who continued to visit them despite the FBI's observation of their every move. Visits with me were three to four months apart. Since no useful purpose was being served by such torture, in the spring of 1954, with careful prearrangement, they were all whisked away from Carrboro in the middle of the night and put on a train to New York, where they were met and de-tailed by expert comrades. In a few days Gladys and I were able to set up housekeeping in the Highbridge section of the Bronx under an assumed name.

· Being reunited with my family was a joyous relief for me, even though most of my time was spent away from them in the South. Gladys got a job as a Macy's comparison shopper under yet another assumed name. Occasionally, with careful planning, we were able to visit with Bea and Bernie (also "unavailable") and, at different times, with Hank, meeting in places such as the Central Park Zoo and even in the bleachers at Yankee Stadium.

Discussions with Hank and Bernie greatly broadened my view of what was going on in the Party and in the world around us. From the way they spoke of Foster and some of the operative leadership, I gathered that sacred cows were fast disappearing. Little was taken for granted; idols had crumbled; and doctrinaire leaders could expect to be humiliated when they offered inspirational flights of rhetoric to Party functionaries in search of hard political answers.

Some of their down-to-earth spirit began to rub off on me. At the next SRC meeting I was gently critical of Ed for his insufficient concern with trade union questions, and Hosea thundered in Ed's defense in a state of authoritarian outrage. I decided that thenceforth I was going to carry out the line of the SRC with more awareness of the capability of the forces the Party actually had, and with more modesty in the tasks and goals I set for my hardpressed comrades. Ed (and Jim) could worry about impressing the Party brass with the "impact" of the southern Party. I was going to look for real achievements, even if only two, or five, or ten people were involved. I was having no more baloney statistics, no more inflated claims for inconsequential actions, no more kowtowing to leaders out of touch with reality or living in the past.

With my new resolves in mind, I began making plans for a long sojourn in Tennessee, starting with Memphis and then working my way east. To vary my travel pattern, I would go South through the Midwest. My first night, I decided, I would spend in Cincinnati.

Part Three

God help that country where informers
    thrive!
Where slander flourishes and lies
    contrive
To kill with whispers! Where men lie and
    live!

Archibald MacLeish, from "The Black Day"

16

Unmitigated Hogwash

And let us reflect that having banished from our land that religious intolerance under which mankind so long bled and suffered, we have yet gained little if we countenance a political intolerance as despotic, as wicked, and capable of as bitter and bloody persecutions.

Thomas Jefferson, First Inaugural Address

E ven with my leg-irons and half my chains discarded, I found my disembarkation at the Greensboro–High Point airport painful. I resented being trussed up like a roped calf and offered as a target for my hometown's newspaper photographers. The marshal who had allowed me to go unfed, immobilized with manacles, threatened, and half frozen on the flight from Memphis hustled me past reporters into a men's room, where he removed the remaining hardware, leaving me merely handcuffed. While he was thus occupied, I looked him in the face and said sarcastically, "Thanks very much for fulfilling your responsibilities so conscientiously and considerately." The marshal wriggled like a bashful child, grinned widely, and replied, "Well, we *try* to do our best, but it's not often we get anyone who's gentleman enough to thank us. I hope you come out of all this OK. Lots of luck." And with that he signed me over to the local marshal, leaving me speechless and pondering the limited effectiveness of sarcasm.

Instead of heading for Greensboro, the marshal drove to Winston-Salem, explaining to me that Forsyth County had just completed a new jail which was the last word in modernity and security. The jail was within easy smelling distance of several Reynolds Tobacco plants, and the pungent odor of cured tobacco served as a persistent reminder of the identity of one of my triumphant adversaries. Mr. Speas, a gruff but kindly man and a paragon of jailers, installed me in a clean, apparently never-used, cellblock, which I had all to myself. Since the second and final meal had been served, Speas opened the kitchen and brought me a hot plate of substantial "country" food, possibly the most-appreciated meal I'd ever had. I made myself at home in my new quarters and soon fell into a peaceful sleep.

My isolation from the world ended the next day with a visit from my mother Not having seen her for nearly two years, I was shocked at how much she had aged. She was pale and distraught and walked with some difficulty when she arrived in the company of Speas, who was required to be present during her visit. He quickly got her a chair so she could sit outside the bullpen bars, and then he stood as far away as possible so as not to be intrusive.

My mother had not been idle; in her distress over my arrest, she had busied herself with trying to secure respectable local counsel to defend me. She was fearful that her son, left to himself, would stage a frightful replay, abetted by northern lawyer-ideologues, of the first Foley Square Smith Act trial presided over by Judge Medina. So skillfully had that judge promoted nationwide the stereotype of Communist lawyers and defendants shouting at, berating, and harassing both prosecutors and the court during the nine-month trial that not only my mother but probably the entire Greensboro bar understood such actions to be the hallmark of Communist court behavior. She had consulted several lawyers of her acquaintance, particularly Richardson Preyer, a family friend whom I much liked and who had married Emily Harris, my favorite cousin. Because he was an intelligent and principled lawyer, my mother had confidence in him; and because he was a kind man and concerned for her, Rich had consulted several lawyers who might, he thought, be willing to accept the Scales case. Never having tried a federal case before, he would not handle it alone. Most lawyers were not eager, in a political atmosphere compounded of heavy portions of pro-segregation sentiment and McCarthyism, to defend a "nigger-lovin' Red," about whom the most favorable opinion likely to be encountered was that he was crazy.

To my surprise, Rich came up with a very prominent member of the bar, about ten years his senior, often a representative of textile corporations against unions, who would consider handling the case jointly with him. The two lawyers came to visit me in jail on December 6. On being assured that I did not believe in force and violence, the senior attorney said that if they handled the case they would do so without soapboxing, in a dignified legalistic manner, and they expected complete control over tactics, witnesses, arguments, and the like; they wanted no compensation from the Party, if indeed they were compensated at all; and I must discourage handbills or other "public clamor." I said I was primarily concerned with an effective, forceful presentation of the truth; that their political views and style did not concern me; but that I would not, under any circumstances, make a guilty plea, since that would perjure and disgrace me. We seemed to have reached an understanding, but agreed to think it over till the next day.

But did we understand one another? I, feeling as though I were trying to make myself heard through soundproof glass, tended to lapse into stridency and political jargon. That, in turn, prompted the lawyers to speak to me as to an uncomprehending child or a mental patient.

The next morning I was driven to the federal courthouse above the post office in Greensboro and locked in a small cage in the marshal's office. When Rich and the other attorney appeared, the elder announced that he did not think they could satisfy me or my friends in the way they would conduct the case. My immediate, uncharitable reaction was that the corporation lawyer was afraid of the adverse reaction of his clients if he should take the case; but when I considered the amount of concern and responsibility the man had shown, and the time and thought he had given to my situation, I was inclined to accept him at his word. I thanked him and he left. Rich said that he would persist in his search to find counsel who might work with him. He seemed to feel strongly that the integrity of the Greensboro bar demanded that it provide adequate counsel for such an unpopular defendant. I held little hope for his success. Even the maverick lawyer from Reidsville whom I'd retained two years before had merely visited me very briefly in jail, attempted to extract five thousand dollars from my mother, and when that enterprise failed, washed his hands of the matter and refused to accept phone calls about it.

When Rich left, my mother arrived and, assuming that I had rejected the lawyers, reproached me bitterly as I was taken into court alone. I told the judge that I didn't have counsel and asked for a week's postponement, which was granted. I then asked for a reduction in my hundred-thousand-dollar bail, arguing that it was wildly out of proportion to amounts set in other Smith Act cases. For example, Martha Stone, head of the New Jersey Party and a member of the national committee, arrested the previous month on the identical charge, had been released in two days on fifteen thousand dollars' bail. After some wrangling, my bail was set at thirty-five thousand dollars.

Rich came up with a tough lawyer with a sterling reputation in criminal practice who would take my case, in association with Rich, for no fee—by court appointment. He said he would not argue for lower bail because he thought denial of reasonable bail and my remaining in jail would create public sympathy for me. I pointed out that in 131 previous Smith Act indictments, not one person had been denied bail; that reasonable bail was a constitutional right that lawyers should fight for; and that accepting such outrageous bail could adversely affect the bail efforts of other Smith Act defendants later on. The new lawyer thereupon bowed out of the case with what I thought was a sigh of relief, and the chance of a defense with local counsel slipped away.

Every day I received letters from well-wishers from all over the country. Among many others, Elizabeth Gurley Flynn, William Z. Foster, and Benjamin J. Davis wrote to me. I was also touched by a concerned message from Dr. Herbert Aptheker, the historian, who had become my friend during the previous six years.

Determined to speed my release from jail, Gladys came to Greensboro despite my fear that she might be arrested under the Smith Act or some state law such as the Anti-Klan Law, which had been drafted primarily for use against the Party. When my mother brought her to visit me, I hugged and kissed her through the bars while my mother sat to one side and engaged Speas in conversation.

Because Rich had run out of prospective attorneys, and because two eminent civil liberties lawyers suggested by the Party were temporarily unavailable, I was finally arraigned without counsel. The judge entered a plea of not guilty for me, and a date was set for argument for bail reduction. That argument never took place. Without consulting anyone, and without my knowledge or Gladys's, my mother posted the thirty-five-thousand-dollar bond in government notes. The next day I was hauled to Greensboro yet again, where my mother and I signed numerous papers; I was then freed. After I kissed my mother goodbye and answered the interminable questions of reporters, Gladys and I boarded a bus to New York, arriving in time to buy a tree and some presents for our daughter's fourth Christmas.

At the beginning of 1955, there was considerable social activity involving the "available" Party leaders in New York, whose numbers were slowly growing. A few were returning from serving Smith Act sentences; many more were abandoning their underground status; all were being welcomed back to normal Party life. The underground Party apparatus was gradually disintegrating as more and more of its participants recognized the futility and foolishness of the entire operation. The dominant opinion among those "coming out from under" was that the three years or so of the underground had been a costly disaster—politically, financially, and personally.

Instead of fighting tenaciously for every vestige of its legality and holding close to its popular base, the leadership had surrendered the Party's legal image, beginning with the planned bail jumping of four of its national leaders and continuing with the massive disappearance of most of its active leaders. As a result, the Party's isolation had increased while its influence had declined. Accumulated Party funds, held in reserve, had been squandered at a great rate to maintain the secret apparatus. But the apparatus was no secret to the FBI, which had infiltrated it and observed it with considerable success. Finally, the suffering and stress borne by the participants and their families had been incalculable. The unnatural life-styles, with one or both spouses living away from home like nomads, the crazy hours, the destabilizing separations—all put severe strains on marriages and, worse, on children. Only years later did many of the psychological traumas suffered by the small children of those Party leaders in the early fifties come to the surface to torment them and their parents. Bitterness and persistent questioning of authority characterized the attitude of many a returned veteran of the underground.

I was not bitter for myself, because I thought that in the South, with its unusual array of hostile forces, exceptional animosity toward the Party, and scarcity of large urban centers, there had been reason for a fair amount of clandestine activity if I were to function at all. Besides, there was no one else underground in my four states except Bob in Virginia; and Bob stayed pretty much in one place. But I could see the disastrous effects, even in the South, of the Party's de facto abdication of its status as a legal party, and I profoundly understood the suppressed anger of my ex-underground comrades.

As a Smith Act victim, I suddenly found myself a celebrity readily accepted in exalted Party circles. Gladys had soon been pulled into the activity of a committee of Smith Act families made up chiefly of the wives of Party celebrities. I had to spend much of my time with the Civil Rights Congress (CRC), the Party's principal defense organization. It was headed by William L. Patterson, a prominent Negro Communist who had become something of an elder statesman and confined himself mostly to public relations tasks. The herculean job of coordinating the work on dozens of pending defense cases devolved on William Albertson, himself on appeal from a Smith Act conviction. A former delicatessen worker who had played a major part in organizing his fellow workers in New York City, Albertson worked tirelessly and ably in the CRC.

The CRC's immediate concern with my case was to help me raise money for my defense and to find me a lawyer. While such problems were being attacked, I began to get better acquainted with many eminent Party people, some of whom I'd known only slightly before: George Charney, the New York State Party leader whom I'd called from Memphis; Alan Max, Joe Clark, Harry Raymond, Max Gordon, Abner Berry, and Rob Hall, all of the *Daily Worker;* my old friend Herbert Aptheker, who had several times made speaking tours of southern universities and had once stayed a week at my Carrboro home during my brief bachelor days; "Doc" Blumberg, with whom I'd met frequently in the underground; Joe Starobin, former foreign editor of the *Daily Worker,* author, traveler, and independent thinker; and many others. The wide diversity of viewpoints among such people was stimulating and helped to put southern problems in a broader perspective.

I also had occasion to talk at length with William Z. Foster and Elizabeth Gurley Flynn, then among the outstanding leaders not in prison or in hiding. My more intimate acquaintance with some of the leading figures among the Party leadership eliminated my naive hero worship of them and gave me a more sophisticated view of the Party generally. Concurrently I began to nurse a feeling that Ed (and Jim) took advantage of me and other southern leaders by trading on our blind faith and political provincialism in order to keep us in line. It was still a time in the Southern Regional Committee when the statement *"That* is the opinion of Comrade Foster" was sufficient to end most arguments. On the New York scene, a typical response to that statement might not have been at all respectful.

Around the beginning of the new year I received a message from Hans, whom I'd not seen for several years, saying that it was imperative that he speak with me. Accordingly, Gladys and I met with him and his likable young wife. Hans had had a harrowing, disillusioning experience with state thought control in eastern Europe, had returned to the West nearly broke, and after a brief stay in Ireland had then made his way back to the United States, where he had eventually obtained a teaching job in New Jersey. He had then met and married the daughter of a world-renowned M.I.T. scholar, and he had broken irrevocably with the Party.

Such matters, however, were not what Hans wanted to talk about. He had followed the accounts of the case against me, had somehow got hold of a copy of the indictment (apparently with less difficulty than I), and had consulted a lawyer acquaintance. The government's case, he reasoned, would stand or fall on my personal attitude toward force and violence. He had shared my house for six months, discussing every aspect of the question with me, and could refute with specificity every facet of the indictment as it related to my knowledge and belief. He believed that he could speak with authority as an expert on Marxism-Leninism, as an ex-Stalinist, and as a former spokesman for the American Party at the University of Chicago and at Chapel Hill.

But that was still not what he wanted to discuss. When he took the stand, he said, he was sure he would be asked the names of his former comrades; he would refuse to name them and would be held in contempt. All those factors he had discussed with his wife, who was in full agreement that he should testify. If his contempt sentence should be no more than six months, everything would be fine; their savings would carry them through that. The question was, if the sentence were longer, say a year, or two, or three, could my defense committee guarantee some minimal financial assistance, if needed, to his wife?

I was overwhelmed. My first inclination was to refuse the offer with profound thanks, but I knew my friend's hardheaded determination too well. We agreed to let the matter of his testifying rest with my lawyer—when I got one.

I had to have a lawyer by the middle of January because the pretrial motions were due by them. The CRC found me one, a sort of utility infielder who had passed the New York bar but had practiced law very little. His assignment was to obtain a postponement while a suitable lawyer was found to try the case. He and I flew down to Greensboro, where the newspapers prominently displayed his picture. The legal community, according to my mother, duly noted that he was from New York, a Jew, and, presumably, a Communist. The postponement was obtained, pretrial deadlines were scheduled, and the trial was to start April 11. The lawyer flew back to New York, while I stayed awhile with my mother and aunt and then resumed my Party activities, visiting my principal comrades in Winston-Salem, Durham, and Chapel Hill.

While I was in Chapel Hill, a comrade took me one night to see two graduate students who wanted to discuss testifying on my behalf. Their faces were familiar, but I could not recall their names. As undergraduates they had both attended one of the numerous small meetings in Chapel Hill churches in which I'd been invited to state my beliefs. They remembered my statements rejecting force and violence in vivid detail, thereby convincing me that they would be excellent witnesses. I asked if they thought testifying for me would endanger their graduate degrees. They both said they did not; their academic work was above reproach; their activities in college were not even remotely leftist. They both had a low opinion of Communism, but they felt that I was sincere and was falsely accused. I thanked them, saying that I would see them again in the spring when I had a lawyer.

The comrades I met with were warm and supportive, trying to be helpful about my approaching trial, nearly all offering to testify. I explained the problems facing a Communist who testified for me. Non-Party friends could testify without having to identify Communists, since they could not know for sure who was or was not in the Party, but in the prevailing atmosphere they could face severe economic and social pressures. I thought it would not be easy to find defense witnesses.

Soon after returning to New York, I made a trip to Washington. There, at the recommendation of the CRC, I retained as my attorney David Rein of the firm of Forer and Rein. Dave was a short, round-faced man who deported himself with natural dignity. His sympathies were with the left, and he and his partner, Joe Forer, were often called "Red lawyers"; but he was scathing in his contempt for numerous Communist Party leaders with whom he had dealt. He also loathed and distrusted the CRC, and he emphasized on several occasions that *I* was his client, not the CRC or the Party.

I never asked about Dave's political beliefs or affiliation (if any); in a short time he had my complete confidence. A few inquiries provided the basic facts: he was a New Yorker, a product of Columbia University Law School; he had been in practice in Washington for many years with Forer. While the House Un-American Activities Committee and the McCarthy committee were reinventing the Inquisition and making a mockery of due process of law, desperate victims of various unpopular political persuasions came to the offices of Forer and Rein. All too often they had no money and few prospects of getting any, though that never was an obstacle to the firm's representing them. Those two brilliant, imperturbable lawyers persisted in reminding hearing rooms full of lawmakers that the Constitution was the basis of the laws, that freedom of speech and belief was a basic constitutional right, that their clients, regardless of ideology or affiliation, were entitled to due process of law (and common courtesy), and that in the English-speaking world a star-chamber proceeding had for centuries been recognized as a shameful thing.

Living near the edge of poverty themselves, they made their services available to all the unfortunates like me who could find no one to take their cases. Scores of clients owed them both legal fees and their gratitude. Indeed, the whole nation owes them its gratitude for courageously doing their part to defend the Bill of Rights at a time when widespread madness threatened its existence and so many lawyers ran away from their consciences and their responsibilities.

Having accepted the case, Dave moved with dispatch. He visited my mother, listened attentively, and to her great surprise, made an excellent impression on her. He then began to prepare motions, including one challenging the sufficiency of the indictment and another challenging the manner of jury selection in the judicial district. The regular judge of the Middle District of North Carolina was reportedly ill, and a special handpicked district judge, Albert V. Bryan of Alexandria, Virginia, was assigned by the Fourth Circuit Court of Appeals to try my case. He was reputed to be highly competent legally, but no other reliable information about him was available. He occasionally affected courtly, antebellum southern manners, as I was soon to observe. Shortly before the trial was to begin, I walked into the dining room of the King Cotton Hotel to have breakfast with Dave. On the way to Dave's table, I was startled to see Judge Bryan rise from his seat, bow from the waist, and murmur with a sharklike smile, "Mr. Scales!" I returned the bow in silence with what Dave thought was considerable elegance. Dave shrewdly remarked, "I think he's heard about your aristocratic family and he's testing you. I also think he's convinced you're guilty of something, but he's not quite sure what it is yet."

I found time to go to High Point to visit Esther Gillen for the first time in three years. She greeted me with the same affection as always, mixed with her concern over my legal situation. Before I could even sit down, she said she was going to testify for me because she knew how phony that "violence" charge was. After bringing me up to date on family news and stuffing me with her delicious biscuits, she took me to see various neighbors, who welcomed me with great warmth. I was deeply touched because I had gradually come to feel that I was a pariah in many of my old haunts. Full of enthusiasm, Esther drove me in her little red auto to a nearby town for a visit with her middle daughter, Carleen, who had married and had just given birth to her second child. I held and admired the new baby while the glowing young mother showed me the same loving tenderness she had as a little girl, before the war. Esther then drove me to Greensboro and dropped me off at my mother's apartment, reiterating her willingness to testify at my trial.

Meanwhile, Dave and I were searching for other witnesses who might testify for the defense. We borrowed my mother's car one morning and went to Chapel Hill. I phoned a non-Party friend, the son of a well-known liberal, who as an undergraduate had had the freedom of my home for a couple of years and knew intimately my views on the subject of "violent overthrow." The young man, then an advanced graduate student, was obviously distressed by the call even before he knew its purpose. He pleaded to be excused as a witness, saying that the publicity could ruin his chances of employment and even jeopardize his degree. Feeling mortified and embarrassed, as though I had done something shameful, I said to forget it, apologized, and hung up.

Next I called a professor friend under whom I had taken several enjoyable undergraduate courses in Greek literature. The professor and I had become quite good friends and had carried on extensive conversations, with me speaking frankly as a Communist. The conversations persisted after I became a graduate student and a public Communist, often causing us to arrive at our homes late for dinner. The professor, who had once been a Protestant minister, was particularly interested in whether the Communists proposed the use of violence in achieving power. The discussions had been helpful to me because the give-and-take helped me formulate my position.

The professor was in an impregnable position in his department and in the Chapel Hill community; he would shortly retire; and any charge that he was a Communist sympathizer would have seemed entirely preposterous (at least in Chapel Hill, where he was well known), even in the prevailing McCarthyist atmosphere. I expected a cordial reception, for I remembered the man at our last meeting, in about 1951, when he had been deeply concerned for my welfare and safety and quite admiring of my advocacy, if not of my cause. When I identified myself over the phone, there was a sound of the intake of breath followed by a brief period of silence. I said that I was in town with my lawyer in search of defense witnesses and asked if we might drop by his house to discuss the matter with him. The professor stammeringly postponed the visit for an hour and a half. I assured Dave that my friend was a man of such integrity, piety, and dedication to democratic principles that there was little doubt he would be willing to relate the content of our discussions on the witness stand. Dave made no comment.

We arrived at the professor's home in the late afternoon and found him awaiting us on the front porch. He nervously invited us inside, where his wife, other family members, and a hostile-looking stranger were assembled. The stranger was introduced as the dean of the Law School. I stated my problem of securing witnesses, and Dave outlined the indictment, explaining that challenging the "knowing" and "intending" clauses was vital. He was several times boorishly heckled by the dean until Dave asked for an explanation of his participation in the discussion. The dean replied pugnaciously that he was there at the professor's request to prevent his being misled by "the two of you." The professor, his face gray and his chin trembling pathetically, hung his head. Dave earnestly told him that he believed that what he could relate about discussions he had had with me concerning force and violence was essential to the case. Sweating profusely and still looking down at his feet, the professor said, "Well, I guess that lets me out because we never talked about *politics*. Did we, Mr. Scales?" I arose, took the professor's clammy hand, nodded to his family, ignored the dean, and left without a word, followed by Dave.

At dinner, Dave tried to be consolatory, pointing out that despite two additional rebuffs from potential substantive witnesses, we had spoken with one tentative character witness. But later we went to see the two young graduate students who had earlier offered to be witnesses and found them a haggard, crestfallen pair. Their offer, they said, was withdrawn. They explained that a few days after I visited them, two FBI agents, complete with belted raincoats and credentials, came to their quarters and asked if they planned to testify at the Scales trial; they replied that they did. The agents had then said that if they did so, allegations would be made, in order to discredit their testimony, that they were homosexuals. They had vehemently denied the charge, explaining that they both had steady girlfriends and that one of them planned to marry once he had his degree and a job. Nevertheless, such a highly publicized charge would put their degrees in jeopardy and ruin their academic prospects. They dared not testify.

Dave returned to Washington to complete his challenge to the jury-selection system, and I returned briefly to New York, where I learned that the *Daily Worker* was sending its Washington correspondent, my old friend Rob Hall, to Greensboro to cover the trial, and that my friend Herbert Aptheker was taking leave from the Jefferson School in order to help out in any way he could. I supposed that with such good friends present the trial might not be the lonely horror I had anticipated, even though Gladys, it had been decided, would not be there, both because of possible danger to herself and because she and I could not afford to lose her salary for two or three weeks.

Dave Rein won a partial victory at a hearing for his motion on the manner of jury selection. By questioning the clerk of the court, he proved that the method used in the Middle District of North Carolina was less representative and less lawful than that in use in Connecticut, where a Smith Act conviction in a federal court had recently been thrown out because of improper jury selection. Judge Bryan upheld the method, but, presumably to avoid reversible error, he ordered that the jury for the Scales trial be drawn from a new venire which had been in preparation for several weeks and which had taken into account the objections stated in Dave's motion.

The amount of space given to the case in the press subsequent to my arrest had been enormous. Although white racism was rampant as a response to the Supreme Court's decisions against segregated education, and although I was widely regarded as a sort of ultimate "nigger-lover," in addition to being the embodiment of numerous other evils as a Communist, most of the larger state papers demonstrated some degree of pretrial restraint. The *Greensboro Daily News* opined that the defendant should "have counsel of his own choice"; the Winston-Salem papers both expressed some concern over my original high bail. But the liberal Jonathan Daniels, unable to contain his personal animus, had concluded an *ad hominem* editorial in his *Raleigh News and Observer* two days after my arrest: "At worst we have a small skunk on our hands whose very stink has been amplified by his hunters."

At the trial there was a considerable group of reporters who seemed to work hard but who had a difficult time keeping facts straight. Dave and I were on friendly terms with most of the newspaper men, and for the most part we considered the reporting surprisingly fair, the principal exceptions occurring when some visiting reporter, slanted by his editor, would spend a few hours in court and then suck an impressionistic piece out of his thumb.

The trial began on a Monday morning, April 11, in the federal courthouse (scarcely three blocks from the house where I was born). Rob Hall and Herbert Aptheker were on hand, and so was a capacity crowd of onlookers. Rob, preoccupied with his job, made himself useful in every possible way when he was free. Herb quickly became Dave's right-hand man. He was available for everything from bringing in coffee at recesses to commenting critically when Dave tried out arguments on him. He made copious notes on testimony; researched legal precedents; occasionally bucked up morale at the defense table; established cordial relations with court personnel, the press, and courtroom regulars; and frequently stayed up half the night helping Dave with anything that was needed. All in all, he made himself invaluable.

The prosecution was headed by District Attorney Edwin M. Stanley, a Republican and an Eisenhower appointee. He was a local man with coarse features and a theatrical, huckstering courtroom manner. His principal local helper was Assistant District Attorney Robert L. Gavin, a tall man with a long head, thinning hair, and small eyes with the expression of a suspicious guard dog. In court, if he was deficient in style and courtesy, he was accomplished in "patriotic" ranting. To add to the platoon of other assistants and a complement of marshals and FBI agents, the Department of Justice had sent from Washington a group of Red specialists, young lawyers who seemingly knew little of their profession but had been equipped with the special mind-set and extralegal skills involved in prosecuting a Smith Act case.

The first business was the selection of a jury. On the lookout for particularly hostile prospective jurors, I had gone over a list of the people constituting the venire with my Aunt Lucy, who knew something about nearly everyone in Greensboro. Except for her knowledge and insights, the defense had to accept or challenge prospective jurors mainly by guess, while the government had a small dossier on each person in the venire. The judge questioned groups of eight or ten, asking them if they were acquainted with a vast number of names, mostly submitted by the government. Many of the people named were comrades, friends, or sympathizers, and I was in agony at hearing those names, with the implication of guilt by association, read aloud several times before a packed courtroom and the press.

A group of questions submitted by the defense was roundly attacked by the DA, who presumed to argue that the question "Do you believe the Bill of Rights should apply to Communists?" was not proper. Dave replied that that was really what the trial was all about. Judge Bryan reluctantly allowed most of the defense questions. As individuals responded to questions, the general lack of political sophistication, the veiled hostility to the Bill of Rights, and the enormous blind hatred of Communism became evident. The judge's bias was shown repeatedly in his refusals to dismiss the most hopelessly biased individuals for prejudice, and the government succeeded in keeping all Negroes off the panel. Selection of a jury and four alternates was completed after a day and a half.

Dave renewed a motion to require the prosecution to give the defense access to the statements and other material supplied to the government by informers who were to appear as witnesses. Stanley, in opposing the motion, declared that "the entire government security system would break down" if he permitted any such thing. Dave quietly pointed out that Stanley could not have it both ways, that if the government was going to use the testimony of such informer witnesses, then it should follow the rules of procedure with respect to them. Stanley said that the Scales case was "special," that if he were trying a moonshiner, he would not object to furnishing the defense with such material, "but this case, Your Honor, goes much deeper." Dave said that it was a violation of the Constitution to offer his client fewer rights than a moonshiner because of the nature of his case. The judge sidestepped the issue by deferring his decision. (He later denied Dave's motion.)

Stanley made a condescending opening statement to the jury. He gave what purported to be a description of the specialized jargon and esoteric terminology used by the Communist movement. He pretended to explain such words as *proletariat, bourgeoisie, petit bourgeoisie, revisionism,* and *opportunism,* pronouncing (or, more often, mispronouncing) them with great distaste. Those terms from his mouth sounded ominously "foreign" and far removed from American life. Marx, Engels, Lenin, and Stalin were introduced, the latter almost certainly the only one identifiable for most jurors. Stanley told them, "This is not the usual run of a case; it is of tremendous importance to the internal security of the country." He said that the government would prove three things: the violent aims and purposes of the Communist Party, Scales's membership in that Party, and Scales's knowledge of the Party's aims and intent. During the thirty-five minutes that he spoke, it seemed clear to me that he had successfully befuddled most of those in court, that he had introduced them into a never-never land of mechanical doctrinaires, labeled Communists, in which everything heartless or perverse was the norm and in which fuzzy-headed stupidity vied with a dangerous cunning that threatened "our way of life."

At the lunch break I encountered several former high school acquaintances in the corridor outside the courtroom. Some were drawn by the sensation of the trial. Two or three wished me well, but most of the people I recognized in the audience avoided me. The pain of being on trial, of being on public exhibit, of being nothing but a helpless target, began to tell on me; I found that I could not eat my lunch. The previous night, after a day of jury selection, I had managed to sleep because of physical exhaustion. But as the hopelessness of winning my case grew on me, as I began to anticipate the ways in which some of my comrades would be exposed and made to suffer, and as I commenced to sense how the whole of my life would be caricatured and hideously distorted while I would be powerless to answer, my anguish and the tension I was under became almost unbearable.

Dave made his opening statement, speaking just under nine minutes, in a quiet, natural voice. My membership in the Communist Party, he said, was an open, public matter; I had been its spokesman at public meetings, in numerous radio speeches, and before the state legislature. I had no knowledge or belief that the Communist Party advocated the use of force and violence. But the party was not on trial; I was. I was born in North Carolina. I went to school in North Carolina, not in Moscow. I read books (available in the public libraries); I read and studied at the University of North Carolina. I was an idealistic youth from a wealthy family who was disturbed about the danger of war, the state of race relations, and the condition of working people without trade unions. I decided to devote my life to the solution of those problems. I left the university, worked in mills, and volunteered for the army immediately after Pearl Harbor. Whatever the merits or demerits of my chosen instrument, my aim was always the promotion of peace, equality, and economic better-ment for my own people.

The DA then called the first witness, John Lautner, who came forward to be sworn. Dave asked permission to approach the bench, and the first of innu-merable colloquies took place out of the hearing of the jury. The diminutive Dave, dwarfed by Stanley, Gavin, and frequently one or more Department of Justice "specialists," would tenaciously argue vital legal questions before the judge, who usually managed to hedge or to rule against him.

Lautner's testimony had become as smooth as glass from frequent repeti-tion in many Smith Act trials. His story was that he had joined the Party in the twenties, had attended Party schools, had become a prominent functionary, and had himself conducted schools. As his biography proceeded he would state that he had studied, taught, or had been told to read various pamphlets, books, or periodicals, which the prosecution would produce, show to him for identification, and then introduce as exhibits in evidence. By midafternoon a table was loaded with Communist literature. After a recess, a Department of Justice attorney read dribs and drabs from works of Lenin and Stalin dealing with different stages of the Russian Revolution and civil wars. Taken out of context, as they were, the passages sounded rather violent and were very difficult to follow; the jurors usually appeared to be hopelessly adrift after the first few words. By the late afternoon several jurors were nodding, and those still awake wore a look of bewilderment.

Finally court was adjourned for the day, and I went home to my mother's Irving Park apartment. There, with the help of my Aunt Lucy, who had sat just behind me all day, I tried to recount the progress of the trial to my mother, who had not been well enough to come to court that day. After dinner, neigh-bors, mostly socially prominent older people, dropped in to offer comfort, encouragement, and goodwill. I was much liked by several aging widows who remembered me from my early childhood. They were especially delighted with me when late one night, toward the end of the trial, a water pipe burst in the apartment of one of them and I stopped a considerable flood with a wrench. Surveying the bathrobed, wet-footed gathering (mostly good Pres-byterians), I had suggested that they join me in a few verses of the hymn "Shall We Gather at the River?" "I just don't understand how such a sweet boy can stand those awful Communists," one of the old ladies told my mother the next day.

Each night during the trial the courtroom events returned to distress me. Fortunately, my mother had a copy of Rachel Carson's *Under the Sea Wind,* and my nightly contemplations of birds and sea, under Carson's perceptive guidance, restored my perspective on the behavior of human beings and enabled me to sleep. I finished the book the night before the trial ended.

The third day of the trial, all day, Lautner expatiated on the structure and ideology of the Party. The testimony on structure was aimed at making the Party look sinister; the jury was furnished with complicated diagrams showing that I was an important figure as Party leader in four states. The ideological testimony was to establish the government's claim that Marxism-Leninism taught that violent revolution was essential. Lautner stated that when Browder's Communist Political Association had been disbanded and the CPUSA reconstituted, force and violence had been reinstated in the Party doctrine. He went on to paint a picture of the inflexible dedication of all Marxist-Leninists to the use of force and violence in their pursuit of power. I could see the foundation being built on which to hang me: Communists believe in Marxism-Leninism; Marxism-Leninism advocates the violent overthrow of bourgeois governments; the Communist Party of the USA believes in the violent overthrow of the U.S. government. Presumably, Clontz and others would say that I believed in the violent overthrow of the U.S. government, and that would be that.

Lautner concluded his direct testimony, as was his custom, with an appalling account of having been falsely accused of being an FBI spy and then of having been terrorized by his comrades at a meeting held in a basement room in Cleveland. Lautner said that he had been a loyal Communist until that time; that he then read of his expulsion in the *Daily Worker;* that his wife repudiated and divorced him; that he became a pariah to his friends and former comrades of more than twenty years. In his bitterness, after six months, he had written to FBI director J. Edgar Hoover tentatively offering his services. At that time I, like most other Communists, scoffed at Lautner's account of his departure from the Party, convinced that he was an imaginative liar; but some years later I was to learn, to my horror, that Lautner's story was true.

Lautner's account of the Party structure was also essentially true, but his explanation of Marxism-Leninism was heavily colored by the requirements of the Department of Justice, which employed him at $125 per week and furnished him with an office in the department in Washington. Probably inspired by his hatred for his ex-comrades and his desire for revenge on them, he excluded from Marxism-Leninism all its classic statements on peaceful, nonviolent roads to socialism, claiming that they were self-serving cover-ups. He was, however, a rather ignorant man, poorly equipped to discuss Communist theory. (For example, he defined *bourgeoisie,* according to my trial notes, as "today's monopoly capitalism and imperialism.") But before a jury far more ignorant, he served the prosecution well enough.

Dave effectively pointed up Lautner's role as a professional informer, eliciting a concerned editorial in the *News and Observer* that deplored the importance accorded to the likes of Lautner, but Dave's point seemed lost on the jury and the courtroom audience. There was little else Dave could do with him, since, to the delight of his employers, his testimony scarcely varied from one trial to the next.

Lautner, driven by consuming hatred, had over the years of his monomania become a minatory presence. Yet he had, while industriously fulfilling his role as theoretician, forgotten that I had known him as a security expert and had spent some time with him, usually in the company of others. I had considered him a tired, slightly pretentious, middle-aged Party hack who did his work passably but without imagination. I remembered his childish delight over a tea tray which, as he demonstrated, could be converted into a usable mimeograph in about one minute. It was hard to believe that the amiable bureaucrat of the late forties had become the "Horrible Hungarian," as one reporter at the press table liked to call him, with a smiling grimace worthy of a mechanical crocodile. Rob thought that Lautner, with his Hollywood-villain looks, had done more harm with the jury simply by appearing as an ex-Communist than by the rest of his testimony. "The jury will figure that if you associated with people like that, you ought to be convicted of something or other," Rob said with a sardonic grin.

Near the end of Lautner's testimony, when Dave was cross-examining him, an alternate juror asked to address the court and stated forcefully that while he was strictly a layman, he couldn't see what any of that stuff had to do with the defendant. The judge quickly silenced him, saying that the court would decide on the admissibility of evidence. Nevertheless, it was satisfying to me to hear some manifestation of homegrown common sense and reasonableness.

The next witness, Ralph Clontz, was no charmer either. "He's got a face like a suck-aig dawg" was a comment Rob overheard from one courtroom spectator. He appeared older than his thirty-three years, probably because of his paunch and the irregular fatty areas in his face, which gave him a mottled look. His witness-stand manner, often self-deprecating and even servile when Stanley questioned him, was usually arrogant and aggressive when Dave cross-examined him. Having spent much time in preparation, Clontz was very sure of himself and appeared quite carried away with what a local reporter described as his "amateur theatrics."

Under Stanley's questioning, he provided a brief autobiography, proceeded to his first meeting with me, and then quickly entered the area vital for my conviction. During his testimony numerous additions were made to the government's pile of exhibits. Clontz would say, "Scales sold me" such-and-such, and it would be admitted as evidence. I was held responsible for the entire contents of anything I supposedly gave, sold, or recommended to the witness.

Throughout, Clontz stuck closely to a factual time frame and a partially factual reference to subjects discussed in his meetings with me. Otherwise, fact and fancy were mixed freely. In his account of his first encounter with me, for example, he related that I had told him my father had been a "capitalist" and I had had to "live down" my respectable family background. I was infuriated, not because such a tidbit would have an adverse effect on the jury (which it probably did), but because it was so monstrously the opposite of what I felt about a very personal matter.

At that stage I began to realize what it was to be on the receiving end of mischief and malice beyond imagining and to have it presented to the public in the solemn dignity of a federal court, backed by the majesty of the U.S. government. To add to my discomfiture, the chance of delivering a rejoinder had diminished. Dave and his partner, Joe Forer, believed that should I take the stand, I would be asked to name my comrades and to tell everything else asked about the Party; I would of course refuse, placing myself in contempt of court; the judge, they assumed, would then send me to jail, whether the case was won or lost at the trial or on appeal. For some of the same reasons, Dave had rejected Hans's offer to testify; he also calculated that in the prevailing political atmosphere the jury would not likely be influenced sufficiently by a recalcitrant ex-Communist's testimony to warrant Hans's sacrifice. Exploratory feelers by Dave to the government lawyers found them adamantly against any agreement to limit testimony and cross-examination so that a contempt situation might be avoided. On the basis of off-the-record conversation with the judge, Dave said he was inclined to believe that Bryan would not hesitate to hand out contempt sentences of three years or worse, should a Communist witness refuse to answer any question.

Clontz pursued his prescribed course, furnishing precisely the testimony required for a conviction. In so doing, he tried to offer as much color and detail as possible in such a way as to denigrate the defendant and at the same time promote himself by showing his aversion to every aspect of Communism. Had any of the jurors been burdened by logical or inquiring minds, or had they otherwise had any incentive to penetrate the clouds of doctrinal nonsense Clontz dispensed, they might have asked themselves several questions. For example, if I said such stupid and inconsistent things as reported (Clontz described one entire discussion with me as "absolutely idiotic"), how could I be a "threat to the security of the United States"? Or, since Clontz was so evidently ignorant about Marxism-Leninism (he referred to Engels as "a philosopher of some kind" and said that Marxism-Leninism was so much gibberish to him), how could his presumed understanding of it be trustworthy? But neither jury nor spectators nor reporters had much idea of what was going on. The newspapers highlighted Clontz's story of my espousal of violence at his second meeting with me—and that was the idea the government wished to impose.

After going through his various meetings with me, Clontz described in detail his activities at the Jefferson School in New York. Because I had recommended the school, I was held responsible for everything he said he had been taught or told to read while there, for a period of nearly two years. The pile of exhibits grew, and the readings to the jury increased accordingly.

Having had from four to seven years to ponder his testimony, Clontz was well prepared for cross-examination. As a practicing attorney, he knew many tricks of the trade and used the occasion to make unresponsive answers by way of counterattack. He named sixteen people as Party members, twelve of whom he said I had identified as Communists in their own presence. (Actually only Hans, Bernie, Hank, and I had been so identified, and they were either public Communists or known Party leaders; of the remaining twelve, at least one had never been a Party member.) Dave reminded him that a little over a year earlier he had testified against the Jefferson School before the Subversive Activities Control Board and had stated under oath that he knew only six Communists. Clontz promptly replied that he had "had considerable time to reflect" and had extended his list. He added that he knew a seventeenth person to be a Communist "for a moral certainty." Apparently there was little awareness of the McCarthy-style arithmetic used for counting Communists, and the press generally ignored the incident. On cross-examination Clontz defiantly stuck to his story; he was soon to begin a career as a superpatriotic expert on Communism, a speaker much sought after by veterans and fraternal organizations.

During his direct testimony, Clontz stated that I'd asked him to inquire of one of his Duke University law professors, Douglas B. Maggs (whom Clontz described as "not a Communist, but very liberal"), whether he would represent me if I were arrested. Clontz said he had done so and that Maggs had said he would either represent me or find me a lawyer. I was surprised because the story was a complete invention, without so much as a glimmer of supporting fact. I had never thought of retaining Professor Maggs; if I had, I would not have retained my Reidsville lawyer; and in any case, I would never have entrusted a matter of such importance to Clontz. I whispered to Dave that it was probably Clontz's way of settling a score with a professor he disliked personally and politically. The next day, in the Durham papers, Maggs made a vigorous denial of Clontz's whole story, and Dave subpoenaed him as a defense witness.

At some point the prosecution read to the jury from a periodical I'd sold Clontz years before. It was an editorial from a newspaper called *For a Lasting Peace, For a Peoples' Democracy,* usually referred to by the few American Communists who had seen it as "Falp-Fapd" or "the Cominform bulletin." It was indeed the voice of the Cominform, ordered by me from a New York importer because I thought it would provide insights into the thinking of the European Communist parties.

A second-string Justice Department lawyer read it with obvious relish. It dealt at great length with the infallibility of the Soviet Central Committee and its peerless leader, Comrade Stalin. After several paragraphs of jargon and clichés came three minutes' worth of such panegyrics to Comrade Stalin as "Long life to the glorious leader of the Communist Party of the Soviet Union, Comrade Stalin!" and "Glory to the all-wise architect of the Socialist world!" Each succeeding slogan was more grotesque, more tortured in the search for adulatory phrases. As the reading continued, I could feel my face turning red with embarrassment. Such sycophantic drivel, I told myself, had nothing to do with the kind of socialism I sought. Why hadn't Stalin himself, I wondered, repudiated that slop? The reading ended at last and a recess was called. As we walked to the corridor together, Rob was gritting his teeth. "We should have had our heads examined," he muttered, "for ever tolerating that crap!" Such a remark from a Communist was not unlike a Catholic's cursing the pope. But I agreed with him. The European parties and the Soviet Party were entitled to their aberrations, I thought, but why should we publicize, praise, or imitate them? That train of thought was sidetracked in the turbulence of the trial, but the Cominform jargon continued to haunt me.

On Friday afternoon the court adjourned until Monday. Dave borrowed my mother's car, and we went again to Chapel Hill in search of defense witnesses. After seeing the government in action for one week, I had taken Esther out of consideration as a witness because of her vulnerability in the mill and the weakness of her union protection. As things stood, we would have precious few people to testify to anything for the defense. While we were driving near the university library, I suddenly asked Dave to stop. I got out of the car and approached a student who was walking toward me, his gaze fixed on the ground. As I neared the student, the young man looked up and appeared to go into shock when he saw me standing in front of him; then, seeing a smile on my face, he rushed forward and threw both arms around me in an uncharacteristic display of emotion.

The student was Charles Childs of High Point, much prized by the Party as one of its few young white workers. Because of his working-class origins and his youth, a great many weaknesses had been overlooked, and few noticed that he was short on his class's strengths and long on its weaknesses. He had been a relatively unproductive comrade, emotionally shallow and seemingly preoccupied with his emancipation from the working class. To inspire him a bit, we had sent him to a Party school which I conducted in the late summer of 1952, but he continued to be a dreary loner. He later enrolled at Chapel Hill, even though his comrades urged him to remain in an industrial plant. Not having seen him for two years, I wanted to say hello; Charles, in impassioned tones, wished me every success in the trial.

Dave and I spoke to Professor Fletcher M. Green, head of the History Department, Professor Raymond Adams, a noted Thoreau scholar, and the Reverend Charles M. Jones of the Community Church of Chapel Hill, all of whom agreed to be character witnesses. We stayed overnight in order to visit one of the university's most distinguished personalities, Archibald Henderson. He was then professor emeritus of mathematics, reputed to be one of the few men in the world who understood Einstein's theory of relativity when it was first published. Subsequently he had achieved fame as a historian, as a drama critic, and preeminently, as the authorized biographer of George Bernard Shaw. He was my cousin, had known me from my infancy, and had been a frequent guest in my parents' home. He had been cordial when I phoned to ask if I might drop by with my lawyer. We found the old man sunning himself on his front porch in the company of a young graduate student. Henderson adroitly steered the conversation away from my trial and spoke of Shaw; I outflanked him by mentioning that Shaw had publicly denounced the trial of the top American Communists; Dave seized the opportunity to explain the defense's problem with witnesses and asked him to be a character witness for me. Cousin Archibald, citing *Saint Joan,* made a stirring denunciation of heresy trials—and refused.

The trial resumed Monday morning with about an hour more of Clontz. When he was dismissed, there was an air of expectancy in court, for the prosecution had informed the press that it expected to call a surprise witness. That next witness was Charles Childs. I was stunned. I had had few illusions about his deficiency in moral fiber, his minimal courage, or his mediocre intelligence—but for Childs to be an informer! It was incredible: after all, he was a *working-class* guy.

As Childs was led through his paces, it soon appeared that his function was to color the picture for the jury. He had virtually nothing to say about force and violence; that, presumably, was Clontz's territory. But in his day and a half on the stand, Childs earned his FBI pay by his effect on the jury. He too had been a career informer, but his manner, in contrast to Clontz's, was low-keyed; he resembled an obediently shrewd puppy.

What pained me was the number of names of comrades he brought smilingly into his testimony, names of people who for years had treated him with infinite kindness. They were all, of course, subsequently victimized. Most of the comrades in the Erwin Mills textile club in Durham were promptly fired, with full union collaboration. In one case, however, the person named was a highly respected shop steward, and the workers went out on a wildcat protest strike, closing the Erwin plants for the rest of the week.

A second source of distress for me was Childs's ability, like Clontz's, to distort and trivialize every incident he described. Factually his accounts were more accurate than Clontz's; he lied mainly about the essence of the things he recounted. For example, he once showed me a rabidly anti-Communist magazine piece written by some professional Red hunters. I read it with some amusement because of its very grossness and said playfully, "Take down their names so we can shoot 'em." The sentence was spoken in ridicule of prevalent anti-Communist stereotypes and was a stock joke with me, as was the ancient vaudeville line, "Comes the Revolution, you'll eat strawberries with cream, whether you like them or not." In his testimony Childs solemnly stated that I had told him to make a list of the authors' names so that someday we could shoot them. Although Childs admitted that he never wrote the names down, the prosecution and some newspapers referred to the nonexistent document as a "death list."

Childs testified at great length about a school I had run three years before on a farm. In addition to several North Carolinians, two women from Virginia had been present, along with Bob, the full-time Virginia Party functionary. One day (as I learned after the trial by consulting people present at the time), when classes had ended for the morning and the students were awaiting lunch, the Virginia women and a few others were chatting about street crime in their cities and how frightening it was to go out at night. Bob, eager to show off his World War II military training, launched into a demonstration of judo techniques, showed how a *New York Times* folded a certain way could become a club and how a sharpened pencil held in the palm could become a dagger. The demonstration might well have continued, but lunch was announced; and the women, properly impressed with Bob, went to table. According to Childs, a demonstration was given at the school, in the defendant's presence, of how to kill a man with a pencil. Esther Gillen had driven over that day to lend her moral support, and she drove me to my mother's when court was finished for the day; as we drove along Greensboro's principal business street, newsboys were selling the afternoon paper with huge headlines to the effect:

COMMUNIST SCHOOL TAUGHT MURDER

The government then produced a second surprise by resting its case. Stanley told the press that the case was sewed up and that there was no point in revealing any more informers. Because the government had listed several more witnesses, Dave was caught off guard; he told the court he was unprepared and requested a recess until the following morning. The judge graciously granted a recess of fifteen minutes. Fortunately, Herb had been working for some time on a collection of quotations from the books and pamphlets in evidence, quotations contradicting those passages selected by the government which appeared to justify force and violence. Dave read slowly, evenly, and with meaningful inflection, no doubt intending a contrast with Clontz's yahoo style.

At the end of the court day, Dave and Herb began a long discussion with the defense's principal witness, Professor Robert Sonne Cohen of Wesleyan University. He had arrived the previous day and was bunking in Herb's room to save expenses. He was a non-Communist authority on Marxism who had volunteered his services when he learned of the case.

The defense commenced with three character witnesses, the first being Professor Fletcher M. Green, who had been my teacher and adviser and who was chairman of the History Department in Chapel Hill. He was a gifted teacher with whom I'd had a warm relationship for many years. He was followed by Professor Raymond Adams, a scholar whose feeling for Thoreau was no mere academic interest, but permeated his character and deeply influenced his way of life. I'd had a strong affection for him since accompanying him, his family, and some friends on a delightful picnic in 1938.

The Reverend Charles M. Jones, the third witness, was a man of extraordinary strength of character. He had been ousted from the pastorate of the Chapel Hill Presbyterian Church because he partially desegregated it (although the synod claimed doctrinal differences as justification); he had then formed his own interracial church, which attracted most of the Presbyterians and many others besides. I had first known him in 1947, when he had tried to aid a Fellowship of Reconciliation challenge to segregated seating on interstate buses, a challenge conducted by Bayard Rustin, Igal Roodenko, and Joe Felmet. After the three had been arrested in Chapel Hill, certain cab drivers had attacked Jones's home, nearly killing his assistant pastor. A non-Communist friend and I organized a detachment of veterans, and while Jones and his family got out of town, we performed around-the-clock guard duty in his house for two days.

All three testified to my reputation for sincerity and honesty. Their testimony in that political climate required great courage, and the student paper, the *Daily Tar Heel,* acknowledged the fact in paying editorial tribute to them.

Bob Cohen, whom I met when he first arrived in Greensboro, took the stand over furious prosecution objections and, under Dave's unobtrusive questioning, delivered himself of a lucid and authoritative exposition of the origins, scope, and development of Marxism. He viewed it as a scientific, democratic body of thought which changed as it grew, its application depending upon specific time and place; he emphasized that advocacy of violence was foreign to, and even hostile to, Marxism. His academic credentials were impressive and impeccable, and he had no leftist connections whatever. I looked around the courtroom and saw my character witnesses and about a half-dozen others following the testimony avidly; the jury and everyone else seemed to be lost. The Department of Justice experts tried to show contradictions in his testimony, but to no avail; they were entirely out of their depth. Even if the jurors and most of the spectators were incapable of digesting that impressive cram course in Marxism, there was no doubt that the thirty-two-year-old professor, with his pleasant voice, his good looks, and his gentlemanly manner, had made an impressive witness.

Cohen was followed by my mother, who had insisted on testifying despite my wishes. Looking older than her sixty-three years because of her poor health, she maintained her composure with great effort. When Dave asked her when and where she was born, she pointedly replied that she was born in Richmond, Virginia—drawing a smile even from the bench. From then to the end of her testimony, there was complete silence in the courtroom as she recounted, in her soft, musical voice, my activities since the war and told of discussions she had had with me about my view of violent overthrow. She quoted me as saying, "Mother, to my mind it would be just plain silly for a little minority group to *try* to overthrow the United States." She said I told her I joined the Party to "give help to my fellowman," that my whole idea was to help the underdog. As to my nature, she said that I was extraordinarily gentle, "the gentlest of all my children." Her testimony lasted about fifteen minutes. After she left the stand she embraced me and went home to bed to calm her overworked heart. I was grateful that the press, without exception, honored my request not to photograph or attempt to interview her.

The jury was dismissed for the day, and a long colloquy took place at the bench to decide the judge's instructions to the jury. Rob's time for covering the trial had run out; he had to leave for Washington. Herb uncomplainingly assumed the task of writing news stories for the *Daily Worker* until Rob's replacement, Harry Raymond, arrived.

The next morning Professor Maggs repeated under oath his complete denial of Clontz's testimony concerning him. Then, shortly before noon, Gavin began the summation for the prosecution. Adopting the ranting style of "hell-fire-and-damnation" preachers and making full use of his considerable histrionic abilities, he gave special emphasis to what heroes the government's three paid informers were: "Take Ralph Clontz, son of a Presbyterian minister, a Carolina boy. . . . Thank the Lord Ralph made the sacrifice he did. And Charles Childs, an orphan, a local boy, felt it his duty to contact the government and inform them of this Communist activity [a public Progressive Party rally, according to Childs]. Nobody has discredited him for the little bit of money he made. . . . Could we ever pay them enough? . . . They are *not* Judas Iscariots."

Near the end of his oration, Gavin's voice had risen many decibels, and the crescendo was still continuing. The thing that shocked him the most, he said, was that "Scales had been well educated by a father who was a lawyer and a capitalist. . . . He was ashamed of his background and yet he calls his aging mother to testify for him. That's the most revolting thing I ever heard of—to turn his back on his family, lie to his mother about his beliefs, and then call upon her to testify for him. Could you have pity for such a man? . . . What you do here will be heard around the world. . . . There is no room for any ism other than Americanism in this land of ours. . . . We don't want the 'Internationale' sung in our schools. We don't want the red star. . . . Tell the world we don't want this unmitigated hogwash."

Speaking quietly and with humor, Dave addressed the jury. He used Gavin's "unmitigated hogwash" to characterize Clontz's testimony, which he carefully analyzed and summed up as "incredible from beginning to end." Aside from the demonstrable lies told on the stand by Clontz, he said, all the government's case amounted to was "that Scales had read Communist literature." The only testimony about my views which was credible and rational was the testimony of my mother. In analyzing the government's case he pointed out that I never *did* anything remotely consistent with Clontz's force-and-violence story.

Referring to Lautner, he said that he would keep his job with the Justice Department "only so long as his service is satisfactory. His function is to obtain a conviction." When he remarked, "Apparently it's now the fashion to work your way through school by informing for the FBI," there was a roar of laughter. Unfortunately, I was so moved by Dave's logic and eloquence that I took few notes on his summation.

The government had both the first word and the last, and Stanley concluded. He was even louder and more mannered than Gavin, haranguing the jury like a tent revivalist. Some passages that I was able to write down from that torrent of words include these:

I approach my task with regret and pleasure. I regret to have to bring before this jury a plot to destroy the government of this country. . . . It is a revelation to me—the acts of a native son of this state. I regret that such a person should advocate such an alien way of life, teaching lying and cheating, . . . teaching betrayal and deceit, trying to destroy the very government which gave him a safe-conduct for his activities. . . . I have the pleasure and privilege of praising the government's witnesses. . . . Clontz and Childs were motivated by their desire to protect their government. Imagine the passion for freedom that possessed these men! Imagine the humiliation of sitting in the Jefferson School . . . of being called a stool pigeon and a liar by the *counsel for a self-confessed Communist* [the last words were hissed out]. Imagine the mental torture of being told by Scales to lie and cheat and steal. . . . If the government brought out one bit of evidence that was not true, why didn't Junie bring down a Communist from New York to refute it? . . . What about Herb Aptheker? Why not put him on? [he pointed his finger at Herb, who was sitting just behind me]. . . . The Commies in China think it's naive to believe that you could bring anything about without force and violence. . . . Why not put Bernie on? Why didn't you bring Doxey down and put him on? [reference to Doxey Wilkerson, Negro director of the Jefferson School]. . . . Instead he brought down Sonny Cohen to lecture to us. . . . Scales should go back where he came from. . . . Interested in the little man, was he? To do what with them? Make slaves of them? . . . Do we want them singing their theme song from Moscow right here in our own backyard? . . . [He suddenly turned toward Dave and bellowed] I resent with all my heart hearing boys like Clontz and Childs called liars and stool pigeons! . . . They [the Communists] lie, steal and cheat. Lord help us if they ever take over. . . . You must show the world that Communism has no place in our own North Carolina. I have never before made such a request to a jury as I make to you: don't only convict this man, this viper, but do it quickly so the whole world may know that this land we love so much shall forever be and remain the land of the free and the home of the brave.

The judge then charged the jury with a staggering list of instructions which previously had been bitterly fought over by opposing counsel. Then, after a dinner break, the jury began its deliberations at 7:35 P.M., just nine days after the trial had started. Herb and I left Dave poring over some papers and joined a crowd of courtroom habitués seated on benches in the corridor. Out of politeness, the hangers-on refrained from discussing the trial, and the talk turned to baseball. Herb soon had them in thrall with his encyclopedic knowledge of the game and the vast stock of stories collected since his student days at Columbia, where he had been a pitcher, probably with big-league potential.

Throughout the trial there had been a contingent of Woman's College students in attendance, whose sympathies had gradually veered toward the defense. Their student paper, under a heading something like "Gallantry Is *Not* Dead," carried an account of how I had held a disabled water fountain in the courthouse corridor so the young women could drink. During that evening's vigil, I saw them in force.

As the wait went on, I observed Stanley return, washed, shaved, shined, and wearing an elegant suit; he was accompanied by his wife, also dressed to the nines, and their twin children, outfitted in their Sunday best to witness their daddy's hour of glory. He resembled a beaming, shoo-in candidate confidently awaiting the first election returns. (Could he have guessed, perhaps, that in two years' time Eisenhower would make him a federal judge?)

The jury returned with its verdict at nine o'clock, after one hour and twenty-five minutes. To no one's surprise, the jury found the defendant guilty. At Dave's request the jurors were polled individually, and all answered, "Guilty"; most seemed smug, some pained; all appeared in a hurry to go home. The judge, over Dave's vigorous protest, and with what seemed to me to be un-judicial relish, revoked my bond and ordered the marshals to take me into custody. I recalled that, of late, when I had encountered His Honor in the hotel dining room, the latter's fancy bows had fallen off to mere nods: probably a warning sign that my stock was falling.

I numbly emptied my pockets, giving the contents to Herb and Dave. My Aunt Lucy and Harry Raymond, who had just replaced Rob Hall, stood by my side while I explained to reporters why I had not taken the stand. "I was sorely tempted to . . . because of the kind of slander I've been sitting here listening to for days. One of the main factors that influenced me not to is that to my knowledge, without exception, every Smith Act defendant who has taken the stand in his own behalf has received an additional sentence for contempt as considerable as three years because he refused to name persons as Communists who would suffer as a result. The other reason is that I think the government failed completely to make a case."

I caught a glimpse of Dave and guessed from his stricken face that he was far past tears. In the audience I saw the somber faces of two of my comrades who had been named by Childs earlier in the week. The judge had set the following morning (Saturday) for sentencing. "How convenient," I thought. "He can still get home to Alexandria for the weekend." Flanked by the marshals, I was escorted across West Market Street to the Guilford County Jail for the night. In the street I was greeted by weeping college girls telling me they were on my side and that I had been railroaded.

Possibly at that very time, editorial writers around the South were sifting their stores of wisdom in preparation for their pronouncements on the Scales trial. My hometown newspaper spoke for most of the others when it said, "He got what he deserved." A more original and thoughtful summation was made by an unknown student editorialist for the *Daily Tar Heel*: "It is next to impossible for a Communist to be tried justly today in the United States. The web of hysteria has been spun too thick. The fear of Russian power to the East, the tattered but still flapping ensign of McCarthy, and public ignorance as to the nature and real threat of Communism throw cases like the Scales affair out of kilter. In the Greensboro trial, a long troop of excited witnesses, paid performers, spies, and incompetent press reporting have made the outcome, as the informed expected, all but inevitable."

17

Of Justice:
An American
Travesty

What is the right of free speech? It is the right
of speaking controversially. It is the right of
controversy.

Bernard Shaw, Speech (1926)

Once one begins to try to suppress some
knowledge or some opinions, one loses all
sense of proportion and relevance in one's obsession with the danger of ideas.

Leonard Woolf, *Downhill All the Way*

G uilford County's jail was atop the county courthouse. Some sixteen
years earlier, when employed by Guilford County, I had made daily
elevator trips to the jail with two or three colleagues to buy sodas from an
inmate-trusty. It had been a dreadful, depressing place then; it had become
worse. When I was taken to an empty cell in the dim, shadowy light, I found
myself besieged with questions from my fellow prisoners. A certain amount
of noblesse oblige was expected of me, a "celebrity" from the outside world,
and I dutifully replied to all who addressed me. A prisoner in an adjoining cell
claimed that I had attended a Greensboro high school with him, thereby acquiring some reflected notoriety; the years of attendance and the name of the
school were both wrong, but in order not to torpedo his story, I said only that
it was good to see him again and inquired why *he* was in. My neighbor on the
other side, whose eyes were clouded over with pain, narcotics, or booze,
complained to me that he was sick but that no one cared. When a jailer came
by, I mentioned the matter to him, but he only shrugged. It was after ten;
things soon quieted down, and the sound of snoring gradually drowned out the
lingering talk.

I intended to think about what I would say to the court before sentencing,
but once I lay down on my bunk, the tensions and emotions of the day overwhelmed me, and I fell into a stupefied sleep, only vaguely aware of intermit-
tent groaning and shouting nearby. I awoke before sunrise and lay thinking of
what to say in court and making notes on a slip of paper. The lights came on
and the jail grew noisy with breakfast preparations. When the meal was

served, it was discovered that my next-door neighbor with the cloudy eyes was dead. There was no great excitement or concern among the jailers. Once the body was removed, the inmates sat subdued and gloomy, and I was shaken out of my self-absorption by the recognition that despite my troubles, life— and death—proceeded much as usual. A humbling question nagged at me: had I not been so determined to sleep, might I have saved a man who had died alone and in pain? A further troubling thought insinuated itself: had the combined cruelties of persecution and imprisonment begun to brutalize me?

I was taken out to see my attorney. Dave, gray-faced and probably sleepless, tried to be brisk and cheery. He had spoken to my mother to try to keep up her spirits. He listened to my proposed remarks, applauded them, and left to have breakfast, saying that he would be waiting for me in court in an hour or so.

The marshals brought me into court early, and Dave, Herb, and I were able to talk at the defendant's table while the courtroom filled. Dave said that he would prepare an appeal to the Fourth Circuit Court of Appeals and that he would immediately appeal the denial of bail to one of the judges of that court. My mother and Aunt Lucy, crushed but stoic, arrived and sat with me.

When the court reconvened, Dave asked for a moderate sentence, saying that because it had been a trial of ideas, errors were especially likely; I was of good character and had never before been convicted of anything; I had served long and honorably in the army during World War II. Then I addressed the court:

> Your Honor, I am innocent of the charge in this case. Insofar as the issues are Marxism-Leninism and my beliefs, I do not think they can be tried in a courtroom, but must be tested in the give-and-take of political life.
>
> No jury is competent to convict a man for his *ideas,* no matter how long a study they make. This jury had small opportunity to even understand my ideas through these rags and tatters of unfamiliar books, introduced and grossly misrepresented by the government. For all the world this has been like a medieval heresy trial.
>
> Mr. Stanley asked the jury to drive Communism out of North Carolina. He disagrees with my views on Negro equality, on foreign policy, on unions, and on many other things. The democratic thing would be to encourage debate on such ideas in public forums; Mr. Stanley asks that my ideas be jailed with me.
>
> I wouldn't belong to an organization advocating force and violence. It is foreign to my upbringing by my father and mother, who educated me in a tradition of democracy, honor, and devotion to principle.
>
> Of all the lies told from the witness stand, the lie that I had broken with my family and was ashamed of my father was the cruelest and most despicable.

I am proud of my Party and its program, which I have tried hard to make public. My life has been devoted to the fight for the liberation of mankind. I and my Party will continue to stand for that objective.

When I sat down, my mother whispered that she was proud of me and that my father would have been too; Aunt Lucy patted my shoulder. Stanley was immediately on his feet demanding a severe sentence. His Honor promptly obliged by sentencing me to six years' imprisonment, the heaviest sentence ever given under the Smith Act. He again refused to continue bail, pending appeal, and ordered the marshal to take me to a place of incarceration at once. I was handcuffed and led off, followed by my mother, Aunt Lucy, and Herb. I had just realized that I had undergone a change of designation; instead of "the defendant" I had become "the prisoner" once more. In the marshal's office I was locked in a familiar small cage. Herb pleaded with the marshal to let me talk uncaged to my mother for five minutes. "No. Who'd watch him?" he replied.

To keep my mother occupied and help her hold back her tears, I asked if she would bring me in jail the handsome edition of Dante which the translator, Professor Huse, had just sent to me, movingly inscribed, and also Fielding's *Joseph Andrews*. While she noted down the titles, I urged Aunt Lucy to take her home, and they left. A few minutes later, two marshals took me out into the corridor, where Harry Raymond, Herb, and two weeping college girls gave me an emotional send-off. Down in the street several reporters said goodbye, shaking my manacled hand, and a TV camera recorded my final wave as the car drove off, headed for Winston-Salem and the Forsyth County Jail.

Mr. Speas greeted me amiably, saying that he had hoped he had seen the last of me the previous Christmas. He placed me in a cellblock with four local fellows, who received me cordially. The two-a-day meal regimen had expanded to three meals, without loss of quality. All my fellow prisoners were likable; some played gin rummy about half their waking hours and devoted another two or three hours to crossword puzzles. I limited my rummy playing to three hours a day, since I was absorbed in Dante and Fielding, my thoughts, and my correspondence.

On her first visit, my mother told me that her phone had rung for two days with calls from well-wishers expressing their sympathy. She said that her sources reported that most local lawyers had only praise for Dave's defense and that many of them (privately) expressed contempt for Stanley's performance. She had written to Dave to tell him so and to express her own admiration of his efforts.

A great amount of mail began to arrive for me. There were daily letters from Gladys, frequent ones from my mother (who was reluctant to burden the accommodating Mr. Speas by visiting more than once a week), and dozens of letters from readers of the *Daily Worker* and *Worker*. *Worker* readers had seen a slightly garbled version (with omissions) of my speech before sentencing and had written, often quite emotionally, to say how much they liked it and to promise to do everything possible to get me out of jail. The number of letters from non-Communists was surprising. They frequently concluded with inspirational quotations; one anonymous letter, assigning me to the "noble army of martyrs," wound up with a moving passage from the Book of Common Prayer: "Grant us grace fearlessly to contend against evil, and to make no peace with oppression; and, that we may reverently use our freedom, help us to employ it in the maintenance of justice among men and nations." The writer hoped that I might find in those simple maxims "a sounder standard against which to measure [my] actions than the ever-shifting intricacies of Communist theory."

Herb Aptheker wrote frequently: an emotional note praising my speech as he was leaving Greensboro; a note to say that he had written a piece about the trial for the May issue of *Masses and Mainstream;* another to say that he and his family had visited with Gladys and Barbara; still another to relay greetings from Gene Dennis, recently released from Atlanta on parole, William Z. Foster, and Steve Nelson, the Party's most famous political ex-prisoner. Foster himself wrote commending me. So did George Charney, Nat Ross, Joe Clark, Bill Albertson, and a dozen Smith Act victims. Ben Davis, just released from jail, wrote me a glowing letter of praise saying that he hoped to see me soon.

I was pessimistic about getting bail. I expected to be sent to a federal penitentiary shortly, and I concentrated on serving my time and reassuring Gladys that we would both survive the sentence. She came down for one brief visit on a weekend and showed in her tired face the strain she was living under. She was valiantly trying to raise money for my legal expenses and was having trouble because the Claude Lightfoot case in Illinois had top priority as the likely test case following the various membership trials. Inasmuch as Lightfoot was a Negro and a principal leader of the Illinois Party, most available contributions from well-to-do civil libertarians or Party sympathizers were being channeled to his defense fund. Dave Rein, nearly broke, as usual, had not yet been paid all his out-of-pocket expenses.

I was waiting, not very hopefully, for Dave to argue the bail question before Judge Armistead Dobie of the Fourth Circuit Court of Appeals. On April 30 that representative of southern justice heard argument in Charlottesville, Virginia, in the very shadow of Jefferson, and denied bail, even though he acknowledged that substantial questions of law were being appealed. Dave immediately applied to Chief Justice Warren of the Supreme Court. On May 12 the chief justice ordered bail reinstated.

I left the jail in high spirits. At my request, Speas took me to the kitchen so that I could thank the Negro woman who cooked so splendidly. Once more I was driven to Greensboro by a U.S. marshal. That marshal, a Quaker of about fifty, did not handcuff me and made polite conversation till we were nearly at our destination. Then he said solemnly, "Mr. Scales, I've known your folks most of my life, and I've watched you all through your trial. I believe you're as sincere in your beliefs as any man I ever saw. But you've never been to Russia where the Communist theories have been put to the test. I've never been there either, but I believe that if you could see Communism in practice, you'd break with it; I think you'd have the guts to reject it if it wasn't what you expected. Whatever happens to your appeal, I hope you'll try to see the Soviet Union for yourself. If you'll go there, I'll contribute the most I can afford toward your expenses. That's a serious offer and here's my hand on it." I was so moved by the man's sincerity and concern that I took his hand and thanked him, saying confidently that I had no doubt the Soviet Union would live up to my expectations, but that it was the Communists in the American Party that I depended on and put all my confidence in.

In the office of the clerk of the court my mother was waiting for me; we signed the necessary papers and I was free again. Newsmen were waiting, asking for interviews. I gave several, one of which was to stay uncomfortably in my memory. On tape, I was asked if I thought I'd have had a fairer trial in the Soviet Union. I replied that I couldn't imagine anyone being tried for his ideas in the Soviet Union, nor could I conceive of a trial anywhere more unfair than the one I'd just endured. I then glibly compared American and Soviet justice to the detriment of the American system, drawing heavily on the 1936 Soviet Constitution for what I thought I knew about Soviet law and procedure.

Once reunited with my family, I found a two-way demand on my time. I could easily have been a full-time defendant (or appellant, as I then was), raising money, organizing a Scales Defense Committee, and publicizing the issues involved. But the political and organizational problems in my four states had intensified: the membership continued to erode, owing largely to the departure from the South of comrades unable to make a living because of political harassment; the Party was still isolated and far removed from the vital centers of Negro, trade union, and other activity; the Southern Regional Committee was functioning, half blindly, in a partial vacuum.

As a professional appellant (and somewhat lionized Party leader, by then of national prominence), I spoke in July at a left-wing meeting of about three thousand on Chicago's South Side and to a smaller gathering in Milwaukee. In September I made a tour of Massachusetts, Rhode Island, Vermont, and New Hampshire, speaking at many small meetings. The tour was well organized by the New England Party, which was resourceful in getting me before other than left-wing audiences. An unpleasant surprise was that I found it difficult to speak effectively about my own case or to ask for money. At a large give-and-take meeting at Goddard College, I was much impressed with the way Otis Hood, the self-searching New England Party leader, refused to defend or apologize for the Soviet Union on any account; he was an authority only on what the *American* Party stood for, he said. Ed Strong would have considered his stance blasphemous.

While I was pleading my cause in New England, Dave Rein was arguing my legal case before the three judges of the Fourth Circuit Court of Appeals, then considered one of the nation's least liberal circuits. The chief judge, who dominated the court, was John J. Parker, a North Carolina Republican notable for his considerable legal ability and his reactionary political views. He had been nominated to the Supreme Court by President Hoover but had been rejected by the Senate because of strong labor and Negro opposition led by John L. Lewis. Though Dave expected to lose in such a court, he wrote of his personal satisfaction in outdoing Stanley in the briefs and in the oral argument. I was able to reduce my debt to Dave somewhat with the proceeds of my midwestern and northeastern trips.

I spent much of July in North Carolina trying to undo some of the side effects of the naming of more than a dozen comrades in my trial. Several had been fired from their jobs, and all had had their work in mass organizations disrupted. As I observed the political currents in the South, I believed that despite a new militancy among Negroes, stimulated by the Supreme Court's decisions on educational discrimination, the worst of McCarthyism was still to come. My own trial, I thought, was the first blast. More could be expected, and my main task was to save the Party's membership and contacts. In North Carolina I took steps to retrench on practical organizational objectives and to deemphasize the functioning of the state and city committees. I advised issuing leaflets only where comrades felt they were right on target and where a meaningful distribution could be assured; my individual advice to my comrades was, "Lie low and hold on."

Similar measures were taken in South Carolina, Virginia, and Tennessee. In Memphis I relied on Nick, who had replaced Fred when the latter was forced to move with his family to the Northeast in order to find a job from which the FBI could not get him fired. In eastern Tennessee I counted partially on an old-time former Party functionary who had occasion to make frequent trips in the area. In Virginia I depended on Bob, despite his obsessive rigidity and other weaknesses. In South Carolina, where there was little organization left, I relied on myself.

When I next met with my comrades of the SRC, I felt more at odds with them than ever before. Part of my alienation was due to my increasing attraction to the political outlook of many of the New York City Party leaders. Through Bernie, Hank, and George Charney I had met many of the Brooklyn, Queens, and Manhattan functionaries, a remarkable group of men and women who had mostly grown up in the Young Communist League in the thirties. The best of them were acute politicians who thought in terms of popularizing issues in neighborhoods, of winning votes, of organizing shops, of influencing union locals, of speaking at street corners in working-class communities. Developing a political line was not, for them, a matter of imitating something in European or Soviet experience, or of acting on a Soviet hint, or of delving into Stalinist theory. They knew that a new Party line had to withstand heckling on a Brooklyn street; it had to withstand the scrutiny of hard-boiled Communist union leaders and shop stewards who must try to sell it to rank-and-file workers; it must survive the criticism of astute Jewish intellectuals and the barbs of militant Negroes. Otherwise there was something wrong with it, something that would further isolate the Party and make it look crazier than ever to the public. Those New York leaders lived and breathed politics. Their methods within the Party were not ideally democratic; they were strong leaders and drove their members hard, once they had aroused their enthusiasm. Three years of the underground coupled with a defeatist line had ruined the Party they had known. They were determined to return to political reality; they wanted political answers; they questioned everything, including sacred cows and Party doctrine (though with discretion). I warmed to their attitude and was less concerned about their Marxist-Leninist orthodoxy (or "correctness," as Ed would have put it) than about whether what they proposed would help to get the Party somewhere near the mainstream of American life and politics and to inaugurate its advocacy of an American brand of socialism.

Even before the underground days I'd been aware of another current in the Party: a plethora of cocksure ideologues who zeroed in on deviations from Marxism-Leninism within the Party's dwindling ranks. Those watchdogs of Leninist rectitude attributed many of the Party's troubles to theoretical laxity. The pages of *Political Affairs,* the Party's authoritative organ, were loaded with their writings. Betty Gannett, whom I had known for years as a fairly amiable assistant national organizational secretary, developed a remarkably virulent polemical style for inveighing against comrades, books, and ideas she considered to be "revisionist"; Pettis Perry's hunt for white chauvinism inside the Party has already been mentioned; George Siskind, my former teacher, staked out psychoanalysis as his territory and helped make psychiatric care off limits to Party members; under a pseudonym Robert Thompson, the war hero who jumped bail and went underground, brutally attacked left-wing union leaders who opposed Party policies in their unions; William Z. Foster conducted a pointless polemic against the economic theories of John Maynard Keynes. Though at first I had been overawed, I became repelled by the doctrinal barrage. It appeared to me that those purists were usually the ones who believed that war with the Soviet Union was nearly inevitable and that the triumph of Fascism in the United States was extremely likely. On the basis of such beliefs, they had insisted upon sending the Party leadership underground, pruning the membership to the hard core, and forcing the left unions to stand alone, outside the CIO—in effect, reducing the Party to a sect with small influence but great ideological purity and a record of unfailing support of the Soviet Union.

In the emerging inner-Party conflict, sides were not then clearly perceived and few individuals had sharply defined viewpoints. I had friends on all sides of the issues. It gradually appeared to me that the main question was whether one believed that major American problems (ending legal discrimination against Negroes, gaining a measure of political and economic democracy, promoting a peaceful foreign policy) could be resolved to a serious degree under the capitalistic system with the participation of the left. If one felt, for instance, as Foster did, that war with the Soviet Union was inevitable and that "bourgeois democracy" scarcely existed any more in the United States, it was difficult to make any sincere approach to solving the principal national issues. The unspoken presumption seemed to be that a cataclysmic event, such as an unlikely revolution or an even less likely invasion by the Red Army, was a necessary precondition. Most restless Party leaders would have agreed that to await the first alternative was absurd; to await the second was contemptible and worse. If, as many of my friends and I believed, the members could survive the current terrors and slowly make our way back into unions, the Democratic Party, Negro organizations, and professional organizations— however loose the organizational (or even the ideological) ties that bound us together—we could ultimately play a positive and honorable role in the future political life of the country.

My disagreements with the other SRC members, who were strong Foster supporters, began to emerge more frequently at the SRC meetings. The differences usually took an organizational form. For example, in my four states, which had the best Party structure in the South, I cautiously suggested further loosening and deemphasizing the elaborate Party committees, as I had already started doing. I brought up an idea I had first urged on the students at a southern training school I conducted in upstate New York a couple of years before: in the South, where the members were so few and the attacks so heavy, every member could expect a degree of organizational isolation and should aim at self-sufficiency, should try to be his or her own theoretician and national committee. My comments were not well received. Hosea replied, "If you don't have a Party organization, you ain't got nothin' "; Ed, Frannie, and some others present agreed. I rebutted, saying that harassment and other forces were destroying the Party's organizational structure throughout the South anyway and that developing self-sufficient, thinking people should take priority over trying to resuscitate an inactive organization. I was told that my argument was pre-Leninist, and perhaps even liquidationist. Privately I recalled the Communist Political Association and wondered anew whether Browder had not been on the right track.

(Some years later I came to know Browder in his old age and liked him very much. He seemed to be somewhat ambivalent in his attitude toward the Soviet Party and was perhaps a bit rigid in seeking to fit everything into political categories. His attempts—brave if superficial—to bring the American Party into the mainstream of our political life both in the mid-thirties and in the early forties seem to have prefigured in some respects those of contemporary Eurocommunists, such as the Italians.)

I was already slightly in the doghouse, as far as the SRC comrades were concerned, for not having met with them (even though I had tried) to discuss the political content of my case before going on trial. When I returned to New York from jail, a condescending letter (courier-delivered) from Ed awaited me. He did not mention the ordeal I'd been through but said rather threateningly that the SRC wanted to go "fully into the character" of my defense (it never did), and then he took me to task for a critical comment about his leadership of the SRC which I'd never made. The letter was a reminder of how cruel and contemptuous Ed could be when he was under pressure and things were going badly.

Chief Judge Parker was quick with his opinion on my appeal. He enthusiastically upheld the conviction in an aggressive opinion delivered on November 7, 1955. He sustained the constitutionality of the membership clause of the Smith Act, saying, "[The clause] is, of course, nothing more or less than a statute denouncing and making criminal a conspiracy to overthrow the government by force and violence." He then explained, "A charge under the membership clause of the Smith Act is a charge of conspiracy. There is no magic in the use of the word 'conspiracy' or 'conspire'; and to charge that defendant became or remained a member of an organization advocating the forcible overthrow of the government is to charge that he became a party to an unlawful conspiracy for the purpose and makes applicable the rules relating to proof of guilt in joining a conspiracy."

Dave Rein replied in his petition for rehearing: "The theory now advanced by this Court, that the crime alleged was a conspiracy, did not occur to anyone at the trial. Accordingly the trial was not conducted on that basis and the jury was not charged in accordance with conspiracy doctrine. As a result, the holding of this Court that the crime alleged was a conspiracy results in the appellant being convicted of a crime for which he was neither charged nor tried." The petition for rehearing was denied on November 15.

Judge Parker's haste caused my case to become the precedent-making test of the membership clause, replacing the Lightfoot case, which was not decided by the appeals court in Chicago until the following January. Because membership indictments were already pending against the Party's general secretary, Eugene Dennis, *Daily Worker* editor John Gates, Benjamin J. Davis, Max Weiss, and other outstanding Party leaders, and because the entire leadership and membership were vulnerable, the Scales case became the Party's most pressing legal business. The national committee discussed the matter and decided that I should obtain counsel of national prominence not associated primarily with the left. I praised Dave's competence and noted that most of his modest fee was still unpaid. It was not a question of competence, they said, but of political effect; a renowned lawyer, preferably a distinguished constitutional authority, was required. I said that the resources of my defense committee were much overextended already and that I would agree only if Dave were paid in full and if the national committee took responsibility for the new lawyer's fee. It was agreed, and I received a long list of lawyers to ask to take my case.

I phoned Dave that night to tell him of the new developments, and he was hurt. I explained that the decision was against my wishes but that the whole Party was now involved—and at least he would be paid. Dave grunted that if *they* were paying the bill he would believe it when he got it, but that I must hurry because time was running out to file my petition for a writ of certiorari, necessary to get my case heard by the Supreme Court.

Beginning in early December a sheaf of refusals by lawyers began arriving in the mail. Some, such as Joseph N. Welch of Boston, Thurman Arnold of Washington, Ray Jenkins of Knoxville, and Claude Pepper of Miami, were kind and seemed concerned; Whitney North Seymour, Sr., was nasty; the rest were merely civil. It became apparent that I was getting nowhere by mail; and Bill Albertson of the CRC urged me to make a trip through the South, not only to find a lawyer but to try to raise some liberal support by pointing out the profound civil liberties issues involved in my case.

I tried, writing first to Mark Ethridge, the liberal Louisville publisher, and requesting an opportunity to discuss my case with him; Ethridge wired back a stinging rebuff which took Louisville off my itinerary. One prominent liberal after another indicated an extreme lack of enthusiasm over having me explain the civil liberties issues involved in my case; the kinder ones suggested that I put my explanations in writing.

I phoned William Faulkner in Oxford, Mississippi, stating who I was and my situation. "If you come here, I will see you," he said gravely. I told him I would arrive two days later. After flying to Memphis, I caught a meandering bus to Oxford; there, observed by a hundred eyes, I walked to the Faulkner home, having remembered its general location from a previous visit to the town. When I arrived there I found the house deserted. I was greeted only by a dog too despondent even to bark at me. Back at the bus station I read in a newspaper that Faulkner was hospitalized in Memphis for an "undisclosed ailment." I phoned an old left-winger I knew, who came to meet me in his car and explained that Faulkner, an occasional social companion, had been taken "dead drunk" to a Memphis hospital—a not uncommon occurrence. The old man, who had followed my trial closely, insisted on giving me three dollars toward my legal expenses. As we sat in the car parked near the bus station, he also confirmed my belief that we were and had been under intensive observation by police, cab drivers, and assorted street denizens. I left on a bus for Jackson, convinced as I had been on my other visits that one of Faulkner's artistic weaknesses was that he understated the menacing horror of everyday life in Mississippi.

After two days spent in New Orleans at the behest of the SRC, trying to resolve some inner-Party problems with the battered membership there, I headed for Montgomery, the capital of Alabama. There the great bus boycott had been going on for months under the leadership of Martin Luther King, Jr., and I reverently observed Negroes loading their people into cars in the shadow of the state capitol and then dispatching them home to Negro residential areas, while hundreds more went proudly on foot. The Montgomery Negroes had joined the battle against segregation by raising the seemingly minor issue of where they might sit on a public bus. The Reverend Dr. King had accurately assessed the unarmed helplessness of southern Negroes and struck the all-powerful white majority in the midst of its "Christian" hypocrisy. In his version of passive resistance the weapons he used against his enemies were moral rectitude, love, common decency, common sense, logic, prayer, courage, and gentlemanly behavior. He prayed for his tormentors; he gave sophisticated, militant leadership to his followers in the street; he was prepared to die, if need be, for his cause (and he proved it repeatedly); he refused to be goaded into meeting violence with violence because it would have meant the destruction of the movement; he continually appealed to the best in whites; and he divided and morally undermined his enemies by putting into practice the

Christian principles to which they mostly paid no more than lip service. Knowing that a Negro Communist had had a hand in organizing the boycott gave me some sense of pride; but I was overwhelmed by a lonely, left-out feeling as I began to realize that the tactics which were moving the great mass of Negroes toward achieving civil rights were being developed by a young Negro minister, while the Party, which had for decades been searching blindly for the road to Negro liberation, lay in ruins throughout the South—its members harassed, its leadership devoid of fruitful ideas.

My purpose in going to Montgomery was to ask Clifford Durr to take my case. He had been an influential member of the Federal Communications Commission in and after the New Deal and had returned to his hometown to practice law. He was then living in poverty, ostracized by his white neighbors because of his forthright support of Negro rights. He was much occupied in giving advice (*sub rosa*) to the Negro leaders of the bus boycott. I had long been acquainted with his wife, Virginia, a militant liberal and the sister-in-law of the Supreme Court's Associate Justice Hugo Black. When I called Durr at his office he recognized my name and met me outside his office, which he believed to be watched and bugged.

We talked on a park bench and he regretfully ruled himself out as my counsel, since, he said, he would lose me one vote before the case was heard: Justice Black would remove himself from consideration of the case because of their connection. Since it was lunchtime and we were having an enjoyable conversation, I suggested we remove to a nearby café. He resisted, and I'm quite certain that he had no money. When I insisted that I had an expense account that provided for taking potential counsel to lunch and that I shouldn't be deprived of the pleasure of his further company after such a long trip, that marvelous southern gentleman smiled and agreed to be my guest.

In Atlanta I visited some young comrades I knew to try to find what was left of the Atlanta organization. The Georgia DO, a man of remarkable courage, was unfortunately endowed with a strong tendency toward aimless contentiousness in nearly all of his interactions. He ascribed his personality problem to a faultlessly consistent class consciousness. Nonetheless, Georgia was the location of a number of stillborn Party plans, a great deal of inner-Party chaos, and an enraged hue and cry after the DO from numerous reactionaries both in and out of government. The SRC had had to remove him for his own safety, among other reasons, the inside joke being that he was "all guts and no brains."

I spent a day in western North Carolina, which I'd not visited for a while, and then flew to Washington, where I called on a noted authority on constitutional law, John Lord O'Brian of the firm of Covington and Burling. To my surprise, O'Brian was in his eighties and could not accept the case, but he was full of intellectual curiosity and discussed Communism with me for a stimulating hour, remarking that I didn't seem to be "a very orthodox Communist," a comment I supposed was intended as a compliment.

I stopped by their office for a brief visit with Joe Forer and Dave Rein, to tell them again how distressed I was over the national committee's decision. Then I phoned Arthur Goldberg, the capital's leading labor lawyer, and Joseph Rauh, a guiding spirit of Americans for Democratic Action; they each politely rejected my case in about thirty seconds. I called Roosevelt's former attorney general, Francis Biddle, who invited me to his home straightway when he heard my business. In his handsome living room, Biddle said that if there were any case that might bring him out of retirement it was mine, but he had disposed of his law library, mistrusted the state of his health, and probably wasn't up to it. "Would you like me to get you a lawyer?" he asked. At my enthusiastic affirmative, he suggested Telford Taylor and Joseph Rauh.

"You can forget Rauh," I said. "He turned me down thirty minutes ago."

"I'll call Taylor," Biddle said. He promptly phoned him in New York and made an appointment for me late that afternoon. I thanked him and dashed for the airport.

Seated in the impressive Madison Avenue offices of Landis, Taylor and Scoll at the appointed hour, I was full of curiosity about my prospective lawyer. From *Who's Who* I'd discovered that besides having been chief Allied prosecutor at the Nuremberg trials (for which I awarded him a couple of pluses), Taylor had been a brigadier general (a minus to an ex-GI) in army intelligence (a big minus). While I was amusing myself by balancing up Taylor's score thus far, I, together with Bill Albertson and another Party defense specialist, was ushered into a large office stacked in orderly profusion with books and papers.

The former general was handsome, tall, and athletic; his manner, though stiff and businesslike, seemed friendly. I told him of the status of my case and of the national committee's concern. Taylor said that he would handle the appeal and that his fee, assuming the Supreme Court would hear argument, was ten thousand dollars. I said that I was very pleased to have him as counsel but that I would have to consult the national committee about the fee. Taylor remarked that it should be clear that *I* would be his client, not the Party, and I agreed. The conversation grew more relaxed, and from a chance remark I discovered that he had a serious interest in classical music, played the piano, and even composed. I marveled at the Madison Avenue lawyer who cared about music and mentally awarded him several more pluses. When he questioned me about some area of international politics, I was startled at the doctrinaire, sectarian ring of my reply in the presence of a man so logical and knowledgeable. "Well, I suppose we'll just have to agree to disagree," Taylor said smiling, as I prepared to rush off to Party headquarters.

At the headquarters, the national board (the smaller, resident body which carried the national committee's powers in between its meetings) was gathered in an urgent meeting. I sent in an emissary to tell the board members that I must have their approval to retain Telford Taylor, who asked a ten-thousand-dollar fee. Instead of inviting me in, the board had the emissary shuttling back and forth relaying messages until I said in exasperation, "You tell them I want an unequivocal guarantee that the national committee stands responsible for the ten thousand dollars, or I'll call Taylor and tell him it's all off, and then I'll call Dave Rein and tell him to start preparing his petition for certiorari. I've got no money and I'm running out of time." Then a message came back that the money was guaranteed; and I had a new, world-famous lawyer.

The political climate in North Carolina in early 1956 seemed, in the opinion of one not very detached observer, to have approached mass insanity. The aftermath of the Supreme Court decision in *Brown* v. *Board of Education* was threatening to tear down the whole profitable structure of segregation, with its accretion of discriminatory laws. Segregationists were counterattacking against the Supreme Court with the Southern Manifesto, which most of North Carolina's congressmen were dragooned into signing. (No politician could afford to forget the defeat of Sen. Frank Graham by an unmemorable racist back in 1950 in a campaign based on Red-baiting and naked racism.) Liberals considered anti-desegregationist came under heavy fire and soon fell silent. Irrational and venal outbursts by politicians, never rare, became commonplace and were duly reflected in the press. For example, a self-inflated right-wing lawyer, a former Boy Scout celebrity and ex-FBI agent, garnered a three-column headline on page one of the *Greensboro Daily News* by raging at the invitation extended to me by the American Friends Service Committee to speak at a peace panel in the county courthouse. Freedom of speech was, as usual, in widespread disfavor; talk of civil liberties was, as usual, suspect.

In such an atmosphere the only thing missing was that shameful symbol of the nation's government at its nadir during three decades: the House Un-American Activities Committee. Warnings of its impending visit had come in January. In early March the first subpoenas were served. John Myers, a professor of languages and golfing coach at Baptist-sponsored Campbell College (he who led hymn singing after Party meetings), was the first target of both the committee and its two star informers, Ralph Clontz and Charles Childs. A third informer, Ralph Long, then far down the road to becoming an alcoholic derelict, had not been called as a witness and missed his star billing.

In a letter to the state's major newspapers, Myers stated:

> I will reveal before this committee neither my own political beliefs and associa-
> tions nor those of anyone else. Political beliefs lie in the realm of personal
> conviction and conscience, and no governmental power has the right to force a
> person to reveal them against his own free will. Wherever such committees have
> held their hearings, the attempt has been made to terrorize people into giving up
> their constitutional rights, into becoming suspicious of their friends and neighbors,
> into lapsing into a "safe" silence, and into refraining from any activity which
> might displease the investigators.

He quoted extensively from the committee's rules of procedure, which denied witnesses almost every right associated with due process of law. He concluded with a question: "Can any self-respecting person seriously consider 'cooperating' with them?" John had refused, when an instructor at the University of North Carolina, to answer a questionnaire which asked if he was then or had ever been a member of the Communist Party. After the university had declined to renew his contract, he had used his savings to go to Paris for a couple of years of study at the Sorbonne, securing his job at Campbell College on his return in 1952. Son of a Baptist minister and himself a regular Sunday school teacher, John was a decorated hero of World War II. He was also a splendid teacher with a profound love and understanding of French literature.

After publication of his letter, only a week before the hearings commenced, the trustees of Campbell College fired him for declining their suggestion that he make a statement "clarifying" his position or take a leave of absence pending the outcome of the hearings. John instead issued a statement saying that he had not accepted this suggestion, "although it was made in a spirit of kindness which I appreciate," because he believed that it was not only the right but the duty of a teacher to take a stand against the violation of constitutional liberties by agencies of the government. He pointed out that to make the statement requested by the trustees would be "to take upon myself the burden of proof" contrary to the American concept that the accused is innocent until proven guilty. "If anyone believes me to be guilty of any crime, let him have me indicted and tried in a proper court, having the advantage of the application of the rules of evidence, the right to cross-examine, and the right to present defense witnesses. I shall then be able to present my defense in an orderly fashion with some hope that justice will prevail."

John could have truthfully denied, had he chosen to do so, that he was a Party member. He had neglected to pay dues while in France and after his return; he had therefore not been a member for about three years. Because he really believed what he had written, he scorned to take advantage of his technical status; moreover, after the hearings, he took care to pay his dues up to date. As his career fell to ruins, his first concern was to assuage the frustrations and fears of his teaching colleagues, who had scarcely raised a finger to protest his firing. Because he was a gentleman and an unpretentious exemplar of charity and other Christian principles, his concern came as no surprise to those who knew him well.

As the beginning date of the committee's three-day visit neared, I learned of more subpoenas. In Winston-Salem, Bill, who was working as a fish butcher, had received his at the fish market. Two Negro comrades had also been served. Having already alerted the CRC that a good lawyer was needed, I phoned to find out whom they were sending and to give them more details. The hearings would be in Charlotte, the state's largest city; three congressmen, Willis (Democrat of Louisiana), Kearney (Republican of New York), and the chairman, Francis Walter (Democrat of Pennsylvania), would be present, with Richard Arens, the counsel (borrowed for the occasion from the Senate's Internal Security Subcommittee), as ringmaster. The CRC said it was sending down Rhoda Laks, a young, extremely pretty attorney from New York, to represent Bill and, on request, any others.

To the surprise of nearly everyone, Laks had company as defense counsel. James Gilliland of Warrenton, a Wake Forest classmate of John Myers, rallied to his friend's defense, insisting on acting without charge. He had not the remotest connection with the left and had not even seen John for some years. But, he said, John was one of the best people he had ever known, and he was not going to see him pushed around by anyone without a fight. Gilliland was a successful lawyer, the county solicitor, a member of the Lions Club, commander of his American Legion post, and a respected civic leader. On the first day, after seeing the committee in action, he offered his free services to all "unfriendly" witnesses.

John Myers was the first such witness called. Arens had Clontz confront him; Clontz waved his finger in John's face as he identified him as a member of the Communist Party. Clontz could of his own knowledge identify as a Communist but one of the many unfriendly witnesses summoned before the committee, and that one person had so identified himself. I never identified anyone as a Communist to another unless he or she was publicly known as such or had expressly asked for the designation, but Clontz apparently realized that an informer who couldn't name names was a negligible commodity. Perhaps that was why his recollection of the people I had supposedly introduced him to as Party members had greatly expanded since 1952, when he had embarked on his maiden voyage as professional witness, a role that subsequently made him the hero of numerous "patriotic" banquets. It was a busy time for him as he swaggered arrogantly about the hearing room shaking his finger in front of witnesses, sometimes shouting melodramatically, "I know that individual to be a Communist!"

He and Charles Childs were listened to with apparent awe by both the committee and the press. In addition to the news story on the hearing, the *Durham Morning Herald* ran a separate front-page story quoting the words of those two oracles. "Childs said . . . 'I consider the Communist Party a greater threat now than it was in the past.' . . . He said the reds are concentrating on the infiltration of various organizations . . . such as the American Legion and the Veterans of Foreign Wars. . . . Childs explained that Communists are now using the technique of influencing organizations from within by taking over top leadership posts." Luckily for Childs, no one questioned those profundities; but he did seem much upset during a recess when he accidentally suffered a face-to-face encounter with a young woman who was a very unfriendly witness. "Charles," she told him scornfully, "you're a physiological marvel: you have no heart, no guts, and no brains!" The three congressmen, however, outdid themselves in praising Childs and assuring him that he was not an informer or a stool pigeon.

All of the unfriendly witnesses followed the prescribed procedure of protecting themselves from contempt charges by invoking the First, Fifth, and Tenth Amendments and by refusing to answer most questions put to them lest they accidentally waive their Fifth Amendment rights.

One witness, who quietly invoked the usual amendments while he refused to say anything about himself, was not a Communist. Joe Blake, a native of Chadbourn, North Carolina, jazz connoisseur and record collector, witty raconteur and good companion, had resigned from the Party more than six years previously. Although he had remained a loyal friend to me and to several others, he had thought the Party too sectarian and rigid and himself temperamentally unsuited to it. He had gone his own way, maintaining no political contact with his former comrades, teaching school first in Durham and later, at the time when he was subpoenaed, in Georgetown, South Carolina. He resigned from his job in Georgetown a week before the committee convened. "I did not want to embarrass my school and community," he explained, "because of my appearance before this committee." Before his early death a few years later he had distinguished himself in his profession, well away from his inhospitable native state.

Witness after witness was called to the stand while cameras flashed and clicked in their faces, committee counsel and congressmen denounced them, and informers pointed fingers. In each case, after a few preliminary questions the victim, consulting the lawyers on every question, avoided likely imprisonment by invoking the Fifth Amendment. Few witnesses escaped the routine invective of the inquisitors. Representative Kearney asked a witness if he considered himself a loyal American. "Yes, sir. I do." "Well, I have nothing but the utmost contempt for your kind of American," the congressman replied. Some of the audience dutifully applauded, and the newspapers picked up the exchange and printed it as though the representative had delivered himself of a bon mot. Attorney Gilliland remarked afterward that the committee's performance was something like tying a guy to a tree and repeatedly slapping his face, knowing he couldn't hit back. While one witness was being questioned, there was a pause for a lengthy colloquy between the witness and counsel. Walter interrupted, shouting threats in strong terms at the lawyers. "Are you trying to *intimidate* counsel?" asked Gilliland, a large man, rising to his feet. "I'm not trying to intimidate anyone," Walter softly and petulantly replied.

There was an apparent division of labor among the three committee members. Walter presided, pontificated, and threatened the witnesses and their attorneys; Kearney, with a set of well-worn lines, set up the witnesses, called them names, and denounced them with righteous indignation; Willis attempted to summarize matters for the press and audience at suitable intervals. After the interrogation of three highly educated North Carolina–born witnesses who had been working at unskilled jobs to survive, Willis announced with an air of astonished discovery, "The conclusion is inescapable that these people are professional agitators, expert emissaries of the Communist conspiracy planted in the Southland. Who said it couldn't happen here?"

Perhaps the most telling blow against the committee came from Gilliland at the end of the first day's session. He rose and suggested respectfully that the committee investigate the status of the public schools in North Carolina, referring to the widespread resistance in the state to the Supreme Court's anti-segregation decisions. "It appears to me to be a very un-American situation. A large number of our officials apparently are in a conspiracy" to deny children their education. Walter shouted that Gilliland was trying to create a diversion. All the same, the press reported Gilliland's remarks widely.

But after three days of the committee's orgy there was no doubt who had won. All the unfriendly witnesses had lost their means of livelihood; the local papers published their pictures and addresses; the state press loaded them with contempt and condemnation (while ignoring the violation of their civil liberties). They were all marked men and women, the potential prey of Ku Klux Klan members and other bigots; their political effectiveness was vastly reduced; their futures looked dark. Some were in untenable positions and would have to leave the state. The courageous Gilliland was shortly to see his hometown people turn against him and destroy his position and career. On a native son whose politics comprised only the principle of fair play for everybody and who had enough guts and misplaced faith in his fellow citizens to follow the call of his conscience, the Old North State was about to bestow a characteristic reward.

Though I had remained inconspicuous during the hearing, I received detailed accounts of the proceedings each night from some of the participants. All the comrades I was able to talk with were frustrated and depressed at their inability to fight back. John Myers was ready to waive his Fifth Amendment rights and chance the likely contempt sentence just for the opportunity to tussle with the committee. I wouldn't hear of it; it was against Party policy. But after a while I began to have second thoughts on the matter. Most people equated "taking the Fifth" with an admission of guilt, and they viewed the accused Communists as guilty subversives who had been caught at some kind of devilment and had nothing to say for themselves. I began to wonder whether some two or three volunteers who had no dependents should not have tried to crack through the committee's stacked rules, tangle with the committee members, and, invoking only the First Amendment, go to jail for contempt. At least there would be a weight on the public conscience at seeing a person jailed for trying to answer charges and for refusing to rat on friends. The Party proclaimed itself a revolutionary organization ready to make any sacrifice for the people. Why not go to jail to defend free speech and show the kind of people Communists really were?

In my mind this question was closely related to one which had troubled me for a year: should I have taken the witness stand in my trial? Certainly I would have gone to jail for not naming names, but would it not have been worth a jail term to testify for two or three days telling what the Party was like and what it stood for? Jefferson had said, "The tree of liberty must be refreshed from time to time with the blood of patriots and tyrants." Sitting in prison would not exactly have been giving one's blood, but it might have strengthened the liberty of thought and speech.

The North Carolina Party had just received at the hands of the committee the worst defeat in its history, simply because it was muzzled and could not talk back. In the face of all that perverted governmental power, should not the Party have found some way of proclaiming its principles? Should I not have done so at my trial?

That was all idle musing under the circumstances. What was done was done. The immediate need was to see to the welfare of the committee's victims. There would be time enough later to brood and talk over what should have been.

But a month later, when I returned to New York, so many cataclysmic events struck the Party that all other concerns were eclipsed.

18

The Tangled Web

Corruptio optimi pessima—the greatest evil is the good corrupted. . . . Communism has its roots in some of the finest of human political motives and social aspirations, and its corruption is repulsive.

Leonard Woolf, *Downhill All the Way*

There is not a fiercer hell than the failure in a great object.

John Keats, Preface to *Endymion*

Most of the North Carolina comrades were determined to stick it out even though the future seemed to offer little hope for their becoming politically effective. A few, endangered and harassed to the point of facing hunger for themselves and their families, had little choice but to leave the state. Still, no one panicked or gave way to despair. For some, adversity gave rise to a resourcefulness and a wry wit not previously apparent. For me, it was an occasion in which distress was mixed with such admiration that I could say but little.

After doing what I could to help my comrades, I visited my mother and aunt in Greensboro and returned to Gladys, Barbara, and Grandma in New York. I was gloomy about my work; I felt like a general most of whose army was on the sick or wounded list. The finances of all my districts, like everything else, were in bad shape. I believed that I should soon get a job and quit drawing my sumptuous forty-dollar-a-week salary.

On the evening of the day I returned I received a visit from Bernie, who wore a desperately funereal face. He had attended a high-level Party meeting at which excerpts had been read from Khrushchev's secret speech at the twentieth congress of the Soviet Party. As he related some of the facts to me—the killing of nearly half the Soviet Central Committee in the thirties, the phony treason trials, the wholesale slaughter of Jewish artists and intellectuals, the anti-Semitic hoax of a "doctors' plot" at the time of Stalin's death—Bernie was overcome with emotion. "I didn't join the Party to condone murder!" he gasped. In summation, according to Khrushchev, most of what the capitalist press and the professional anti-Soviet experts had been saying about the Soviet Union for years was *true*.

I scarcely slept that night. Stalin—my revered symbol of the infallibility of Communism, the builder of socialism in one country, the rock of Stalingrad, the wise, kindly man with the keen sense of humor at whose death I had wept just three years before—*Stalin,* on the admission of his former idolators, had been a murderous, power-hungry monster!

Yet it never occurred to me in 1956 to doubt what Khrushchev had said. Khrushchev, after all, was head of the Soviet Party and therefore the fountainhead of political wisdom, the very source of policy. Having long been a good Communist, I was still accustomed to reacting to such authority with willing belief. Besides, what Khrushchev said made sense and explained many mysteries: how, for example, "spy" trials held in many of the Eastern European countries under Soviet domination could result in the execution of top Communist leaders who, after Stalin's death, were exonerated and "rehabilitated"; how Tito could be in the Soviet press in 1948 a "fascist criminal" and in 1955 "a devoted Communist son of the working class." Past strains on my credulity clamored for my attention: the nonnecessity of civil liberties in the socialist Soviet Union (might not Stalin's liquidated opponents have felt them necessary?) or the demonology of Trotsky's career as retailed by Soviet "history." My idol had crumbled to dust forever.

That was only the beginning of the questions which tumbled over one another in my mind. If Stalin were so corrupt, what about his surviving comrades? Where were they when his crimes were taking place? If such as they were running the Soviet Party then, why trust them later? Could Foster's and Dennis's devotion to the needs of Soviet policy partially explain why so many honest workers rejected the Party as an American radical organization? Was Earl Browder dumped in 1945 because he attempted to Americanize the Party at the possible expense of its pro-Soviet slant? Piece by piece the whole once-trusted structure began to disintegrate, leaving me desolate and lost. Gladys, though equally dismayed, tried unsuccessfully to distract me from my brooding.

Bernie was raging at the mealymouthed hypocrisy of such Party functionaries as cautiously balanced Stalin's achievements against his crimes. He wanted a complete rethinking of every question of theory and policy with no holds barred; then, he believed, maybe there would be somewhere the Party could go, some service it could render. Hank, with his heavy responsibilities among the distributive workers, felt much the same.

My friends at the *Daily Worker,* John Gates, Joe Clark, Alan Max, Rob Hall, and Lester Rodney, together with the former foreign editor, Joe Starobin (who had formally left the Party in 1954), were exceptionally well informed about what was going on in the Soviet Union and in the international Communist movement and were bitterly critical of its chicanery and especially of Soviet interference in the American Party. John Gates, who along with Gene Dennis had recently completed his parole after serving four years in the Atlanta Penitentiary, was back as editor and had become the rallying leader of those who wanted to question everything and revise the Party's theory and policy. Dennis wavered somewhere in the middle and, true to years of conditioning, was never really critical of the Soviet Union. Foster flaunted his Soviet loyalty and was the natural leader of the there's-nothing-basically-wrong standpatters.

In the SRC the attitude was business as usual. I spoke privately to Hosea of my distress over Khrushchev's secret speech; Hosea, in his most reassuring manner said, "Listen. I been around a long time and I seen a lotta fusses raised; they all blowed over, and *I'm* still here. This'n 'll blow over too." Frannie and Sylvia, her chief assistant, seemed undisturbed. Ed, a balancer of Stalin's good and evil aspects, generally supported Foster and refused to treat Khrushchev's speech as a matter of any great importance. He was more concerned with the return of his friend Jim from his Smith Act conspiracy trial to active leadership of the SRC.

Jim returned, projecting a sense that the first team was back in the lineup and that everything would be fine. Better informed about the internal situation of the Party than Ed was, he steered a course that tacked between Foster and Dennis. Jim and Ed called a southern Party conference for May 28 and spent a considerable amount of money providing travel expenses for Deep South delegates. Frannie and Sylvia had made excellent preparations, and about a dozen delegates showed up from Florida, Texas, Louisiana, Alabama, Virginia, and North Carolina. The person who joined me in representing North Carolina was Bill (the one who had become a textile worker). Most of the delegates were seriously lacking in Party experience, and five were not southerners but "colonizers." Apart from Bill, they were generally ignorant of Khrushchev's speech and its implications and could be expected to follow the cues of Ed and Jim on such weighty concerns.

Jim led off with a report on the Party in the South with which, though it had not previously been discussed with the SRC, I had little quarrel. It concluded with the proposal that the southern Communists try to build, instead of the Party, a loose association of socialists and Marxists with a broad program which would not antagonize the NAACP or the unions—in other words, essentially what Browder had proposed for the South a dozen years before. I spoke in favor of the proposal without referring to its origin. Later, on the question of the work in the South, Bill spoke gently but critically of the SRC's lack of attention to trade union problems and of Ed's leftist, condescending, ill-informed attitudes when the two had met a year before. Bill outlined what he thought should be the Party's approach to the unions in the South, drawing on his own six-year involvement with the textile industry, his editing of the *Textile Workers' Voice,* and his experience as a shop steward and rank-and-file leader in a textile union.

Delighted with my friend's cogent, insightful remarks, I joined in, injecting a sweeping criticism of the SRC leadership's narrowness of vision (such as the earlier scoffing at Martin Luther King, Jr.) and the lack of democracy in the committee. Ed and Jim reacted like scalded hogs, and Hosea threw his considerable weight behind them. Previously such a combination of three national-level leaders (who were also Negroes) would have crushed the opposition almost automatically, but Bill and I fought back with voluminous, bitter examples of Ed's and Jim's bureaucratic high-handedness. Our moral outrage and aggressiveness were not characteristic of either of us: there was the thrust of resolute desperation in our demeanor. Frannie entered the fray, but the expected lynch spirit failed to develop. The southern delegates were getting an eye-opener on matters which they had never even considered.

The meeting took place in a spacious, comfortable basement room of a Negro couple's home in Queens. When it neared time for cars to pick up delegates and take them to their prearranged quarters in different parts of the city, the meeting was adjourned and the delegates collected upstairs at the front door. Bill was still in the basement in intense conversation with one of the Alabama delegates when I reached the top of the stairs. I heard Jim ask in a stage whisper that caught everyone's attention, "Who *is* this Bill? *I* think he's an FBI agent!" I stood in the stairwell astounded, as Hosea, doubtless inspired by his leader, hastily characterized Bill and me as liars, a charge he had failed to make during the heated debate.

The next day, since we two dissenters had not been made outcasts, Jim and Ed changed their tactics and treated us more respectfully. However, one delegate, new to the South, chose to attack Bill on the charge of white chauvinism because he had sharply disagreed with Jim, Ed, and Hosea. According to my notes on that meeting, I rose and demanded to know why being a Negro made a comrade immune from criticism, especially since Bill's comments—unlike the retorts of the three—had been courteous and respectful. I also demanded to know why the comrade had not included me in his absurd charge. Was it perhaps because he considered me a big name or a privileged character in the Party? Brushing aside the charge of white chauvinism as a waste of precious time, I insisted that privileged-character, big-shot, one-man rule had saddled the southern Party with a leadership grown arrogant and blind because of the absence of the democratic freedom to criticize. I cited Ed's and Jim's numerous superficial analyses, including their still-patronizing estimate of Dr. King.

I pointed out the growth of favoritism in the Party, using as examples Frannie's gradual installation as Ed's alter ego when such a role was clearly beyond her capacity; she was merely a capable organizer. I also mentioned a tendency to promote incompetents so long as they questioned nothing and were admiring of Ed and Frannie. I complained of the lack of comradely warmth in the SRC, the frequent contemptuous references to developing comrades, and a condescending approach to organized workers who failed to revolt against bad union leadership. I characterized such manifestations as "elitist leftism," which derived from the leftist, Soviet-oriented line followed nationally.

After my blast I was roundly denounced by Ed, Jim, Hosea, and Frannie. When I finally got the floor again, I declared that the arrogance growing from power not subject to criticism not only made my SRC colleagues hypersensitive at the moment, but had resulted in the past in insensitive and even unprincipled behavior. I illustrated with the case of Carl, who had been a valuable, thoughtful addition to the SRC until his wife had suffered a nervous breakdown and needed psychiatric care. Partly because psychiatry was a dirty word in the Party, Carl was in effect demoted and virtually dropped from southern work. I suggested that an additional reason for his fall was that he tried to do his own thinking.

There were exchanges about whether the southern Party's line had been leftist and sectarian. Bill and I heaped scorn on those who maintained that it was not. Jim finally suggested that "in some respects it tended to be." Never in my Party experience had there been such an exchange of opposing views with such frankness, and I thought that Bill and I were gaining ground among the delegates.

Midway in the afternoon there was a violent disturbance upstairs, and our hostess called down that the FBI wanted Ed and was breaking down the front door. Feeling myself a veteran in such matters, I went over to Ed, who was understandably shaken, and took his papers, notes, wallet, watch, and everything else of value, shoving them into my jacket pocket. I then escorted him up the stairs, closing the basement door behind us, and confronted several FBI agents, three of whom looked remarkably seedy and goonlike. Two agents took Ed into custody, telling him to put his hands against the wall and calling him "boy." "He's 'mister' to you, Mac! And don't forget it. Let's see your warrant." The warrant was produced and I studied it carefully, sharing it with Ed. Meanwhile, two agents were starting for the basement door. "Do you have a warrant for anyone else?"

"No."

"Do you have a search warrant?"

"No."

"Then get away from that door and get out of here!" The FBI demanded to know who I was and I replied, gesturing toward Ed, "I'm his lawyer." I assured Ed that his things would be turned over to his wife, that efforts would start immediately to arrange bail, and that he should relax and have a good rest while waiting. We walked together to the front door and embraced, whereupon the agents prepared to handcuff Ed's hands behind him. "Why don't you do it in front? Isn't six-to-one good enough odds for you?" They handcuffed him in front and drove away in two cars. I phoned the news to the national Party office and to Ed's wife at the *Daily Worker,* where she worked, tried to reassure my courageous hostess about her shattered front door, and then rejoined the meeting.

Everyone gradually calmed down and the meeting was resumed. After Jim's and Ed's behavior of the night before, I had determined, with Bill, that they should not get off too lightly, even though we had decided against mentioning Jim's low-blow remark that Bill was an FBI agent. I had prepared a written statement, a point of personal privilege, which I presented just before the meeting broke up:

> I had written the bulk of this statement this morning, but because of Ed's arrest I had decided not to read it, since we all feel so raw about that event. What changed my mind was ———'s proposal a few minutes ago that the meeting go on record against Bill's and my point of view in the discussion last night [the proposal had been defeated].
>
> I think that discussion was valuable insofar as it produced deeper thinking on questions of tactics and principle. I learned from it. I think Bill and I were right.
>
> However, what I want to raise here is the manner in which two national leaders, Jim and Ed, participated in that discussion. I don't think national leaders should be muzzled; they should participate forcefully and make available their knowledge, experience, and thinking. But I do believe that they have a responsibility not to try to crush an opposing opinion by such methods as extending the framework of the discussion to imply our total alienation from nearly everything—ranging from Marxism to democratic rights—or to try to hold us up to ridicule and contempt. I feel that Jim attempted to do this last night in a pompous and pontifical manner. I believe it was wrong of Jim to imply stupidity, scholasticism, panic, cowardice, and possible white chauvinism in opposing our points of view.
>
> I think it was equally bad for Ed to demand with great vehemence that the meeting "record itself as to whether we have been faced here with a tactical or a *principled* question." Although he retreated from this position later, under pressure, his tone was such that it could only lead toward forced unanimity and the clobbering of the dissidents.
>
> I am not raising this to belittle Ed and Jim in any way. Nor are my feelings hurt.

I want to be part of a Party in which the comrades are encouraged to think for themselves; where there is the right to disagree with the leadership without having one's integrity held up to question; where one has the right to make mistakes, to be wrong, without being "worked over" politically.

Many of us comrades, however ill-equipped, are trying to learn to think for ourselves. I'm one of them. I'll make mistakes and will undoubtedly prolong discussions many times in the process. I want to be told my mistakes and I will be responsive to convincing argument. But I will never again say I agree to something until I'm convinced; and I will *not* be bulldozed.

Inner-Party democracy is not a side issue. It is vital to collective leadership, which I think we have not had in the SRC. It is even more necessary if we are to release the creative initiative of our comrades, if we are to get into the mainstream of our country's life. We *must* feel free to raise the problems closest to us.

There has, I feel, been a long history in our Party in the South of bureaucratic, sometimes high-handed dealing with our people. We must make a profound change in this state of affairs. I might add that since Communist discipline is primarily *self*-discipline, Party discipline need not be weakened by such a change.

I did not want the comrades to leave without knowing my views about the meeting.

There was a brief silence and someone moved that the meeting adjourn. For once, I had had the last word.

A noticeable factional hostility had begun to permeate the Party in New York. Formerly, to imply to a comrade that so-and-so was also a comrade was sufficient to arouse a response of warmth and trust, but an additional question was now usually implicit before such a response was forthcoming: "Where does he stand?" Early in June 1956 the State Department released the complete text of Khrushchev's secret speech and the *New York Times* published it in full. Although the Party leadership had known the gist of the speech for many weeks, most of the Party membership had read only news stories in the commercial press, which, as usual, they considered lies. Once the text was published without repudiation, it could not be ignored, and the Party vibrated with shock, dismay, and controversy. On the morning that the text appeared in the *Times,* Gladys, five-year-old Barbara, and I were on a train bound for Brewster, New York, for a weekend with left-wing friends. The actual text was far more shocking than the bits Bernie had relayed to me. As I read, Gladys tried to distract Barbara's attention while I pounded the windowsill in fury till my fist was sore and swollen.

The people gathered at the summer resort, mostly intellectuals, were stunned by what they had read. Shaken to the depths, I launched into a vehe-

ment attack on the Soviet Party leadership, declaring that while it had supposedly been building socialism in the Soviet Union and leading the struggle
for peace, it had used the American Party for its own immediate ends in total
disregard of the American Party's responsibilities in its own country. I con-
tended that American Communists had ceased thinking for themselves and
blindly accepted as Marxist-Leninist gospel whatever was dished out by a
mass murderer, or his successors, in Moscow. So shocking were my words
that people began arguing pro and con all at the same time, till the great Negro
scholar and activist W. E. B. Du Bois, then eighty-eight years old, and also a
guest, cooled the feverish tempers. He felt that, while Khrushchev's revela-
tions were deeply disturbing, there was no reason to doubt the basic integrity
of the present Soviet leadership or their progress in building socialism or in
leading the world's peace forces. I was dying to engage in battle, but because
of the enormous admiration and affection I had for Du Bois, I bit my tongue
and said no more.

The "Khrushchev report" was the topic foremost in the thoughts of most
comrades. I discussed it tirelessly with everyone I could. Herb Aptheker
seemed moderate and somewhat noncommittal privately. Later, at what was
probably an enlarged national committee meeting, where there was much criticism of some of the Party's past actions and of Foster, Ben Davis, Bob
Thompson, and other rigidly leftist Party leaders, Herb, speaking very slowly
and almost as if in a trance, said that he thought that the comrades should
remember that there was such a thing as befouling one's own nest; and then he
sat down. Many people shied away from the caustic confrontations in their
club meetings and quietly stopped attending them. More and more the mood
in the Party became one of hostility toward anyone with a view opposing one's
own. So pervasive were those differences that Gladys and I discovered acute
tensions even when meeting socially with Frannie of the SRC and some others
of her political persuasion. At one gathering, when the conversation shifted to
a French murder movie which we all had seen, a harsh, angry disagreement
arose about the underlying values of the film makers.

I told my views frankly to as many of the comrades in North Carolina as I
could, stating that they were my own personal views and that as far as I knew
everyone on the SRC disagreed with me. There was near unanimity among my
Carolina comrades in support of my stance. I also told them that I was going
to try to find a job and get off the Party payroll. In that decision I was encouraged by Bill Albertson, who was so outraged by what he considered the duplicity of the Party leadership (excepting John Gates, who had published the
Khrushchev report in the *Daily Worker*) that he withdrew from full-time Party
work and returned to his old trade of delicatessen butcher.

During the summer Jim got an increased subsidy for southern work from the national office, and it was decided that my salary would thenceforth be paid by the SRC and increased to $42.50 per week, the highest pay I ever received as a Party functionary. I wondered privately whether getting my money from the SRC rather than from my districts was intended to make me more pliable with the committee.

For several months I had a remarkable relationship with Jack Stachel, whom I had known formally for years as national educational director and a member of the ruling national board. Jack had played a major role in the Party's history in the twenties and thirties and had served a term in prison along with most of the other first-string Smith Act defendants. I had come really to know him and his sweet-natured wife, Bertha, through friendship with their son, a near neighbor of mine. I became quite friendly with the older man, who was afflicted with a severe heart ailment; we would spend whole afternoons together minding Jack's toddling grandson while he played in Central Park. Seated on a bench, Jack would bitterly denounce the stupidities of the Party's line for the previous decade or so. He was contemptuous of Foster, except as a trade union leader after World War I. He believed Dennis to be spineless. He was markedly more revisionist than was John Gates and laughed at "Marxism-Leninism" as a body of theory. He remarked that the Party was virtually nonexistent as an organization and that the furious inner-Party discussion was really a great to-do by ex-leaders over a political corpse; he believed that the Party was so isolated and so deservedly discredited that it would take years of redeeming itself before it could earn even a tiny footnote in American history.

The discussions in the park recurred throughout the summer and into the fall until the cold winds precluded sitting out of doors. I noticed that the political discussions occurred exclusively when there were just the two of us and the grandson. Once, when Gladys accompanied us, the conversation remained nonpolitical despite my efforts. Having considerable admiration for Stachel, and sharing some of his views on the Party, I ventured on one of our last afternoons together to ask his advice about what I should do, considering my disillusionment with the Party and Marxism-Leninism. Jack's reply was that I should stay in the Party; many leaders would be leaving, thereby creating open leadership positions; I was young (thirty-six) and celebrated as a Smith Act case; I was that rare Party breed, a southerner; and above all, I was a non-Jew. As Jack saw it, the Party would necessarily be attempting to reenter the main currents and there would be a high priority for non-Jews to place in top Party positions. I would, he thought, be elected to the national committee at the next national convention and could go far. My privileged background was a slight handicap, but considering my past record and the likely revision of Marxism-Leninism, there would probably be less rigidity in such matters. By all means, he said, I should remain in the Party and refrain from taking any extreme positions publicly.

I felt hurt that he had judged my concern with the Party to be a crass, careerist one, and I dropped the subject. However, in that period, several of my friends surprised me. Bill Albertson, for example, one of the first to leave the full-time payroll, found himself barred from employment in delicatessens by the very union he had helped organize many years before. After a few weeks of unemployment, he returned to the Party payroll to assume the top job from which Bernie had just resigned for the very reasons Bill had espoused earlier.

Meanwhile, my case had been accepted by the Supreme Court, Telford Taylor was writing an impressive and extensive brief, and printing bills mounted alarmingly. The need for fund raising was ever-present, so much so that Sylvia of the SRC staff spent a large part of her time working ably in the Scales Defense Committee, even though she probably considered me some kind of apostate after my blasphemous remarks at the southern conference.

Fund raising became increasingly difficult because the period of Smith Act trials had passed and people were preoccupied with the Party's internal situation. Still, some people, including Hank and Bernie, were adept at securing contributions from unions. Nat Ross, over a seven-year period, raised an extraordinary amount of money from sympathetic individuals. But fund-raising meetings and parties were continually necessary and were organized in every borough of the city. In torment, I found I would have to speak about my case and ask for money. I usually did a wretched, self-conscious job of it and undoubtedly reduced the financial take in the process. Fortunately, Paul Robeson, who for eight or nine years had been denied his passport by the State Department and had had the concert halls of the United States closed to him through political pressure, somehow heard of my plight. One night when I was boring an audience of about a hundred or so in a wretched hall in the Bronx, a great black giant entered the auditorium, mounted the stage with a glowing smile, and crushed me with a bear hug. "Excuse me for breaking in like this," he said to the meeting, "but I must tell you something about this young man which his modesty prevents him from saying. I have known him for many years. We are old friends. In all that time he has been fighting the good fight—*our* fight, his and mine—against racism and for democratic rights in the South. He has spent his adult life speaking for the oppressed in the *South,* where for generations few have dared to stand up for the right."

The people in the audience, somnolent a minute before, were like tautened musical strings played on by a master hand.

"His roots and my roots are in North Carolina—my ancestors, slaves; his, slave owners. We stand here tonight as two brothers in the struggle for human decency." His gigantic arm embraced my shoulders. "I am merely a peoples' artist trying to do my part. I came tonight to say to you that Junius has been victimized; he is in trouble; he needs our help. While I sing a few songs of my people—if you will permit me [wild applause]—let us show him that he does not stand alone." An accompanist appeared carrying her music and sat down at a battered piano, and the audience was at once transported by a rich, warm, bass voice singing spirituals: "Didn't My Lord Deliver Daniel?" "Water Boy," "Go Down, Moses," and "This Little Light of Mine." That great voice and the generous spirit which activated it had spoken to the hearts of people the world over for three decades; once again, using the music of his enslaved forebears, Robeson moved an audience, predominantly of Jews, so that they would treasure the occasion as long as they lived.

The money raised was three or four times what I had expected. Moreover, that was only the first of many Scales fund-raising meetings that Robeson transformed with his matchless alchemy. He seemed to have his own radar that told him when my committee was having a meeting, and more often than not, if he were in New York, he would attend. Time and again he would use his incredible gifts with soul-stirring passion to aid an obscure southern Communist, while his own career was virtually on the rocks and he himself was prey to God only knew what despair about the state of his country and that of the Party for which he had once had such high hopes.

Discussion raged and dissension grew, so that even an upcoming presidential election received little attention in the Party. I was forcibly reminded of what the Communist-hunters were up to when, in late July, the House Un-American Activities Committee, meeting in Atlanta with its usual hostility toward civil liberties, clobbered several North Carolina comrades whom they had missed in Charlotte. The North and South Carolina registration figure of dues-paid members then stood at fifty-odd, perilously close to the figure ten years earlier when I had been discharged from the army.

During the summer and fall the *Daily Worker* and *Worker* carried on an uncensored, free-for-all discussion, printing letters from all over the country, and the New York Party issued irregularly a magazine called *Party Voice,* filled with provocative discussion articles. The Gates revisionists, among whom I counted myself, were at first a majority of what remained of the Party. Many of them, including me, believed that the Party could be radically changed; but many others saw no hope of changing a membership so accustomed to following unthinkingly, and on faith, where it was led. The latter group left the organization in great numbers. A national convention was scheduled for February 1957, and a "Draft Resolution" was prepared as a basis for preconvention discussion. The Draft Resolution was a compromise between the Gates and Dennis forces, but it chiefly reflected Gates's views; Foster opposed it with increasing vehemence.

In the SRC, Jim and Ed (who had been quickly released on bail) opposed most of it but agreed to use it as a basis for discussion. As an enthusiastic revisionist, I was treated coolly in the committee. At an enlarged SRC meeting in late September and two weeks later at a second enlarged meeting, which included some members from Florida, Alabama, and Virginia (no one could come from North Carolina), Jim denounced the New York district as liquidationist and white chauvinist, implying that I "went along" with the New Yorkers and wanted to dissolve the Party in the South owing to my "faintheartedness." I replied that at the southern conference four months before Jim had proposed dissolving the Party in the South and substituting for it essentially what Browder had proposed and instituted in 1943. In the interest of comradely and fruitful discussion, I said, I was not going to label Jim a Browderite, a liquidationist, or a coward. Jim, I said, had proposed a "basis of unity" in the SRC resting on acceptance of the Draft Resolution as a basis for discussion; however, he and Ed had already rejected nearly all the fundamentals of the resolution, labeling them Keynesianism, Browderism, liberalism, and other isms. Where, I asked, were there any grounds for agreement among Jim and Ed and me? And how important was it anyway? The Party was in a state of collapse and not as a result of a sectarian error here and there or a mistaken estimate or two. The cause was quite evidently the failure of Marxism-Leninism as a guide to action, a failure to adapt the Party to the American scene. How else could one account for a mass leader of Hosea's stature in the thirties, whose whole subsequent history was one of declining influence among the people after he became known as a Communist? Jim and Ed, as student leaders, were cases in point. I too had been an influential student leader until I became a public Communist. Must not something be wrong, I asked, with an organization that inevitably destroys the influence of its leaders? The only solution was a complete, democratic revision of all Party policies and theories and a redirection of its energies.

I had no illusions that I would get far with southern DOs or the three or four handpicked delegates; they were too isolated politically to realize that the Party was politically bankrupt. But I wanted to expose them to reality as I perceived it, and I would hope for the future. They had bravely stood up to white citizens' councils, the KKK, and McCarthyites, and they would not easily surrender the illusion of a Party with all the right answers and the patented model for a future of socialism. I did not blame them; I wondered what *I* would do if the Party could not be rebuilt as a viable, democratic, rational, independent, radical organization—a tall order indeed.

That dilemma was closer than I'd thought. By the end of October mass protests had been erupting in Hungary, and the Soviet Union suddenly intervened militarily. After discussing the situation with John Gates, Joe Clark, Sam Sillen, George Charney, Sam Coleman, Bernie, and others, I was convinced, as several of them were not, that all hope of reorienting the Party was gone. The best people were leaving in droves; many of those who remained did so from inertia and from awe at the Soviet Union's display of naked force. A few days later, Soviet tanks were firing on workers in the streets of Budapest. I happened to drop by the Party's national office at that time to see Ben Davis, with whom I had a superficial but cordial relationship, about some minor matter or other. After I had spent a few minutes pleasantly with him, he invited me to sit in on an important meeting about the "Hungarian affair." He escorted me into the meeting room with his arm about my shoulders. The meeting was in recess and people were standing around in clusters; Foster was holding court, seated at a table, and I heard him say in his hard, arrogant way, something to the effect that the Red Army would soon take care of "this CIA 'revolution.' " I burst out, "Those are *working* people the Red Army is shooting down!" Then, more quietly, through clenched teeth, I added, "If I were in Budapest now, I'd be throwing Molotov cocktails at Soviet tanks!" My face red with anger, I walked out on an infuriated Foster. Thirty minutes later I was in Telford Taylor's office for a meeting about my case. I asked Telford if the law firm had lost clients because he was defending me. Telford acknowledged that there had possibly been a few. "Then I think you should be the first to know that you will shortly be defending a *former* Communist." Telford showed surprise, and I said, "The only world Communist figure I feel like calling 'comrade' right now is Imre Nagy [the Hungarian Communist leader and premier], and the Soviets will probably kill him."

The prophecy was only too true; the opposition was soon crushed in Hungary. In the American Party the tide was turning against the revisionists who remained. In New York the level of bitterness between politically opposed comrades had no limits. Old friends ceased to speak to one another. So harrowing were the disputes in some club meetings that longtime Party members walked out and did not return. A valued friend drifted away from me at that time. Herb Aptheker, apparently at Dennis's behest, had written a hasty, poorly documented book defending Soviet intervention in Hungary. Whatever it was intended for, *The Truth about Hungary* damaged Herb's credibility with thousands of people who greatly respected him as a pioneer in the field of Negro history. At that time he began to avoid me.

I made one last trip to North Carolina as DO and SRC representative. Meeting with most of my comrades in small groups, at each gathering I made a three-minute speech summarizing my view of the situation in the Party and asking what they wanted to do and what they thought I should do. The response was usually something like, "Don't leave yet; go to the convention and tell Foster and Dennis, for us, to go to hell!" Among all the comrades I was able to meet with, the response was similar. I used Party discipline one more time to extract solemn commitments from two of my leading cadres that they would complete the Ph.D. studies they had interrupted to take on Party assignments. (Happily, they kept their promises and later achieved distinction in their fields of work.) Parting was a painful wrench for me, even though everyone promised to "keep in touch."

Back in New York, I made a terse, accurate report on my trip to Jim (Ed was sick), turned in a few dollars which belonged to the SRC, drew my last pay, and began job hunting. Advised by the sympathetic head of a small employment agency, I applied for a Christmas job at Saks Fifth Avenue and was hired as a salesman in boys' furnishings. Gladys had been working as a window decorator at Ohrbach's and had become the fashion coordinator for all their windows and displays. At night the two of us either worked at fund raising or engaged in political discussions with our friends. The news from the New York Party was painful to hear, so ugly had the confrontations become. Bernie returned from one such meeting declaring that "if these bastards [Foster, Davis, Dennis, et al.] had state power in their hands, they would *kill* us! They'd stand us against the wall!" There was little doubt in my mind that he was right. I wondered what Jim, if he had absolute power, would do to me "for the good of the Party." I thought Ed might at least hesitate, because he and I had been close at times.

Christmas and New Year's passed and I began looking for another job, since the temporary employees at Saks were dismissed after the post-Christmas sale. To my surprise, I was asked to stay on because they liked my work; I was switched to boys' suits at a substantial increase in pay and would work on a commission basis in a few weeks. Knowing nothing about clothes and caring still less about fashion, I had, of necessity, to pick the brains of my colleagues in order to learn some minimal catchwords to bandy about with the well-heeled mothers of the boys I must clothe. The job was not unpleasant and apparently I was doing well, for after a month I was told that I was going to be trained as a junior executive. A week after that, on a Friday afternoon an hour before quitting time, I was summoned to the personnel office and fired with profuse apologies and a great many contradictory explanations. Recognizing the FBI's handiwork, I looked at the eyes of the oily personnel chief and said, "I think I know what happened." The man became confused and stammered. I asked for my pay, cleaned out my locker, and left the store without ever becoming a junior executive of Saks Fifth Avenue.

The national convention began the next day, and being unemployed, I decided to attend. Bernie and I subwayed to Houston Street. As we left the train we encountered a Comrade Harry, known for his amiability; I had known him intimately since first joining the Party. Harry greeted me with a snarl, "Well, Junius, I see you're traveling in pretty crummy company," he said, gesturing at Bernie, a famed revisionist. I barely had time to say that I liked my company, when Harry assumed an unintentionally comic boxing posture, and I stepped between the two to prevent Bernie from pulverizing his antagonist. As Bernie and I proceeded toward the hall, Bernie groaned with pained foresight, "I can already see the kind of meeting this is going to be!"

Once at the hall, Bernie joined the New York delegation, while I discovered that there was to be a "southern caucus" later in the morning and that I had been named cochairman of the credentials committee. The committee, composed of outstanding Party activists, was equally balanced between "right revisionists" (supporters of Gates's position) and "left sectarians" (supporters of either Dennis's middle-of-the-road Soviet-oriented position or Foster's ultra-left Soviet-oriented position); the opposing cochairman shook hands with me, excused himself, and never returned, leaving me to preside.

There were numerous rival delegates from around the country who challenged one another from opposing factional positions. The committee heard them all, and if both sides seemed to represent any significant group, as was often the case, I would recommend that both delegates (or delegations) be seated; where there was obvious chicanery (usually by Foster supporters), I would recommend denial of credentials. I was supported by a two-to-one vote on almost every issue. On one occasion a Foster delegation, sponsored by Charles Loman, a Negro leader from Brooklyn, failed to convince anyone of its legitimacy. Loman and I had had cordial relations for years because of our friendship with the late Gene Morse. After the unanimous rejection of his group, he approached me at the committee table and asked me quietly to seat them anyway. I indignantly refused, saying that the committee didn't do business that way. Loman replied that he was prepared, as he put it, to knock me on my "ass" and indicated that he had support from a couple of heavyweight white guys a few feet away. I replied, "I guess you'll have to do it then. You're not going to intimidate this committee." Most of the committee arose and surrounded us, and Loman withdrew cursing and threatening. (Later it was widely reported that he had refused to return approximately a quarter of a million dollars entrusted to his care by the Party in the underground days. He then turned up in Chicago, the owner of a profitable fleet of trucks and, reputedly, a "house black" in the Mayor Daley machine.)

I excused myself from the committee long enough to discover who and what was the "southern caucus." I found Jim meeting with two people whom he had incongruously designated "southerners." One was James Allen, a prominent Party intellectual who had written a book on the Negro question back in the thirties. The other was Ted Bassett, a nice old guy who had taught me in my Party school in 1940. I greeted them both and then demanded of Jim why they were representing southern comrades, saying that I would take bets that neither had been south of Washington more than once in the past twenty years. I apologized for challenging them but said that they really should not allow Jim to use them to misrepresent a constituency. They were embarrassed and Jim seemed upset. Nevertheless, Jim proposed that the "southern caucus" nominate him and Ed for the national committee. (Ed was still sick and was in the hospital undergoing tests.) Jim made a glowing speech about Ed's fine personal qualities. I replied that I agreed with most of what Jim had said about Ed, but that membership on the national committee was a political position and that Ed's forlorn qualification was that he had been wrong about two-thirds of the time. I said that I thought a good many of Ed's political errors came from having too much confidence in the judgment of his friend Jim, but that his leadership of the SRC, despite his sincerity, sacrifices, and devotion, did not warrant his promotion. Jim winced and asked for a vote. I said I did not recognize that caucus as having the slightest legitimacy, that I would denounce it subsequently, and that I was voting in it only to prevent their claiming unanimity. I voted against both nominations, left the room, and returned to the credentials committee.

One leftist woman committee member was so filled with factional virulence that she hated to agree with me that it was time for lunch. That woman, a near neighbor, still uses every chance encounter, twenty-eight years later, to demonstrate her hatred of me—even though in the interim she once begged for my help in a personal matter and received it. Much of the rest of the convention was an exhibition of how basely decent people can behave toward one another when obsessed by ideology. The revisionists behaved somewhat better because we were in the process of discarding much of our ideology and were essentially making an appeal to rationality; but even so, pent-up bitterness, ingrained habits, and response to provocation often numbed both reason and altruism.

The well-worn arguments of innumerable preconvention discussions were repeated with new eloquence, new cunning, and increased bitterness. Along with a number of others in the New York delegation, I just sat it out, sometimes wondering what we were doing there and occasionally laughing at the foibles of some of our one-time friends. Eugene Dennis, for example, when a controversial vote was approaching, seemed to disappear into the men's room and could be found haunting the urinals with a sheepish look on his face. I decided against speaking, despite the mandate of my Carolina comrades. I did, however, expose the phony southern caucus by meeting with most of the larger delegations: New York, California, Illinois, and New England. Bernie spoke for many when, on Sunday night as we watched a savage procedural wrangle, he exclaimed, "*What* are we doing in this nuthouse?"

We toughed it out to the end. I had to speak for a few seconds to decline nomination to the national committee made by California, Illinois, and New England. "It is a great honor," I said out of courtesy to those who nominated me. A few months earlier I would truly have considered it so. Finally, Bernie and I dutifully voted for Gates supporters for the national committee and walked out in the winter cold in the company of an exhausted acquaintance from Schenectady, who said, "Well, there goes twenty-seven years shot to hell." "Twenty-five for me," Bernie said. "Eighteen for me," I echoed, somewhat lamely.

I needed a job and started looking for one the next day. During the week I secured two, both of which, contrary to my intentions, were discussed over my tapped telephone. In both cases, after successful interviews, I was fired with lame excuses before I began—the FBI trademark. I then got a job delivering coffee and sandwiches at a small restaurant owned by a left-winger. Though the FBI couldn't get me fired, I developed painful varicose veins after three months and could no longer make deliveries.

Finally, I secured a job as copyholder at Pandick Press, a large printshop in the financial district, where I was to read copy to a union proofreader at exactly half the proofreader's pay. On my first day I was assigned to work with a kind woman proofreader who became my friend for the rest of her life. Thirty inches to my right, I discovered, also copyholding, Phil Bart, a longtime Party functionary with whom I had worked closely in the underground. Phil had been disgusted with the internecine warfare in the Party, had removed himself from the Party payroll, and had been working at Pandick for four months.

But I had scarcely settled into my job when Gladys was fired from hers immediately after having received a substantial raise. Her boss admitted that he fired her because of pressure from the FBI. She wanted to be a teacher and had already earned a teacher's certificate while at the University of North Carolina. To find out what sort of a recommendation she could expect from there, she asked the left-wing director of a private school to ask UNC for a recommendation. Her former adviser in the Education Department promptly replied that she had made excellent grades and was a "person with superior intelligence and drive," and spent the bulk of his letter relating that "her husband was the head of the Communist Party activities in North Carolina. . . . I do not know whether or not Mrs. Scales was a Communist. . . . I believe that she has the ability to do an excellent job of teaching, but I feel honor bound that I should give you the information that I have given above." Such was one teacher's honor in 1957. So Gladys, her UNC degree being useless, secured a temporary teaching job at a Jewish parochial school while she pursued a master's degree in education at Yeshiva University.

Meanwhile, I was to see my former SRC comrades together once more. The occasion was a tragic one: Ed's funeral. He had died of cancer while still in his early forties, leaving a splendid wife and four children. The old SRC crowd ended up in the same car in the funeral procession, and once again there was some slight mutual warmth—we shared a common grief.

Learning to live outside the Party was an extremely painful adjustment. Gone was the sense of living each day with the utmost intensity in the selfless service of a great purpose. Gladys and I had anticipated that loss before leaving the Party and felt that we simply must face the truth as we saw it: the belief was dead and with it had gone the innocence and joy forever. The truth as we saw it was that the American Communist dream had become a cruel, convoluted hoax.

Facing that truth was not so simple. Though the lesson had been learned painfully, it was easy to adjust to the fact that Marxism-Leninism had become a Stalinist hodgepodge which meant at any moment precisely what the Soviet Politburo said it did. But so many years of mental and emotional conditioning had gone into determining my response to certain stimuli that for some time thereafter I continued to feel a warm response at the mere mention of the Soviet Union. Since my mind was once again on cordial terms with objective facts, I was bombarded with data which proved that my romantic dream of socialism in the Soviet Union was false; that the USSR was in a terrible state, lacking most democratic rights; that it was a country in which the government killed, persecuted, or regimented its artists and intellectuals; and that its government preyed on weaker neighbors as brutally as any imperialist power. But my mind and emotions resisted every fact, every bit of evidence. Deeply painful was the loss I felt as each encrusted illusion about socialism in the Soviet Union fell apart.

What was needed, I thought, was time to examine myself closely, to separate the phony from the genuine in my Communist past. Gladys gradually focused her altruism and her passion to better the world on one small, vital area: she would teach the children in her care, with all the love, gentleness, and skill she could command, how to be better people than those in the preceding generation.

But I couldn't sort myself out so easily. For one thing, I was still in grave danger of going to jail for six years. I thought that if my case could be won in the Supreme Court it would break the back of the Smith Act and provide a great victory for American civil liberties. The Party would be the first beneficiary because all the pending membership cases would be thrown out; that was fine with me. Although I'd separated my life from the Party, it never occurred to me to think of it as an adversary. John Gates, George Charney, Max Gordon, Doxey Wilkerson, Doc Blumberg, Joe Clark, and many another good friend had remained inside, fighting a good, if hopeless, fight to transform it into a democratic socialist organization.

Through months and years I mulled over my Party experience. Several years later, Dwight Macdonald gave me one of his books inscribed: "To one failed politician from another." I never got a chance to discuss with Macdonald, whom I admired, his reasons for the inscription. But I'd already arrived at that evaluation of my own political career.

My eighteen years in the Party had spanned military and political defeats for Fascism, significant improvements in the welfare of working people, and the beginnings of a Second Reconstruction of the South that ended the disfranchisement of Negroes and largely eliminated racism from the body of the law. In those historic achievements I had played a positive role as a Communist. In the effort to advance a foreign policy to oppose the cold war and the drift toward atomic war, I, with my Party, generally floundered. As for advancing the principles of socialism (the heart of my political outlook), I had seized blindly on an unworthy model, had mired myself in indefensible dogma, and had often allowed the needs of the moment to betray the ideals of my goal. Considering the strength and virulence of the opposition, some excuses might be made for the failures of my Party as a whole.

Where I felt *my* real failure lay was in my lack of intellectual courage in thinking out political and cultural questions for myself; my fear of trusting my own conscience; my slavish, opportunistic following of the Party line when I knew it was wrong or inadequate; my ineptitude in playing the Party leader, a role I felt was unsuited to my temperament and abilities. I had, along with some few achievements and some joyous and proud memories, enough failures to provide me with grief and guilt for decades to come. Much of that grief and guilt should be shared, I believe, by those who led our country during that same period.

(At this writing, even the "achievements" seem less solid: my native state seems to be dominated politically by ultra-right-wing racists; the labor move-ment in North Carolina and the nation is less substantial than it was forty years ago; the poor are getting poorer and more numerous; blacks are still at the bottom of the heap; the country is ruled by an administration firmly gripped by the negative ideology of anti-Communism; fear of the Soviet Union and Com-munism is offered as justification for any outrage, military or legal, foreign or domestic; the Bill of Rights—indeed, the Constitution—is under deadly at-tack; life on the planet is threatened both by pollution and by atomic war—and there are intellectuals in droves to defend and praise the way things are going.)

Had my Communist experience been worthwhile, on balance? The Com-munist Party made me keenly aware of the danger of Fascism, the misery of the Negroes, the plight of the workers, and the desirability of democratic socialism. Elsewhere I might have found a satisfactory way of opposing Fas-cism, of aiding the organization of workers, or of promoting socialism. But when it came to opposing white supremacy, there was nowhere else to turn.

In my youth the most glaring injustice facing a southern white was the mistreatment of Negroes. The horror of it was palpable and everywhere. Be-cause the Party showed me this horror firsthand, there was no alternative for me but to fight it. Many principled southern whites were unaware of the extent of the outrage that permeated every facet of their society, and they could look the other way, deplore racism privately, while applying their talents in admira-ble and creative ways. Unfortunately, most southern white liberals found that they could live with a slightly altered version of the Declaration of Indepen-dence: "all men are created [separate but] equal." Thus they failed to attack the heart of Negro oppression, and abjectly helped to perpetuate the most corrosive wrong of our time.

Had Bart Logan, my first Party leader, been an insensitive hack instead of a passionately feeling person, I might have stayed relatively sheltered and largely oblivious of my surroundings. And I might have become a liberal history professor. Instead, I joined the *only* organization committed to full economic, political, and social equality for Negroes; and that is still a matter of pride. For that, more than for anything else, I think my Communist experi-ence was worthwhile. Gladys, who suffered the most, thought so too.

In the summer of 1957 the need for funds for my case had increased while the ability to raise them had declined sharply. Still owed to Telford Taylor was $4,000 of the $10,000 which the Party had guaranteed. Having raised all my committee and I could, I had no choice but to ask the Party leaders to stand behind their commitment. The national organization secretary refused bluntly, saying, "What do you want us to do? Stop publishing the *Daily Worker* so we can pay your legal bills?" Evidence was coming in with increasing frequency to the Scales Defense Committee that Party functionaries were sabotaging our fund raising. A neighbor of ours whose Party club had raised nearly $150 for my case was severely reprimanded for instigating the contribution. Keeping the money tightly in her hand, she resigned from the Party after twenty-five years of membership. Dorothy Healey, chairing the California Party, was attacked by the national office and others because her state committee contributed $200 to my case.

Some friends organized a large money-raising picnic for me at a sort of left-wing vacation colony in New Jersey; it was attended chiefly by former Party members and their families. A well-known Negro woman Party functionary, long a leader without a constituency, stood at the edge of the picnicking crowd and chanted like a taunting child, "Ol' Junius Scales won't go to jail. Naw! Junius Scales won't *never* go to jail, 'cause he's a renegade bastard, an' he's done left the Party!"

19

Strike Three!

I confess I am a little cynical on some topics, and when a whole nation is roaring Patriotism at the top if its voice, I am fain to explore the cleanness of its hands and the purity of its heart.

Ralph Waldo Emerson, *Journals* (1824)

Alas, from what high hope to what relapse
Unlook'd for are we fall'n!

John Milton, *Paradise Regain'd*

In the autumn of 1957 the Supreme Court reversed the conviction in my case. The government admitted error in denying me access to the notes, records, and other material submitted to it by its informer-witnesses. The other membership appellant, Claude Lightfoot, had his case reversed on the same grounds and was never retried; but the Eisenhower Department of Justice announced through Robert L. Gavin, the new U.S. attorney for the Middle District of North Carolina, that I would be tried a second time. I was not surprised; I guessed that the government doubted its ability, after the Supreme Court's decision in the Yates Smith Act case in California (requiring among other things more rigorous evidentiary standards), to obtain a second conviction of Lightfoot in Chicago. In my own case, however, having at hand an unsophisticated, handpicked jury in a backward southern state where most political leaders were busily scheming how to defy the law and continue to violate the civil rights of Negroes, and where the Circuit Court of Appeals was the most reactionary in the nation, the prosecution would have a heavy advantage. I thought that the Department of Justice had a far more accurate assessment of the nature of my state's politics than did those liberal editorialists, politicians, and scholars who so enjoyed telling North Carolinians (and the rest of the nation) what an "enlightened," "liberal," "tolerant," "advanced" state it was. In my opinion the last tattered claim for North Carolina as a politically progressive state was torn away in 1950 when Dr. Frank Graham was defeated for the Senate in an orgy of white racism worthy of Mississippi in the days of Bilbo or of North Carolina more than fifty years before.

My immediate problem was to secure defense counsel. Fortunately, Telford

Taylor was willing to handle the trial, preferably joining with local counsel. The overwhelming problem was the lack of money. My defense committee was full of fight and had received offers of help from ex-Party activists from coast to coast who were searching for a worthy cause; my mother was also in a fighting mood and offered to settle the residual debts and to pay for local counsel. The defense committee had managed to reduce the debt to Taylor to three thousand dollars when I discovered that the Party had reneged on paying what was owing to Dave Rein (just over one thousand dollars), so that the Party still owed four thousand on its solid commitment to me.

The North Carolina newspapers still referred to me as a Communist Party leader. I had never publicized my departure from the Party and had told only family and friends, hoping, should my case be won, to drop quietly into political obscurity. However, in the face of a second trial, I had no intention of being publicized as a Communist. Having thought for a while about how to break the news, I decided to write a letter to the editor of the *Greensboro Daily News*. My letter appeared on December 18, 1957, in a news story under an eight-column, front-page headline, "Scales Reports He Has Quit Red Party":

> All over the country courts have been throwing out Smith Act cases. In the last few months the Department of Justice itself has dropped cases in Boston, Pittsburgh, Philadelphia, and California. Only this month the department moved to drop a membership case in Indiana. In view of this distinct and welcome trend, it seems surprising that the department has singled out mine to be the sole Smith Act membership case to be actively prosecuted. . . .
>
> It is still more surprising to me that the Justice Department's move comes nearly a year after my departure from the Communist Party. . . . While the events of the past eighteen months have brought about an irrevocable parting of the ways for me and the Communist Party, I have departed from none of the democratic, humanist ideals which I once identified with it. . . . I earnestly hope that public opinion will put an end to these prosecutions and that the courts will declare this law to be unconstitutional. . . .
>
> As for my own case, I hope that it may help to send the Smith Act to the same historical graveyard occupied by the Alien and Sedition Acts and reserved for undemocratic and thought-control laws everywhere.

U.S. Attorney Gavin (Edwin M. Stanley had gone to his reward, in a manner of speaking, having been appointed a federal district judge by Eisenhower) responded that he would continue preparations for the trial. Telford Taylor and I drove down to Greensboro to attend a hearing on pretrial motions and to examine the possibilities of securing local counsel. Three or four distinguished attorneys had indicated that they would consider joining my defense with so eminent a lawyer as Taylor. He and I visited several, each of whom had some strong points and all of whom were mainly acceptable to Telford. My preference was unhesitatingly for McNeill Smith, a trial lawyer of exceptional reputation and a member of one of the state's outstanding law firms. Smith was politically a liberal and a man of character and principle. What attracted me to him in addition, however, was that he pedaled himself to and from his office on a bicycle and carried his lunch in a brown paper bag; if circumstances required it, he would take clients to one of Greensboro's best restaurants and would break out for himself, without the slightest self-consciousness, his homemade sandwiches wrapped in waxed paper. Such refreshing independence of spirit and freedom from convention, I thought, could only be an advantage.

The political climate in Greensboro had noticeably improved since 1955, when Dave Rein, assisted by Herbert Aptheker, walked bravely into the lion's mouth. Dave had been as helpful as possible to Telford, and he had spent an evening with Gladys and me on his last visit to New York. From Aptheker, by then a major functionary in what remained of the Party, I heard nothing, not even a postcard wishing me well. From my ex-Party friends I received much support, moral and financial. My friends who had stayed in the Party were dropping out one by one, finding the narrowness, rigidity, and vilification they encountered intolerable: George Charney in May, Joe Clark in September, Doxey Wilkerson in November, and at last, in January 1958, John Gates, who resigned when the national leadership voted to kill the *Daily Worker,* which he edited.

When Gates learned that I would be retried, he went to Telford Taylor and told him that he had been present at a state convention in North Carolina at which a delegate had really advocated "force and violence" and that I had vigorously opposed the delegate's position and had later carried out his expulsion from the Party. Knowing that I would have vetoed his testifying at the trial because of the virtual certainty of a contempt sentence from Judge Bryan, Johnny told Taylor that defense counsel alone was to decide whether his evidence was to be given, and asked that the matter be kept from me until a decision had been made. I first learned of his offer well after the trial had begun, when Mac Smith and Telford were assessing possible defense witnesses; they had decided against using Johnny because, in their opinion, the jury would be likely to discount anything he said, seeing that he had been a non-Communist for only a month. Moreover, though his testimony would go to the heart of the indictment, it still would not be worth the probable cost of two or three years in prison for contempt once he refused to name names on cross-examination. For me the incident was one of the few bright spots in my second trial—the knowledge that an admired friend who had already served four years in prison was ready to give up his freedom once more to aid in my defense. (It is characteristic of the man that when I reminded him of the occurrence more than twenty-two years later, it had completely slipped his mind; it had been a matter of no great importance—merely the decent thing to do.)

The law firm to which McNeill Smith belonged plunged energetically into the case. Mac had the assistance of Bynum Hunter and Richmond Bernhardt, both keen junior partners in the firm. A Smith Act case was wildly exotic for law partners so conventionally oriented, but they faced up to the crude behavior of the opposing lawyers, their dubious interpretation of the law, the paid informant witnesses, and the unwonted ideological zeal of the Justice Department's anti-Communist specialists. Taylor, however, was not new to Smith Act cases or to the peculiar brand of law practiced in them, nor was he overly disconcerted by the spectacle of one arm of the government turning against its own laws and constitutional principles. (He was the author in 1954 of *Grand Inquest,* a major study of congressional committee investigations/witch-hunts.) Altogether, the defense was a remarkably effective team.

In several ways the second trial was more painful for me than the first. No longer was I defending a Noble Cause with a wisp of martyrdom clinging to me; nor was I capable any more of viewing my political past through self-justifying, rose-colored glasses. I was in the early throes of that painful process of self-analysis and review (which probably lasts a lifetime) common to many who break with the Communist Party. I assessed the viewpoints and attitudes I had held during the period covered by the indictment sometimes with ambiguity and often with repugnance. When Telford and Mac would question me about some leaflet or statement issued between four and eleven years before, I involuntarily would try to justify the position I had then held while being embarrassed at the holes in my logic, the questionable facts on which I had relied, the stereotyped expressions, and the sectarian jargon. My attorneys would look at me incredulously; I would despair of explaining my ambivalence and become morose, convinced that men I liked and respected considered me a jackass.

I was staying in my mother's Irving Park apartment, while Telford was at the King Cotton Hotel. I had secured indefinite leave from my copyholder's job "to take care of a pressing personal matter" without having to be more explicit. Barbara was told that I was in Greensboro on business. Gladys was teaching but planned to join me for the last few days of the trial. Although my committee still carried on valiantly in New York and around the country, my mother bore the brunt of my legal expenses. Her health had markedly improved since the first trial, and she followed with firm assurance every step of the preparation for the second one. I myself was not optimistic; I sensed that much of the changed atmosphere had to do with my famous and influential counsel. I also noted with some amusement that Judge Bryan's courtly bows had not accompanied the defendant's second presumption of innocence; a curt nod seemed to suffice whenever we met.

The pretrial hearing took place on January 18, with Telford arguing most impressively for his motion to dismiss the indictment. February 3 was set for the trial date, and lawyer and client returned to New York for a few days— Telford to prepare for a three- or four-week absence and I to rejoin my family and job. In a short while we were back in Greensboro to plan the defense case and seek witnesses.

I took Telford to High Point to visit Esther Gillen as a prospective witness. As we drove up to the little mill village house and mounted the steps, nostalgia for my past joyous associations with the Gillens overwhelmed me, and after embracing Esther I sat silent and thoughtful while she and Telford discussed the details of what she might testify to. It was soon clear that she liked and trusted him, for having seen him referred to in the papers by his army reserve rank, she was completely at her ease, calling him "General" as though that were his first name. She reminisced about me and told him that I had had such a sheltered upbringing that I didn't realize that people could be selfish, often "ornery," and usually motivated by less-than-idealistic principles. She was quite determined and almost enthusiastic about testifying, and there no longer appeared to be any threat to her job if she did.

A trip to Chapel Hill with Telford secured agreements to testify from the same character witnesses as in the first trial, along with my friend Professor Joseph Straley of the Physics Department. In subsequent days Mac and Telford were phoning all over the country in search of non-Communist witnesses. Ken, a close college chum who, as a graduate student, had spent countless hours discussing every aspect of my politics with me, could not have been more ignorant of that subject when Mac reached him. Waiting on an extension phone to be called into the conversation, I felt my heart sink as my erstwhile friend said that he had had only a "casual" acquaintanceship with me. I hung up the extension phone with a sense of shame and nausea, unable to find the words to explain to Mac that the man had published a gimmicky textbook which had won him a fragile, transitory reputation that he feared might be damaged if he stuck his neck out for me.

The next call was to a couple of close college friends then living in the Midwest. The man, who had achieved a modest success professionally, was ill, so the wife spoke for them both. She had refrained from joining the Party only because her husband forbade it, fearing damage to his career. When Mac explained the purpose of the call, she replied in a patronizing, club-womanish voice, "I'm glad you called, Mr. Smith. I think you can salvage that young man—" At that point I again hung up my phone and listened dully as Mac tried politely to say that he was trying to save me from a prison term, not my former ideology, and that he needed *witnesses*.

Next on the line was a well-known history professor whose student I had been and whose aid I had vainly sought in my first trial. He was a Norman Thomas Socialist with whom I had often discussed my views on force and violence. As a graduate student, I had helped organize a farewell dinner for him when he left Chapel Hill; the professor had been so moved to find that I respected him and cared for him, despite our strongly opposed politics, that he had given me several of his books warmly inscribed. However, when Mac explained the purpose of his call, the professor irrelevantly recalled some supposed slight to him by Herbert Aptheker when he had spoken at Chapel Hill in the forties, and worked himself into an incoherent tantrum. Mac finally hung up in disgust.

Still another call, one which I did not hear, was made by Mac to a college political adversary of mine, a very bright young student, Allard Lowenstein, whose anti-Communism had seemed obsessive even for those times. In the late forties I had been invited to speak to a Presbyterian student group in the basement of the church. Only about twelve to fifteen people were present; Lowenstein attended for heckling purposes. I spoke of my views on a number of moral questions specified in my invitation, including the use of force. The heckler interrupted rudely saying, "Let's get this discussion out of the clouds!" I responded amiably, "Al, I'm sure *you* can bring it to a very low level." That drew a general laugh and put him on the defensive. A debate ensued over "Communism's record of violence"; I denied (mistakenly) the facts adduced and pointed out that the term *socialism* (Communism's objective) was inherently humanist and implied the ascendancy of reason, democracy, and peace, while ruling out the use of force except defensively. My opponent lost his temper, became abusive, and made an ass of himself—a most extraordinary thing for him. If only for that reason, I was sure he would remember the evening. But he told Mac that he could remember almost nothing of the discussion. At the time I cynically ascribed such memory loss to a rising young politician's ambition or perhaps a desire to strike a blow at someone remembered as a Communist. (Subsequently, he became a national figure, deservedly admired as a courageous, crusading liberal, and a man of evident principle. Because he suffered a violent and untimely death, I will never know what caused him to suppress that evening. Did vanity cause him to forget it because he was bested? Or was his anti-Communism then so intense that he expunged from his memory anyone whose stance seemed contrary to that of the stereotypical Communist?)

The trial began on February 3, 1958, with the selection of a jury. Gloom and hopelessness settled over me as soon as I got a good look at the panel from which the jury would be chosen. They looked dismally like the panel of three years before. They appeared to be nice-enough, plain people who would be just as bewildered as those jurors the last time, and would cast their votes against Communism; I could already imagine their being polled individually and somberly answering, "Guilty!"

As the judge's dreary questioning droned on, my mind wandered. Since I was in the process of reexamining everything I had ever believed, I demanded of myself, in the manner of a cross-examining prosecutor, whether I had ever wanted force and violence to resolve the difficulties holding back American socialism. Certainly I had felt rage toward Nazis, Ku Klux Klan members, inhuman mill owners, McCarthyites, lynch mobs—but when I cooled down, I realized that violence created more ugliness than it could ever eradicate. I would defend myself and others against murderous attack by such people, but only as a last resort. I had long believed that the only way to storm the symbolic barricades of power was to have the minds, hearts, and active, organized support of a majority—quite an order! In the 1940 Party school I had attended, George Siskind, rigid Russian-style Bolshevik that he was, had never said that violence was necessary or desirable for establishing socialism. In fact, back in my most fanatical days, nobody I knew except about three or four leftist nuts had ever opted for the violent aspects of Marxism-Leninism. Yet here I was, for the second time, on trial as a man of violence.

Jury selection occupied all of the first day. That night at my mother's apartment I began reading a new Rachel Carson book which my mother had thoughtfully provided. The next day the jury was impaneled and Gavin made the government's statement in the afternoon. Compared with Stanley's earlier effort, the presentation was almost dignified; otherwise it was similar in outline and content.

Mac Smith's opening statement was brief and contained the following reflections:

> I hope, when you hear all the evidence in this case, that you will get a picture of somebody riding a bus, meeting two or three people here and there, small groups, larger groups, in the basements of churches—anywhere he could get— talking out, trying programs, in a very ineffective way, to secure certain rights for working men and for Negroes, trying to stop the war in Korea (as a lot of people wanted to do) . . . but the point is: was he intending by his actions to try to do good, however stupidly and ineffectively, or was he trying to overthrow the United States government by an armed uprising?

I didn't like to be referred to as stupid by my own lawyer, but I reasoned that no one who had idealistically been a Stalinist could claim omniscience. The trial was already taking on a surreal quality: I was sitting to one side watching a very different person who was being weirdly misrepresented and slandered. It would have been comforting if I could have observed the nightmare fantasy in detachment with a mixture of disgust and amusement. But I couldn't remain aloof, for there was no mistaking that my enemies, in deadly earnest and spurred by a right-wing missionary zeal, meant to destroy me and my family.

The first witness was John Lautner. As Telford said in his summation, he was no longer a professional witness; he had become a phonograph record. After hearing him in 1955, I knew exactly what would come next. The pile of books and pamphlets, identified and numbered as government exhibits, grew as it had before. From the mass of all that irrelevant material the government would have the witness read passages intended to shock decent people with the ruthlessness of the Bolshevik Party. Lautner himself was an aggressive witness obsessed with the need to repeat the words *force and violence* as often as possible and motivated by a vengeful hatred against his former comrades which gave him an appearance in sharp contrast to the somewhat lethargic Party hack I remembered from the forties.

After more than two days on the stand Lautner was excused and ex-Communist Barbara Hartle, a woman of fifty from the state of Washington, went through a drab account of her Party history—schools, meetings, classes— each episode bristling with force and violence. Yet under Telford's patient cross-examination, which for an hour appeared to be getting nowhere, it was suddenly revealed that she had several times stated that she had been unaware, until becoming an FBI informer, that the Party advocated the violent overthrow of the government; that during her eighteen years or so as a Party functionary she had never believed that it did. A minor tidbit was that when she had entered on her spree of name-naming, she had named her former husband (whom she had every reason to believe had left the Party long before) and her lover of relatively recent vintage.

She and Lautner both gloated over their "expertise" in matters relating to the Party; both could remember precisely who was at such and such a meeting or school and when, yet their recollections were of a Party life barren, drab, and devoid of any love, idealism, or passion. It was hard to believe that those twisted, bitter relics had been, as they claimed in perfunctory statements, devoted, "dedicated" Communists until disillusionment set in. In retrospect, I believed that when the two, for different reasons, had made rapid 180-degree changes in their courses and had decided that what had been good had become bad, and vice versa, that friends had become enemies, and vice versa, those changes had been deeply destructive and unsettling, leaving them both emotionally dead, dying, or, at least, quite unstable. Their sole surviving passion seemed to be vengeance on their own past lives and on everyone associated with those lives.

The government sought to present them as selfless, patriotic figures and implied that the future greatness of this country rested on people like them. Lautner, in particular, bridled with pleasure when complimented by a government lawyer. In addition to being emotionally involved in a case designed to destroy a "Communist," they were both obligated to and dependent on the FBI: Lautner for his comfortable living and the satisfaction of his egotism; Hartle for income and to avoid losing her parole and going back to prison. (Believing herself guilty, she had severed herself from the other Washington Smith Act defendants on appeal and had gone to jail for twenty months while they had won their case and remained free.)

The FBI and the Department of Justice provided voluminous testimony that the teaching and advocacy of force and violence was prevalent in the Party and that virtually all leading Communists thought that violent revolution was the sole road to power. From my own experience as a Party leader, student at a national training school, and director of state, district and regional schools, as well as from having questioned hundreds of Communists and ex-Communists, I was convinced that the American Party (at least while I was in it, from 1939 to 1957) widely proclaimed at least the possibility of a democaratic, peaceful road to socialism. There was theoretical fuzziness on the question because of seemingly conflicting statements made in differing times under various circumstances by Marx, Engels, and Lenin; but I never heard any authoritative Party teacher or leader make statements such as those related by Lautner, Hartle, and the bevy of paid informers who followed them. Nor have I since been able to find other former Communist leaders who ever heard of any such reliance on force and violence by responsible Party leaders.

After two days on the stand, Hartle was followed by an informer named William Garfield Cummings, who had infiltrated the Party at the instigation of the FBI. In 1945 he had attended a Party school taught by George Siskind, who had, Cummings said, repeatedly told his students that the capitalist class must be overthrown by force and violence. Cummings was unable to testify about those classes of twelve years before without referring numerous times to summaries prepared by him at the time. Under cross-examination by Mac Smith, it was revealed that nowhere in those summaries did the phrase *force and violence* or any remotely similar one appear. The man did, however, provide some unintentional humor with his fastidious concern about his status:

Q. In your own mind you considered yourself an informer, did you not?
A. Oh, I did not.

Q. You did not?

A. I did not.

Q. You were making reports and giving information, weren't you?

A. Oh, I was.

Q. You were informing then, weren't you?

A. I was informing, yes; but I wasn't an informant. No.

Q. I see. You were informing, but you were not an informant; and you were getting paid for it, for the information that you furnished?

A. That is true.

The government then brought on its star witness, Clontz, as brash and menacing as three years before. He went through his familiar paces, although perhaps a bit more circumspectly, since he knew that the defense was checking his FBI reports for consistency. I half listened, pondering the skill, or duplicity, needed to paint such a basically false picture of the Party. The simple truth revealed quite enough wrong with the Party: it was hopelessly mired in a rigid body of doctrine continuously interpreted by Lenin's vicar-on-earth in Moscow. For the American scene, that body of doctrine was mostly poisonous and tended to adulterate such constructive activities of the Party as organizing unions and fighting for Negro rights. The Party had done a lot of bad things too: it had propagandized for, apologized for, and misrepresented as socialist one of the most tyrannous governments of the twentieth century; it had often practiced the brutalizing, cynical, morally degrading doctrine that the socialist end justified almost any means of serving it, no matter how rotten. From such morality arose disabling conflicts for many Communists and corresponding enmity from great numbers of intelligent, socially oriented, scrupulous non-Communists who should have been allies in constructive pursuits. It had ruthlessly dominated the American left for years, absorbing, suppressing, and polluting independent radicals and the various socialist and reform movements. Such real sins were sufficient, I thought, without dragging in false, laboriously concocted ones, or portraying the Party as though it were a cross between the Ku Klux Klan and a collection of mental patients. In spite of all their weaknesses and failings, the Communists included in their number some exceptionally fine human beings, courageous and self-sacrificing, who on balance played a generally positive part in the life of their communities.

From the collection of unhappy, egocentric, dehumanized witnesses, an unsuspecting juror, assuming that he was even interested, could only surmise that the Party did little besides "plot" vaguely and listen to its leaders and teachers proclaim the overriding need for force and violence. For two days Clontz was on the stand, a study of efficient, if illogical, malice. A Mexican-American from Denver and a Negro minister from St. Louis, both seasoned testifiers unknown to me, went through their monotonous school experiences, continually seeking the aid of notes on the most elementary matters. Odis Reavis, a High Point native and a transfer Party member from Detroit, was a pathetically weak, frightened person who had sought out the FBI in Detroit as a sort of insurance policy after he had followed his conscience and joined the Party. His testimony had no weight or substance, though his addled responses on both direct and cross-examination were embarrassing to me because, after all, Reavis had once been a (most inactive) Party member. One of the FBI agents who had arrested me testified briefly, as did the proprietress of a motel near Durham where I'd stayed a couple of times; the purpose of her testimony was to let the jury know that I'd registered under an assumed name. Then Charles Childs, for two days, repeated his testimony from the first trial—still making much of that potentially murderous pencil—even though his reports to the FBI showed that he'd forgotten to mention the incident to them.

Finally, on February 18, the government completed its case. I had been emotionally numbed for fifteen days; at night I used the sea and Rachel Carson's books about it to transport myself temporarily from the unpleasant realities I faced to the far more important realities of intricate, slow-changing nature. Being of little use in the trial, I read voraciously. In a much-thumbed anthology the familiar lines of W. B. Yeats painfully reflected my own mood while Clontz was testifying:

> Be secret and take defeat
> From any brazen throat,
> For how can you compete,
> Being honour bred, with one
> Who, were it proved he lies,
> Were neither shamed in his own
> Nor in his neighbours' eyes?

My mother showed these lines from "To a Friend Whose Work Has Come to Nothing" to Mac Smith, who found them extremely moving. Meanwhile, I continued with the reexamination of my life as a Communist.

Two incidents recurred in my mind persistently. Some months before I publicly proclaimed my Party membership, I'd been sitting one afternoon in a coffee shop conversing with another graduate student and fellow veteran when the subject of Communism came up and I enthusiastically defended it as a philosophical concept; my companion, whose name was Paul, asked me if I were a Communist. I might well have answered yes to Paul, requesting that he not publicize my reply; or I might have declined to answer, saying that in such repressive times the question was better neither asked nor answered. Instead, out of some perversity, I lied outright and said no, looking him in the face as I did so. That deception of a friendly acquaintance had tormented me for years (and still does), sufficiently so to prevent many another degrading deceit I might otherwise have let slip.

The other incident dated from 1941, when I was living in High Point in the mill village. I was visiting Esther Gillen one morning when we heard a child's screams which seemed to come from the Tituses' privy, a couple of houses down the street. The Tituses were the poorest family on the block, usually sick or hungry; Carrie, the oldest child, was indeed screaming wildly in the privy: nine inches of gut protruded from her anus. While her mother and Esther held her, I replaced the intestine with my fingers and the small handle of a hearth broom. Her pain subsided and no doctor was called because no one had money to pay him; besides, the doctor had earlier prescribed fresh vegetables for Carrie and there had been nothing in the house to eat except white beans and corn syrup. That scene, which haunts me when complacency about the lot of working people threatens to settle on me, served to remind me during the trial that what had truly moved and incited me and most of my comrades was the hope of bettering life for the living and the unborn. Marxism-Leninism, we naively thought, was the medicine that would bring relief.

As the government prepared to close its case, Victor Woerheide, the chief specialist from the Department of Justice, read for about thirty minutes from a pamphlet called *I Saw the Truth in Korea,* which I had received as a free sample from a non-Communist importer in New York. Clontz had seen it at one of our meetings, and I had given it to him without ever looking at it. The writing was graphic and shocking; it ascribed to the American army numerous atrocious acts such as later became commonplace in the Vietnam War. The impact in the courtroom was palpable; the Australian reporter-author held everyone's revolted attention. At the end of it Mac Smith asked for a recess, and when the jury withdrew, Taylor moved a mistrial because of the reading, charging that the material was unrelated to any issue in the case, was prejudicial, and was calculated to inflame the passions of the jury and deny the defendant a fair trial. The motion was denied.

The defense then called its first witness, my aunt, Miss Lucy Pell, who had then completed her thirty-fifth year as a Presbyterian church worker. She gave a memorable account of the FBI's bullying of my mother and her at their home in September 1951. She also testified to my leaving the Party in 1957. Emily Harris Preyer, my cousin, beloved from early childhood, testified as a character witness. She was the wife of Richardson Preyer, then a judge; she had just been president of the Greensboro Junior League and was one of the best-known and most-admired women in the city. She testified that I was a "wonderful person." My junior high school chum Billy was another character witness. He had the courage to testify, even though he was doubly vulnerable as a realtor and a Jew. Since Professor Douglas Maggs, the Duke University constitutional law authority, was in Japan, a portion of his 1955 testimony giving the lie to Clontz was read into the record.

Then Esther Gillen recounted simply her acquaintance with me, beginning with a first meeting in the union hall in 1939. She told how I had lived in her home, had moved to her mother's home, and had helped nurse the old lady until her death. Esther had known I was a Communist and had often discussed Communism with me. When asked by Telford Taylor what I had hoped to accomplish in High Point, she replied, "He thought that everybody ought to have a decent place to live, a good place to work, and be paid decent wages—enough to buy their children milk and bread—and he knew that the only way would be through organization. He was very much interested in the labor movement." To Woerheide's clumsy attempts on cross-examination to imply that she was a Communist, she retaliated by sticking to the truth and showing herself to be far more adept than he at verbal sparring.

Next, UNC physics professor Joseph Straley testified that he'd inquired of many colleagues and neighbors about my reputation in 1947 when I'd announced my Party membership. "I was amazed, for my own part, to find that his reputation was uniformly very, very good. Everyone regarded him as a gentleman and a scholar. Of course, since that time I dare say his reputation is tainted by his membership in the Party because this has not been a popular party to belong to." Straley described a private discussion in my house in 1951, when he had dropped by unexpectedly despite the extensive FBI surveillance of the place: "His position seemed to be about as follows: that our school systems are primarily oriented toward adjusting people to society as they find it. Our churches have a philosophy of brotherhood which no one practices. Our psychiatrists try to adjust people to society as they find it, and Junius said that sometimes society may be so bad that one should *not* adjust himself to society as he finds it; that rather, it is his responsibility to attempt to reform it."

The Reverend Charles Jones, repeating his previous character testimony, testified more extensively on other matters, including the attack on his home by white cab drivers in 1947.

Inasmuch as the prosecution had sought to make my possession and distribution of Marxist books a sinister, secretive thing, Mac Smith subpoenaed the librarian of Duke University. He testified that the library had readily available thirty-eight titles by Engels, eighty-seven by Marx, seventy-five by Lenin, and sixty-four by Stalin; that the periodical room offered the current *Daily Worker, Political Affairs, Pravda,* and *Izvestia,* as well as bound back issues of all of them. Whether or not the ladies and gentlemen of the jury perceived the irony of the librarian's testimony is questionable, but Mac made the most of it.

Throughout the trial, in a show of family solidarity, numerous relatives in addition to my mother and aunt joined me. I had had to plead once again with my brother, who had a high government job, to stay away from the trial so as not to jeopardize his position. During the last two days of the government's case, and during all the defense case, Gladys was able to sit with me in court. She was appalled at the spectacle of the government eagerly preparing the destruction of her husband. Fortunately, several members of the press were especially kind and attentive to her without attempting to exploit her in their stories. One redheaded reporter, who wrote good, objective news accounts, was particularly friendly to both Gladys and me, frequently telling us press-table gossip and giving his candid opinion of how things were going. When my mother took the stand, "Red" reported that he and other reporters were deeply moved by her testimony. Under Mac Smith's questioning, she gave an account of my isolation in early life, of my political idealism, and of many political discussions with me in which the question of how the Communists proposed to take power was dealt with. In some detail she described the varied harassment of the FBI. The near arsenal in my Carrboro home that Clontz had described was reduced to two totally inoperable shotguns, one a gift to me at the age of seven. On cross-examination by Gavin she managed to improve on her direct testimony, even getting into the record that I had left the Party and had advised my comrades to do the same, and that in the forties I had been instrumental in the expulsion from the Party of three persons who really had advocated violence. Being in much better health, she testified far more effec-tively than previously; she expressed to me, my sister, and Gladys her satis-faction at having spoken well.

A former radio announcer who'd recorded some speeches which I'd made in the forties was the next witness. He and I had been friendly as students and had discussed politics when I was a public Communist. Mac Smith asked, "What did he say as to how socialism or Communism might come?"

"Well, my question to him, and I asked it in a somewhat facetious way, was how was he going to bring about the revolution, and he smiled and replied, 'Well, if it ever comes, it will come with words.' " The ex-announcer also testified as a character witness.

On February 21 the defense had one remaining witness, a Baptist minister. He had known me since 1946, and as adviser to the Baptist Student Union he had several times invited me to address the group and had once engaged me in a debate in a dormitory. As to the give-and-take of the discussions, he recalled my challenging the Baptist students to surpass the Communists in building a better world and in fighting racism and injustice, saying that if they did, I would leave the Communist Party and join the Baptist church.

The defense then rested its case and the summations began. In contrast to its procedure in 1955, the government eschewed hysteria and adopted a more reasonable tone. Woerheide led off by giving the jury a history lesson in which the Justice Department's expert on Communism appeared to be confused about who the country's wartime enemies had been. He seemed to regard World War II as a Communist plot against the United States and the alliance with the Soviet Union as a tragic mistake: "During this period when our efforts were helping the Communist Russians, the Communist Party members cheerfully took part in our war effort. . . . Communist Russia had been saved by the sacrifices of American life and treasure." I was surprised not by the warped history but by the phobic, doctrinaire tone, the skewed fanaticism, of the man. *I* was supposed to be the ideological zealot called to account by my peers for my extremism. Yet there was my prosecutor, his lawyer disguise momentarily slipping, mouthing a right-wing extremist view of history as though he were addressing some "shirt" organization.

Telford Taylor spoke eloquently, with logic and humor. The speech was so good that I was surprised to note that I had an acute feeling of depression and sensed the same in Gladys, who sat next to me grimly holding my hand. We both decided later that the reason for our despair had been the perception that reason, logic, and wit were unwelcome visitors in that court. Mac Smith, speaking in the homey, winning way for which he was famous, could only offer more logic and humor as he picked apart the government's case. "Red," the reporter, said the two lawyers were "devastating" and that he was much encouraged.

After lunch Gavin concluded for the government, using much of Stanley's approach of three years before, minus some of the ranting and screaming. He was too shrewd a politician merely to ape his predecessor, and he knew his jury well. Coloring and stretching every prejudicial piece of testimony, he wound up with such histrionics as "I don't want to swap the red star of Russia for that flag you see there in this courtroom!" He asked the jury for a prompt verdict. Evidently he was effective, for following an endless, bewildering charge from the judge, the jury filed back into the courtroom only one hour and nineteen minutes after they had left it. "Red," who had been talking with Gladys and me about his enthusiasm for Italian opera, looked closely at the jury, took Gladys's hand, and said earnestly, "Coraggio!" ("Courage!") The verdict was guilty, and Mac made a plea for leniency. Judge Bryan again sentenced me to six years in prison. Bail was continued as before, pending appeal—and the trial was over. As the crowd left the room, Gladys could no longer hold back the tears and wept bitterly, saying, "They're trying to *destroy* us!" As I sought to console her, I saw, sitting apart, a young partner in Mac's firm, holding his head in both hands and sobbing.

Gladys and I returned to our home and jobs, and life continued with welcome uneventfulness. Telford went to work on his appeals court brief, and the Scales Defense Committee continued its money-raising efforts. Despite the loving concern of Gladys and many good friends, it was hard for me to shake off the pain of the trial. Concurrently, the aching process of sorting out my life as a non-Communist continued. It was expected that my case would be on appeal for about two years before my fate was decided; actually, suspense shadowed my life for more than three years.

To my surprise, I received four thousand dollars, owed to me by the Communist Party. My friend George Charney had been entrusted by the Party in the underground period with a large sum of money to be kept for emergencies. He had left the Party; the money was not his; so he decided to return it. Knowing of the Party's obligation to me, he and his wife invited Gladys and me to dinner and handed me the four thousand in exchange for a signed receipt acknowledging payment in full by the Party of its obligation to my legal defense. Later he presented Party representatives with the large amount of money, minus four thousand dollars and plus my receipt. According to George, their howling and raging was impressive, but having no alternative, they accepted the receipt. I repaid the money to my mother.

One of the pleasanter things about my new mode of life was the considerable number of visits my mother made to New York. They were a joy for everyone concerned; she had completely won the love of Barbara and Gladys. She liked the theater, opera, and ballet and would arrive with a sheaf of tickets for each ordered in advance by mail. Although she suffered from a variety of heart ailments and had difficulty in walking, she loved New York and what it had to offer. Unlike me, she was optimistic about my appeal, although she had expected nothing from the Fourth Circuit Court of Appeals, which upheld my conviction. She was confident that the Supreme Court would throw out the case against her son. But she was never to know. In February 1960, two years after she had testified for me so ably, I received a phone call from my sister: our mother had died instantaneously of a cerebral hemorrhage.

My job as a copyholder paid poorly, and it was a dead end. The only way up in the printing trade was to get into the printers' union, the International Typographical Union (ITU)—a very difficult thing to do. However, the kind-hearted ITU shop chairman asked me if I'd like a chance to take a proofreading test; if I passed it, I might get a union card when and if a job became available. The test lasted three days and was, as I'd been warned, designed to keep me out of the union rather than let me in. Two weeks later l was told that I was the only one of the tested group who'd passed. Six months elapsed before a proofreading job was offered me, but during that time a young Canadian proofreader put me through an intensive apprenticeship on the job, letting me read while ostensibly holding copy. Finally, in June 1960, I got my first union job and became a journeyman printer.

The Supreme Court temporized over my appeal and ended the 1960 term by ordering reargument of the case which had already been memorably argued by Telford Taylor. For some time I had been restive about what to do with my life while the Court kept me on tenterhooks. Having learned a skilled trade that I respected and could rely on to support my family, I wondered if I might still salvage some part of my academic career. Although too many years had passed, in my estimation, for me to pursue historical scholarship, pedagogy, especially as it concerned teenagers, had always interested me. So I made an appointment at Columbia University's Teachers College, applying as a candidate for a Ph.D. or doctorate in education. To my surprise, I was given something approaching red-carpet treatment. I spent most of a morning talking with a dean with whom I felt considerable rapport and who was most reassuring that the ten-year hiatus in my academic work would be no obstacle to my future career. I was so pleased with the enlightened dean that I decided to tell him of my political past and my pending appeal. The extreme warmth of the interview evaporated, and in heavy frost the dean told me that I would hear from him shortly. True to his word, he sent me a nasty two-liner saying that Teachers College wanted no further dealings with me until I had completed my "litigation with the United States government."

Leading the life of a spectator on the political scene while working as a well-paid printer and living a "normal" life with my family proved mostly agreeable. What continually blighted my life was the time bomb ticking in the Supreme Court. Telford argued the case once again before the Court, but as the term neared its end there was still no decision. After working in several printshops, I'd returned to Pandick Press as a proofreader, a sort of "local boy who made good." When the final Monday for Court decisions of that term arrived in June 1961, I'd been working the "lobster" shift (midnight to 8:00 A.M.) and was at home when I heard on the radio that my conviction had been upheld by five votes to four, with Justice Frankfurter casting the decisive vote; Justices Warren, Brennan, Douglas, and Black were the minority.

The majority opinion, written by Justice John Marshall Harlan, was widely considered to be a sharp setback for civil liberties. Essentially it relied on the legal reasoning provided by the appeals court six years before, that membership, if "active" and "knowing" and if with "intent" to bring about violent overthrow of the government, amounts to conspiracy and complicity in the organization's aim. Justice Harlan apparently was much impressed with such "evidence" as the pencil story. Justices Black and Douglas both wrote vigorous dissents. Justice Douglas declared: "Today's break with tradition was a serious one. It borrows from the totalitarian philosophy." He added this hope: "What we lose by majority vote today may be reclaimed at a future time when the fear of advocacy, dissent, and nonconformity no longer casts a shadow over us." Summing up his view of the case and the majority opinion, he wrote:

> When we allow petitioner to be sentenced to prison for six years for being a "member" of the Communist Party, we make a sharp break with traditional concepts of First Amendment rights and make serious Mark Twain's lighthearted comment that "it is by the goodness of God that in our country we have those three unspeakably precious things: freedom of speech, freedom of conscience, and the prudence never to practice either of them." . . .
>
> There is here no charge of conspiracy, no charge of any overt act to overthrow the Government by force and violence, no charge of any other criminal act. The charge is being a "member" of the Communist Party, "well-knowing" that it advocated the overthrow of the Government by force and violence, "said defendant intending to bring about such overthrow by force and violence, as speedily as circumstances would permit." That falls far short of a charge of conspiracy. Conspiracy rests not in intention alone but in an agreement with one or more others to promote an unlawful project. . . . No charge of any kind or sort of agreement hitherto embraced in the concept of a conspiracy is made here.
>
> We legalize today guilt by association, sending a man to prison when he committed no unlawful act. . . .
>
> This right of revolution has been and is a part of the fabric of our institutions. . . .
>
> Of course, government can move against those who take up arms against it. Of course, the constituted authority has the right of self-preservation. But we deal in this prosecution of Scales only with the legality of ideas and beliefs, not with overt acts. The Court speaks of the prevention of "dangerous behavior" by punishing those "who work to bring about that behavior." That formula returns man to the dark days when government determined what behavior was "dangerous" and then policed the dissidents for telltale signs of advocacy. . . .

Within hours of the announcement of the decision, an FBI agent visited the president of my local union to urge him to find a way to expel me. The lame-duck president, who had scarcely two more weeks in office, imperiously summoned me to union headquarters and informed me that he was taking action to have my card revoked on the ground that I'd lied in 1960 when I applied for membership and signed a paper saying I was not a Communist. I told him I had not been a Communist for nearly four years when I signed that document. I then proceeded to bawl him out furiously, until he turned red in the face and began to retreat. "I've got to have evidence," he whined.

"You didn't need any when you were ready to dump me out of the union. But you'll get it. You're a disgrace to this union: just because the FBI asks you, you try to take away the livelihood of a lifelong union man who is already down on his luck."

I sent the president nearly a dozen photostats of 1957 newspapers which announced in big headlines that I had left the Party. An official of the American Civil Liberties Union (ACLU) called the president to say that his organization was going to take my case and that the ACLU would, if necessary, seek an injunction to stop him if he persisted in trying to take away my card. The same official orchestrated phone calls by more than a dozen prominent New York labor leaders who urged the president to drop his persecution. He did drop it, although he lacked the grace to inform me of the fact. I learned of it from a friend in the union office who also told me that the incoming president would have nothing to do with the matter.

Meanwhile, Gladys and I were swamped with calls and visits from friends and well-wishers, including several who had remained in the Party. Among those was Phil Bart, my former fellow copyholder, who asked to meet me for coffee in the Times Square area. We met, Phil expressed his sympathy and regrets, and we sat for three-quarters of an hour reminiscing over our years at Pandick Press and exchanging news of friends and acquaintances. Phil said that he had gone back on the Party payroll, that he had recently seen Henry Winston, who had inquired warmly of me. He also said that the Party had a special fund to pay for *New York Times* subscriptions for Smith Act prisoners, to which I would be entitled. I declined the offer with thanks, and we parted.

With my remaining days of freedom fast disappearing, I got a thorough physical examination from some excellent left-wing doctors who were untroubled by my non-Party status. I required some minor surgical procedures, which were performed with dispatch and humor by Edward K. Barsky, the renowned surgeon who had made medical history in the Spanish civil war.

McNeill Smith and Telford Taylor had requested a hearing before Judge Bryan in his home court in Alexandria, Virginia, to ask for a reduction of sentence. I'd been suffering from what I'd supposed were stomach-ulcer symptoms brought on by the acute stress I had been under. My astute doctor had just discovered, however, that my distress was caused by a gallbladder packed with stones. Mac, who met Gladys and me in Washington, made an eloquent appeal for a reduced sentence, pointing out the relatively light sentences in other Smith Act cases, and even reading the Yeats poem my mother had shown him. The government, represented by the redoubtable Woerheide, said in reply that the FBI had reason to believe that Scales kept "surreptitious" contact with Communist Party members and had refused to inform against any Communists. By way of illustration, he then read from an FBI report how two FBI agents had observed Scales meet, a couple of weeks before, with one "Philip Bart, known to be the national organizational secretary of the Communist Party," that the two entered Hector's Cafeteria on Forty-second Street and engaged in conversation for some forty-five minutes. On that note the government sat down. Mac began a spirited rebuttal based on whispered information from me; but the judge interrupted him, saying that he had no sympathy for the defendant, would not reduce his sentence, and did not want to go into any other matters. All Mac could gain was a stay of sentence until October 2, 1961, so that I could have my gallbladder removed.

One of the most painful tasks for Gladys and me was to tell ten-year-old Barbara that she was going to lose her father for six years (or four and a half, with time off for good behavior). She had not known that her father had once been a Communist and had been tried twice. She took the blow bravely and was soon off to her beloved summer camp, where campers and staff were from both Communist and former Communist families. The camp, in southern Vermont, was run by a wonderfully sensitive man who happened to be the brother of Mike Gold, author of *Jews without Money.* Mike and I, though we seldom saw each other, had been good friends since 1943.

Visiting day at camp was two days before my surgery appointment, and Gladys and I drove up to Vermont with friends. I was as welcome as a corpse at a banquet to some of the Party parents, who went to extraordinary lengths to avoid meeting me. I spent most of my time nursing my symptoms in the shade, in the company of Mike Gold, while Gladys let Barbara take her in tow. In the afternoon, when the guests were already leaving, my old adversary Jim Jackson and my old friend Herbert Aptheker, both visiting daughters who were counselors, almost walked into Mike and me. Since there was no way of ignoring one another, I said hello rather coolly. Jim muttered gracelessly something concerning "regrets about the case." Herbert, who had avoided me for more than four years, chirped brightly, "Oh, Junius, how nice! We must get together soon!"

Part Four

"Aw, June-Bug, don't even try to tell your folks what it's like in the pen. I tried it and it's no use. Nobody can believe how awful it is unless they've been through it themselves. You can't tell them what it's like. The *ugly* stuff is all over us like the fog—you can't pin it down. And even if you could, it would only hurt them.

"So just tell them about some of the crazy people and and some of the funny things we laugh about, or how snafued everything is. After all, laughing about it is how *we* stay sane.

"You don't want them to know, what it's *really* like—at least not while you're inside. Maybe when we're out we can try to tell what it *is* like, but I bet it'll be a long time before we'll even want to try."

Carlos Pfohl Johnson, Lewisburg (1962)

20

"Landry"

The inexorable October 2 surrender date approached, seldom mentioned but depressing everyone in the Scales family.

Convalescing from my surgery, still weak and tiring quickly, I one day received a phone call from Henry Winston. Winston, by then the national chairman of the Communist Party, had recently been released from a federal penitentiary totally blind, a condition resulting from the faulty treatment of a brain tumor by prison doctors. The call was personal; politics were not discussed. We talked about our children, who had been friends for years, and about each other's health. We reminisced about a favorite Spanish restaurant that Winnie had introduced me to before the war, and then about our return from a meeting in Birmingham in 1941—dark-brown Winnie and blond, fair-skinned Junius, sharing a double seat in the jim-crow car of a Southern Railroad train, something unthinkable at that time. We laughed, remembering how after many hours a new conductor (officious in blue) discovered us and announced that I would be put off at the next stop if I didn't leave the jim-crow car immediately, and how I told him to go to hell (to the amusement and approval of the other passengers), knowing that the next stop was High Point, North Carolina, my destination.

Winnie had then been youthful, warm, generous, and truly modest. There had ever since been a special affection between us, and when Winnie as one of the top leaders of the Party had jumped bail and gone underground, the Carolinas Party had "adopted" his young son Larry, to try to ease his being deprived of his father. The phone conversation lasted twenty minutes or so and ended with Winnie's wishing me well and saying he was confident I would make out all right in prison. It was heartwarming to know that at least one top leader in the foundering Communist hulk had not lost his civility.

Visits from and to solicitous friends were often disastrously gloomy for all concerned. What could they say to a friend whose family would shortly be torn apart and whose individual future was hazardous and dim?

The remaining September days flew by. We spent the last full day (a Sunday) with Richard and Lia and their boys picnicking near the palisades of the Hudson. Richard took snapshots of Gladys, Barbara, and me. It was agreed that we could not correspond, since Richard as yet had no tenure at his college and might be vulnerable to FBI harassment.

The fateful Monday morning dawned. The family arose and breakfasted at the usual time, and I saw Barbara off to school with a special, but tearless, goodbye.

At about 10:15 A.M. Ab and Minna Abernethy arrived to drive Gladys and me to the federal courthouse in Foley Square, where I was to surrender in the U.S. marshal's office at noon. Just as I was saying goodbye to Grandma, the phone rang. It was James A. Wechsler, the author, columnist, and editor of the *New York Post*. Apologizing for calling at such a time, he said he had just discovered that this was my last day and that he wanted to write a column about my case. After chatting for fifteen or twenty minutes, I said I really must go, and hung up.

Ab and Minna managed to make the rushed trip almost cheerful, and we arrived in front of the courthouse with nearly ten minutes to spare. Then came the hardest part: a not altogether tearless farewell to Gladys. I said I was not going to look back, and as I turned away from the car and started up the broad, high, granite stairs, I saw Bernie waiting for me, standing by a large stone column.

Bernie, who knew this would be the most dismal walk of my life, was on hand to offer moral support and friendship and to join Gladys in the car later to console her. We walked slowly to the marshal's office, arriving at 11:59. I identified myself to a polite secretary who addressed me as "mister"—the last time that that title would be applied to me for a long while. A turnkey came and opened a locked grating. A handclasp and a hug from Bernie, and then I passed through the door. Down the corridor to a corner, a last wave and smile to Bernie standing forlornly at the grate; then I was locked into a cage to begin my career as a nonperson.

About four-and-a-half hours later, defendants in various cases began to be brought into the detention area, and the place started to fill up with both male and female prisoners. About thirty of us were handcuffed in pairs and herded into a prison bus parked at an enclosed side entrance. I was faint from hunger,

Gladys, Barbara, and Junius on October 1, 1961, the day before he entered prison (This photo, taken by Richard Nickson, appeared in a syndicated column by James Wechsler, editor of the *New York Post*.)

having forgotten to eat lunch, and I felt an acute pain in my incision as my cuff-mate stepped up into the bus and I pulled myself into the doorway. At that precise juncture, two photographers shouted, "Hey! Scales!" and caught me with a look of anguish and desperation—to this day the preferred photo of many North Carolina newspapers.

The bus wound through side streets to the West Street Federal House of Detention, where the admitting inspection seemed designed to be as humiliating as possible, prisoners being forced to strip naked and subjected to rectal searches with a flashlight.

The prison was miserably crowded. I was given a work-assignment slip sending me to the laundry—a pretty tough job, according to other inmates. My quarters were changed to a large, crowded cage. A neighbor told me that the *Daily News* had run a picture of me struggling up the steps of the prison van together with a short, inaccurate, nasty caption; another said that the *Post* had a whole column on me by James Wechsler which was favorable.

Gladys visited me the next day, trying to look cheery though apparently having been subjected to some cruel bureaucratic harassment. "Visiting" consisted of sitting on stools on opposite sides of a solid wall, looking through a small, filthy, inch-thick glass panel, and trying to speak to each other through a wretched phone that rasped and rattled with every word. It was hard to imagine how the jailers could even make an intelligible recording (which a man in the control booth was obviously attempting).

By then I had been informed by some deputy warden that I would be sent to Lewisburg, Pennsylvania, the nearest federal penitentiary, and I hoped for an early departure. Meantime, the laundry job was a killer, the location being a steamy basement where the temperature ranged from 100 to 120 degrees Fahrenheit.

I became friendly with a Negro man some years my senior. That man, Mack, a dope pusher high in the Harlem drug hierarchy, had spent much of his life in prison. His way with serving cocoa and vanilla wafers would have put many an elegant host to shame. As a conversationalist and raconteur he was superb. His charm and graciousness were accessible to anyone who did not abuse them, but when he liked someone who had won his confidence, his loyalty and concern were monumental. As he said, "What matters most in life are the woman (or women) you love and your friends." I was to learn in the months to come how a week's acquaintance with this man (though I never saw him again) was to result in innumerable kindnesses from Negro prisoners who had got "the word" from Mack. Later, at Lewisburg, I found that torn, ill-fitting, button-missing, or stained prison clothing was constantly replaced with new and superior items; through none of my doing I was called into the clothing room and fitted with the best-quality new prison shoes; any news items in the press concerning me were passed on within hours of receipt. After months of puzzling, I was able to trace these kindnesses to three or four Negro friends of Mack's who had done them for his sake as a matter of course and expected nothing in return.

One of the first things a political prisoner had to learn was not to be overly judgmental about a fellow prisoner's crimes. Mack had become involved in drug peddling in early youth and had tried to maintain a separation between his trade and the rest of his life. He wasn't proud of his trade, but he was proud of his proficiency. He was perhaps most comfortable in prison, where he could forget about the trade, be his own man, and develop his gentlemanly social instincts to the fullest possible extent. There his chief suffering was being deprived of the society of women (though he would hardly allow any-one to know that he *suffered* from anything).

I had an amusing conversation with a young man in his twenties. We began by exchanging the usual polite inquiries: How much time did we have? where would we serve it? had we done time before? Somehow we got on to the subject of studies while in prison. Since he had several years to go, I remarked that he probably could master some skill or profession during that period. "Hell! I got a profession on the outside!" he said.

"Oh!" I said, "what's that?"

"Boigular!" he replied.

Two days later a prison bus arrived from Atlanta en route to Leavenworth by way of Lewisburg. I was loaded aboard and handcuffed to a Negro man, who was in turn cuffed to a metal frame. The bus went through the Lincoln Tunnel, and from the Jersey side I saw the New York skyline fade away, an emotional moment for me. The sight of the city from the Jersey side, begin-ning with my teenage years, had always filled me with excitement over ap-proaching a cultural "promised land." At forty-one, I was leaving that view behind, leaving most of what was dear to me, with little prospects of seeing it again for many years—if ever.

My Negro traveling companion, about sixty years old, was a professional check forger with the eyes of a voracious crocodile, who regaled me with descriptions of his techniques of emptying out private checking accounts and passing phony checks. Other traveling companions, Mafia bigwigs Salerno and Cavalcanti, who had served about half of their twelve-year sentences at Leavenworth, had been at West Street during appeal proceedings for a new trial. They had lost the appeal, as expected, but they had had a pleasant change of scenery and checked up on Mafia discipline in the various prisons en route. They were to be in Lewisburg for about two weeks, during which time they indeed got VIP treatment: sheets on their beds, extra blankets and towels, daily papers, and books. Those serene men occupying the seats in front of me were friendly and informative during the trip. They mentioned that they had heard favorable comments about me from Tony M———, a Mafioso I had met at West Street.

When the bus arrived, it was let in through a side gate in a huge, high wall which surrounded the whole prison. As the gate closed behind the bus, a Negro prisoner in an awed voice said in the general silence, "Man, we is in the *penitentiary* now!"

The prisoners were herded inside, still handcuffed together, where the first thing I noticed in the stone-and-masonry room was a large iron-framed canvas basket with one flat wheel and a ripped panel. Wretchedly stenciled on the side was the one word LANDRY. As I was later to learn, no object better symbolized the operation of the penitentiary: nothing was done well; nothing worked properly; ignorance and misinformation predominated; the administration was fuzzy-minded; directives were ambiguous and illiterate; no one in authority appeared to give a damn; sloppiness reigned supreme.

When cells were assigned, I found that my bed had no mattress cover or blanket. A broken metal desk, a shaky metal chair, and a metal trashcan completed the furniture. There was a barred window and a barred opening, about eight inches square, head-high in the heavy door, a toilet with no seat, and a wash basin. An inmate on duty in the corridor as orderly weighed about 225 pounds and looked like a badly made up hunchback of Notre Dame. When I went to the grille in my door to tell him of my shortages, Quasimodo was diagonally across the corridor, holding the upper plate of his dentures in his hand, performing fellatio on another inmate through the grille—for which privilege he offered either candy bars or cigarettes.

The two Mafia soldiers, who shared a cell directly opposite from me, were solicitous about my situation and frequently invited me to eat with them. Salerno was cool and unflappable and seemed always to be sorting out and evaluating things. Cavalcanti was thin, cold-eyed, sharp-featured, and tense; even his rare smiles could be disturbing. A Hollywood casting director would have given him a part as a hit man without hesitation. They were inseparable comrades and intensely loyal to each other. There was, however, no likelihood of homosexuality between them. In fact, as far as I could tell, homosexuality seemed to be almost nonexistent among the Mafiosi and most Italian-Americans. They were interested in any news of "the street," even whatever a square like me could tell them. A couple of days after arrival, during the assembly in the corridor before breakfast, they discovered that I had no sheets, no pillow or pillowcase, and only one blanket. "Speak to Joe when we go downstairs," said Salerno sotto voce to Cavalcanti. Breakfast was pleasant, and I regaled them with an account of *Fiorello,* a Broadway musical to which some kind friends had given Gladys and me tickets, just before I entered prison. Though it seemed a misspent evening then, my audience was enthralled as I reenacted the wisecracks, the tunes, and nearly everything except the choreography.

When I returned to my cell I was astonished to find two pillows, two pillowcases, two sheets, an extra towel, and an extra blanket, which was most welcome on cold nights. I mentioned this to Salerno and Cavalcanti later that day and thanked them in case they had anything to do with it. "I wouldn't give it a thought," said Salerno. "It was probably the tooth fairy," suggested Cavalcanti. They changed the subject and mentioned that I might be seeing Tony (who had been on laundry assignment with me at the West Street prison) again before long if what they heard was true.

A few days later they shouted goodbye from across the corridor and headed west on a prison bus, probably to Chillicothe, Ohio, the next stop on their return journey to Leavenworth.

Through my radio earphones world news began reaching me, mostly infuriating: Khrushchev's big bomb threat (and apparently few, if any, mass demonstrations against it around the world), his preparations for a Stalin-style witch-hunt purge, prizes given to East German children for informing on people trying to get to West Berlin (how to raise a new generation full of socialist ideals!), and strong demands here that we start above-ground testing of A-bombs.

My prison medical examination was short of reassuring. "You've had an operation recently," the youthful-looking doctor observed triumphantly as he stared at the ten-and-a-half-inch flaming red scar down my middle. He put down vital information, such as height, weight, age, blood pressure, previous ailments, and operations on a medical form with such painstaking care that I was favorably impressed—till I noticed that the form applied to an inmate named "Corcoran, James." I called this discrepancy to the doctor's attention. Somewhat abashed, he then wrote a card for "Scalise, Julius I." and began entering the information from memory (since, in his embarrassment, he had torn up Corcoran's card), filling in the blanks with significantly different figures.

"Maybe I better take your blood pressure again." He took it again, with a thirty-point variation in each figure from the previous reading. He then consulted his stethoscope and noted down "a significant heart murmur." "How long you had that murmur?" The previously undetected murmur was never observed by any doctor subsequently.

"Anything wrong with you now?"

"Just a case of GI dandruff dating from World War II."

"That's psoriasis," he said, glancing up at my scalp—a diagnosis that had been decisively rejected four months earlier by a renowned dermatologist.

"Any psychological problems?" he asked, coming to the last line of the form.

"Well, for the past few years I've had the feeling that someone was out to get me," I said with a straight face.

"Paranoid tendencies," the doctor wrote in the appropriate blank.

"Wanna see the psychiatrist?"

"No thanks," I said. And the examination was over.

I was by then profoundly convinced that my survival in prison depended, in some measure, on staying away from the Medical Department.

During my protracted isolation in AO (administrative orientation, a quarantine area for new arrivals), I had plenty of time to contemplate and assess the situation in which I as a new penitentiary prisoner found myself. As I saw it, I had been placed legally and physically outside the society of which I had been part and whose welfare and improvement had been my prime concern during my adult life. My efforts at social betterment having admittedly been clumsy and often mistaken, most of my fellow citizens (I had not yet realized that as a convicted felon I was no longer a citizen) apparently considered me to be an adversary of society, an object of no value and troublesome, even dangerous, at that. Most certainly that was the view of my society's designated representatives: wardens, social workers, and other jailers.

My fellow prisoners and I were generally regarded as less than human. The impersonal way we were counted several times a day spoke volumes about our status. Communication with many jailers was mostly one-way, much like a dog's or cat's with an insensitive owner or a zoo inmate's with its keepers. Generally, the jailers viewed me (and every other prisoner) not only as an enemy of society and the good things in it, but as *their* enemy, one with whom the best relationship was a one-sided armed truce. I was not trusted in anything and was suspected of everything. I sensed that the prison administration was ready and perhaps eager to try to crush me by exercising its nearly absolute power through either subtle or crude means, or perhaps both.

I repeatedly reexamined my assessment as the weeks passed, considering particularly whether its bleakness reflected the paranoid reactions of an isolated new prisoner. I carefully observed how much my treatment differed from that of the other prisoners. Because of the unprecedented length of time I had been kept in AO I guessed that the administration had not yet decided how to handle me. But from the attitudes of social workers, the difficulty Gladys was having in arranging a visit, and the number and tone of the unjustified rebukes

I had received from the mailroom, it was apparent that there was plentiful hostility "up front."

I gave some thought to means of surviving six years in such a place and wondered if there were not important differences among my jailers, not yet detected, which might improve my chances. I was sure, however, that survival in anything more than a physical sense depended on keeping my personal integrity and sense of dignity intact, and that this in turn involved a continuous critical self-evaluation accompanying a rejection of my jailers' evaluation of me. Such things were matters I would not discuss with Gladys on a visit; she had more than enough to reckon with. I believed that prison survival was a lonely, individual problem and thought it unlikely that I would find help in the form of friendship from any in the collection of prisoners I saw around me.

My fellow inmates could be trusted only in the most limited areas. Many were profoundly conditioned to exploiting, preying on, and betraying their associates. Only after time and careful observation could one chance some degree of trust in another prisoner and then hope that there might be some shared interests or values. While I was gregarious and was even sought out as a mealtime companion, my best acquaintance in Lewisburg at first was a little Italian-American guy in his forties, too lowly and disreputable to be included among the Mafiosi. He had been in prison many times and was experiencing his first federal rap. He was undeniably stupid and had the table manners of a hog, but he had a kind, generous heart (he shared his science fiction with me) and was beloved of a large family of brothers and sisters, two of whom had already visited him, although, as he told me, "I've never been nuttin' but a bum and a tief."

One day, while still being processed in AO, I was told to report to X-ray in the Medical Department. Since I had already been X-rayed thoroughly a couple of weeks before, I was puzzled. When I arrived, an inmate technician told me my first X-rays were blurred and would have to be done over. I was then shown into an inner room by the technician, a dark-haired, skinny little guy about five feet one inch and ninety-eight pounds, who closed the door, introduced himself as Carlos Pfohl Johnson from High Point, North Carolina, said he had been following my case for years, and handed me a cup of coffee.

Carlos was a sort of non-Communist radical who had gone into the army in his early teens, had done occupation duty in Japan, and had later been much decorated in Korea. Then he'd been sent to Austria, where he took a furlough and illegally went into East Germany and Soviet-occupied Austria to see for himself what it was like behind the Iron Curtain. An Austrian friend who was a Communist had more or less fitted him with rose-colored spectacles, so he liked what he saw. Then, after being AWOL two or three weeks, he returned, a starry-eyed "Bolshevik," expecting to lose his master sergeant's stripes and perhaps catch a couple of weeks of KP. But some brass got wind of his pro-Soviet enthusiasm and decided to make an example of him, so he ended up with a general court-martial, an eighteen-year sentence, and confinement first in the Fort Leavenworth stockade, then in the federal pen at Leavenworth, and then at Lewisburg. On appeal, his sentence was reduced to fourteen years. He had been at Lewisburg for eight.

We at once began talking about High Point and discovered numerous mutual acquaintances, including a girl Carlos had been in love with, whom I had known and loved when she was only eight years old. Despite the exotic-sounding names, Carlos was North Carolina working class through and through. He was an educated man—self-educated. He had read widely and enthusiastically and trained himself by means of correspondence courses and practical experience to be proficient in nearly every skilled job in a hospital lab, and in addition he held certificates as an X-ray technician and as a physiotherapist.

Carlos had a keen sense of humor and was remarkably sensitive, insightful, generous, and warmhearted; he was a man of high principles and courage to match, truly a companion to treasure anywhere—but in prison, it was incredible. There was no way that I could communicate to Gladys till her visit my joy at having found a potential friend.

At last, in mid-November, I was transferred from AO to a huge dormitory shared with about seventy others and assigned to work in the kitchen, pending permanent assignment. The new quarters were painfully crowded; the third-floor dormitory was a large rectangular room with double-decked beds close together all around the sides and a footlocker in front and behind each. Down the middle was a tight row of single beds with footlockers. At one end next to the barred door to the stairway was a twenty-by-twenty-foot concrete-floored bathroom with ten washbasins, eight toilet bowls without movable seats, a long urinal, and about eight shower heads which squirted into a slanted trough for drainage. For those who showered daily it was a struggle to get wet, soap up, and rinse off because of the crush at each shower head. There was also an uncomfortable feeling of being watched closely by pederast-rapists who were taking mental notes for future, less-crowded circumstances.

In less than six weeks mail from Gladys became a veritable lifeline for me. Its importance was indescribable. Her letters, written with complete naturalness and charm, were never constrained by the thought of hacks reading them and were masterpieces of affectionate conversational style. Two days without mail led to wild speculation about illness or other disasters at home;

three days could shake me to the core. When I moved to my dorm, although none of my fellow transferees had any problem with their mail, my anonymous persecutors in the mailroom held back my incoming mail for four days.

While there was nothing exciting about moving from one part of prison to another, "hitting population" (becoming a regular inmate) was very different from the relatively sheltered existence in AO quarantine. A regular inmate could proceed anywhere on the huge main corridor during certain hours: to the dining hall, the caseworkers' offices, the Medical Department, the Education Department. He could, of course, be stopped and shaken down at any time and at any place by any hack for any reason. The reasons ranged from personal animosity and bullying to a reasonable suspicion of transporting contraband, such as "shivs" (knives, homemade or otherwise) and pills (uppers, downers, or anything between).

The ugly atmosphere created by the hacks on security duty on the grounds, in the corridors, and in the dormitories and cellblocks was based on their opinion that the inmates were, by definition, scum, subhuman, and devoid of any claim to self-respect, dignity, or privacy. Much of this attitude was institutionalized in the specific security rules and procedures in force.

Fortunately, many of the hacks, especially those in the various nonsecurity departments, were suspected of humanity with good reason. Often they were quite decent, particularly when confronted individually. They were mostly local men, sons of farmers or miners, who had needed jobs and had been tragically trapped in the prison system. They served time too, but instead of talking of release dates, as the inmates did, they spoke of their retirement dates. The educational and IQ requirements must have been pathetically low. But what was remarkable with them, as with the inmates, was that some few retained their decency under terrible pressures, and a very few managed in addition to keep relatively high spirits and to be outgoing.

Early on I realized that there were many differences of pacing between penitentiary existence and jailhouse existence. In a penitentiary there was a slower tempo. There had to be less frenzy and turmoil, fewer comings and goings, a more rigid inmate code of behavior. Most of the short-termers with six months to a year were weeded out and sent to Allenwood or to the Lewisburg Farm just outside the walls, where they were never seen by the "close-confinement," "hardened-criminal" long-termers inside.

Since I had only a "nickel and penny" (six years), I scarcely qualified for inclusion in the Lewisburg elite, where a "nickel" was sort of minimal and where less time was by many considered "just visiting." In Leavenworth I would not have "rated" much at all, since a "dime" was reportedly minimal and a "quarter" or the "whole buck" (life) were quite common sentences.

Looking over the inmates, one might have been inclined to generalize them as morons, pathetic jerks, slobs, or goons. But though there were plentiful examples of such categories, all inmates in touch with reality knew that they were all different and all human and, above all, that each inmate was *one of them*.

21

Taking the Count

Wouldst thou dive into the secret villainies of men? Lie in a prison. The good may be made better there, but the bad are sure to be worse.

Thomas Dekker, *Lantern and Candlelight* (1608)

The visiting room was large, with sofas and armchairs scattered around and a hack seated at a desk keeping time and watching to see that inmates embraced their guests only at arrival and departure. Visitors were shown in politely, and they waited until the inmates were called on the prisonwide loud-speaker system. The inmates were herded into a room and forced to strip bare. This was annoying enough before a visit, but to have to go through the procedure a second time while in a state of euphoria after a visit was truly maddening. Sometimes there was even a rectal search.

Since there was no wall or glass partition, couples could sit opposite each other, with a coffee table in between; but they were not permitted to hand each other anything, except at the desk with the hack's permission. Thus the visits were robbed of most of their naturalness and dignity. Gladys was much upset by the surveillance and rightly suspected that the "Potemkin Village" behavior of the hacks in the visiting room hid much greater indignities behind the scenes.

She had decided to come alone on her first visit so that she would be better able to shield Barbara's sensibilities when she brought her for the first time. When the visit began, I was strained and tense, still raging inwardly from a sadistically slow and painstaking body search. We each tried too hard to protect the other, but Gladys soon broke the tension with her precious stories about our child and our friends. A campaign was getting under way for my release, and soon she was glowing with enthusiasm as she told of favorable responses from some North Carolina liberals whom she had recently visited (especially Dr. Frank Graham). Nationally, Wechsler had become a sort of publicity director, while the experienced and tireless Norman Thomas was commander in chief, using his great influence to enlist the support of ever-more-prominent intellectuals and political figures. Many good friends were using their past Communist Party organizational skills to do a staggering job of issuing promotion materials, handling mailings, and raising money for the campaign. Gladys reported that some Communists were supportive and active in my behalf, though the Party leadership had consistently obstructed fund-raising efforts. Meanwhile, she was working conscientiously at her low-paid teaching job and was spending the rest of her time with Barbara and at endless meetings concerning my freedom. Grandma had been invaluable with her loving care of Barbara.

When the visit ended I felt that I was not completely forgotten on the outside and that the campaign and publicity for my freedom, while having no chance of success, would at least put the prison administrators on the spot so that they would be inhibited in any particularly vicious plans they might have for me. I felt then that I could handle anything they might throw at me, provided Gladys's health held up. The warmth and elation of the visit lasted for days. Soon after, I was at last classified, being assigned to the library effective the following week.

While I was still on kitchen detail, serving on the chow line one day just after Thanksgiving, some newly arrived AO-ers dressed in white coveralls came in for lunch. To my utter astonishment I saw coming down the line Frank Wilkinson, who had been my next-door neighbor and a friend for several years. Behind him was Carl Braden, a Kentucky radical of Socialist Party background, whom I had met in Frank's home. They had both opposed the House Un-American Activities Committee on principle and, when hauled before it, had refused to answer questions on First Amendment grounds. They had been cited for contempt, convicted, and sentenced to a year (which boiled down to about nine months, with the usual time off for good behavior). Both had been transferred from a minimum-security camp in South Carolina and were en route to Allenwood Prison Farm, a similar establishment about eighteen miles away (regarded by Lewisburgers as something between a country club and a rest home).

There was general amazement among us at the chance meeting, and Frank and Carl were not sure whether they should pretend not to know me. When the AO-ers had been served, I went over and joined them at their table, and we had a long talk about prison experiences and our families. I felt they were doing "hard time" (not adjusting to the circumstances of prison life), and I assured them that all the noncriminal types, like Kentucky moonshiners and short-term first offenders, were sent to Allenwood, and that restrictions there were minimal.

Later when I was more prison-wise and had become a sharp "con," I was able to arrange to have Frank sent in to Lewisburg for a day on some phony pretext and to spend a couple of very pleasant, relaxed hours visiting with him.

Intensely concerned about every aspect of Barbara's upbringing, I filled my letters with questions and suggestions about her. Since the thought of missing a single day in the development and flowering of such a beautiful child was almost insupportable, it was with great reluctance that I gradually gave up trying to have a say in everything she did and accepted the inevitable loosening of the carefully cultivated intimacy. All the same I was determined to write to Barbara before Christmas, since a letter was the only present I could give her. Writing a thoughtful letter was difficult, since my dormitory (E-3), known as "the jungle," was miserably crowded and the noise level while the lights were on was deafening.

I wanted to tell her how much Christmas had meant to me and my parents and to give her a vivid, detailed account of my tenth Christmas, but the concentration necessary for such an exercise in recall was impossible in the midst of that bedlam. The noise subsided at "lights out" and concentration was then possible—but it was dark.

I resided in an upper bunk in front of a window. At night, floodlights almost parallel to the walls lit up the outside of the prison buildings, as a safeguard against escapes. By holding a pad at arm's length, I was able to catch a ray of this light on the paper and to scrawl my recollections on it over a period of three nights. My writing was so small that I received an admonition and a threat from the mailroom of a week's loss of writing privileges.

My new job in the library was a blessing. The library itself was extraordinary for a prison. The physical plant was large and handsome with high ceilings and large windows on both sides of the top floor of a long, rectangular building. The books were well classified according to the Dewey decimal system, and the reading tables and benches were plentiful and comfortable. Individual chairs were scattered around generously. In quarters behind the checkout desk was a complete bindery and repair shop, where two inmates worked constantly trying to keep pace with the destruction wrought by inmate "customers."

The librarian, Mr. Adams, was a remarkable man who cared about the library and its functions. He was largely self-educated and, like most of the hacks, had lived all his life in the locality. He was a member of a narrowly fundamentalist religious sect, but he would never remove a book from the shelves because he disagreed with its point of view. He was a real Jeffersonian democrat who considered his job a public trust. He had acquired truly professional qualifications as a librarian and, according to widely experienced prisoners, had made his library by far the best in the federal prison system.

He and I established a cordial, mutually respectful relationship. He often spoke of the famous psychologist Dr. Wilhelm Reich, who had been imprisoned for fraud (concerning his "orgone box") and who had died in Lewisburg. He came to Adams not long before his death, led him to a library window, pointed to a weather balloon floating high above the prison and gleaming in the afternoon sun, and said with an air of quiet confidentiality, "See? They're coming for me."

"Who is?" Adams asked.

"Ah! That's *my* secret!" he said.

Adams, a tough but sympathetic man, had grown quite fond of him, but he observed that his mental deterioration was rather rapid shortly before he died.

I casually mentioned to Adams that the last two issues of my *Nation* subscription had been held up by the mailroom without explanation. I had subscribed to it for some years at home, and it was on the approved prison list of publications. That afternoon, according to inmates working nearby, Adams walked into the mailroom, confronted the censors, whom he outranked, and demanded to know who had authorized them to violate the Bureau of Prisons rules, who had authorized them to administer special punishment to Scales by depriving him of his mail and harassing him. The decibels from the altercation apparently reached astonishing levels. The next day when I came into the library, Adams quietly handed me two issues of the *Nation* and said merely, "I don't think you'll have any more trouble."

But trouble I had, and soon.

I was removed from my job in the library. A notice was handed to me announcing a job change from the library to the storeroom, where all the institution's supplies were received and where some were kept. My removal from the library job was the warden's reply to a Wechsler column in the *New York Post* which had created something of a sensation among the inmates. The warden, an old prison hand, was probably no better and no worse than the average warden, according to experienced hacks and inmates. With his bushy black eyebrows, low forehead, and coarse manner, he seemed to be not very intelligent. Every time I had anything to do with him, he appeared to be struggling with some inner rage which was about ready to burst into violence. My caseworker told me that the warden was "furious" over the *Post* article, as if it were not already obvious enough to me that I was "getting the business."

Actually, the new job proved physically unbearable. I was still very far from recovering my strength, and the lifting was extremely painful. Fortunately, I was much experienced in warehouse work from having worked in hosiery and textile mills, and I knew lifting techniques. Otherwise, I could hardly have got through the day. By early afternoon I was staggering and seeing stars every time I lifted anything. At the end of the shift I drew the hack in charge to one side and said, "Look, I'm not going to holler 'uncle' to anybody, you included, and I'm not going to crawl to medical, but I can't do this job." I pulled up my shirt and showed an angry red incision from my upper rib cage to my abdomen. The hack winced. "My God! Why didn't you say something? I'll see what I can do."

The hack's name was Wagenseller, a good man. He had had a couple of years in a small college, had run out of money, and did not want to go into the mines. Interested in social work, and hearing that there were job openings at Lewisburg, he applied for a hack's job, full of belief that he could be of service to his fellowman by helping reform some of the not-too-hardened criminals in the pen. Bright and astute, he suffered such disillusionment during his first six months that he lived in near despair. He had volunteered his spare time for every kind of self-help, self-betterment, self-education project, where he thought he might help at least one inmate, while it gradually appeared to him that he had become a zoo keeper in a human zoo and that he had imprisoned himself as well, because his whole life revolved around, or inside, the big cage. Meanwhile, he had married and had children; jobs were scarce; compared to his neighbors, he was well-off; he already had accumulated six years toward completing his "time"—he had caught a wolf by the ears and couldn't let go. He was witty, charming, sophisticated, and completely unpretentious. He kidded and joked with the inmates, but he always followed the rules (even though he followed the most humane interpretation possible).

So I was put in the storeroom office, where I was not really needed because a young man named Rudy handled the office passably by himself. Rudy was the son of a prominent Harlem minister and had got involved in various rackets, including drugs (for the peddling of which he had been convicted); he was nearing the end of his five-year sentence. Since he was so "short" (had such a short time to serve), he had applied to be transferred to Allenwood for the end of his sentence and was expecting each week to have his request approved. Meanwhile, he wasn't anxious to have a college-educated potential rival in the office. He thawed out in a few days, however, became friendly, and offered to be the go-between with Rep. Adam Clayton Powell, Jr. (his friend), who could, he said, get me out—for a price.

When I finally "hit population," I met one other man who was to become a dear friend. He was Andy, Carlos's closest friend, who worked in the Education Department. Several years older than I, of Italian ancestry, Andy had graduated from City College in the thirties and was sophisticated politically and in most other ways. He was the best bridge player and best tennis player in the place, stood rather aloof from things, and was much respected. He had been at Lewisburg twelve years and was immensely prison-wise and wise generally.

He had lived in Washington, D.C., running a profitable real estate business. Shortly after an immature marriage, his life began to come apart emotionally. He became a father; when the child was a year old, he and his wife, both in emotional turmoil and despair and in acute need of psychiatric care, made a suicide pact and turned on the gas in their apartment. Someone broke open the door and found them near death; the child was dead. Andy lied, exonerated his wife (who promptly divorced him), took the rap, and was sentenced to twenty-five years for murder.

He had arrived at Lewisburg, as he himself put it, a "raving lunatic" who hardly knew his own name. Fortunately, he had a loving sister and two loving brothers, but it was essentially by his own bootstraps that he pulled the pieces of his life together. While I knew him he was, by far, the sanest man at Lewisburg.

Carlos, Andy, and I became inseparable friends and shared nearly every meal and nearly all our free time together. Their advice and counsel were priceless to me, and they kept their neophyte friend from many a misstep. For example, they advised me not to apply for a locked cell, because in a couple of months I could apply to leave "the jungle" and go to semihonor quarters, and in three more months I could apply to move to honor quarters, where there were private rooms to which the doors were never locked and many other privileges. In every crisis they were supportive, constructive, and nearly always right. We three were selfless where the welfare of any one of us was concerned.

As Christmas approached, cards addressed to me began proliferating. Then, all of a sudden, they stopped reaching me, and on December 19 I was ordered to the office of the associate warden, a hack no more intelligent but less unpleasant than the warden. He confronted me with a clipping of a letter from Gladys published in the *New York Post* in which she invited friends "known and unknown" to send Christmas cards to her husband. The warden's stand-in said that his boss was "much concerned" about federal prisoners receiving mail from "unknown" persons and that this was impermissible. I pointed out that hundreds of inmates received religious tracts in the mail from evangelical zealots they had never heard of. Be that as it may, said the official, I must examine each Christmas card addressed to me, and if it were from someone I knew I must identify the person and I would then receive the card. I refused, saying that I would not "finger" my friends. Then the cards would be destroyed, my adversary said. "You have no right to destroy my mail. If you do, I'll consult my lawyers about what legal action can be taken. Why don't you return the cards and see if you can explain to the senders why I alone am not allowed to receive Christmas cards?" I also pointed out that it was a bit late for my wife to retract her letter, and that part of the discussion ended in a stalemate. (About a month *after* Christmas, I was summoned to the mailroom and presented with a cardboard carton containing more than four hundred Christmas cards.)

But that was not all that troubled the warden; his subordinate said that the boss was disturbed by Wechsler's statement that Mrs. Scales's visit had been for a whole morning and afternoon instead of the stipulated three hours and that this embarrassed the prison administration. I noted that neither my wife nor I had any control over what Mr. Wechsler wrote and that I had never even met the gentleman. However, I said, it seemed to me that the warden had received publicity which merely demonstrated his generosity and humaneness. In any case, I assured the man that my wife and I had no wish to embarrass the administration and that I would write to her about the warden's concern. That pleased the associate warden, and he terminated the interview.

Although I enjoyed talking back to the warden through his deputy, I had no illusions about the relationship of forces, and I knew that the warden held all the trumps. I therefore wrote Gladys a straight-faced account of the warden's worries, knowing that he would probably read it and that Gladys would detect the tongue in my cheek.

A penitentiary Christmas may have been a bit lacking in goodwill, but at least there was a change. The security hacks were a little less dismal than usual, and an older one near the dining hall (who was by now as familiar as the doorway) responded warmly to an impulsive "Merry Christmas" from me. Meantime, the packages from Federal Prison Industries were distributed, pleasantly under the circumstances. Andy got the cigarettes, and the candy went to my Negro lower-bunk neighbor, who had had a prodigious sweet tooth ever since he'd been "cold-turkeyed" off drugs a few months before. He had been hooked on drugs in Harlem and then forced into pushing when his money ran out; he had been required to make risky deliveries and was arrested in his first week. He had adopted me, willy-nilly, as his psychotherapist. Christmas was a sad day for him because all he could think of was his beautiful wife, Lucille. He feared she would divorce him (as so often happened to inmates) before his two-year sentence was served. Two days later, to his complete surprise, she visited him, and I was able to meet her in the visiting room.

The visiting rules were much relaxed during Christmas week: instead of the announced one-day visit, the inmates (I included) were allowed three and a half visits. Bernie, who had driven Gladys and Barbara from New York, was also allowed to see me briefly.

Back in New York, on Christmas Eve, the doorbell had rung at our co-op apartment, and when Gladys opened the door, a neighbor from another building in the co-op handed her an envelope and said, "This is for a Merry Christmas for you and Barbara," ran to the elevator, and disappeared. Gladys opened the envelope and found $250 in cash and a Christmas card signed, "Love from some of your neighbors." About two hours later the doorbell rang again. This time there was no one in sight—only a package in the doorway. It was a beautiful and expensive book for Barbara from "a friend."

Later, when Gladys got the mail, there was a Christmas card with $60 enclosed which said: "Dear Barbara, This is a Christmas present to you from some of the guys who worked with your dad and think he is a great guy." It was signed: "The 'Boys' on the day, night and lobster shifts at Pandick Press." This was at a time when Gladys was not sure how to pay the expenses of the next trip to Lewisburg. She wept.

One night when I had finished writing and there was still some time before lights-out, I lay on my belly with my head toward the center of the room and tried to break down the chaos of sound and activity into its components. While writing, I would sit like a tailor facing the window at the head of my bed, tuning out the steady uproar by tremendous efforts at concentration.

Now I opened my ears and let my eyes roam the huge room and its seventy-odd occupants. To my left, at the far end, was the concrete-floored bathroom and to the left of it, the locked, barred door to the staircase. From the showers came a cloud of vapor and the caterwaulings of shower-bath Carusos. Along the wall in the bathroom was a row of eight "thinkers" lined up on their pedestals, looking solemn and earnest. Opposite them at the basins were the shavers who didn't want to buck the morning rush. Interspersed among them were pimple-squeezers and other narcissistic types.

In front of the stairway was an illegal dice game with its own delegated lookout standing at the stairway door. The dice were rolled against the side of a footlocker; the currency was cigarettes. There was no merriment there: just cold, ugly, silent business. At the opposite end of the room was a much-larger illegal card game, with cigarettes again the currency. The somber-faced card-sharks also had their lookout at the door, but they were not so quiet. Ugly altercations, accusations, and counteraccusations usually accompanied the disposition of every "pot" of cigarettes. Their table was a blanket spread over two footlockers. The animosity and tension around it were almost tangible.

Directly before me, on one of the row of single bunks down the middle of the room, sat John, a sixty-five-year-old Maryland bank robber, holding his grizzled head in both hands and covering his ears, a hunched-over image of despair. His wife was divorcing him.

On my left, three bunks down, newly erupted from an ordinary bull session, a screaming dispute raged over who was president in 1927. Just when the only likely outcome appeared to be extensive mayhem, one of the disputants roared, "Ask Scales!"

"Oh, my God! Thanks a lot," I thought. Would I suffer the combined wrath of the three Hooverites and the three Hardingites? Damn the torpedoes! I struck a blow for enlightenment and survived it: Coolidge proved acceptable, and the discussion subsided to its earlier, merely deafening level.

On the lower bunk to my right, Henry, a West Virginia bootlegger, was watching a young man in the middle row write a letter while letting a long cigarette butt smolder in an ashtray right behind him on a footlocker. The young man, intent on his letter and a studio photograph of his pretty wife which he looked at continually, reached back absentmindedly and snuffed the butt. For all of his sixty-odd years, Henry was on his feet, snagging the butt, and back on his bunk lighting it before a guy could have hollered "Snake!"

Henry, knowing I had observed him, said softly, "You see, I ain't got no money in the commissary, so I have to watch for a good leftover. Got hooked on the weed over forty years ago." I nodded understandingly. "You know, this is my fourth time in the pen, and it don't seem right. I done what I know to do best, makin' whiskey. My family's always made good whiskey, father to son. I 'member my great granpappy, and he said his father had made it afore him. It's just 'cause these outfits like Schenley's can't make as good that they put the likes of me in here. You taste some of mine an you'd *never* touch their rotgut no more."

This was a familiar story to me. In the double-deck bunks opposite was a Kentucky moonshiner in his forties with a similar story. They were both mountain truck farmers who relied on their superior booze for their income. Other members of their families were carrying on the trade during their absence. They would soon be sent to Allenwood, where life would be easier for them. In a matter of months, the old masters would be back at it themselves.

The young man who had unwittingly contributed most of his cigarette had finished his letter and was reading his handiwork with approval. He was a college graduate and CPA who had been making it in the lower levels of Washington society with the aid of his extremely pretty young wife. Somewhere along the line he had embezzled twenty-odd thousand dollars from the firm that employed him. He had made partial restitution but had still got eighteen months. His wife was keeping up appearances and moving in the same social circles, or trying to. He was thirty-one; his wife was twenty-six.

At least once a day he got frantic, wondering what she was doing back home. One evening he described to me a social affair he had attended with his wife in happier days. The climax of the party was the brief appearance made by Attorney General Robert Kennedy. "My God! You should have seen the way he looked at the women! He burnt holes in their clothes with his eyes. And my wife thought he was the cutest thing she ever saw. And—" His voice trailed off; he left the story unfinished and lapsed into a funk of despair and rage; but it was obvious that he had been overcome with jealousy at the thought of his wife's admiration of the attorney general. He then embarked on a campaign to keep her faithful to him by mail and regaled me with a couple of slushy excerpts from his letters to her.

Near the opposite wall to the left, a verbose Negro inmate was providing three or four rather resigned neighbors with a loud and heavily revised account of what he had told the judge before sentence was passed.

At several points near windows the perpetual battle raged over whether the windows should be open or shut. It was bitter cold outside, but inside the air was blue with cigarette smoke and redolent of dirty shoes, socks, and feet and assorted bathroom and body odors. Moisture accumulated on the inside panes and ran down in streams, making puddles under the radiators. A fresh-air advocate would occasionally lower a window a crack at the top as an exhaust, but someone would usually shut it in a matter of minutes. I had a steady cold as a result of these ups and downs of the temperature.

It was nearly ten to ten, time for the count. Crap and card games dissolved; inmates headed toward their bunks from all over the room. In the midst of the hustling, my friendly downstairs neighbor on the left arrived, smelling of soap, shaving cream, and toothpaste. "Oh, if Lucille could only see me now when I'm so sweet and clean! She'd eat me *up!*"

Just then the door opened and three hacks appeared. "Attention for the *count!*" one shouted. There was instant silence. One remained by the door and two marched up the far side, counting the men; the inmates either sat on their beds or stood beside them. When the hacks got to the far end, they retraced their steps and counted the men in the single bunks in the center. When they came up my aisle and reached my bunk, I handed the second hack my outgoing letter. "Well, they got it right the first time for a change!" murmured Lucille's husband to me, as the hacks, pleased with themselves, headed for the stairs.

When the door closed behind them, the noise immediately erupted again as the inmates prepared for bed. It was two to ten. Nearly everyone slept in his underwear, except for a handful who slept raw and one or two who kept their shirts and pants on.

At last the lights went down, and there was a gradual diminution of noise. I had an agreement with the lower-bunk neighbors on each side of me and directly below that I would crack the window from the top after lights out. This I stealthily accomplished. "You're a good kid, Juniass," whispered Lucille's husband approvingly.

Henry, the bootlegger, was already snoring comfortably. One bunk over from Henry, there came a loud, deep-voiced complaint from the Negro lower-bunk occupant to the white, rat-faced occupant of the bunk above him: "If you'll kinely finish beatin' yo meat, I'd like to git some sleep. That is, if you don't shake me plumb outa this muthafuckin' bed!" That drew a few discreet snickers from around the room but no reply from Rat-face.

The cold air drifting from the top of the window onto my hard, lumpy pillow made breathing a pleasure again, instead of a betrayal of my lungs. Conversation had ceased. A couple of red glows indicated insomniac smokers. Alternating groans and whinnies gave evidence that old John was having his first nightmare of the night. Someone exploded on a toilet. Just below, Lucille's husband, in a high-pitched voice, pleaded with her, "Don't leave me, honey! Lucille! Lucille!" The red glows had gone. The radiators began klunking in different rhythms as the steam died down. I turned over on my stomach and felt sleep overtaking me. Just as I drifted away I sensed a quick flash of light on my face; it was eleven o'clock already, and the hacks were taking the first of several bedchecks and counts.

Beyond the pane and bars, above the batteries of floodlights that bathed the prison buildings, and above the spotlights on the high wall, a nearly full moon was serenely taking the count on us all: eighteen hundred miserable convicts and our wretched guards.

22

Iron Bars and
Unnamed Names

E ver since I had been in prison Gladys, her sister and brother, and dozens of friends had busied themselves almost continuously at running an intense campaign for my release. Norman Thomas, Reinhold Niebuhr, Robert Goheen (president of Princeton), and Grenville Clark (a nationally known Republican lawyer) were a sort of "leading committee" (which was surprisingly active). James Wechsler of the *New York Post* had become the "field commander" and was endlessly resourceful. Harry Golden, the witty editor of the *Carolina Israelite* and author of bestselling books, undertook a campaign in North Carolina at great cost to himself (know-nothings withdrew much advertising from his paper), securing the support of a number of people: two federal judges; Jonathan Daniels, editor of the *Raleigh News and Observer,* FDR's former press secretary, and my former hostile adversary; Carl Sandburg; Paul Green, the playwright; and many others. Early signers of the nationally circulated petition for executive clemency, who also wrote directly to the president, included poets W. H. Auden and Archibald MacLeish; A. Philip Randolph; Martin Luther King, Jr.; Frank P. Graham; Harry Emerson Fosdick, nationally prominent Protestant minister; J. Frank Dobie, Texas historian; and Pablo Casals. Gladys also told me that Eleanor Roosevelt had written to the president a "very strong" letter on my behalf.

The campaign was gathering steam, and though I had little expectation of any concrete results, it was enormously comforting to know that some people cared that I was in jail.

One day after lunch, as I was walking down the main corridor amid heavy traffic, on my way back to the storeroom, a familiar leather-lunged voice behind me bellowed, "Hey! c-o-m-r-a-a-a-d-e!" I guessed without too much difficulty that *I* was being addressed. I turned around and there was Tony M—— from the West Street House of Detention, who ran up, knocked the wind out of me with a klop on the back, hugged me before I could inhale, and then crushed my hand in a handshake.

Subtle Tony. One day at West Street, during a work break in the steaming laundry, I had noticed a tall, strongly built inmate with his handsome face puckered by intense concentration as he worked over a pressing machine. He was the only one working in the intense heat. He repeatedly sprinkled, shook out, pressed, and inspected a pair of ordinary boxer-style underwear shorts. Finally the hack called time and work began again. The man disgustedly jammed the shorts into his pants pockets.

At the next break he was at it again, and this time he triumphed: no underpants had ever had a more perfect crease. He smiled, folded the shorts carefully, put them in a brown paper bag, and hid it away safely.

I thought that anyone so fastidious and compulsive must be an interesting character at the very least, so at the next break I flopped down near him and was trying to think of a way to start a conversation when he said, "Hey, ain't you the Commie I seen on the back of the *News?* You looked like you had your pecker caught in the wringer." I explained that I was once a Communist. We introduced ourselves: names, type of rap, time to serve, and so on. Tony was in for parole violation of a previous sentence and was awaiting trial on a very serious narcotics charge which would likely get him twenty-five years. Especially since he was Italian, he said. Did he have a good lawyer? The best and lots of them; but if you had an Italian name and were up on a narcotics charge, they figured you were Mafia and you got the maximum, Tony replied ruefully. Perhaps the American Civil Liberties Union would be interested, I suggested. Oh, they were; and they were filing an *amicus* brief later on, but they had pointed out to Tony that his outfit's lawyer fees exceeded their entire annual national budget and that there was not much else they could do.

"What if the judge is Italian?" I asked.

"They're the worst. They're so busy proving they got no gangster connections they lean over backwards as soon as they hear your name."

"From what I can observe," I said, "it takes about ten or fifteen years for new ideas to penetrate the judiciary. Why don't you get your lawyers to speed up the process and get hold of a new book by Daniel Bell, the Columbia sociologist, called *The End of Ideology?*" I proceeded to outline in some detail the chapter called "The Myth of the Mafia," which makes a powerful case against any significant existence of the Mafia in the American crime picture. Tony listened, entranced. When I had finished he said with the utmost intensity, "Scales! *Write dat down!*" I wrote it down, even remembering the name of the publisher, and added, "Now the name of that chapter is 'The Myth of the _____' " Don't write *dat* down! I'll remember. Scales, dis is terrific! I won't forget you for dis."

Tony must have been at least a soldier in the Mafia hierarchy because he was important and got special treatment from some of the hacks and from all the Italian-American inmates. He had great self-confidence and considerable charm, and he was a delightful conversationalist. He even had a rare sense of humor, if one excepted certain subjects (notably, himself). His quick and violent temper was proverbial (he later made front-page headlines by smashing a courtroom chair to matchwood in front of the U.S. attorney during his trial). He must have been formidable in many circumstances, but in the few days that I had remained at West Street I had encountered nothing but his amiability as we ran the sheets through the big mangle together.

Now, when I could breathe again, I gasped, "So what are *you* doing here?"

"Just got outa AO this morning, and I was keeping an eye out for ya. Ya know The Book ya put me on to? I got a copy for every one of my lawyers, I got a copy in the jungle here, and this afternoon I'm going up to education and pick up three more I had sent. I'm gonna make every one of my guys in the place read it." Tony said he probably wouldn't be at Lewisburg more than a couple of months because his trial was coming up. "But I'll see ya around. How ya making out? Anybody giving you any trouble?"

"Only the warden and the mailroom," I laughed. "I have to go back to work now. I just 'took over' the storeroom office."

I was becoming better adjusted to Lewisburg life. I warmed to the friendship of Carlos and Andy, kept busy and intellectually stimulated, and tried to keep an eye on what was going on in the world outside. I called Gladys's attention in January to a letter to the *Times* urging my release written by Theodore Draper, author of two scholarly books on the history of the American Communist Party which I had found profoundly enlightening. I also recommended Koestler's *Darkness at Noon,* which I thought stood up amazingly well as a political novel after twenty-two years. I felt it was a book we all should have read many years before.

After her first visit, Barbara remarked to her mother that she wanted to visit every month, which delighted me. On her first visit, when Gladys got up for something, Barbara said to me, "Daddy, when we came in, out by the front desk, while we were waiting, I looked up the stairs and there's a mirror and in it I saw some *bars!*" I replied casually that there were bars all over the place and that those were to the Education Department, or something of the sort. The idea of bars apparently shook her considerably. I thought my comment minimized the importance of them as far as I was concerned, but I warned Gladys to be on guard in case she was still a little upset about them.

The sight of bars apparently triggered more than we then realized. I learned many months later that fearless little Barbara, after that visit, insisted on moving her bed near the door of her room and slept with her door open while a light burned in the hall. At the same time her behavior with her mother often became contentious and angry, a quite unprecedented situation.

Gladys took her to a psychiatrist (an old friend) who, after talking to her alone, told Gladys that her behavior was not neurotic but a healthy reaction to a threatening, irremediable situation. The sight of the barred door had suddenly brought home to her the reality that her father was indeed caged like any wretched animal in a zoo.

My job seemed to get gradually busier and left me little spare time. It was also tedious: a little typing of forms and a lot of filing, ledger keeping, and the like. Wagenseller and his assistant hack, Hardnock (a roly-poly, sweet-natured, carefree sort, were commended for their superior performance, and they knew that much of the credit was due to my hard work. They became genuinely friendly and asked if it was OK to call me Junius. To return their friendliness, I made a point (except when other hacks were around) of never calling them by their correct names. Wagenseller was always ("Mr. Wagonwheel," "Mr. Waggintail," "Mr. Wagginsnapper," "Mr. Whippersnapper," "Mr. Wotthehellsyourname," or the like. Hardnock was "Mr. Hardtime," "Mr. Hardnockers," or most often, "Mr. Hard-on." Relations between guards and the guarded could scarcely have been pleasanter.

I fixed an old hot plate which had been thrown out because of a broken wire, secured a kettle and covered saucepan "on loan" from the kitchen, arranged a daily 9:30 A.M. delivery of a gallon of coffee (in exchange for cupcakes) through the door to the kitchen's storeroom. I had become the custodian of a large supply of day-old packaged cakes kindly left every other day by one of the deliverers for the loading crew (seven inmates and two hacks). All day long anyone wanting coffee (or tea) and a snack could be served in the storeroom office. I could also serve inmate friends who were able to find a pretext to get outside the buildings and come to the storeroom. With a fine lack of discrimination, I also would even break out coffee and cake for several friendly, rather special, visiting hacks. But if Lieutenant S—— (the "Horrible Hack") dropped in, we had always just run out of everything.

Such amenities did much for morale. Even the aged hack from upstairs and his moronic inmate-assistant who stayed locked in with the prison's office supplies above the storeroom joined us daily. (The old hack's assistant had formerly been Alger Hiss, still a Lewisburg legend because of his brilliance.

Knowing and being around Hiss had doubtless been one of the memorable experiences of his life. The old man, partly from despair, partly out of irony, had dubbed his near-moron charge "Alger."

My mailroom tormentors were at it again, and I more or less challenged them by again describing their devilment in detail in my letters to Gladys. The delay and the "mix-up" over letters was simply crass harassment by a couple of censorious hacks in the mailroom. They were punishing me because Adams, the librarian, had chewed them out for refusing to deliver the *Nation*, because I had received five hundred Christmas cards, and because (one hack had said within earshot of an inmate) they "didn't like the attitude" in my letters and I "needed to be taught a lesson." So, with the unfailing instinct of nasty little men with power, they hit where it hurt worst.

In February the *New York Times* became interested in my case (possibly owing to Wechsler's prodding) and editorialized, asking the president for executive clemency on my behalf. I was delighted with this clear-cut position in favor of my freedom, thinking that it would mean a much-broadened campaign, that other papers and journals would then have the courage to follow suit, and that individuals would be less timid in support of clemency. In any case, I told Gladys that I was confident that with the editorial and about four more years behind me, I would get out of prison.

Observing life in the jungle sometimes had its rewards. It was incredibly crowded and noisy, but there was much of interest to be seen and heard in all that bedlam. One day, by an adroit flanking movement, I secured the end toilet, furthest from the showers. This most popular seat had two significant advantages: one did not get splashed by showers, and at worst, one had but a single neighbor. (The toilets, without partitions, were less than twelve inches apart—so close, as one inmate put it inelegantly, "you weren't sure whose ass you were wiping.")

While enjoying my triumph, I listened to a monologue emanating from a nearby bench where showering inmates left their towels. It was earnestly delivered by a Negro man in his late sixties to a Negro under thirty, who listened attentively and respectfully.

"The trouble with a lot of you young dudes when you get sent up is you wastes yo' time. You lie aroun', you rap mawnin' till night, you drink that home-brew shit, you take all them upper and downer pills till you don't know if you's comin' or goin', you play wid yosefs, and you talks about what you'd do wid de gals if you was in the streets. You jes wastes yo' time.

"Now what you oughta be doin' is studyin' and learnin'. They's a heap of smart cats in here what got a lot to teach you if you jes' listen."

I was entranced with the force and vehemence of the old man's remonstrances. I began nodding in approval, reminded of many a Negro preacher I had heard reprimanding a wayward congregation.

"Now that fella las' night—he done planned a *good* bank job, but 'cause he had jes' one dumb muthafucka workin' with him, it got all messed up. An thas why *he* here. Now you got a chance to learn how to do better. I'm too ole, time I get outa here. But you's in yo' prime.

"Now that tall mother, next bunk to you—he been burglin' fifteen year an' ain't never been busted till now. An' I tell you why: he know *locks*. I seen him open one a them combination footlocker locks yistiddy wid a shoestring! He could teach you mo' about locks while you in here than you *ever* learn in the street.

"An' don' you jes' hang aroun' wid de culluds. They's plenty white cons 'll tell you what they know if you treat 'em right. Right here's where you can *better* yoself. You ain't got foevah. Next time you pull a job, you wanna come back here? You talk to some a them *smart* cons that ain't always blowin' off their mouf; they tell you what you done wrong on them jobs you already done. You gotta use yo' time to make sho' you don't get caught no mo'. Now you mine my words. I *know!*"

"Yes indeed," I thought with a sigh, "there's nothing like education for the perfection of the mind and the refinement of the spirit."

By mid-February the problem of how to study and write was worsening. The dormitory was a little more crowded and somewhat noisier than before. Unfortunately, some of my fellow inhabitants, getting to know me better, made increasing claims on my time for proofreading of their letters, aid in letter writing, settlement of factual disputes, and advice on personal problems. There were wretched fellows doing "hard time" for whom the principal relief was wasting another's time in endless talk, usually autobiographical. I seemed to receive a large share of such confidences. It would have been like denying bread to the starving to refuse a sympathetic ear, because, at least during the telling, the guy grew in his own estimation and probably believed his rationale of his life story. The trouble was that I never had enough time to read or write and do the things I wanted, and the pathetic futility of those earbendings became quite frustrating.

The problem was not that I couldn't concentrate sufficiently to keep out the distractions, but rather that some solitude was a positive need if I were to feel really alive. Solitude I hadn't had for nearly three months. I felt as though I'd become a walking storage warehouse of unfinished thoughts and unexplored feelings which had been hurriedly shelved owing to inappropriate surroundings.

The news of the spy exchange of Gary Powers for Colonel Rudolf Abel was of interest to me, partly because of the chance that it might be a significant overture by Khrushchev for better relations with the West and partly because, while still in AO, I had received what I believed to be a bona fide communication from Colonel Abel (a.k.a. Willy Fisher), the Soviet master spy who was imprisoned in Atlanta and who was apparently much respected there for his brains and strong personality. While I was waiting to go to supper, a medium-sized, middle-aged man whom I took to be a Mafioso came over to me and asked if I were Scales. He then introduced himself by an Italian name and said that he had lived near Abel in Atlanta and had been asked by him to give me a message. "He says to tell you he knows that you and he disagree on many things, but he would like to send you his greetings, as one political prisoner to another, and convey his admiration and respect for your courage and adherence to principle. Now that's exactly what he said. He made me repeat it back to him till I got it right." He then described Abel as a most magnetic figure who made doing time easier for everyone who knew him. I thanked the man but never had a chance to talk to him again because he left in a prison bus for points west shortly afterward. Besides, I was sure the FBI or the warden or some of his stooles would love to cook up some tie between a Soviet agent and me. So I had resolved to be very cautious about any response to the colonel's courtesy.

During the next visit Gladys told me that McNeill Smith was meeting with high officials in the Department of Justice to ask for a reduction of my sentence and that he would visit me afterward. We discussed my situation: Gladys was optimistic, as usual; I was pessimistic, as usual.

I had just learned at lunch that the *New York Mirror* had printed an article by Fulton Lewis, Jr., opposing clemency in my case. It was my feeling that the American people would eventually, in some slurred way, again disapprove (as they had done with the Alien and Sedition Acts) the banning of political viewpoints, but I feared that the change would come at some time after my sentence had run its course. Still, we were carrying the ball on the issue, and it was a good fight; so we should take what joy we could in that. It was one of the few meaningful things about the whole case: opposition to absurd bigotry enacted into law, corrupting the courts, and destroying the lives of the victims.

McNeill Smith, after spending some time at the Department of Justice and conferring with Deputy Attorney General Katzenbach, had made a comfortless, sleepless trip in heavy snow to Lewisburg to confer with me. I felt quite pessimistic about prospects of clemency after Mac's report on his soundings. Katzenbach was no more impressed, he said, with one's having left the Communist Party than with a burglar who had renounced stealing—a brilliant analogy arrived at by applying criminal law to unpopular political beliefs.

The department was apparently divided on the Scales case: Robert Kennedy was sympathetic to clemency appeals, but J. Edgar Hoover (whose spokesman

Katzenbach seemingly was) insisted on his definition of an *ex*-Communist. This involved a 180-degree turn: what had been good must become bad, and vice versa; names of old friends and associates must be named, regardless of cost to them, in order to show one's "sincerity." According to Katzenbach, old-school-tie loyalty to former associates was unacceptable. But I, he said, could be released in a matter of days if I would name just a "token" number of names. Mac explained that he felt obligated as my attorney to bring this proposition to me. I thanked him and said I'd rot in the clink before I'd accept such a proposal. That business out of the way, the rest of the visit was pleasant, and Mac was altogether charming.

23

A Bum Rap

O ften I was asked, by inmates and others, after a certain minimal acquaintance, what my crime was. A sort of composite of the conversation went like this:

Q. What are you in for?

A. I'm in for six years.

Q. No, I mean *why* are you in?

A. Because of my political views.

Q. You're kidding! Nobody goes to jail for what he thinks. What do you mean?

A. I'm in for being a "knowing" member of an organization advocating the violent overthrow of the government.

Q. What organization?

A. The Communist Party.

Q. Why do you advocate violence?

A. I don't and never have.

Q. But the Party does?

A. Not that I know of. If it ever did, it was before I joined it in 1939.

Q. But the government claims the Party advocates violence, and you are a member of the Party, right?

A. I was when I was indicted in 1954, but I had left the Party a year before I was convicted in 1958.

Q. Why did you leave?

A. Because Khrushchev's speech about Stalin proved that Stalinism was most of the things I had said it wasn't, and the suppression of the Hungarian Revolution and the American Party's attitude toward it completed the disillusionment.

Q. Well, I didn't think the government could put you in jail for what you *thought*. I thought you had to do something or conspire to do something. Then you really are in jail because of your beliefs?

A. No, not because of my present beliefs, but because of my past beliefs—or rather—no, that's not right either; I'm in jail for beliefs that I never remotely held. I'm in jail for a belief in violence as a political principle, which a single paid informer said I announced to him in 1948, after an acquaintance of approximately a half hour. But of course, that isn't quite it either; that's just the way a politically ambitious prosecutor secured my conviction. The real reason is that I once had a belief (which I made no bones about) that the Communist Party was out to build the brotherhood of man.

At that point the whole business would sound so farfetched that I wouldn't even have believed it myself—if I hadn't been there in jail. So I'd change the subject. After all, the most ruefully sarcastic jailhouse joke is the cry "I'm in on a bum rap!"

In addition to being asked some of those honest questions, I received the attention during my sojourn in prison of a large number of would-be informants. Who sent them was uncertain, though some appeared to be inspired by the FBI. They were constantly implying that I was still in the Party, and they praised the way Reds stuck together, in the hope of hearing me praise Communism and the Communist Party. Some were fairly adroit; others were hopelessly inept.

I had a consistent policy toward the likes of these (unless they were so gross and clumsy as to preclude any discussion). I would be sure that a third person I trusted was listening, if possible, and I always spoke my views truthfully and quite the way I would to my closest friends. Generally, I kept those that my instinctive "radar" warned me against at arm's length.

In the dormitory this was rather difficult. Rat-face, the shifty-eyed inmate who lived a couple of bunks away, had a long sentence to serve and thought that he might ingratiate himself with the prison administration if he could provide them with information that I was agitating or preaching Communism. Fawning, pretending admiration, doing little kindnesses, constantly underfoot and continually inquisitive, he became a serious nuisance. Then suddenly he disappeared for five months. He worked "in industry" (i.e., in a metal furniture factory in the prison, where he received wages and considerable time off his sentence; of course, close-confinement prisoners like me were not even considered for such privileges). He had apparently not confined his ratting activities to any limited area. He had become known in the plant as a consistent stoolie for the hacks against all and sundry. One day someone removed nearly all his teeth and most of his lower jaw with a heavy iron bar in the presence of a half dozen inmates, and yet no one saw it happen. When he returned, he looked like a leftover prop from a horror movie and seemed to have given up on me.

Another would-be stoolie at least had politics as his excuse. I had found out through a Black Muslim acquaintance that this one had been newly recruited by the members of George Lincoln Rockwell's American Nazi Party who were doing time at Lewisburg for various violent crimes. They considered it an obligation, I was told, to do in a "Commie" (or "ex-Commie"), if at all possible. However, this particular one (volubly anti-Negro, anti-Semitic, anti-Italian, and anti-Hispanic) found himself isolated. He was rather crafty and quite persistent, all the same. One day I got him alone and said, "Look, you've asked me about my being a Communist a half dozen times and I told you I broke with them years ago. That's the truth. It's none of your goddam business anyway, and I don't even care whether you believe it. But I do know your gang is out to stir up race trouble in here, and I can make plenty of trouble for you, starting with you and your buddy 'Red' [who worked in the storeroom]. I don't go for your 'superior race' crap, and I don't want anything from you or your bunch. I'm serving my time and I want to be left alone. Now if you have any of that 'guts' and 'manhood' you're always bragging about, quit trying to rat me out, tell 'Red' to quit his two-bit backbiting on the job, and remember we're all inmates. If you don't want it that way, I'll meet your whole Nazi Party, one at a time, in the storeroom and knock the shit out of you! Just name the date and time."

I left him without waiting for an answer. The bravado worked. The would-be informer stopped his questions and was polite, distant, and respectful. "Red," a southerner, hopelessly blighted by every imaginable form of bigotry, became positively obsequious in his efforts to please me. The other Nazis kept a respectful distance. If I'd had to carry out my threat, I might well have succeeded, even though I knew nothing about fighting, because those *Übermenschen* were a laughable, scrawny quartet.

In February I wrote to Gladys on the twelfth anniversary of our marriage: "By far the worst thing about prison is the separation from you and Barbara, and yet the only thing that makes it bearable is the existence of you two." Then the following month I had occasion to send a proud commendation to Barbara, who had entered a citywide competitive admissions examination for Hunter College High School, a superlative girls' school run by the New York City Board of Higher Education. She passed easily and was admitted.

Meantime, visits at Lewisburg, according to custom, lasted a full day, which allowed time to build up an easy atmosphere for talk, and especially small talk, with the little girl. Three hours a month for visits was, however, the rule—and suddenly the rule was rigorously imposed. Such a change, seemingly minor, could make a crushing difference to inmates whose families visited them. But an explanation of the loss of amenities was rarely given. On one occasion it was rumored that drugs had been smuggled to an inmate during a visit, and months of increasingly onerous searches followed. Most often, according to word that came down through security officers, it was an ugly mood of the gloomy warden— "a wild hair"—that caused so much suffering for inmates and families.

No wonder, then, that my birthday late in March seemed bleak enough, though I was pleasantly wakened with a "happy birthday" and a couple of useful and thoughtful gifts from Lucille's husband, who had somehow remembered the date.

The campaign for my release had stepped up, and in my letters I mentioned with pleasure receiving favorable articles in the *Harvard Crimson* (February); a *New York Times* editorial of February 7; an editorial in the *Washington Post* in conjunction with a long letter from Joseph Rauh, the prominent attorney and leading spirit of Americans for Democratic Action (February 15); and an editorial in the *St. Louis Post-Dispatch,* which also carried the Rauh letter (February 26). I was especially pleased that Arthur Miller, Mike Wallace, and Thurman Arnold were among the newest signers of the petition to get me out. I was also pleasantly surprised to see a large paid ad entirely concerned with my case which appeared in the *Washington Post* of February 26, titled "Wanted: Presidential Clemency." It was a public service editorial from the International Latex Corporation, signed by A. N. Spanel, Chairman.

A group of inmates (including some Smith Act Communists) had founded some years earlier the Literary Forum, as it was called, for the purpose of discussing cultural matters on a serious level. Through ups and downs it had persisted over the years under the supportive supervision of Mr. Adams, the librarian, meeting from 7:00 to 9:00 P.M. in the library. Since my arrival, the forum had become chiefly a one-man performance by Harry Gold, who would ramble on, mostly unprepared, about some book he had read in his youth or recently. Discussion would be desultory at best, and attendance had dropped to three or four inmates each week. Adams felt that he was no longer justified in closing the library for two hours for such a small gathering. He asked me to take over planning and running the forum and said that if I would, he in turn would find a graceful and painless way of easing Harry out.

Harry Gold, as a young physicist, had testified that he was the link between Klaus Fuchs, the atom spy in Britain, and the Rosenbergs, testimony that was very damaging to the latter. He himself had received a thirty-year sentence and had been at Lewisburg about ten years. Small, perpetually frightened, he spent nearly all his time in the hematology lab. Although he was dull and commonplace and displayed a strikingly banal set of viewpoints in his "book reviews" at the forum, a legend had spread in Lewisburg (doubtless encouraged by Harry) that he possessed one of the great scientific minds of the age—somewhat on a par with Einstein's. He masked his fear of the general population by an apparent devotion to his hospital duties, at which he worked long and irregular hours.

Some of my inmate acquaintances, including Carlos and Andy, told a story of how several hospital workers (Gold among them) had filched a chicken from the dining hall and were cooking it in an instrument sterilizer. The delicious smell led a hack to look in unexpectedly. Gold panicked, turned pasty white, and began stuttering incoherently and pointing an accusing finger at the other inmates. While Carlos kicked Gold devastatingly but unobtrusively in the behind, Andy and the others cordially invited the hack to join them for a chicken sandwich and coffee. The hack declined with thanks, suggested they open a window so the smell wouldn't get all over the hospital, wished them goodnight, and withdrew. Gold, since that incident, had withdrawn even more, surfacing chiefly at the Literary Forum, where he basked in the worship of three or four idolaters.

To provide something interesting, informative, and well prepared every week for the forum was not only a tremendous task but would require great support and participation from friends and acquaintances. Nonetheless, I tentatively accepted the challenge out of a desire to see something done well in Lewisburg to counter the ingrained negligence in every aspect of prison life.

I decided that the first program I'd undertake would be an abridged performance of Puccini's *La Bohème,* using a record of excerpts I had found in the Education Department. First I had to get something like a high-fidelity phonograph. With the support of Mr. Adams and Mr. Graham (Andy's boss in the Education Department), and with the help of a friendly southerner in the Electronic Repair Department, I was able to repair—nearly rebuild—a quite old amplifier and speaker. We created a real hi-fi set that made a splendid sound in the huge library, well worth the infinite sweat and red tape involved.

Reflections on the Supreme Court and the Communist Party commingle in a letter I wrote to Gladys on April 1:

> I suppose you've followed Mr. Justice Whittaker's retirement, and perhaps you thought as I did that if it had come a year earlier, lots of five-to-four decisions might have had better endings.
>
> I've just been reading of the arraignment of Gus Hall and Ben Davis. It's ironic that these two empty shells should be provided by the government with a gift of spurious dignity through their prosecution under such an appalling law. Inevitably

they must acquire a certain aura of rightness only because the government victimizes them with a law that is so *wrong,* so anti-democratic. Can you think of two less likely defenders of democratic practices? Yet that's the billing the government insists on giving them.

I saw in the *Washington Post* that "recent estimates" give the Communist Party 8,000 to 10,000 members. I believe that figure is inflated and that half of what they do have is sixty years old, or over. And yet, in order to suppress this bunch, our lawmakers are willing to undermine most of the Bill of Rights!

Ben Davis had been a brilliant man of great capacity. A Negro lawyer from Georgia, the well-educated son of a famous father, he had become the Party's leading Negro Communist by the forties, when he was elected to the New York City Council on the Communist ticket.

While I was sitting in the Winston-Salem jail after my arrest, Davis had written a friendly letter to me, and he had done so again after my first trial when bail had been revoked. It was the late spring, summer, and fall of 1956 that I became disillusioned with him. At first he had seemed inclined to support Foster and crush the questioning opposition by weight of his and Foster's authority; then he shifted his position and abandoned Foster; and throughout the summer and fall I felt that he had become pathetically unsure of himself while making a loud and ominous noise—the ruin of a fine man.

Gus Hall, whom I had known since the late forties, had seemed to me a rock of unpretentious common sense and honesty. However, when he had finished his Smith Act sentence, he returned to lead the Party with a sectarianism, a pro-Soviet devotion, and a dullness that startled those who had known him earlier.

Shortly after moving into my new semihonor quarters, H-3, with its four-foot high partitions fencing me off from neighbors, I was on my way past my old jungle quarters when once more Tony M——'s earsplitting "Hey C-O-M-R-A-A-D-E!" rang out behind me. I turned and went back to where Tony was standing in the stairwell of E dorm (the jungle).

"What's up, Tony?"

"Well, I wanted to say goodbye, Scales. I'm coming up for trial in a month and they'll probably be shippin' me back to West Street tomorrow. But before I go I want you to meet some of the boys." Tony turned and said in a lordly and peremptory manner to two young fellows, "Go round up the boys. NOW!" They were off like the wind.

Tony briefly questioned me about how things were going and commented, "I heard you was doin' OK for yourself; gotta coupla good buddies, got outa the jungle, got a good job—you're doin' all right."

"How does it look for your trial, Tony?"

"Not good; not bad; you can read about it in the papers."

Meanwhile "the boys" had been arriving in accord with some sort of pecking order. The lowly ones came almost at a run, the more important ones at a walk, and last of all, at a leisurely roll, The Chin, who was (though far outranked by Tony) the operative head of things at Lewisburg.

"Fellers," said Tony to the assemblage which filled the stairwell to the second landing, "This here is Scales. He's the guy what put me on to The Book." There was a murmur of appreciative recognition; then came individual introductions and a prodigious amount of handshaking (mostly real grips, not limp-fish jobs). Last of all, The Chin, whose hand was the size of a small ham, squashed mine, applied his other hand for emphasis, looked me in the eye and said solemnly, "Anyting at all, Scales, *Anyting* at all!"

Tony said, "Now look out for my buddy," to a general nodding of heads. I said that it was a pleasure to meet them since I had already seen most of them with their families in the visiting room. This brought a deluge of compliments on my "beautiful little girl" and "really classy wife." Then the meeting dissolved. I wished Tony well, received a crushing handshake and a shattering slap on the back, and went my way.

Gladys sent me another box of books, which I had to put aside temporarily because of my preoccupation with my opera program. I did, however, find time, in correspondence with Max Gordon, to reassess the probable time of my release, estimating that with good luck I might be out by the end of 1965. To Gladys I recommended that she pace herself accordingly while living as fully as possible, and I urged that she not let our daughter feel that she was playing second fiddle to an empty chair.

The *La Bohème* evening finally took place. My preparations were most elaborate: several readings of the libretto in Italian (with a good Italian dictionary handy) until nearly all of the music came to life in my memory; then a reading of every conceivable commentary in the library from Grove's Dictionary to Kobbe's opera book; and a couple of additional hearings of the recording, which consisted of excerpts from the 1946 Toscanini performance with Licia Albanese and Jan Peerce.

I drew on my recollection of many live performances at the Met and of Murger's novel, from which the libretto was fashioned. Finally I began to work out in my mind how to hold an inmate audience, none of whom had probably ever heard an opera and all of whom were probably considerably prejudiced against the form as a pretentious, earsplitting amusement of the idle rich or "longhairs"—largely because of the silly nonsense which Hollywood usually made of it.

I planned every word I would say. It had to sound conversational and not didactic; it had to be informative without being an encapsulated dose of facts; there had to be implied enthusiasm and yet no value judgments (like "this is great" or "this is a beautiful tune" or "this is very moving").

At seven o'clock about twenty-four inmates seated themselves in two long rows of chairs near the side wall, roughly twenty-five feet from the hi-fi set so as to get the best sonic effect. I stood next to the set. After a brief introduction, I described the action and then paraphrased the words to be sung. While playing the first aria, I studied the faces in my audience—as rigid as marble busts and apparently as responsive.

Despite a twinge of despair growing somewhere in my viscera, I pushed on with an overwhelming single-mindedness, as though I were Puccini, minus a piano, trying to convince a group of influential producers of the power of his work. I sang (with no voice) bits of the Italian text so that they would recognize them when they heard them. I whistled or hummed what the orchestra was doing at significant moments. I acted and mimed the decisive dramatic passages. And when I played the recorded portions, I was as enraptured as if I had written, sung, and conducted the music myself.

So intense was my involvement that the seeming lack of audience response never fully caught up with me until Mimi was singing out her life in the last act. Then all my misgivings fell in on me. "My God! what a colossal bomb this has been. While I've been carried away, they're bored to the point of paralysis!" I looked at Adams, seated out of sight of the audience behind rows of bookshelves, leaning forward in his chair. "He can get himself a new man. I'm not letting myself in for this zombie treatment ever again!"

As Rodolfo was crying out in agony over his beloved's death, I was thinking only of how quickly I could get the hi-fi set and the record put away and retreat to my quarters.

At the last chord the audience rose as one, applauding (a sound I had seldom heard at Lewisburg). Several had tears in their eyes; a tall, gangly eccentric wept openly. I was mobbed. "This is the best thing I've been to in five years at Lewisburg!" "You've just made my whole week." "How about *Tosca?*" shouted an Italian-American from Syracuse. "Vy not *Carmain?*" implored an elderly Corsican drug pusher. A dozen volunteers hoisted the heavy set up three marble steps, where Adams locked it away. I was congratulated, backslapped, handshaken—and bewildered. "This was the biggest, most-attentive audience, and the best program since the forum began," said Adams. "It was just grand!"

I returned to my quarters like a sleepwalker, in company with Andy and Carlos. When I expressed my earlier certainty that people must have been bored to death, Andy explained that a jailhouse audience was usually fishy-eyed and poker-faced. Carlos said, "Hell, I knew you had 'em in the first five minutes. Nobody moved a muscle. I didn't either. Most of them have probably never been to anything anywhere so thought-out and real—certainly not in Lewisburg!"

"Let's face it," Andy said, "After this you're a celebrity. But can you keep up that quality without killing yourself?"

Back in bed in my cubicle, I had a victory celebration in private: I had been able to bring something beautiful to light at that dung heap and had helped communicate it to a handful of others. It was a great personal satisfaction, but more important, it was profoundly subversive of the whole tone and spirit of prison existence—of the Lewisburg way of death.

One Saturday night in H-3, being weary, I went to bed early, gave my neighbor Tomás my letter to mail with the hack, turned my face to the wall, and slept through the count and lights-out. I awoke at about eleven o'clock to a drunken uproar. A violent brawl was going on in a cubicle at the far corner from my bunk; furniture was smashing and glass breaking. Soon the hacks arrived, turned on the lights, and hauled two of the "D.C. Gang" (Negroes from the District of Columbia), who were slugging away at each other, to the hole, which was then a solitary basement cell with no furniture and no plumbing facilities, save a flushable hole in the floor.

After the hacks had gone, it was obvious from the silly, blurry talk that most of the fellows were sloshed. Everyone who said anything at all sounded boozed up, except for Tomás, always the responsible family man. He whispered furiously to me, "These son-of-bitch keep on, we lose our visit, then I *kill* someone!" I reassured him, and finally, as things quieted down, we were able to sleep. The next morning Tomás described for me how, after lights out, some of the guys had reached up to the dish-shaped, clouded-glass light fixtures and had taken out condoms heavy with home brew, made from raisins and prunes, and had proceeded to pour everybody who wanted some a full tin cup of the mess.

From Andy and Carlos I learned that making home brew was an ancient tradition in the pen. To make the "mash," raisins, prunes, potatoes, beets, apples, oatmeal, or almost anything organic would serve. Then there had to be some sort of container for it to "cook" in and "harden up." The remaining problem was that it gave off a powerful odor of fermentation and could be detected in a closed room.

The morning after the drunken fistfight, a "booze-detection squad" of three hack specialists with bloodhound noses arrived and checked over every inch of the dorm. They found two leftover condoms of the brew in the light fixtures and a third at the bottom of a barrel where the inmates placed their dirty socks to be laundered. The bootleggers had thought that the odor of the socks would mask that of the mash, but those specialists were formidable. While I was in H dorm, they won every subsequent round.

An unsolved mystery lingered: how did the bootleggers get the condoms? Certainly they were not made available at Lewisburg for prophylactic purposes, inasmuch as several known epidemics of gonorrhea occurred during my stay there.

Tony M——, meanwhile, had been sent back to West Street, as anticipated, to await trial. About five weeks later, The Chin stopped me in the hall for a chat. He was slightly formal but friendly and wanted to know how things were going with me. As we talked, it was apparent that he knew everything about my situation. He knew that I had a good grasp on my storeroom job; he spoke approvingly of my handling of the American Nazi boys; he congratulated me on my "opera thing" and said that his grandfather had been an opera nut and had lots of Caruso records; he knew of the *New York Post* and *New York Times* editorials in my behalf. He questioned me politely about my semihonor quarters, H-3, and asked whether it was quiet and if I had had any trouble with anyone. He also complimented me on my wife, who never missed a visit, and my beautiful little girl, whom he had seen in the visiting room.

I was amazed that he knew the names of many of the inmates in my quarters and was so well informed about everything. Andy and Carlos said that as the leader of the best-organized group in prison, he carried considerable weight with the administration, which made concessions to him in return for his services in keeping the peace and acting as a barometer of inmate sentiment.

There were other organized groupings as well. The Puerto Ricans had some cohesion, but they seemed to be split between "straight" guys and homosexuals and lacked organization and leadership.

Negroes were even more fragmented. They all shared a general loyalty toward another black-skinned inmate, but they fell apart in many other ways. There were different homosexual groupings: aggressive pederasts with a preference for "white ass" and homosexuals who quietly had homosexual relations with other Negroes. There were straight guys who shunned the homosexuals and numbered whites among their friends, and there was also a small but rapidly growing group of Muslims. The Muslims were intensely antiwhite and sectarian. They had gradually won the right to hold religious services. Though they probably numbered only twenty when I arrived at Lewisburg, their numbers and influence steadily grew. They were straight, refused pork, and observed endless rituals collectively and individually. They hated "whitey" and all his works, and this common opposition gave them a revolutionary purpose and dedication which undoubtedly saved many of them from the gradual personal disintegration so common in prison. They derived strength and purpose from their intense racism. Aside from beards, they were generally distinguished by notable individual dignity, cleanliness, and neatness.

At the opposite pole was the dreaded "D.C. Gang." The members were mostly between twenty-seven and thirty-five years old; they had been convicted in the District of Columbia; and most of them had spent more than half their lives in the federal prison system, usually starting with the National Training School near Washington, graduating to various reformatories, then to the penitentiary for youthful offenders at Chillicothe, Ohio, and finally to the big-time maximum-security pen nearest Washington—Lewisburg. Most were in for violent crimes: rape, deadly assault, homicide, armed robbery, and arson. Since the District of Columbia had no equivalent of state courts or penitentiaries, such convicts were channeled into the federal prison system, where, among other things, they served to warm up considerably the climate of senseless violence. Some were severely retarded; some were psychopaths; all were dangerous. Apparently without exception they had experienced pederasty very early in life, both passively and aggressively. So the term *D.C. Gang* also had its sexual connotation.

I had a D.C. neighbor in the cubicle across the corridor from me. Dan was light-skinned, about six feet five inches, 225 pounds, and rather slow-witted. I had noticed him because he regularly carried on a deafening after-lights-out conversation with four or five other D.C.-ers around the room and had once described how, on the first night of one of his infrequent and brief intervals out of jail, he had jumped into bed with his then wife, rolled her over on her belly, and sodomized her, "jes' outa habit, and she squealed like a scalded hawg!"

One night I returned to my cubicle from the library, where I had been working furiously on my next forum program, and found a note on my bed. I read it in disbelief; it was an unsigned, semiliterate mash note that ran: "I seen your bare ass last night while you was asleep and I watched a long time and almost raped you cause I wanted you so bad. I bin watchin you in the shower and the way you walk. Won't you be mine?"

I saw Dan watching me with a silly smile. I walked into his cubicle.

"Is this yours?"

"Yeah," he grinned.

"I guess you made a mistake. I don't go for guys at all. Never have. Never will. I've always been half crazy for women as long as I can remember."

"You putting me on! The way you walk graceful-like and all them books and things—you *must* be queer!"

"You couldn't be wronger. So here's your note. Let's shake hands and forget the whole thing."

"Well, OK, but you sure fooled me." And he offered a huge, limp hand.

I gave it a brisk, hard clasp. As I turned to go I said, "By the way, Dan, I'm glad you didn't try to jump me last night. I keep a razor blade under my pillow and whatever you might have done to me, I think I could have killed you."

"Well, I'll be a *motha*-fuckah!" he laughed, with genuine good humor.

I was still vibrating violently inside, like someone who had just stepped back from the edge of a precipice, when there was a tap on the partition separating me from Tomás, for whom I had done many favors, from writing letters (his English was faulty) to soothing his worries about his family. Tomás was a passionate family man, sickened by the sounds of sodomizing to be heard in the quarters almost nightly. His dark, violent, leonine face appeared over the partition contorted with fury. "I heard!" he whispered. "He try anything, I cut his guts out!" I assured him the danger was over. But after that, I was hard put to keep the peace between the two, because Tomás's hostility was as wholehearted as his loyalty. Tomás had been suckered into driving the getaway car in a bank job because he thought he could thereby give his wife and children a better home and "not hurt no one."

24

Publicity and
a Parole

While I was working on the next forum programs, which I would conduct myself, I was busily arranging what I hoped would be more interesting programs of the traditional sort—book reviews followed by discussion and the like. I corralled a bright, rather unstable young man, a *Catholic Worker* disciple of Dorothy Day, and asked him to review a recent exposé of the auto industry's program of planned obsolescence, false advertising, shoddy engineering, and usurious financing. The lad, who was homosexual and rather timid, was lucid, witty, knowledgeable, and quite indignant about the frauds perpetrated on car buyers.

When the question period opened, a man about thirty, doing his second "bit" for mail fraud, arose and said, "I don't understand what you're getting so hot about. We're all cons here; we're *all* criminals. How else are we gonna make it unless we take it out of the next guy, the same as these big auto companies do? Sure, they're crooks, but so are we. I've been a con man all my life. That's what it's all about. What's wrong with that?"

The young reviewer was nonplussed. Another con in the audience came to his aid. The man, a bank robber getting "short," said that when he got out he would be able to afford a car after pulling his next job, and he didn't want to get taken by the big car makers. Besides, he robbed *banks,* he said, not people. Finally the discussion got off, blessedly, onto the engineering deficiencies of the current cars, and the program ended much to my relief. I was glad I'd be doing *La Traviata* the next Sunday.

I had been shocked by the unchallenged defense of criminality, but I had learned a little more about the alienation and loneliness that a political (or noncriminal) prisoner can feel in prison. And I also learned a dimension of my audience I had never really thought about. The practical idea occurred to me that at my own programs I would not invite too much discussion. The prisoner began to weigh, ironically, the advisability of restraint.

By late spring, however, I felt myself to be a veteran con. I had learned a great deal about prison life. I had long since acquired, from simple observation, many basic survival maxims. In fact, I could have compiled a book of them.

For example:

Don't intrude on a twosome you're not acquainted with under any circumstances. Much prison violence is caused by homosexuals who think someone is trying to "beat their time."

Avoid the proximity of obstreperous, belligerent sorts. They often want the satisfaction of a fistfight and care little who their adversary is; the nearest person will do fine. And then both will be sent to the hole.

Don't do any favors for strangers, unless you have at least observed them closely. The wildest misunderstandings often result from paranoid reactions to well-intended kindnesses.

Cultivate glassy eyes and a poker face with any security hacks, especially when they're shaking you down. They look for inmate reactions with a penetrating eye, and if they detect any they don't like—and they don't like *any* reactions from inmates—they'll "shoot" you (cite you for disciplinary action) on the spot.

Attract the attention of security hacks as little as possible. If one of them happens to be in a vile mood—a not infrequent condition of the species— he'll pick on the nearest guy who looks familiar.

When possible, avoid asking questions of hacks. They probably won't know the answers, and having their ignorance exposed often infuriates them.

When possible, avoid asking questions of inmates. They probably won't know the answers either, but they will readily give you an earful of misinformation. If you ask a question of ten inmates, you will probably receive ten contradictory wrong answers.

And so on.

However, it took constant association with two such prison-wise stalwarts as Carlos and Andy for me to begin to realize the areas in which I was ignorant of many all-important subtleties.

To take a complicated example, there was the question of race relations, on which I considered myself to be an expert. I had been a militant integrationist, a fighter for equal rights, and an outspoken opponent of racist slurs since my teens. Besides, I had always liked Negroes generally and sought their company; in particular, I had come to love and admire a considerable number of them on a personal basis.

When I came to Lewisburg, the Bureau of Prisons was beginning to clean house and had cracked down on at least the appearance of racist treatment of Negroes. There was no official segregation—quite the opposite. Yet in the huge double-building dining room with four doors and chow lines leading to four cafeteria-style serving banks, there was still a residual, voluntary segregation. From the left, the first line was almost all Negro; the second had about 40 or 50 percent Negroes; the third had a rare sprinkling of Negroes; the fourth was almost all white. It was entirely a matter of choice which line one went down and where one sat.

Andy and Carlos tactfully informed me when I first "hit population" that for me frequently to go down the first line (which I did, just to break the solid black phalanx) was understood by Negro homosexual studs to mean that I was offering myself sexually. I was aghast and stayed out of the first line. No such implications were involved in going down lines two and three (which the three of us usually used). Line four was used by relatively aggressive racists (southern or otherwise), but they were such a small handful that there was no racist stigma attached to using even that line. Seating (each table accommodated four) was far less segregated and took place quite naturally.

Nevertheless, race relations, while placid on the surface, were often near the boiling point. In the recreation halls, where I rarely went, were several TV sets with chairs in place in front of them. For certain favorite TV programs there was apparently a prearrangement by which several strong Negroes, as soon as "inside recreation" was announced over the PA system, would dominate the seats in front of the sets and tell whites that they were reserved until all had been occupied by Negroes. TV watching, competitive sports, and dormitory quarrels provided situations where racial stresses rushed to the surface and often threatened to erupt into massive violence.

Years later, I was amazed to hear that my friend Frank Wilkinson had made a speech saying that the United States had solved the problem of race relations in its prison system. Carlos and Andy would have guffawed cynically at that. I realized, however, that Frank had spent his time in two easygoing, minimum-security prisons with the most noncriminal, nonviolent prison populations imaginable, and it might very well have seemed to him that race relations were going along without friction. But that was not the situation inside Lewisburg in 1962.

I was enlightened in numerous other ways by my two buddies. One day at lunch while we were eating and conversing, a violent fight broke out between two inmates on the serving line: first there were loud, violent threats; then trays crashed to the floor; then they went at each other with table knives raised over their heads; and finally, hacks rushed from everywhere and hauled them off to the hole. I was appalled. "My God, I thought they were going to kill each other!"

Andy and Carlos laughed. Neither had more than glanced at the fracas. "Not a chance," said Andy. "Such punks never take chances. They yell first so that all the hacks start running to them; then, when they see the hacks are nearly there, they start the overhead knife act so the hacks can grab the knives out of their hands. If they meant business they would have held the knives low and jabbed at the guts. And how much damage could they have done anyway with these dull, blunt table knives?"

A week or two later, in shocked tones, I broached the subject of the attempted suicide, in a cellblock, of an inmate we all knew slightly. "Yeah, I saw him in the hospital this morning," said Carlos. "He cut just one wrist very superficially. I talked to the cellblock officer on duty, who said the guy had timed it for just two minutes before he was due to make his rounds and hung his wrist out of the bed so it would show and there'd be a little puddle of blood when he shined his light through the door."

"Aw, you're just cynical," I said, half joking.

"I ain't so cynical. Hell, June-Bug, there's a lot of paper tigers in here and you might as well know them. You'll rest easier." Then he added with a grin, his eyes twinkling through his large black-rimmed spectacles, as he flexed his skinny, ninety-eight pound physique, "Now you take me—I'm a *real* tiger!"

Meanwhile, a number of other things occupied me. In May I was awarded "meritorious good time" (as far as I knew, the first such award for a Smith Act prisoner), which would bring me out of jail about five months earlier than I had figured, possibly by the end of 1965.

Having been approved for honor quarters (J dormitory) early in June, I waited eagerly for a vacancy. The honor consisted of not having been "shot" (reported for disciplinary action) for six months and of having received a generally favorable report.

I took time to follow the newspapers closely. The campaign for my freedom, pursued incessantly by Gladys, was reaching an important point with the filing of a petition to President Kennedy asking executive clemency. That petition was delivered to Attorney General Robert Kennedy on June 11.

The effect among inmates depended on what paper they read. Those reading the UPI story (or at least some of them) seemed to think that I had somewhat demeaned myself by describing myself as a "person who has not been and is not now dangerous." Those who read the *Times* story had an opposite impression. I didn't care much because I felt that press reactions to any event or statement, and public reaction to the press's account, were unpredictable and mostly meaningless. And I never attached too great importance to "public opinion" (whatever that is).

From my first days of imprisonment there was a general awareness that I was jailed because I would not "rat" on my friends. This made me a minor hero, especially to the Italian-Americans. As time wore on, it also became widely known, particularly through the Wechsler columns and editorials in the *New York Post,* that I remained in prison because of this refusal. This added to the esteem in which I was held by those who read newspapers, and it produced several side effects.

Because of my reputation, I was the frequent recipient of extraordinary confidences about criminal actions from inmates I scarcely knew, given trustingly, apparently without a qualm, which would have been most damaging to them had the information fallen into the hands of prison authorities. These matters were usually revealed when the fellow prisoner needed some jailhouse-lawyer advice. I treated such information as though a lawyer-client relationship existed, and I never revealed it to anyone.

There was a widespread supposition that since I was so firm about not naming names of present and former Communists I must be well taken care of by my "gang" (that is, the Communist Party). Some believed my accounts of how the Party leader had sabotaged my defense efforts and left me deeply in debt, debt incurred at their insistence. Some did not.

Many cons could not conceive of such stubbornness arising from mere self-respect. They preferred to imply, with the slippery perception of a J. Edgar Hoover and a Nicholas Katzenbach, that I was *still* loyal to the Communist Party.

Lastly, I discovered, by observation and secondhand information, that those inmates who gushed most loudly in praise of my loyalty were the ones most likely to run to the security hacks to offer their services in ratting on me.

Once the publicity had gradually died down, leaving me in a more peaceful state of mind, I contemplated my future in a letter to Bernie, who was completing his Ph.D. in psychology:

> As usual my interests are widely diversified—or perhaps just unfocused. I have a great hunger for understanding, knowledge, and enjoyment of so many things— but aside from being a professional victim and prisoner, my life seems directionless. I have no realistic compulsion to *master* anything. Teaching is an impractical goal, and from what I see of others' experience (except Gladys's), largely devoid of the satisfactions I formerly sought in it. Since one must have a job and earn a living, I suppose my old trade, if it's still open to me then, is as good as any: the hours are relatively short and the pay is relatively high. But as for

anything more purposive than just earning a living, I'm rudderless. I'm too compulsively social-oriented to live the life of a hedonist (outside of prison, anyway). I don't have enough on the ball to try to be a socially useful, skilled professional at forty-five or forty-six (even if such professions were open to me—and they aren't). Still I hate to just eat and sleep and watch life dribble away as "a feverish, selfish little clod of ailments and grievances," as Bernard Shaw puts it, "complaining that the world will not devote itself to making me happy."

Meanwhile I will try to get satisfaction out of some slight signs that a small segment of the intelligentsia is in danger of having guilt feelings because our country imprisons a person, with all due process, for political views which he supposedly held at a former time, but never actually held at any time. They also serve who only sit and gripe—I hope.

Meantime, Barbara had received the highest award that her school could give. Her teachers and principal knew where her father was, and that knowledge gave the honor an additional quality: perhaps partly a demonstrative repudiation of "guilt by association," perhaps an appreciation of a gallant little girl who never told her troubles. Shortly after, when she was graduated from P.S. 125, she received the lion's share of all the prizes, marching back and forth incessantly from her seat to the platform. And to top it all off, her mother was presented with a corsage by the faculty.

Adams, the librarian, asked me to take over formally the responsibility for the Literary Forum, planning, supervising, and presiding over all the programs. That was merely recognition of what I actually had been doing for some time. My reservations concerned whether Harry Gold, who was mildly ailing, could be replaced gracefully without loss of face. No matter how low an opinion I had of him, I thought he was entitled to whatever dignity he had earned in prison. So I agreed to be "acting" head for a time. At a subsequent forum, Harry, pleading ill health and pressure of work, announced his resignation and graciously commended his successor.

The even tenor of the summer days was ruffled at one point by the warden, who, quite possibly, had gone crazy with the heat. One day he sent a lieutenant to the storeroom for me. The lieutenant escorted me forthwith to a sort of guardroom (not the warden's office), where the warden fumbled through several pieces of mail with his face contorted by rage. As soon as the lieutenant left, he exploded incoherently: "Goddam mail! Supposed to keep this black-and-white thing under control! What in hell are you getting this mail for? Don't you know this is forbidden? I won't put up with it! You'll get disciplinary measures!"

"I don't know what you're talking about, sir." Which was true enough.

"Why are you getting this mail?"

"I haven't gotten it. I don't know what it is or who it's from. I can hardly answer your question."

"It's race literature!"

"What's that?"

"It's hate stuff, stirring up trouble, colored and white—just what the bureau wants me to keep quiet. Look at this!"

I looked over several items of Ku Klux-type literature addressed to me with return addresses from Arkansas and Mississippi. "Well, what do you want me to do? It's a matter of record that I've opposed racism all my life. People that put out this sort of stuff have tried to kill me. What do you want *me* to do about it?"

"Tell them to quit sending it!"

"You want me to write to these Ku Klux outfits and tell them to quit sending this filth? They only do it to embarrass me."

"Well, do you agree to destroying this?" He seemed calmer.

"Of course."

"Well, what about this?" He shoved a couple of tracts from an evangelical, somewhat hysterical, religious sect, with a brief covering note urging me to read and be converted. It was from a couple of textile workers I had known long ago in High Point.

"Do you know them?"

I was not about to leave anyone exposed to the irrational wrath of such a lunatic, so I unhesitatingly lied, "No."

"Then why did they send it to you?"

"It's no secret where I am. Anyone with a stamp can write to me. Every month or so I get an envelope full of biblical tracts and the like from various old ladies who want to 'save my soul.' Besides, this is just harmless stuff anyway."

"Well, I'm going to issue orders to the mailroom that you're to get mail only from authorized correspondents."

"That's fine with me. I thought that was the rule anyway. *I* never asked for those Bible tracts."

"Well, if this happens again, you'll *hear* from me!" he shouted, furious again.

"If *what* happens?"

"That *race* stuff!" he roared. He signaled that the interview was over.

That man was head of a large government institution, and for all practical purposes had very nearly the power of life and death over me and every other inmate—and he was a nut.

Small wonder that life insurance companies consider imprisonment a hazardous occupation and refuse to insure prisoners.

The Lewisburg yard was large. There was an eighth of a mile of oval-shaped cinder track, two tennis courts, horseshoe-pitching areas, bocci-ball courts, a baseball diamond, a football field within the cinder track, and lots of grassy area where inmates could sit and talk or sunbathe.

When spring arrived and the weather was mild, "outside recreation" was allowed, and inmates by the hundreds would come trooping out in a variety of athletic attire, ranging from track shorts to long, knitted sweat clothes. Many also came in their regular prison garb just to take the pleasant air. Andy was usually one of the first on the tennis courts, where he reigned supreme in doubles and vied for supremacy in singles with a Long Island bank robber named Ron, twenty years his junior. Sometimes I was a tennis spectator. Most often I walked around or sat and talked with Carlos.

Old-timers generally stuck to horseshoes and bocci ball, the latter widely played by the "Italian" fellows of all ages. Many others walked for miles around the track in twos and threes. Some took no exercise at all, except to walk outside and then back to quarters. Homosexual couples frequently sat cozily on the grass near the wall, sometimes furtively holding hands. The high wall often gave back weirdly distorted echoes of the shouts and noises in the yard. Sometimes I would sit alone and watch the show.

There were three inmates, called by Andy and Carlos "the three zombies," who had an almost addictive fascination for me. I had never seen them except on the track. Two Negro men and one white, they ran ceaselessly around the cinder track, the two Negroes side by side, the white man behind them. The invariable costume was long-sleeved, long-legged, light gray sweat clothes. They were no longer young. The larger Negro, about light heavyweight size, ran with his body and head slightly forward, and both arms moved with the predictability of a windmill as he threw jabs into the air with both fists. At his side, the other Negro (ebony black) loped along with head tilted far back, chin thrust forward, his elbows high and pistoning with his steady stride.

Six feet behind came the white man, smallest of the three, teeth clenched and with an immutable look of agony on his cadaverous, sunken-eyed face. In all weather, they ran at the same steady, measured pace, never speeding up, never slowing down. Their faces were entirely expressionless, like stylized death masks, and their dead, empty eyes were fixed on space, apparently unseeing.

I observed them almost daily from early spring to late fall on their tireless, mindless, futile pursuit of that track. At first they reminded me, with some amusement, of the empty, hollow eyes of Little Orphan Annie characters. Then, as their mummified faces and blank eyes began to grow on me, I thought of Albert Ryder's eerie painting *Death at the Race Track*. Still later I began to wonder if they were not three ghostly Flying Dutchmen condemned to run that circular track through eternity. Finally, I became nearly obsessed with them as symbolic of the full horror of prison life: an endless, purposeless, measured race to oblivion.

Nearly a quarter century after leaving Lewisburg, I can still see, with eyes open or closed, that hopeless threesome running unhurriedly around that track. May they some day rest in peace.

The end of July brought a sort of joyful disaster to Andy and me: Carlos was paroled and left Lewisburg. After nearly nine years, he was a free man. For once the lard-headed parole board had slipped up and freed a man who deserved to be freed and would not return.

The last three weeks or so were both treasurable and sad. Carlos was already half out of Lewisburg, full of ebullience and future plans. When the anticipated/dreaded day came, Andy and I waved out of the Education Department windows as cocky little Carlos, wearing a blue suit made of something very much like paper, and carrying what he called a "gitaway bag," walked to the front gate, turned and waved, grinned, and left Lewisburg forever.

Andy and I, in a depression for days, were somewhat cheered when Van Graham, the assistant superintendent of education and Andy's boss and good friend, received from Carlos a joyful letter from North Carolina, obviously intended mainly for us, radiating self-confidence and humor. But we had barely been able to adjust to Carlos's departure when Andy became ill and had to have his gallbladder removed. Since all postoperative care would be in the Lewisburg hospital, the dangers were immense. I was as concerned as I was helpless.

As on many another occasion, Van Graham came through splendidly. A man full of compassion and patience, he did far more psychotherapy than did the contemptible psychiatrist and psychologist, who merely dispensed tranquilizers and other pills—just by being human and accessible. He called Andy's family daily, visited Andy several times a day, and even smuggled me in for a couple of visits. Graham also called me every day in my storeroom office until Andy had recovered and was back in his own quarters.

Andy recovered with remarkable speed, and it was all I could do to keep him off the tennis court the first week he was out of the hospital.

I was having trouble with one of the D.C. Gang. One evening as I was seated at a table in the library working on *Carmen* for a forum program, a young Negro man with incredibly wide shoulders and enormous biceps slid into a seat beside me and began to tell me how much he went for me, how much he liked my looks, and so on.

I didn't even know the man, but I had seen him often with other D.C.-ers (and later learned that he was twenty-seven years old and had been out of prison less than eighteen months since the age of nine). I told him he'd picked the wrong guy, that I didn't go for men, and to forget it. The fellow got mean and sinister, and I saw that this was not going to be as easy as was the encounter with Dan and his silly note.

After an exchange or two with increasing heat, the D.C.-er put forward his proposition with elegant simplicity: "Well what's it gonna be, shit on my dick or blood on my shiv?" I told him to get lost and saw the man's eyes narrow to slits and his mouth turn down, ugly and menacing. He left without a word and rejoined a sidekick who was waiting a few yards away. When I left the library he was waiting at the top of the stairs and literally stalked me to the door of my quarters.

The stalking continued steadily for two days. Stories of attacks by such pederast-rapists at knife point were too widespread to be ignored. So I broke a double-edged razor blade in half lengthwise and adhesive-taped it to the inside of my right-hand middle finger. If I opened my hand and slapped I could carve a frightful gash. To protect myself I put a Band-Aid loosely over the blade so that it could be instantly pulled off. Believing I would be attacked, I decided I would rather die than give in. I determined to try to wound or even kill my adversary if necessary.

Andy was then still in the hospital, and there was no one else I wanted to discuss the matter with. The stalking continued, and I was sure a confrontation was not far off. The following day the stalker was nowhere to be seen, nor was he around on the next day. The third day he saw me approaching him in the hallway and turned tail as if pursued by devils. His avoidance of me was as conspicuous as his previous stalking. Although I couldn't understand the change, I gave up wearing the taped razor blade. I remained mystified until Andy was released from the hospital. Andy immediately surmised that The Chin was behind the dramatic turnabout.

About a week later The Chin stopped me for our regular chat and asked how things were going. "Maybe you know better than I do," said I.

The Chin smiled. "Don't worry about a thing." He added reassuringly, "Everything is fine now." Then he spoke at length about how the Kennedys were lousing up organized crime and leaving things open for amateurs. Although I wasn't sure what he was talking about, I was not then in a mood to disagree with The Chin about anything.

The attempt of James Meredith to enter the segregated University of Mississippi aroused great interest at Lewisburg, especially among Negroes. I followed every scrap of news I could get on the radio and in the press. On the last day of September 1962, President Kennedy addressed the public on that subject, thanking on behalf of the nation those who had in the past fought to end segregation in colleges and universities. That speech vividly called to my mind a Party meeting at one of the student clubs at Chapel Hill early in 1947, with the entire agenda, at my proposal, devoted to planning a campaign to desegregate the University of North Carolina. The Law School or one of the other graduate schools seemed the best target. From that meeting onward there was never a time when those same members (or replacements) were not actively working toward the goal. Of course, many others, a large majority of whom were non-Communist or anti-Communist, participated. For once the Party worked correctly: no attempt was made to gain political capital for the Party; we Communists compromised on everything except the goal; every effort was made to prevent internal dissension; Communists generally stayed in the background on ad hoc committees, did "Jimmy Higgins" work, and gently prodded slow or indecisive leaders. Since I had also played an advisory role from 1948 in movements that led to desegregation in two other southern universities, the irony of hearing the president's praise while I was in a maximum-security prison as a close-confinement prisoner struck me as sobering, though it could be fully appreciated only by me and by Gladys and a few others. To Gladys I then wrote:

> It seemed to me that the President's speech was a bare minimum of what was needed, sticking mainly to the Constitutional issue. I suppose it is asking a lot to expect a politician to attempt to clean out Augean stables with the accumulated dreck of generations. For that's what the White South is—a half-disguised horror that's mainly laughed at in the hope that it will go away, its bigotry wedded to a historical tradition, a repulsive myth seldom challenged except by "outsiders."
>
> I'm not quite sure how to acknowlege the nation's thanks, relayed by the President, for my services in desegregating Southern universities, especially the University of North Carolina. Of course there were others more specifically active in that endeavor but, in all modesty, if any individual can be credited with *starting* it—that's me! After all, I was denounced all over the state as the instigator of all that radical devilment by all sorts of respectable conservative elements—so it's very nice to be thanked by the New Frontier. I remember a meeting of the ruling body of the UNC Board of Trustees in 1947 or early in 1948 which asked my views on desegregation of educational institutions. I told them that I was unreservedly in favor of it and planned to do everything to bring it about as soon as possible.
>
> The events at Ole Miss should have surprised no one, but they may serve as a reminder to some of what a sordid lot we are as a people. Some of the early editorial reaction I've heard—even when opposed to Governor Barnett and Co.—usually boils down to little more than concern over "our image abroad," or "what

will the neighbors say?" Of course the cold warriors are only concerned with how the Reds will "use" all this to make us "look" bad. No one has bothered to point out *why* all the hullaballoo: that Negroes in Mississippi live and have lived for generations under a terror far worse than that which the most colorful journalists can conjure up for the opposition in Castro's Cuba, and that this is a small step toward eliminating a howling horror which has been winked at, ignored, self-righteously deplored, defended, praised, studied with scholarly detachment and denounced—but generally ignored. As though there were not an encysted area in most deep-South white Southerners where unreasoning human madness reigns, and that varying degrees of this make all of us whites "Ugly Americans." I've just been aghast that no one seems to have thought to say publicly that Meredith should attend Ole Miss because it's his *right* to attend and that by doing so he starts reversing, in one tiny area, the generations of inhumanity to his people and our people (since we are all Americans). The failure of the President in his speech (or even worse, subsequently) to mention the moral issues at stake is a wretched evasion. I believe that shame is one of the tools which may eventually work as a lever to pry many Southerners loose from their sickness. If so, the President should certainly take the lead in stating his views (which I think must be quite strong), and in that way call forth moral expressions from others.

My big news was that I had been transferred to J-3, honors quarters, for which I had waited so long. There were no locked doors, and the rooms were relatively large. Mine contained a bed with a drawer under one end of it, a cabinet to hang clothes in with shelves on one side, a table of steel, a wooden desk chair, and a sink with hot and cold water.

Then on October 2 came the first anniversary of my entering prison.

Thus coming of age as a con, I tried to assess what had been happening to me during that first year.

Each morning of that year I had awakened with an acute sense of pain overwhelming my first moments of consciousness. No matter what the anticipations or pressures of any particular day, the initial pain was unvarying. No matter where my dreams had taken me or how free and pleasant they had been, they always dissolved into that agonizing, inescapable first consciousness.

Whence the pain? Was it the mere fact of jailers, bars, locks, walls? No, because I had not felt that pain in my two sojourns in jail. Then, there was anguish and anger; the imprisonment was temporary; it would and must be righted at the end.

But after seven interminable years of straight-faced "due process," my fellow citizens had decided that six years of my life should be expunged, that I

should not be allowed to live, but only to exist—written off, buried, eliminated from society, torn from my family and friends, humiliated, degraded to
the status of a pariah with no rights any man need respect. And all that had
been done with overwhelming approval, with the enthusiastic support of most
of the free press, with the ultimate solemn approval of the highest court. I
knew what manner of men were my prosecutors, accusing witnesses, and
judge, and whom they served. Nonetheless, they had gotten away with it; they
had brought it off. They had expelled me from society, from life, and had truly
made me despised and rejected of men.

True, there was a handful of people who had opposed my imprisonment and
favored my return to life. True, even in prison I led a richer existence and had
more love and joy in my life than most of my persecutors. Still, the crushing
fact was that I was there, in prison, at the will of my fellowman. And that was
the hurt, the source of the pain.

Had I "grown" in prison? All I knew was that I had survived one year, and
that bitterness and hatred had not yet shriveled and dried up my heart. But I
knew my Achilles heel: Gladys. How long could her frail body support that
indomitable spirit? If her health failed, how could anything at all survive in
me? What would I or she be like after two years? Or three? Or four? And the
six or eight months after that?

The conventional wisdom was to take each day as it came. Some wisdom!
There was damned little else I could do. But I was not a mole. I needed to
know my objective. Gladys still pursued a miracle called "presidential clemency," but that seemed almost beyond possibility, and parole, her backup
hope, entirely so. So there was the objective: quite simply, to survive intact
three and one-half years more—1,278 days—one day at a time.

But all the while I was feeling an acute sense of loss: Barbara was growing
up even as I began dwindling from a vital presence into a kind of sterile
symbol, if not an object of pity. The ripening of a prison term, with its increasing awareness of the ties being severed between you and the ones you
love, is most harrowing with children, because their development is so rapid.
The joy of their growth and flowering is tempered by the selfish regret of
feeling less and less of yourself invested in that process.

Gladys visited me with her sister Arline on October 20, a delightful occasion. In the course of it I told them of two of my extraordinary encounters of
the previous week.

The Chin had stopped me for our regular chat. The Chin, incidentally, had
been Vito Genovese's "chauffeur" before they both went to prison. Reputedly, his most famous assignment was to knock off supergangster Frank Costello. The then-current story was that he had followed Costello into the lobby

of his fancy Central Park West apartment house, fired at him from a distance of six feet—and missed.

A Lewisburg legend (reliably witnessed) recounted that Costello was in AO, en route through Lewisburg (probably to the Springfield medical facilities), when a crowd of Mafiosi (The Chin among them) gathered in the corridor at the time the AO-ers went to the dining hall to see and greet the great man. Costello received the respectful obeisances graciously until he saw The Chin, whereupon he spat at his feet and ignored him. The Chin was deeply offended. "What's he mad at *me* for? I only did what I was told!"

As affable and kind as The Chin was to me, he may not have been so to everyone. At least, his organization was pretty rough. One day in one of the jungle dorms, an inmate who was believed to have ratted on "one of the boys" was found by hacks at lunchtime bleeding by his bed with his skull fractured. The weapon: a combination footlocker lock wrapped in a sock. Though twenty inmates had been present, discretion prevailed; no one saw what had happened.

Anyway, on this occasion, after another monologue on how the Kennedys were leaving the country at the mercy of amateur criminals by not dealing with organized crime, The Chin said, "By the way, Scales, you've been in about a year now, haven't you?"

"Plus two weeks, Chin."

"Well, I just want to tell you you're serving your time like a gentleman. You doin' all right."

I thanked him for the compliment, and we parted with a handshake.

Later in the week Andy mentioned to Van Graham, while the three of us were chatting, that I was into my second year. Graham took my hand, clasped it, and said, "Well, Junius, you've got something to be proud of. You've been serving your time like a real gentleman!" Andy and I cracked up at the choice of phraseology but wouldn't let Van in on the joke.

Experienced prisoners are slow to reach firm value judgments about their fellows until about a year has been served. By then there are few strengths and weaknesses that are not revealed to a sharp con (or hack), and I was pleased that at least in some quarters I had "arrived" and was respected.

25

A Christmas Eve

G ladys spoke hopefully of the growing force of the movement to free me. Hundreds of distinguished names had been added to the petition for clemency addressed to the president, and scores of prominent individuals had mailed to Gladys or her sister copies of letters they had sent to the White House. Dwight Macdonald, Seymour Martin Lipset, Maxwell Geismar, Ashley Montague, Mary McCarthy, Bayard Rustin, A. J. Muste, Linus Pauling, Rabbi Joseph Prinz, George Biddle, Alice Hamilton, Oscar Handlin, Gerald Johnson, Clarence Pickett, Raphael Soyer, Saul Bellow, James Baldwin, Van Wyck Brooks, Henry Steele Commager, I. F. Stone, Mark Van Doren, Edmund Wilson, C. Vann Woodward, Harvey Swados, Paul O'Dwyer, Marianne Moore, August Heckscher, Norman Mailer, Robert Heilbroner, William Ernest Hocking, Irving Howe, Arthur S. Link, Howard Mumford Jones, Martha Gellhorn, David T. Bazelon, Eric Fromm, Osmond K. Frankel, Dorothy Day, Jules Feiffer, Edward T. Cone, Babette Deutsch, Alexander Calder, Charles G. Bolte, and Martin Buber were among those who had recently written personally to the president. The United Packinghouse Workers, the Brotherhood of Sleeping Car Porters, and the Central Conference of American Rabbis had adopted strong resolutions urging clemency. Finally, Walter Reuther had had the United Auto Workers convention pass a clemency resolution.

Perhaps most encouraging was the fact that Attorney General Robert Kennedy had sent for Norman Thomas (Thomas later gave me an amusing account of their exchange). Kennedy's first words were, "Stop the pressure!" Thomas's cagey response was, "In exchange for what?" After a discussion Kennedy had said that he would consider clemency and Thomas had promised nothing. When Thomas reported the matter to Gladys, she firmly refused to relax the pressure created at so great a cost.

Soon she was to report that one of Wechsler's columns on the Scales case (with a snapshot of the Scaleses taken by Richard Nickson) had deeply moved David Dubinsky, president of the powerful International Ladies Garment Workers Union; he had phoned the attorney general, pouring out his sentiments forcefully and at length. Dubinsky then spoke persuasively to George Meany, president of the AFL-CIO, and they both wrote the president in support of clemency. Slowly the campaign seemed to gain momentum.

More than a month after my move, I was still reveling in my honor-quarters private room on the third floor of Building J (J-3). Andy was in J-1, and we met downstairs for breakfast and supper. Regulations permitted visits only between those living on the same floor. J-3 had a generally considerate group, but it included none of my close acquaintances. Thus I found myself with much more time for reading, letter writing, and preparing my forum programs.

I also received occasional visitors, including Joe, who lived in the very last room at the far end of the corridor. Then in his late forties, Joe had spent the past fifteen years in Lewisburg for murder. He played the organ (just passably) for Protestant services and was perhaps the most aloof inmate at the prison. He walked alone and ate alone, and I had never seen him speak to a living soul. He kept a perpetual shield of solemnity, coolness, and dignity around him, sufficient to maintain his complete privacy. To the rash fools who could not see the obvious and did not respect that privacy, he could, reputedly, be frighteningly ugly. He had no friends and indeed knew no one, but he was highly respected nevertheless.

I was understandably startled when one night Joe knocked on my door and asked if I could spare a few minutes. I seated him in my desk chair, broke out some cookies, tin cups, and some instant cocoa, and put a rubber band on the spring faucet to let the water run hot. Then I sat on the bed and waited expectantly. Joe said he wanted to ask me some things about the street since I had been in only a year or so. He inquired about employment, what kind of jobs were open, what prevailing wages were like, and how much a nice furnished room might cost in Philadelphia. Were things any better in the job situation for Negroes than they had been in 1947? I answered as well as I could, blushing a bit at the generally negative reply to that last question. After serving the cocoa and cookies, I must have betrayed an unasked question in my manner.

Joe said softly, "This is a kind of celebration. I got a notice I was paroled this afternoon." I stammered my congratulations. Joe clinked cups with me and smiled! It was as though an ancient glacier had cracked and disintegrated. I could feel the controlled excitement pulsating inside him and the need, at long last, to share an emotion with another human being. Gradually, as we conversed, I discovered a man of warmth and charm and extraordinary inner strength.

Two days before his departure Joe entertained me in his room. On the momentous day itself, I alone walked him to the control center and waved good-bye as he was escorted down the long corridor to the front gate.

The weekly broadcasts over the "earphone network," set up by me some weeks before, apparently began to attract many listeners who would never have thought of attending the forum. Some inmates would turn out their lights, go to bed, and lie in the dark letting the music sort of wash over them for two hours, having no idea of what they were hearing. I had arranged for space to list the selections on the back of the weekly menu beginning in January, but until then I could do nothing about the matter.

I began to discover the impact of my "concerts" when total strangers (and many unlikely ones at that) began stopping me in the corridor or coming to my table in the dining hall to ask myriad questions about the music played and to make requests for future broadcasts. Such occurrences became so frequent that they began to be something of a nuisance, delaying me when I was in a hurry or even cutting into valued mealtime conversation.

My days were busy and full. The forum taxed me heavily, even with my increasing expertise. I tried to keep in touch with the world outside through the *Times,* and *Post,* numerous other periodicals, and the radio. I was apparently in noticeably good spirits much of the time, for I was widely nicknamed "Smiley." I had arrived as a personality and had a distinct, respected niche in my society: I was meaningfully employed in dispensing music. I was in private quarters without the oppression of crowding. Outside, my wife was becoming a brilliant teacher, and our daughter was becoming an ever-lovelier child. Outside also, Gladys and my friends were unceasing in their efforts to secure my release and had rallied astounding support for presidential clemency. I, the persistent pessimist, even had a thin hope (not even admitted to myself) that I might be on the presidential clemency list, traditionally released around Thanksgiving.

Gladys, visiting me with Barbara on November 24, had information which eliminated that faint hope. Not only was I not on the clemency list, but a counterattack was brewing (apparently engineered by J. Edgar Hoover). I was to be hauled before the Eastland committee, asked innumerable questions about individuals I had known in the Communist Party, and forced to take the Fifth a few hundred times, so that J. Edgar, Eastland, et al. could then dare the administration to free such an obviously unregenerate Red. I tended right along to expect the worst, but in my anticipation of the worst I'd at every stage omitted some basic, undreamt-of refinement. I'd failed to keep in mind the injunction Dante found inscribed over the gates of Hell.

At that bleak moment an excellent *Times* editorial, "Time to Free Scales," made the point that no serious question had been raised about the genuineness of my withdrawal from the Communist Party. But some government agent might even so be uncovering the sinister fact that I had the habit of saying hello to, and shaking hands with, Communist leaders whenever I encountered them—another "cause" to suffer for: the right to the uncertain pleasure of shaking hands with Communists.

The comparative stability and peace in which I had been living was coming to an end. The Eastland committee project meant that I would lose the "privacy" of prison and be put on public display again. This was more of a wrench emotionally than I had thought possible, and I first realized how much my still-unformed postprison plans centered on withdrawal into obscurity and enjoying my family and friends in private.

The Eastland hearing hung over me like a sword of Damocles. Aside from the prospect of being once again exhibited in a cage, it was no joy to know that by refusing to name names I would automatically dissipate a great deal of the pressure on the administration for clemency which my friends had so painstakingly built up, and that it would send my last hope of executive clemency down the drain, probably for years to come.

Perhaps most disconcerting was the uncertainty and the lack of communication. I saw the Wechsler column, dated Wednesday, November 28, on Thursday; the column said the hearing was scheduled for Friday, and yet on Thursday night there I was, still at Lewisburg and with no letter from Gladys. By Saturday, December 1, I was beginning to lose my cool and get snappish. Gladys's letter of the previous Tuesday would have told me everything I needed to know: the hearing would probably take place in Washington the following week; Senator Keating, the only subcommittee member available, would preside; the poisonous J. G. Sourwine, counsel for the Senate Internal Security Subcommittee, would be doing the dirty work; Telford Taylor would be my counsel, and the postponement had been granted at his request. But the watchful mailroom turned the letter over to the warden, who sat on it and only allowed it to be delivered Monday night, December 3. It was hard to believe, in view of subsequent developments, that there could have been any other reason for withholding the letter than the warden's sadistic malice.

The news story in the *New York Post* of Saturday, December 1, that the hearing was dead because Senator Keating had denounced it and had bowed out, gave me information that the warden did not have. So when he summoned me to announce that I would be transferred, I realized that for all his pompous manner, he was only a small cog in an extremely inefficient machine and knew nothing of what was really going on, while I now realized that the transfer was a snafu resulting from the ignorance of the Bureau of Prisons about the changed situation. (Only later did I learn how Wechsler had persuaded a liberal Republican congressman to explain to Senator Keating, a decent man, what the true purpose of the hearing was.)

An editorial in the *Washington Post* of December 1, appealing for clemency for me, made the following perceptive point: "The argument against clemency for Scales seems to be that he has never proved his repudiation of the Communist Party by naming the persons who had been associated with him in organizing Negroes and attacking segregation in North Carolina. It is now rumored that he is to be hailed before Senator Eastland's Internal Security Subcommittee in executive session in another effort to compel such disclosures from him."

When the warden sent for me, he had three or four of his henchmen present. He read the transfer order in a sort of bullying, half snickering way. When he finished, he said he would notify Mrs. Scales, and then he added, "I don't suppose this will please you or your friends too much, will it?" I answered cheekily that how I felt about the transfer was a private matter. If the warden wanted to know how my friends felt, I said, "You can write them. I'm sure you have plenty of names and addresses." The bristling eyebrows lowered; the coarse mouth scowled heavily (he was probably debating whether to charge me with insubordination); and the interview ended.

That night I told Andy and Van Graham goodbye, and they assured me that if I didn't come back for any reason, they would ship my precious letters from Gladys and my books home. The next morning I got a call from the control center that the U.S. marshals were waiting for me. The storeroom gang and Wagenseller and Hardnock gave me a cheering send-off.

Reporting to the control center, I was told to leave everything I owned (even my pen and $3.50 watch) in my room in honor quarters. The hack locked my room, wished me good luck, and said he hoped I would be back soon. I hurried back to the control center and to the marshals, who apologized for putting handcuffs on me, saying that it was "regulations" and they could be fired if they didn't. I passed through the Lewisburg front gate for the first time and got into the back seat of the marshals' car alone.

As we drove along, I was fascinated with the stories they told about the duty they had both done at Ole Miss trying to make sure nobody killed James Meredith. One of them had literally been Meredith's roommate and had come to have a great respect for the man's guts. "Come on," I said. "You can tell me. I won't rat you out. You probably got to *like* him a little, even if he is a Negro, didn't you?"

"Well, yes, by God, I did. Inside he was as white as any man I ever knew!" said the marshal, and Meredith thus received the white southerner's supreme compliment!

The conversation was amiable all the way to Washington. In the city I fell silent. We passed by various familiar landmarks, including Union Station, and I had the eerie feeling that I had returned from the dead and was looking on all the bustling activity of my nation's capital as a disembodied spirit. There seemed to be something unreal and a bit improper about my looking at life "in the street," from which I had been banned. I thought of Scrooge's journeys with the spirits of Christmas past, present, and future.

Upon our reaching the ugly D.C. jail, there was a signing of receipts and releases for the freight delivered and received, the marshals said goodbye and wished me luck, and I was taken to a huge processing room and turned over to a Negro officer in charge. I was fingerprinted and mugged (the usual full-face and profile photos).

While undergoing this routine, I observed a scene reminiscent of a Doré illustration of Dante's *Inferno*. There was a deep, terraced cement depression in the floor. At the bottom were several shower heads and a filthy floor. Newly arrived prisoners were told to strip and were sent through the showers like sheep being herded through sheep-dip. I noted a particularly onerous and painstaking body search, which overlooked no single aperture. After the mugshots were taken, the Negro officer came for me, led me around the lower depths, and without a word seated me at a table where a Negro prisoner-assistant was filling out forms.

The activity in the room gradually diminished; the processed prisoners were taken to the main part of the jail; the jailers all disappeared; and only the prisoner-clerk and I remained. The trusty was a bright local lad in his early twenties who had been charged with burglary on such vague evidence that even the D.C. prosecutors did not want to go to trial, yet they had never got around to dropping the indictment. He had been held eight months. Even in such a hard-boiled jail, he was believed to have a bum rap. He and I exchanged a few pleasantries, and finally I asked him why I had bypassed the crummy shower and inspection. Was something even nastier in store for me? "Shit no, man; you's gettin' it *good*!"

Before he could elaborate further, the Negro officer, smiling broadly, came in wheeling a food cart with three dinners and a pot of coffee. The officer locked the door behind him and then passed out the dinners, poured the coffee, and sat down. "Well, they tell me you're in trouble with Senator Eastland," he remarked to me. "We been reading a lot about you in the *Washington Post*," he added. "It's good to know you." And he held out his hand.

The young officer had had a couple years at Howard University before financial need had forced him to take his jail job. He had risen in the ranks and had command of a large number of other jailers. He was highly literate and politically sophisticated. He was married and had a brand-new child (he showed a snapshot) and hoped to get transferred out of the jail, which he said was beginning to get to him. Someone in his family had been a Communist sympathizer, although he himself shared many of my views and was an ardent supporter of Martin Luther King, Jr.

The friendliness of the two was so warm and genuine that I told them about my situation and answered all their questions on a whole variety of subjects, especially my life in the South. Before we knew it, it was 9:15—after lights-out—and the officer said he'd have to hurry and get us inside before the 9:30 count.

Both said that they'd be seeing me again, that they didn't think I'd be around more than a week, and that they'd do what they could for me. I was turned over to a jailer who took me up to the fourth tier of cellblock number one. In the dim light, I could barely see enough to remove the dirty mattress cover and replace it with the clean one I'd been given. This elementary housekeeping finished, I fell asleep, exhausted.

"Allah is great! Allah is great" delivered by a big voice reverberating through all the tiers of the cellblock awoke me before daylight the next morning. The ritualistic monologue seemed to go on endlessly (it actually lasted a bit over ten minutes), sometimes broken by responsive answering chants from numerous voices. That was the Black Muslim morning ritual, which cost every non-Muslim prisoner fifteen minutes of sleep. I was surprised that no one howled in protest at the racket and that the jailers permitted it.

I soon began to understand. When the lights came on I saw that at least 70 percent of the inmates I could see were Negroes and that probably a majority of the jailers were also. The Muslims were tightly organized and had been isolated on the first tier, which they filled to capacity. They refused to eat pork and derided those who did. They even refused to leave their cells for meals at which pork was served.

I sensed that there was widespread respect among both Negroes and whites for the Muslims because of their organization, militance, and persistence. The jail administration found them tough customers and gave in to them on point after point. They were a mean lot and radiated hatred for both whites and "handkerchief-heads" (which term seemed to include most non-Muslim Negroes). The doctrine evinced by the morning ritual was absurd and pathetic, with its near-deification of "Mr. Elijah Muhammad." Still, they had the guts to fight "whitey's" image of them by challenging their oppressors and jailers with open contempt for their professed Christian ethic and other hypocrisies, shrewdly using the constitutional guarantee of religious freedom as the legal cornerstone of their struggle. They were alienated men with nothing to lose, rescued from lives of senseless criminality by a simplistic movement which offered them brotherhood and a purpose. Despite the inherent ugliness of their racism, their courage and steadfastness gave them dignity, individually and collectively, in their prison world. I could even forgive them the daily loss of sleep they caused me.

While waiting for breakfast, I got acquainted with my neighbors on each side. They were doubled up in their cells and seemed friendly enough. At breakfast I got acquainted with several more neighbors. No one treated me as anyone unusual. But by mid-morning, one of my friends of the night before must have got word to someone, because the Negro trusties on the fourth tier, as well as my neighbors, began showing me noticeable consideration.

Then one morning I was summoned to the captain's office and was told that I had a visitor. I was led to a small booth which had a thick glass window opening onto a huge visiting room seemingly as full of turmoil as the New York subway at rush hour. Suddenly I saw a confident little figure striding toward me. Gladys seized the phone and we conversed cryptically, looking through the glass and assuming that we were being taped. She looked beautiful and her eyes were shining, but she was not well. She coughed constantly. I urged her to try to short-cut the usual red tape and see if I could be sent back to Lewisburg. Our time was severely limited, and I was ordered out of the booth after ten precious minutes.

The next day a note from Gladys, dropped off at the jail, told me that she had spoken with a Mr. James Symington in the Justice Department, who had admitted that the entire transfer from Lewisburg was "a flub," that the subcommittee hearing had been postponed indefinitely, and that I would be on a prison bus to Lewisburg on Tuesday, December 11. Meanwhile the smaller, local wheels of justice ground blindly on. Late that afternoon I was taken out of my cell to the discharge section, where I was measured for a suit of clothes in which to testify. My officer friend, who came over to visit, laughed heartily when he heard the latest news of the "flub" and the promised return to Lewisburg.

How was I making out? I said it was rough on an old con with a lot of time to live in the frenzy of a jail with the newly incarcerated (brazen and garrulous or in a state of shock); those going on trial (pleading their cases to everybody); those convicted (in mortal depression); the plea bargainers (cursing the prosecutors and their own lawyers and horse-trading aloud); and so on. The officer was reassuring. "You won't be here long," he said. "There *is* a bus due on

Tuesday. And Martin Luther King and all those other good people are going to get you out of this for keeps. Now I know what's going on and I hear things. And while you're here you don't have a thing to worry about. With my folks—and this is prisoners, staff, and even the Muslims—if Eastland is out to get you, you're A L L right! Hell, if you were running for office you'd carry this jail."

The officer said he'd have to say goodbye, since Tuesday was his day off. He told me the bus would leave around ten. Then he shook hands and assured me I would be out soon. "Just remember, Martin's pulling for you!"

Tuesday night I was back in AO at Lewisburg and bowled over at the friendliness with which I was greeted. Back at the storeroom for the next couple of days I labored furiously to get the work caught up; but at the coffee breaks, before and after lunch, and before quitting time, I regaled the whole gang, including Wagenseller, Hardnock, and the old hack upstairs, with stories of my adventurous week. Soon things had settled down to a normal routine, with Christmas only a bit over a week away—Christmas with its extra visiting privileges. All was right in the Lewisburg world.

But at lunch there was no Andy. I went to the Education Department; Van Graham thought he was at lunch. In some alarm I went to Andy's quarters (against the rules) and found him looking sadder than anyone I had ever seen; on his bed was a form letter denying him parole! After thirteen years of exemplary behavior, respected by everyone at Lewisburg, strongly recommended by all the high prison brass, supported by a loving, dedicated family, he had been denied by a board with an almost perfect record of paroling the wrong men!

Then late that afternoon at mail call I got a scrawled, shakily written note from Gladys which said she was sick and little more. The annual Christmas jam-up in the mail was delaying letters up to five days. I was frantic. With the Christmas rush I knew I might not get mail for days.

Andy and I went to supper together, probably the two most morose people in Lewisburg, each trying to cheer the other up. Our mutual suffering and the need to bolster the other's morale probably helped us both survive the next few days.

My anguish was finally cured by Van Graham. On his own initiative, Van (who had met Gladys and Barbara on their previous visit) made a call to New York from his home and talked with Barbara, Florence (my step-grandmother), and Gladys herself. The next morning he called the storeroom, telling Wagenseller he needed Scales in his office urgently and at once. When I arrived, breathless, Van and Andy were all smiles: Gladys was much better; she had had double pneumonia, a bad case; she was over the crisis; the doctor (a dear friend) had come three to four times daily and said that she must not rush her recovery and that if she followed orders she could visit after Christmas.

When, in a euphoric state, I returned to my office, Hardnock waited for a private moment, produced Wechsler's latest column, clipped by Mrs. Hardnock from a Pennsylvania paper, and asked if I would autograph it for her, saying that they both hoped the president would get me out soon. Later the same day, Wagenseller produced a packet of clippings about my case which he thought I might not have seen because of the New York newspaper strike. He thought things looked very good and hopeful and that the president might act favorably at New Year's. Deeply moved, I explained that all my information indicated that it was quite unlikely.

I worked away at my Sunday night program, Handel's *Messiah*. I did not have the text of the arias and choruses, so with the aid of a biblical concordance I tracked them down and copied them from the Bible. I had advertised the program two weeks in advance with posters on the bulletin boards and with items on the back of the widely read mimeographed weekly menu. But hitches began to develop. First I found that I would have to compete with a special showing of a two-hour film of the highlights of the 1962 World Series. Secondly, the Catholic chaplain had denounced *Messiah* as "Protestant blasphemy" in his homily at services on December 16. I had to find the young priest and convince him that the entire text was from the Bible (even though it was the King James version—the only one available to Handel, I told him). I even played him excerpts. Finally, after consulting higher authority, the chaplain withdrew his denunciation, and on Sunday morning urged his flock to attend the forum that night. I then worked all Sunday afternoon practicing where to put the needle down on the records for each piece.

That night the library was jammed. The official house-counter reported approximately eighty-five, not counting ten off-duty hacks seated behind the bookcases. The hi-fi set wore Christmas decorations. Just out of curiosity I asked at the very beginning how many had ever heard *Messiah*. One hand went up. I spent four minutes explaining who Handel was, the nature and popularity of the work, and its association with Christmas, stating that Part Three, more appropriate to Easter, would be played at that time, while that evening the performance would end with the chorus "Hallelujah!" I mentioned the two and a quarter centuries of veneration for the work, especially in England, where the audience always stood during the "Hallelujah Chorus." I then played the overture, and before every chorus, recitative, and aria I simply recited the text with as much inflection and feeling as I could, without adding another word.

Undramatic as *Messiah* is in concept, I could sense a rising emotion in the audience and could even see tears being wiped away. As I read the ringing words of the final chorus and put the needle in the groove, I looked up and was startled and moved to see the entire audience standing at the first "Hallelujah." I followed suit with a lump in my throat. At the end there was a roar of applause and cheers.

It had been an extraordinary evening, a degree of communication, collective emotion, and sympathetic feeling unparalleled in my experience.

The next morning, Christmas Eve, at breakfast, I was widely greeted by my Literary Forum fans as "Reverend" Scales.

Christmas Eve was a holiday for most offices and departments at Lewisburg; but because quarterly supplies were pouring in, the storeroom was to stay open at least half the day. After breakfast I walked Andy back to honor quarters (the first floor), where he planned a lazy morning of reading and writing. I went to my third-floor room, got my worn ex-Navy pea jacket, and went past the guards at the door out to the storeroom.

Wagenseller had the day off. Hardnock came in, decided it looked like a nothing-doing day, called the gate and told them to accept no deliveries, sent the unloading crew back to their quarters, and left Jim, my new assistant, and me to answer the phone. Hardnock then called his lieutenant, got excused for the rest of the day, and asked the old hack upstairs to keep an eye on things and to close up for the day at lunchtime. He wished Jim and me a Merry Christmas and went home to decorate his tree and be Santa Claus for his young children.

The phone rang. "I'll get it, Jim. Stay where you are. Storeroom, Scales speaking."

"Scales, 28398?"

"That's right."

"Report to the control center *on the double!*" said the hack at the other end.

"I wonder what that goddam warden is up to now," I said as I slipped into my jacket.

"Did it sound like trouble?" Jim asked, concerned.

"Yeah. It sure did. Be back as quick as I can."

As I approached the control center (a large booth enclosed in bullet-proof glass in the center of the corridor), I recognized the hack on duty, a rather nice guy who knew me.

"Hey, Scales, we just got a telegram from Bobby Kennedy, and he says we gotta get you home by tonight in plenty of time for Christmas. Your sentence is commuted and—. Hey, wait a *minute!*" The hack rushed out of the booth because my face had gone white and my legs had turned to rubber. He half dragged me over to a bench against the corridor wall, talking all the while to keep me from blanking out. "Wait, I'll read it to you!" The hack ran and got the telegram which I heard through a sort of buzzing haze. Then I came to life again.

"You feeling better? You OK? Now look, there's a bus to New York at 2:15, and its 10:15 now. We got a helluva lot to do, so why don't you start clearing out your room, and I'll send someone down with a coupla big cartons and some rope. When you finish packing, come back here because we gotta get you some clothes. You OK now, Scales?"

I was more than OK; I was bursting with exuberance and joy, my heart pounding and my thoughts racing. I charged off like the wind, right past the quarters hack to Andy's room, where I burst in with the news. Andy's face was stunned, overjoyed, sad, and joyful again all in a matter of seconds.

We went up to my room on the third floor and started packing. The two cardboard boxes arrived, and we barely managed to get everything squeezed in. I had nearly fifty books on hand, although I had mailed home fifteen the previous week. Andy took three or four books as mementos and took about twenty more to ship to me by way of the Education Department. He did nearly all the packing because I was fumbling around and didn't half know what I was doing. We hauled two staggeringly heavy cartons to the control center, where the officer suggested we go eat early lunch because he had just reached the clothing officer by phone, and he had to come in from his home some miles away.

The prison grapevine quickly spread the word that "Scales is sprung." So Andy and I went to our table in the chow hall and ate nothing, while I stood and shook hands with an endless line of well-wishers, at the same time winking back the tears which threatened to be the only outlet for my confused emotions. A few men pressed phone numbers in my hand with written messages for wives, family, and friends. (These were a sacred trust, later meticulously carried out.) Finally, when it was time to return to the control center, a guy who had sat under my nose at the previous night's forum pumped my hand with a steely grip and said in an aggrieved voice, "Hey, Scales, what about duh toid parta duh *Messiah?*"

Back at the control center, I had to say goodbye to Andy. Though both of us were normally undemonstrative, we hugged European style, and I quickly grabbed my boxes to hide my emotion and followed the clothing hack to the basement.

The hack, one of my forum regulars, refused to so much as examine the boxes and gave me the best clothing he could fit me into from his meager supply. The pathetic suit of navy blue crinkled like newspaper at every movement. The white shirt was thin and transparent. The rayon tie (rather loud for my conservative taste) would never have survived a second tying. The new black shoes, made in the Leavenworth pen, looked old before I finished tying them. The navy blue topcoat seemed made of some recycled fiber, not woven but pressed together like felt. As I walked toward the front gate, my heavy box rubbed against the topcoat and a pile of blue fibers collected on top of the carton. The hack thoughtfully carried the other box to the front door, shook hands, said he sure was "gonna miss all that good music," and added that "lettin' you out is the most Christian thing Kennedy's done since he's been president."

It was getting late. The prissy hack on duty at the front desk entered my name in a ledger with a semiliterate scrawl. He had been my first quarters officer, and the dislike between us was hearty. He was some sort of religious extremist, but he had showed a remarkable lack of simple decency to those dependent on him in prison. As for Christian charity, there was not a trace. He wrote "time served" and the date. "Think you'll be back?" he asked sneeringly.

"If I ever am, it won't be to visit crumbs like you," I snapped contemptuously. The hack reddened and his knuckles showed white; but he was powerless at that point, and I turned my back on him and walked through the door.

The other hack, who was to drive me to town, helped me with my boxes to the double-doored, barred front gate. The prissy "religious" hack called over a public address system to the control tower above the gate: "Going out: Scales, Julius, 28398; presidential commution." ("The jerk never got anything right before," I thought to myself. "Why expect a miracle now?")

The inside barred gate rose, and as it closed behind me, I turned around for a final look and saw Andy and a dozen others leaning against the bars of the Education Department windows waving rags, sheets of paper, and even a dustpan, and silently mouthing, "Good luck." It would have been unwise to shout. They were right above the administrative offices; and besides, the Education Department was supposed to be closed. Resourceful Andy!

The fifteen-minute drive to Lewisburg and the bus station was accomplished with five minutes to spare. While the hack picked up my ticket, I borrowed a dime from him and rushed to an outside phone booth to call Gladys, collect. It required a struggle to remember my phone number but I did, just as the bus came into view. Gladys answered, shouted "yes!" she would accept charges. "Honey, I'm on my way home and my bus just came and I've got to run or I'm going to miss it. I love you. I gotta run!" I hung up while Gladys was still shouting half hysterically for me to hurry. I hadn't even told her what bus line I was on or when I was due in New York.

I got aboard with my boxes, shook hands with the hack, returned his dime—and the bus roared out of Lewisburg. I was so emotionally drained that I didn't even want to explore the implications of my new freedom. I pried one of my unopened Christmas books out of a carton and was soon absorbed in John Strachey's *The Strangled Cry*. Following the stimulating text with all my mental faculties, I savored my rebirth with a sort of visceral glow, as though I were digesting a satisfying meal.

Sometime later, after dark, during a brief rest stop, I called Gladys again and said, "Would you believe that I'm in Jim Thorpe, Pennsylvania?" She would have believed anything. This time I told her I would be in New York at 9:30 at the Greyhound Station on Fiftieth Street.

Back in the bus in the dark, meandering toward New York, I put away my book and tried to think soberly about what I would do next. But my thoughts kept soaring off in unexpected directions like roman candles. How wonderful to be part of the world again? Had I explained to Jim my new way of making the coal-tonnage reports? Would Gladys be warm enough in this bitter cold? Would Carlos know I was out? Would this sensational arrival disrupt Christmas for Barbara? What would Christmas Day be like for Andy? How did that duet "O namenlöse Freude!" from *Fidelio* go? Would my friends in New York know about me without newspapers? What were the things a convicted felon couldn't do?

There, suddenly, was the magnificent New York skyline I had thought I'd never see again. Through the Lincoln Tunnel, up Eighth Avenue—and I could see them under the floodlights: Gladys, Barbara, Arline, Moe, Bea, and Bernie. I remember a tearful bout of hugging, kissing, and pounding, and speeding up Amsterdam in the back seat of Moe's car, snuggling Gladys and Barbara. The apartment: Florence, Grandma, the Christmas tree. I removed my disintegrating topcoat. Everyone talked at once. Richard and Lia had just left to put their sleepy boys to bed; they had heard the news on the radio. Calls from Mary Leigh, from Arch, from friends in California—and, finally from North Carolina, Carlos crowed, "Hey, June-Bug! You're big news down here, buddy!"

Epilogue:
A Quarter Century
Later

The active political life of Junius Irving Scales ended long before his imprisonment, and it has not been reactivated. One consequence of this withdrawal has been an advance in his reflective faculties. Moreover, most of his reflections have been intensely concerned with precisely his political years, the years from the late thirties to the early fifties—years that for many signify the distant, the hazy past. For Junius, they are palpable, still here, still now. They constitute the heart of his memoir. The decades since the commutation of his sentence have afforded him scope for sorting and evaluating his commitments and actions, painful though that labor has often been. The results of reliving those days are to be found in the memoir, where, for some readers, a credible evocation of the way things were may emerge. With this possibility in mind, these pages were written. Though one person's point of view molds the record, the recording aspires to be one of high fidelity to the actual by the only means possible: rendering it as it now seems to have been.

Judging the fairness of the rendition rests with the individual reader, who may care to know something further about Junius Scales and his nonpolitical life during the intervening twenty-five years. For that reader, the following summary is provided.

Soon after the prisoner's release, shortly after New Year's Day 1963, a welcome-home party was held for him at the Barbizon-Plaza, presided over by James Wechsler and attended by some 150 friends and well-wishers, including Norman Thomas, Earl Browder, Dwight Macdonald, a number of former Communist leaders, and several prominent Communist intellectuals. The amiable occasion was highlighted with a notable handshake as two seasoned adversaries—Thomas and Browder—met in all conviviality.

Picking up the threads of a raveled life, Junius returned to the printing trade, deposited his union card at the *New York Times,* and rejoined the working class from which he had once expected so much. He worked for two decades as a proofreader—a well-paid blue-collar job—until he retired in 1983. Gladys continued in her work, and for Junius a paramount reward of those years was savoring her dedicated career as teacher and reading coordinator of a school district in Westchester County. A happy family life, made all the pleasanter by a welcome obscurity, frequent travel, and treasured opera- and concert-going, rounded out the years. Barbara, who remained in Montreal after completing her bachelor's and master's degrees at McGill University, visited (and visits) often. The family and their many friends found indispensable relaxation at a restored country house on a mountainside, next to a pond, in upstate New York.

The obverse side of these advantages was the steady decline in Gladys's health, which ultimately evolved, in 1973, into lymphoma. Despite superlative medical care and the patient's indomitable determination to remain at work, she died in 1981 but two weeks after a last full day of teaching. The writing of this book was dear to her heart, and she enthusiastically read a good portion of it.

Our indebtedness to Lia Nickson, from first to last, we also gratefully record. The friends who—whether as readers or not—provided advice and encouragement at the time of writing are too numerous to name here. Each one will continue to receive our thanks in person without being implicated in print in any of the errors and weaknesses of the book.

And we would like to thank those readers who read these pages free of as much prejudgment and prejudice as possible. Someone with a cause at heart is all too likely to arouse misgivings and hostilities in persons who disfavor or oppose the cause in question. Yet there are few indeed who have known or who know Junius Scales that have felt animosity toward the man. And even such animus as he and this book may still arouse might just be tempered with a reflection on the sentence imposed on him, and that it remains in effect. The prisoner was released; the man was not pardoned. The commutation meant a reduction of the penalty. Short of a pardon, a convicted felon remains a felon. Three decades have passed since the initial sentence was pronounced on Junius Irving Scales; to this day he is barred from exercising his right as a citizen to vote. But he has chosen not to petition for a pardon, believing as he does that any possible pardon is one he himself might extend to those who connived to convict him of a crime he did not commit.

R.N.

Index